CW00432187

Praise for Modern French Phi

"Robert Wicks has done us all a great service with the *Philosophy*. It is a book that we have needed for many years, and Wicks has done a superb job in summarizing the history of philosophy in France from surrealism, existentialism and structuralism to the virtual surrealism of recent postmodernism. Obscure and difficult texts are 'translated' into comprehensible English; cross-connections and historical references, many of them unexpected, are laid out for our appreciation; cautious criticisms, interspersed with the exposition, are offered for the student's consideration. For those of us who teach courses in modern French philosophy but despair of making the material readily accessible to our students, Wicks' book is a welcome pedagogical gift."

Robert C. Solomon, University of Texas at Austin

"This book surveys the complex and bewildering field of twentieth-century French philosophy and manages to pick out significant trends without sacrificing attention to detail. Existentialism, structuralism, poststructuralism and postmodernism are important components of our own intellectual context, but they are more often than not only loosely understood. Robert Wicks remedies this situation by providing a lucid, comprehensive account of French thought in the last century. The book is written with admirable clarity, and the analyses of both individual thinkers and broader movements are impressively accessible and authoritative. This book can be recommended wholeheartedly to anyone interested in the subject."

Colin Davis, University of Warwick

"The book is an extremely readable account of a vast panorama of thinkers, presented in a clear and comprehensible fashion without sacrificing too much in the way of detail or complexity. Relationships as well as differences are brought out, historical affiliations and influences are lucidly explored, and it is carried out with a keen eye for the whole as well as its parts."

Christina Howells, University of Oxford.

Modern French Philosophy

**From Existentialism
to Postmodernism**

Robert Wicks

ONEWORLD

OXFORD

For Ingryd Valentina and Gladys

MODERN FRENCH PHILOSOPHY: FROM EXISTENTIALISM TO POSTMODERNISM

Oneworld Publications
(Sales and Editorial)
185 Banbury Road
Oxford OX2 7AR
England
www.oneworld-publications.com

ISBN 1–85168–318–6

Cover illustration by Andrzej Klimowski;
cover design by Perks-Willis Graphic Design
Typeset by Saxon Graphics Ltd, Derby, UK
Printed and bound in Spain by Book Print S.L., Barcelona

Contents

Part 2 Structuralism

Part 3 Poststructuralism and Postmodernism

Preface

Much of twentieth-century French philosophy can be understood as a quest for freedom, stimulated by the problem of understanding one's place in the world as both an individual and as a social being. This quest was peculiar, though, because it was formulated against a confusing background, namely, an array of scientific and technological developments that appeared inconsistently to be both supportive and threatening to human well-being. The present study, unlike most surveys of this period, will highlight underappreciated continuities, as well as recall familiar discontinuities, between the various segments and strata of twentieth-century French philosophical thought. The hope is to develop a more satisfying understanding of modern French philosophers, by revealing a greater coherence to this intellectually vibrant time period than is usually noted.

It often happens that wide-ranging histories of philosophical thought sacrifice detailed analysis of argument for expository flow, and are formulated at a level of generality that precludes readers from appreciating the argumentative nuances of the philosophical theories under consideration. In light of this often-encountered condition, the present critical and integrative exposition of twentieth-century French philosophical thought aims to achieve balance in a different way: as a rule, we will examine key arguments from each author, and these will be situated within a broader exposition of the author's viewpoint. The resulting narrative atmosphere will compare to a helicopter excursion:

sometimes we will ascend to survey the extensive landscape; sometimes we will descend to cruise along the treetops for a closer and more rapid view; often we will stop to explore carefully, and with some patience, the intellectual gardens and shapes of the tiny flowers of thought. We will continue in this way until we reach the end of the century, when we will look back to formulate a surrealistic and freedom-centered meaning that will comprehend the survey.

French philosophical thought during the twentieth-century is more varied and thematically interesting than some other comparable segments in the history of philosophy, for the influential writers were confined neither to academic settings in general, nor to university philosophy departments in particular. And yet, all of the writers were deeply reflective in spirit. We will consider the ideas of psychoanalysts, artists, novelists, linguists, essayists, literary critics, anthropologists, sociologists, and political activists, in addition to those who worked in academic philosophy departments. A remarkable feature of French philosophical thought during this period, is that its representatives come from every intellectual avenue, influencing the entire scholarly scene, and much of the popular intellectual scene. As a testament to their stature and recognition beyond the French national boundaries, several of these thinkers, namely, Henri Bergson, Albert Camus, and Jean-Paul Sartre, were awarded or were offered, Nobel Prizes in Literature, which indicates their notable place within the wider French, European, Western, and worldwide cultural settings.

The historical and descriptive categories that have applied traditionally and conveniently to our complicated subject – 'French thought,' 'twentieth-century thought,' 'existentialism,' 'structuralism,' 'poststructuralism', and 'post-modernism,' among others – are useful and familiar schematic designations. As rigid and abstract terms, however, they also tend to mislead us into over-looking the complexity, multidimensionality and multi-interpretability of the cultural and philosophical phenomena at hand. To take a small example, consider how conventional calendar markings such as '1900' and '2000,' along with related designations such as 'twentieth-century French thought' or 'twen-tieth-century European thought,' can generate the expectation that major calendar divisions will match significant cultural and intellectual transitions. We can easily question, though, whether there are any clear 'joints' within the cultural sphere which naturally correspond to calendar divisions, if only because so many momentous discoveries and important historical events happen unpredictably, by accident, and on arbitrary dates.

At the same time, conventional manners of marking time are not without substantial influence. Most people organize their lives according to determinate calendars, and cultural transitions sometimes issue from the template of calendar divisions in the manner of a self-fulfilled prophecy: one acts and anticipates the future, as if a major event ought to happen, simply because the calendar indicates the arrival of a new year, decade, centennial or millennium. The European calendar is one among many alternative ways of measuring time, and to the extent that our expectations rest upon this particular structure, they rest, and also noticeably float, upon a socially constructed foundation.

Adding to the complication of understanding a long-term philosophical episode such as modern French philosophy, is how historical change can be slow and subtle: a cultural group could be living at the dawn of a new era without having a clear awareness of their world-historical place, merely because it is too early to realize the significance of what is happening. The widespread social implications that accompanied the discoveries of the wheel, gunpowder, the stirrup, Roman and Gothic style arches, interchangeable parts, the telescope and microscope, the photographic image, the telegraph, antibiotics, the telephone, the motion picture, the motor vehicle, the steel girder, the airplane, the television, atomic energy, and the computer, among other innovations, were not clearly imagined when these items first appeared on the social scene. The full significance of some historical events emerges only with long-term hindsight, and examples abound of individuals whose later cultural influence remained unanticipated by the majority of their contemporaries.

Such interpretive restrictions temper every study of the present kind, which aims particularly to comprehend the highlights of philosophical thought in France during the twentieth century. Prevailing intellectual categorizations have been adopted, hoping that this does not prevent us from appreciating some of the wider, along with the more subtle, currents that helped shape the century's philosophical concerns. In contrast to a strongly interpretive, abstract, and topical history of the period, the following pages present a selection of philosophical authors who frequently speak for themselves, to allow a more open-ended and revisable conception of the time period. Excerpts from the main philosophical texts of each selected author will be quoted and summarized to convey the author's crucial propositions, and these expositions will be augmented by critical reflections. The authors will speak for themselves as much as possible, to set the context for drawing independent thematic connections between the ideas as they appear in the original texts.

The selection of representatives from twentieth-century French philosophical thought has been determined according to the variably weighted criteria of respective historical influence, philosophical depth, comprehensiveness of vision, contemporary relevance, available writing space, and possible future relevance, in conjunction with a desire to illuminate thinkers who have been partially obscured by traditional conceptualizations of the philosophical era. The authors chosen vary in the degree to which they embody these criteria, but underlying this study is a conviction that the Dada and Surrealist movements of the early twentieth century exercised a strong, and still-underappreciated influence upon French thought throughout the century. For this reason, the study begins with a short account of Dada and Surrealism, focusing upon their intellectual aspects as expressed in their various manifestos. The influence of Sigmund Freud's psychoanalysis is also of important note within this context.

Owing mainly to the limitations of space, some twentieth-century French thinkers do not appear in the following pages with chapters of their own, such as Louis Althusser, Georges Bataille, Simone de Beauvoir, Guy Debord, Julia Kristeva, Emmanuel Lévinas, Gabriel Marcel, Jacques Maritain, Maurice Merleau-Ponty, Paul Ricoeur, and Simone Weil. My hope is that these theorists will nonetheless be rendered more understandable, if only indirectly, since the ideas represented by the authors in the present volume constitute either a close background or an immediate development of their respective theories, and therefore an intellectual entrée into their outlooks. In two instances, I have chosen to include Emil Cioran and Teilhard de Chardin in place of more mainstream figures, because they effectively represent the extremes of individualistic nihilistic pessimism and global social optimism in the early part of the century. During any turbulent times, de Chardin's hopefulness continues inspiringly to remain both psychologically intriguing and refreshing. And Cioran unforgettably expresses the dismal view of life whose hard realism touches, if only briefly, upon everyone at some point in their experience.

This study originated as a guide for students of twentieth-century French philosophy at The University of Auckland, New Zealand. Their enthusiasm for the subject has been a major inspiration, and this book would not have been written had it not been for their academic presence and dedication. I would also like to thank the following individuals for their scholarly advice on various chapters, and for discussions of some of the ideas contained herein: Thomas Christiano, Fred Kroon, Chris Martin, Timothy Rayner, Geoffrey Roche, Maree Scarlett, Martin Schwab, Jeremy Seligman, Ivan Soll, Karl Steven, Mel Thompson, Paul Warren, Thomas Wartenberg, Terry Winant, and Julian Young. Particular thanks are due to Lisa Guenther and Stefano Franchi, who commented extensively and informatively on large segments of the manuscript, along with an anonymous reviewer. I would also like to acknowledge a more wide-ranging intellectual and professional debt to Charles McCracken, Ronald Suter, and John F. A. Taylor†, who originally set me properly upon a philosophically directed road. Finally, I would like to thank Robert C. Solomon for his continual encouragement over the years in connection with this project.

Auckland, New Zealand
May 2003

Introduction: Time, Progress, and Disillusionment

To appreciate twentieth-century French philosophical thought, we can begin by recalling that a general feeling of progress inspired the nineteenth-century Western cultural spirit. Although the roots of this attitude trace back to the biblical idea that the world is unfolding benevolently according to a divine purpose, in more recent times this sense of cultural advancement was intensified by the seventeenth- and eighteenth-century developments in scientific and technological thinking. Together these helped stimulate the industrial revolution of the mid-to-late eighteenth century and they contributed to reinforcing a stronger awareness of historical development that emerged near the end of that century.

The wider themes of twentieth-century French philosophy reveal how the nineteenth-century faith in human progress became tempered, if not close to undermined, by the tragic experience of two World Wars, and by the grim realization that dehumanization and authoritarianism can also follow in the wake of technological progress. Twentieth-century French thinkers became keenly aware of how both rationalistic and irrational styles of thought can be disfigured to undermine human dignity, even though these thinkers frequently retained enough optimism to look back upon the nineteenth century in an effort to find inspiration for social improvement and liberation from what they perceived to be increasingly oppressive authoritarian regimes and doctrines. With such

1

hopes, French thinkers often cited the works of German-speaking theorists such as Karl Marx (1818–83), Friedrich Nietzsche (1844–1900) and Sigmund Freud (1856–1939) – theorists whose influence emerges repeatedly throughout the complicated history of twentieth-century French philosophical thought.[1]

Among the late eighteenth-century theoreticians who expressed the optimistic view that human society is inevitably progressing towards a more perfect condition was the Marquis de Condorcet (1743–94),[2] who believed that progress towards a thoroughly democratic condition is inherent in human nature, and that scientific and technological advances will inevitably assist this progress. Condorcet also maintained that we can discover the rational principles of human nature through the science of psychology, arguing that the tools of mathematical probability are the best for understanding human behavior.

Similarly, Auguste Comte (1798–1857) – the founder of 'sociology' and an advocate of a now-familiar position which he labelled 'positivism' – believed that the quest for knowledge is essentially progressive and scientifically aimed.[3] In the 1830s, Comte claimed that the development of human knowledge involves a gradual process of demythologization whereby cultural expressions of what is ultimately true pass through three stages: first, there is the 'fictitious' or theological stage, typical of many religious outlooks; second, there is the 'abstract' or metaphysical stage, typical of most traditional philosophical expression; third, there is the 'positive' stage, which is expressed by the most advanced scientific views of the time. For Comte, religion transforms into philosophy, and philosophy gravitates into science. Anthropomorphic and mythological visions tend to become more precise, logical, observation-based standpoints, and literary modes of expression tend to solidify into literalistic ones.[4]

With an optimistic spirit akin to Condorcet and Comte, among the most famous and influential of the nineteenth-century thinkers who expressed a faith in human progress, and who also significantly influenced twentieth-century French thought, was the down-to-earth materialist and theorist of communism, Karl Marx (1818–83).[5] According to Marx, human beings organize themselves into social groups, and inevitably enter into interpersonal relationships that stem from their elementary and natural activities of producing food, providing shelter, creating tools, making clothes, transporting goods, etc. – relationships which when taken as a whole, constitute the economic structure of the social organization. Marx believes that this economic structure of the society is basic, and that we can understand a good part of any society's legal system, religious system, philosophical system, forms of art, and forms of politics – the society's ideologies, as he called them – as expressions of economic conditions and relationships within the society.[6] In his later years, Marx developed an extensive, mathematically grounded economic theory, and believed that upon its basis, he could scientifically understand social tendencies and thereby foresee the potentials for social transformation and progress.[7]

But Karl Marx was not only an economically focused social theorist. He began as an advocate of human freedom who dedicated his writings to the elimination of exploitation and self-estrangement. For Marx, it is of utmost importance that human beings feel at home in the world, and he believed that social conditions and social systems that interfere with this realization should be revealed for the dehumanizing systems that they are. Hence his continuous criticism of the capitalistic system, exploitation and the institution of private property, which he believed alienated workers from the products of their labor, and alienated people from one other. As a remedy, and as what he believed to be a foreshadowing of the future, Marx formulated a communal social vision wherein ownership of factories and the means of production is shared by all of the workers, wherein exploitation is eliminated, and wherein people have the freedom to develop their potentialities, whether these involve writing poetry, going fishing or working at a craft. In Marxist thought, revolution and rebellion are put into the service of human freedom, community, social harmony, and the feeling of being at home in the world.

In conjunction with Marx, further overtones of progress reside in the more sober evolutionary biology of Charles Darwin (1809–82). In *The Descent of Man* (1871) Darwin claimed that human beings, having risen to the summit of the organic scale, have reason to hope for a still higher destiny in the distant future, even though our bodily frames carry the stamps of our less-exalted origins in the lower primates. Each of these theorists – Condorcet, Comte, Marx, and Darwin – shared the general view that the scientific mode of inquiry, as one based on detached and objective observation, and guided by the use of logical or mathematical reasoning, is the main intellectual discipline for properly understanding the individual human being and human society. In association with their faith in scientific method, they variously recognized a developmental, or progressive dimension to human life in particular, to life in general, or to the universe as a whole.

During the initial years of the twentieth century, up until the First World War, advances in theoretical physics, the visual arts, and mathematical logic[8] – radical advances that undermined many centuries-old assumptions – further supported the nineteenth-century anticipation that the twentieth century would mark a genuinely new and culturally-advanced era.[9] For instance, the scientific revolution in theoretical physics blossomed at the beginning of the twentieth century, even though it had some of its important sources in the mid-nineteenth-century work of the mathematician, G. F. B. Riemann (1826–66). Riemann's achievement was to be among the first to develop a coherent, not to mention revolutionary, non-Euclidean geometry that took as its model, not the relationships between straight lines drawn on a flat surface, as had been the tradition since the times of Euclid, but the relationships between the straight lines drawn upon a spherical, as opposed to a flat (i.e., Euclidean) surface.[10]

It took some time for Riemann's geometrical theory – first formulated in 1854[11] – to be applied to problems in theoretical physics by far-seeing scientists such as Albert Einstein (1879–1955), but the applications of Riemann's non-Euclidean geometry were astounding, not to mention paradoxically challenging to the imagination. In the history of physics, it was momentous to discover that this non-Euclidean geometry of curved space – a geometry that had been initially not much more than a mathematical curiosity – more precisely describes our physical universe, in contrast to the Euclidean geometry of flattened space.[12]

With respect to reinforcing the idea of progress, this realization led to a revolutionary transition in theoretical physics at the beginning of the twentieth century, namely, from the Newtonian conception of physical relationships that had developed in the 1600s[13] to a more contemporary relativistic or Einsteinian conception.[14] Physicists began to speak of a single entity called 'spacetime,' instead of two independent entities – 'space' and 'time' – and they no longer assumed that space and time were absolute and invariant. As is known, the sublime power of this new model of the physical universe eventually contributed to the capacity of the human being to recreate the atomic energy of the sun upon the surface of the earth, thus marking a double-edged, Promethean advance in power for humanity. Upon discerning the almost god-like possibility of harnessing atomic energy, the faith in the effectiveness of scientific styles of inquiry was further strengthened.

Comparable in cultural magnitude, and similar in imaginative spirit to the early twentieth-century revolution in theoretical physics, was a revolution in the visual arts that stemmed from the French art world. This, in particular, was the development of the cubist style of painting by Georges Braque (1882–1963) and Pablo Picasso (1881–1973) which challenged the long-standing tradition of Renaissance perspective.[15] Rather than representing objects as seen from a single observation point taken at a single time, Braque and Picasso painted objects as seen imaginatively from several points at once, generating a multi-aspected, fragmented image, where an object's front-view could be immediately juxtaposed to, or combined with, a side-view or back-view in a mosaic-like, disconcerting fusion. By coalescing together in a single, tension-ridden image, a set of multiple perspectives upon an object taken at different times, the Cubists artistically represented what it would be like to see an object all at once, as if one were somehow located at a vantage point which stood above the passing of time from moment to moment.[16]

The enthusiastic attitude sparked by these, and other scientific and artistic developments, was soon questioned. Although the eighteenth- and nineteenth-century optimism that science would help create a better world initially shaped the twentieth-century spirit of the times, there soon arose a distinct uneasiness about the positivistic promise of scientific, and especially of technological, advancement in light of a further observation: scientific thinking also has the capacity to dehumanize people and to turn them into mere cogs in the social machine. Such reservations towards science and technology were not altogether new,[17] but they intensified significantly as a consequence of the devastation of the First World War, where men fighting on horseback in the nineteenth-century style battled alongside armored units, aircraft, machine guns and poison gas.

Philosophically, we can locate the seeds of distrust towards scientific thinking that sprouted later during and after the First World War, to the beginnings of the nineteenth century and the emergence of a closer attention to the sheer passing of time. For during the late 1700s and early 1800s, a more distinct awareness of time's passing led to a more intense sense of the train of history, and a sharper sense of history's linear progression. With this intensified sense of time came an accompanying difficulty in conceptualizing time's passing in rational, logical or mathematical terms. The earlier calculus of Newton and Leibniz did much to achieve this understanding, but it could do so only by regarding time atomistically as a series of infinitesimal points, rather than as a pure flow. A way to understand time in a manner that captured its continuous nature remained resistant to mathematical reason, and this was noted by the first theorist in our survey, Henri Bergson.

In reaction to what boiled down to the problem of understanding the nature of flowing time, early nineteenth-century theorists such as G. W. F. Hegel quickly developed a new style of logic that modeled itself on the melting together of opposites (e.g., in the way metals are fused together in an alloy). Other theorists, finding the idea of a logic grounded upon the blending of opposites to be either too much in conflict with mathematical thought, or, at the other extreme, still too insensitive to the seemingly non-logical reality of human emotional life, rejected Hegel's attempt to understand time in a rational, and yet fluid and 'living' manner. Having found Hegel's middle-ground objectionable, some theorists adamantly retained an allegiance to the more traditional mathematical forms of rationality in conjunction with a commitment to the idea of historical development, while others rejected the idea that history has an ultimate goal at all, advocating instinct, emotion, and chaos aligned with a conception of time as a force of destruction and endless revolution.

So during the nineteenth century, alternative ways to understand the nature of time issued from the growing awareness of time's passing, and these ways were embodied in the scientific rationalism and empiricism that remained committed to mathematical reason and the scientific method of the eighteenth century, in the dialectical rationality that took both idealistic and materialistic forms, and in a more extreme anti-rationalism that appeared as romanticism, instinctualism, and mysticism. As representatives of these diverse intellectual forces – sometimes appearing in a complicated intermixture – we can associate the three thinkers mentioned above who significantly influenced the course of twentieth-century French philosophy: Sigmund Freud, who embodied the scientific mentality tempered with an awareness of the importance of human instinct, Karl Marx, whose dialectical materialism preserved the idea of a harmonious goal for human society, and Friedrich Nietzsche, whose intense respect for life and instinct led him to challenge the value of purely rationalistic and mathematically centered approaches to the world.

On the whole, the nineteenth century preserved a prevailing faith in human progress along with an accompanying enthusiasm for scientific inquiry as a way to achieve this progress. But this faith in progress was never total, since almost from the very start of the industrial revolution, dehuman-izing forces were also associated with the forces of science and technology, and the notion of time itself remained puzzling. As the century wore on, a gradual questioning of the unqualified value of scientific inquiry increased, giving rise to more distinctively intuitive and poetic ways of understanding the nature of existence. So upon arriving at the initial years of the twentieth century, we witness a growing ambivalence towards science, for almost simultaneous with one of the greatest advances in theoretical physics was one of the most devas-tating of wars – a war fueled by the newest technologies of destruction.

Throughout twentieth-century French philosophy, we find an ambivalence towards science expressed in a series of reactions against scientific, and espe-cially technological, thinking – reactions which, ironically enough, sometimes ground themselves upon mechanical models of analysis that reflect the very technological mentality under criticism. We encounter repeated pleas for greater social responsibility, side-by-side with expressions of futility in recog-nition of human irrationality and the overall irrationality of the world. Numerous rejections of authoritarianism in general punctuate the century, some of which are accompanied by an appeal to be guided by the authority of 'language itself,' and some of which deny the absolute validity of all theorizing, while yet acknowledging an inexpressible reality beneath the appearances.

PART 1

SURREALISM, EXISTENTIALISM, AND VITALISM

1

The Surrealistic Setting: 1916–38

It is a recurring historical phenomenon that individuals who find themselves initially located in society as outcasts, radicals, subversives, criminals, and other kinds of non-mainstream types, often later become legitimated and honored as culturally vital heroes who once stood among the avant-garde. Once-obscure poets, novelists, and playwrights emerge to assume places at the center of the prevailing literary canon, fringe-party political revolutionaries rise to become world-historical heads of state, once-underappreciated musicians move into fashionable current to begin a previously unimagined cultural sound, and people who were once frowned upon by the social elite become overnight sensations as they are ushered into the limelight. On the negative side, the public recognition of protest-groups sometimes undermines the protesters by rendering their causes legitimate, as they slowly become redefined, digested, assimilated, and disarmed by the terms of acceptable language and acceptable media.

Such was the dual fate of the Dada artistic group which originated in the midst of the First World War, during the end of 1915 and the beginning of 1916. This artistic circle established itself in Zürich, Switzerland, as an attempt to raise a voice against the ongoing war in Europe, not by arguing positively for peace, but by protesting against the general cultural scene – one that they perceived to be responsible for the war. The Dadaists comprehended the established cultural atmosphere, as noted in the introduction above, in reference to an alienation-generating amalgam of rationalistic thinking, science, and technology that adhered to the preservation of order, systematicity, and methodicality. They opposed the standing arrangement of the social (dis)order during their time, and they believed firmly that European cultural values were not worth preserving, given how they were fueling the war that was then devastating Europe.

The most frequently encountered label that has been attached to the Dada movement is 'nihilistic:' the Dadaists have been perceived, and indeed they perceived themselves, as being against 'everything,' as they joked, recited nonsense poetry, danced around on stage in absurd costumes, and insulted their audiences. They embodied outrage and negation, gathering together regularly at the Cabaret Voltaire on Zürich's Spiegelstrasse, where it was possible to witness escapades such as the following:

> On the stage, keys and boxes were pounded to provide the music, until the infuriated public protested. Serner,[18] instead of reciting poems, set a bunch of flowers at the foot of a dressmaker's dummy. A voice, under a huge hat in the shape of a sugar-loaf, recited poems by Arp.[19] Huelsenbeck[20,21] screamed his poems louder and louder, while Tzara[22] beat out the same rhythm *crescendo* on a big drum. Huelsenbeck and Tzara danced around grunting like bear cubs, or in sacks with top hats waddled around in an exercise called *noir cacadou*. Tzara invented chemical and static poems.[23]

The Dada scenes conveyed a feeling of chaos, fragmentation, assault on the senses, absurdity, frustration of ordinary norms, pastiche, spontaneity, and posed robotic mechanism. They were scenes from a madhouse, performed by a group of sane and reflective people who were expressing their decided anger and disgust at the world surrounding them. The Dadaists organized a steely toned carnival in their Swiss café, mimicking the chaotic insanity of the First World War in an effort to criticize it. But in place of bloody violence, they substituted zaniness, absurdity, laughter and jokes, as they tried to defuse the seriousness of the general cultural chaos. They criticized the cultural scene by making light of it, perhaps in an effort to psychologically diffuse for themselves the horror it was generating.

To comprehend the Dada mentality, we can note its close and usually unrecognized coincidence with what Hegel described a century earlier as the 'skeptical' attitude. In his *Phenomenology of Spirit* (1807), he wrote the following:

> [The skeptical attitude] declares the nothingness of seeing, hearing, etc., but it sees and hears, etc.; it declares the nothingness of moral principles, and yet it behaves in accord with these very principles. Its actions and its

words continually contradict one other … If likeness is pointed out to it, then it points out unlikeness; and then if one indicates that it had just pointed out unlikeness, then it turns around and points out likeness. Its talk is in fact like the quarrelling of obstinate children, one of whom says A when the other says B, and then says again B, when the other says A, and through the contradiction *with themselves* buy for themselves the fun [*Freude*] of remaining in contradiction *with each other*.[24]

In tune with this skeptical and contrary attitude, the Dadaists claimed that in times of war, the slogan of Dada is peace, and in times of peace, the slogan of Dada is war.[25] Whenever they encountered a positive thesis, they immediately defined themselves against it. And predictably in tune with this form of skepticism, self-contradictory phrases sprinkle themselves across the Dada manifestos – phrases which proclaim that everything is false, that Dada is nothing, that there is no ultimate truth, that everything is absurd, that everything is incoherent and that there is no logic. They are phrases that present themselves in the manifestos as being true, meaningful, coherent, and logical, while they deny all truth, meaning, coherence, and logic.

When conceiving the Dada movement as a form of active-and-antagonistic skepticism, as a form of playful contrariness, and also as a form of intellectual violence, rather than as a kind of hopeless and indifferent nihilism, this artistic movement's influence upon subsequent French thought is more readily perceivable. We shall see, for example, that Hegel's discussion of skepticism also resonates well with the definitively poststructuralist conception of deconstruction advanced by Jacques Derrida in the 1960s. A Dada influence colors the 1970s writings of Gilles Deleuze and Félix Guattari as well. And more generally, a skeptical attitude characterizes the wider sphere of twentieth-century French thought, insofar as there was a continued effort to secure a sense of freedom by taking a stance against the establishment by saying 'no' to the oppressive status quo, as it was conceived in various guises.

As will also become evident, such 'anti-establishment' sentiments appear not only in Derrida, Deleuze, and Guattari, but in Roland Barthes's view that language itself is oppressively 'fascist' in how it determines our styles of thinking, in Michel Foucault's 'negative' conception of power as an external social force of mental and bodily manipulation, in Luce Irigaray's conception of European languages as being inherently sexist and oppressive towards women, and in Jean-François Lyotard's conception of the scientific establishment as a one-dimensional and exclusionary enterprise that violently silences its opposition by denying people the very vocabulary in which to express themselves. The Dadaists' earlier attempt to free themselves from the cultural array that was perpetuating war throughout most of the

European mainland, stylistically parallels later attempts to combat the oppressive cultural arrays that were perceived to be damaging the health of the Western cultural spirit, namely, the forces of capitalism, fascism, sexism, science and technology.

Given that the Dadaists set themselves against whatever happened to come their way – they even set themselves against the art establishment itself –[26] it is no surprise that the earlier Dadaist manifestos (*c.* 1918) are antagonistic to Sigmund Freud's psychoanalysis, which had been growing in popularity. At the time, psychoanalysis remained a kindred spirit nonetheless, for Freud intended psychoanalysis to be subversive: although its critics pointed out that psychoanalytic theory conservatively located its understanding of the human psyche within the contours of the traditional family unit, psychoanalysis still carried an intellectual and revolutionary bite. For perhaps more influentially, Freud maintained that to understand the human psyche, it is essential to understand human instinct, which he believed has a murderous aspect. This Freudian concern with human instinct led to a theory that, for the late Victorian era, involved a radical, upsetting and offensively microscopic and (allegedly shameless) attention to sexual energies and social taboos. Psychoanalysis drew attention to what it believed to be the source of these energies, namely, wild and unconscious states of mind, and this aspect of the psyche soon captured the interests of the surrealists, owing to the connections Freud discerned between unconscious energies, and creativity, spontaneity, dreams, non-rationality, and liberation from civilized norms.

Although Freud eventually refined his theory of mind from a two-aspect 'conscious vs. unconscious' model (*c.* 1900) to a three-aspect 'ego, superego, and id' model (*c.* 1923), each component of which could have unconscious aspects, he characterized the core of unconscious life – an aspect of the psyche which he termed the 'id'[27] – in a manner that underscored its socially threatening nature:

> [The id] is the dark, unapproachable part of our personality ... we call it a chaos, a cauldron full of bubbling excitations ... it has no organization, summons up no collective will, only the endeavor to produce the satis-faction of instinctual needs in accord with the pleasure principle. Concerning the goings-on in the id, the logical laws of thought have no application, above all the law of contradiction. Opposing movements exist next to each other, without reconciling each other or drawing energies away from each other ... In the id, one finds nothing that corre-sponds to the representation of time ...
>
> One can take for granted that the id recognizes no values, no good and evil, no morality.[28]

Even to the Dadaists, the subversive nature of Freud's theory of the unconscious soon became clear, as is evident from later Dadaist statements that praise unconscious energies as being inexhaustible and uncontrollable, and that regard creative energies as being among the chaotic and illogical manifestations of life, as they stand in the same spirit as wild tribal dances.[29] In the waning phases of the Dada movement, their representatives admitted the importance of unconscious energies, and their own adherence to contrariness and irrationality gradually intermingled with the sentiments of the surrealists, who, as central to their artistic vision, expressly advocated the need for artists to tap into their instinctive, non-rational energies.

Complementing the Romanian Dada-manifesto writer, Tristan Tzara, André Breton (1896–1966) – French poet, essayist, critic, and editor – emerged as the main author of the surrealist[30] manifestos during the 1920s. For Breton, Freud's emphasis upon dreams, along with the psychoanalytic therapeutic technique of 'free association,' was of the most striking artistic importance. Seeking to explore the contents of his patients' unconscious thought-processes more effectively, Freud often asked his patients to relax upon a couch and to associate freely whatever ideas came to mind. This free association was done in relation to some given stimulus idea that was perceived to be central to the person's troubled mental condition. Freud's therapeutic hope was to generate a cluster of associations that would emerge without the interference of the filtering and censorship mechanisms that a person ordinarily has comfortably and controllingly in place. His aim was to stimulate the person to 'dream' out loud, to speak from his or her unconscious, in order for obscured and repressed meanings to emerge, thus revealing more explicitly the inner tensions that were troubling the person.

Breton was interested specifically in the nature of artistic creation, and he found the method of free association, or 'automatic writing,' to be a method of pure expression. Using it to stimulate his own literary creativity, Breton used this method to generate texts, with results that surprised him in the degree to which they embodied high emotion, a wide-assortment of images, a vivid graphic quality and periodic levity.[31] By tapping into his unconscious energies, Breton discovered a more authentic mode of artistic expression – one that conveyed a revolutionary quality as well, for given Freud's theory, the unconscious was also regarded as being notoriously free from social constraints, censorship, reason, and moral norms, and therefore, as an energy well-suited to dynamite the values of the established society within which he found himself.

By locating the source of authentic and liberating thought in the unconscious, and by understanding dreams to be expressions of the same, the surrealists aspired to integrate these unconscious energies into the social scene at large to illuminate, and also change, the standing social condition. Hence originated the term 'surrealist' as signifying a resolution and blend between dream and reality into what was hoped to be a truer, more liberated, daily condition. In a manner to be developed in later years by Roland Barthes, Michel Foucault, Jacques Derrida, and Luce Irigaray, one of the surrealists' aims was to show that prevailing social norms are mostly artificial and fragile, and are thereby eminently changeable and reformable. By dissolving the myth that the standing social order is somehow natural, inevitable, and unchangeable, one opens the door for alternative social arrangements.

During the later 1930s, the French surrealist movement transformed to adopt communistic ideals in its desire for social reform, and it framed its revolutionary aspirations in the Marxist terms of an attack upon both capitalism and fascism, identifying the proletarian workers as among the foremost powers of social liberation. In general, by blending dream with reality, surrealistic thinking aimed to stimulate a more passionate and instinctively energized consciousness of the ordinarily experienced world, and it intended to use its thought-provoking imagery to demythologize the illusions upon which rested the capitalist and fascistic social orders. Such socially reforming aspirations were shared by the remnant Dada artists who returned to Germany and who contributed a voice against Nazism during the 1930s; later, they were embodied in Roland Barthes's thought of the 1950s, when he attempted to identify and undercut the myths supportive of French colonialism.

Contrary to the surrealist's communistic intentions of the 1930s, there are conflicting revolutionary tendencies in at least one major style of surrealistic expression, namely, that which portrays an imaginary scene in a manner that makes it look 'real,' as we find in contemporary virtual reality technology, surrealism's twenty-first-century grandchild. This surrealistic style does not obviously render our perception of the ordinary world more realistic, as the communists would have surrealism serve their interests; rather, it substitutes an artificial reality of different content for the ordinarily lived world, by constructing an unnerving blend of dream-imaginary states and the scenes typical of daily life. Just as René Descartes once questioned the veridicality of his immediate experience and wondered whether he might in fact be dreaming, as he actually sat before his fireplace, this virtual-reality-centered, or 'photorealistic', style of surrealistic expression can undermine our confidence that what we are experiencing here and now is the true, natural, or actual world.[32] Here, for instance, the artists intentionally confuse artistically generated forms with naturally occurring forms such that in the end, a world which appears at first to be natural, can be revealed to be a gigantic stage-set, and bodies that appear to be living and breathing, can turn out to be robots.

The Dada movement's predilection for the bizarre and the insane comes into play within this form of virtual reality, or photorealistic, surrealism. This mode of photorealistic–surrealistic portrayal can nonetheless be appreciated as a revolutionary style of expression on those occasions when it stimulates people to question a particular political regime or social situation that has been previously accepted as 'normal.' This is the result desired, although they often use other means, by thinkers such as Barthes, Foucault, Derrida, and Irigaray – all of whom argue that our daily world is more artificial and socially constructed, than it is naturally given. The photorealistic–surrealistic style can, as noted, also foster a more private, idiosyncratic, disconnected and alienated relationship to the prevailing social world, for it can simulate a world of madness. And yet, when its devices are known and recognized as such, it can also be used in a merely entertaining and healthy way, as it plays less deceptively upon the difference between illusion and reality.

Despite its various employments, the influence of the surrealistic mentality in popular culture throughout the twentieth century – especially in the form of 'photorealistic' surrealism – can be seen to have continued long after the art-history-named movement entitled 'surrealism' transformed into an allegiance with communism during the late 1930s in France, and after its representatives migrated to other countries during the Second World War. If we consider the art-form of the motion picture, for instance, examples are present in the 1950s that offer a blend of dream and reality, and even more numerous examples of the surrealist spirit emerged thereafter to accumulate to the present day. All of which requires us to consider the extent to which surrealistic thinking runs throughout twentieth-century French philosophy.

To appreciate the presence of this surrealistic spirit in Western popular culture in general – one whose intensity appears to be sharply increasing – we can consider movies such as *Forbidden Planet* (1956), *Kwaidan* (1964),[33] *Juliet of the Spirits* (1965), *Solaris* (1972/2002), *The Sacrifice* (1986), *Jacob's Ladder* (1990), *Lost Highway* (1997), *The Matrix* (1999), *Existenz* (1999), *Vanilla Sky* (2001), *A Beautiful Mind* (2001), *Memento* (2001),[34] and *Mulholland Drive* (2002),[35] all of which portray how the world of daily life and the world of imagination can be brought into such a close coincidence, that one's confidence in what counts as 'real' becomes undermined. If such a condition is globalized, and one hypothesizes that an entire cultural condition can be describable as 'surrealist' (or in more contemporary terms, 'hyperrealist,' following Baudrillard), then one can wonder, taking Freud's psychoanalysis as the inspiration, whether estimations are in order about whether some governing aspects of the social condition are operating at a stronger level of fantasy and imagination – and hence, at a greater level of confusion and misapprehension of what is objectively happening – than previously has been the case.

That the former can be true, that the standing social condition can be regarded as containing notably disoriented and disorientating aspects, is a central theme expressed by the psychiatrist and social phenomenologist, R. D. Laing (1927–89). He wrote in *The Politics of Experience* (1967) that the process of socialization whose result is the accepted definition of normality, can be construed as a set of variously structured processes that deform human experience, rather than actualize it into a condition of maturity and fulfillment. Which is to say that, given the lead of our above examples, what is accepted as 'normal' in a photorealistic–surrealist culture, namely, inversions, confusions, transformations, and blends between the rock-hard, physically tangible world and the imaginary world of social construction, can be regarded as 'abnormal' when seen from a more down-to-earth condition, for the latter standpoint tempts one to conclude that the contemporary powers of imagination, fabrication, and rhetorical 'spin' are operating in excess. Those who can perceive the social order as being disconcertingly 'surrealistic,' are in a position to understand the degree to which the social order has been artificially constructed, just as a psychiatrist can understand 'from the inside' the mental states of his patients, but also contrast those states with his or her own states of mind which are presumably more reflectively perceived and soberly understood.

In the pages that follow, we will note the influences of Dada and Surrealism upon key twentieth-century French thinkers, and implicitly introduce the question of whether present-day, early twenty-first-century Western culture, to the extent that it displays surrealistic qualities, remains therapeutically open to the style of demythologizing social criticism that was advanced in the 1950s–1990s by thinkers such as Barthes, Foucault, Derrida, Irigaray, Deleuze, Lyotard, and Baudrillard. With this suggestion, we will underscore the phenomenon of how an intellectual movement which was once revolutionary, can become socially entrenched to the point where it has assumed the role of the status quo, and where, in turn, it stands itself in need of criticism and reform. By pointing out the surrealistic undercurrent in twentieth-century French thought, some illumination, and a potential critique, of twenty-first-century surrealistic–hyperrealistic culture can be brought to the surface. In the latter respect, this fundamentally historical survey and analysis of the various French theorists serves as a signpost for social criticism in the spirit of those French theorists. By wondering about the degree to which mainstream Western society has become surrealistic, we can begin to discern the degree of artificiality, and thereby, the degree of potentiality for revolutionary reform, that characterizes our present cultural situation.

2

Henri Bergson, Philosopher (1859–1941)

Life and works

Henri Bergson was born in Paris on October 18, 1859: his mother was English and his Polish father was a composer and music teacher. During his youth, Bergson received an education of excellent quality, and after graduating from the prestigious École Normale Supérieure[36,37] at the age of twenty-two, he was appointed to teach philosophy in a *lycée*[38] in Angers. For nearly the next twenty years, Bergson taught in various *lycées*, mainly at the Lycée Henri IV, where he worked from 1890 to 1898 (ages 31–39). When Bergson was thirty-nine, he was appointed to teach at the École Normale Supérieure, and two years later (1900) he became a Professor of Philosophy at the Collège de France (founded in 1520), where he worked until his retirement in 1921 at age sixty-two. During the course of his career, Bergson wrote a series of philosophical works which became widely known, and which eventually brought him the status of being one of the most highly respected philosophers in France. In connection with this achievement, he was awarded the 1927 Nobel Prize for Literature. At the age of eighty-one, Bergson died from pneumonia on January 4, 1941 during the German occupation of France, after having stood for hours in line in the cold weather, as he waited to register with the authorities as a person of Jewish heritage.

Evolutionary theory and Bergson's ambivalence towards science

Bergson accepted the evolutionary theory of his time to the extent that he regarded the human intellect as having emerged from the adaptations of our primate ancestors to their natural environment. Specifically, he maintained that the human analytical intellect is primarily a bodily capacity for solving practical problems, such as those involved in finding food and in securing a means of protection from environmental threats. This practical and puzzle-solving feature of the intellect's workings led him to question whether this capacity of the human mind is naturally well-suited for other, more speculative, activities, such as apprehending the ultimate truth of the world.

Bergson believed that the intellect, along with the styles of scientific–mathematical inquiry that issue from it, may help us physically survive, but he was skeptical about its effectiveness in acquiring knowledge of the universe's core realities. He wondered whether the mathematical, analytic, practically oriented intellect – the kind of intellect that would be useful if one were an engineer – is appropriate for philosophical knowledge. There was a serious question in his mind regarding the power of the analytical, logical understanding with respect to its ability to answer questions about the nature of reality.

Bergson's philosophy consequently explored the powers of the calculating, practical-problem-solving intellect (he is comparable to Immanuel Kant in this respect)[39] to discover exactly what kind of knowledge the intellect can provide. He reasoned that if analytical thinking is not powerful enough to illuminate metaphysical problems, then we must find some other way to grasp the basic truths of existence, if they are accessible at all. To begin his inquiry, and to distinguish more precisely between the discursive intellect and that part of the mind which he believed can allow us to apprehend metaphysical truth, Bergson contrasted two kinds of knowledge, namely, absolute knowledge and relative knowledge.

Knowledge: absolute vs. relative

According to Bergson, there are two ways of knowing a thing:

> If we compare the various ways of defining metaphysics and of conceiving the absolute, we shall find, despite apparent discrepancies, that philosophers agree in making a deep distinction between two ways of knowing a thing. The first implies going all around it, the

second entering into it. The first depends upon the viewpoint chosen and the symbols employed, while the second is taken from no viewpoint and rests on no symbol. Of the first kind of knowledge we shall say that it stops at the *relative*; of the second that, wherever possible, it attains the *absolute*.[40]

When I speak of an absolute movement [i.e., absolute knowledge of movement], it means that I attribute to the mobile an inner being and, as it were, states of soul; it also means that I am in harmony with these states and enter into them by an effort of imagination.[41]

It follows that an absolute can only be given in an *intuition*, while all the rest has to do with *analysis*. We call intuition here the sympathy by which one is transported into the interior of an object in order to coincide with what there is unique and consequently inexpressible in it.[42]

The above remarks assert that we can acquire absolute knowledge of something only when we enter into it, as opposed to merely circling around the outside of it. We can acquire this knowledge when we become the thing itself, or are that thing in some sense, such that we perfectly coincide with it. Supposedly, such absolute knowledge does not use symbols, representatives or substitutes of the thing we wish to know; absolute knowledge is a direct, immediate, internal, experiential and intuitive knowledge of the thing itself.

Bergson's conception of absolute knowledge might seem to be easily understandable and achievable, and it has implications for how we should address philosophical questions. It implies, he believes, that answers to philosophical questions will not be found in any book. Philosophical answers will only be found in having a certain kind of direct experience that is recognizable as authentic, truthful, revealing, and foundational. In this connection, he introduces the idea of sympathy (or, more precisely, empathy) as a means of grasping absolute truths. If one can empathize with another being fully, then one becomes that other being, understanding from the inside what it is like to be that being, and thereby dissolving all alienation and feelings of otherness with respect to that being. Achieving this coincidence in sentiment is to achieve absolute knowledge of the being in question.

As we can see, Bergson's focus upon empathy differs from the attempt to understand something 'from the outside' using symbolic thought, as we would do, for instance, when using mathematical or scientific symbolism to understand some phenomenon or relationship in nature. He urges us instead to consider things from the first-person perspective of whatever we are trying to understand, such that we have the first-hand experience of what it is like to be that kind of being, or experience the world through that kind of perspective.

The limits of intellect-based modes of knowledge

In science, the mistake of 'spatializing' time

Bergson maintains that space and time are typically conceived of as individual entities (since it is commonly recognized that space, and time, is each a whole with parts), which are mathematically divisible into regular intervals in accord with the numerical sequence (1, 2, 3, 4 ...). Which is to say that Bergson recognizes how space and time are usually understood to be two sets of sequential points. He acknowledges that this mathematical understanding is accurate enough with regard to space, but he is also convinced that it misrepresents the nature of time. He argues that (real, lived) time cannot be captured by mathematical descriptions, mainly because time-as-experienced (or what he calls 'duration') is dynamic and flowing, whereas space is static. In Bergson's estimation, mathematical thinking misleadingly tends to atomize, freeze and ossify whatever it describes, and insofar as it has this effect, it misrepresents the continuous flow of time:

> I was indeed very struck to see how real time, which plays the leading part in any philosophy of evolution, eludes mathematical treatment. Its essence being to flow, not one of its parts is still there when another part comes along. Superposition of one part on another with measurement in view is therefore impossible, inconceivable ... Ever since my university days I had been aware that duration is measured by the trajectory of a body in motion and that mathematical time is a line; but I had not yet observed that this operation contrasts radically with all other processes of measurement, for it is not carried out on an aspect or an effect representative of what one wishes to measure, but on something that excludes it. The line one measures is immobile, time is mobility. The line is made, it is complete; time is what is happening, and more than that, it is what causes everything to happen. The measuring of time never deals with duration as duration; what is counted is only a certain number of extremities of intervals, or *moments*, in short, virtual halts in time. To state that an incident will occur at the end of a certain time *t*, is simply to say that one will have counted, from now until then, a number *t* of simultaneities of a certain kind. In between these simultaneities anything you like may happen. Time could be enormously and even infinitely accelerated; nothing would be changed for the mathematician, for the physicist or for the astronomer. And yet the difference with regard to consciousness would be profound ... But this duration, which science eliminates, and which

is so difficult to conceive and express, is what one feels and lives. Suppose we try to find out what it is? – How would it appear to a consciousness which desired only to see it without measuring it, which would then grasp it without stopping it?[43]

Since mathematical thinking is a style of symbolic thinking, and since symbolic thinking allegedly provides only a relative, as opposed to an absolute knowledge, Bergson does not believe that mathematical thinking can provide answers to philosophical questions, since the latter demand absolute answers. Since he also maintains that abstractive mathematical thinking does not capture the concrete reality of time-as-experienced, he inquires whether the direct experience of time can alternatively provide a kind of absolute knowledge that can open the way toward answering some basic philosophical questions. Bergson thus turns to the examination of temporal experience as an avenue toward metaphysical knowledge, and concentrates upon the lived quality of our personal encounter with time.[44] This attention to the direct experience of time was to become one of Bergson's most influential contributions to twentieth-century French philosophy.

The intuition of pure duration and self-knowledge

Bergson writes:

There is at least one reality which we all seize from within, by intuition and not by simple analysis. It is our own person in its flowing through time, the self which endures.[45]

What I find beneath these clear-cut crystals and this superficial congelation is a continuity of flow comparable to no other flowing I have ever seen. It is a succession of states each one of which announces what follows and contains what precedes. Strictly speaking they do not constitute multiple states until I have already got beyond them, and turn around to observe their trail. While I was experiencing them they were so solidly organized, so profoundly animated with a common life, that I could never have said where any one of them finished or the next one began. In reality, none of them do begin or end; they all dove-tail into one another.[46]

When Bergson reflects upon his immediate experience, he apprehends a continuity of conscious states beneath the 'clear-cut crystals' – those sharply defined aspects of awareness that arise when we look specifically at this object, or at that object, or think of this idea, or of that idea, or turn our attention in this direction, or in that direction. These latter objects of awareness are discretely contoured items in our consciousness, but Bergson's experience is that at bottom, they all merge together as time flows continually within our consciousness without any sharp breaks or interruptions. He also notices that the items within consciousness present themselves as being sharply distinguished from one another and as strongly articulated, only when we reflect upon what is happening. Otherwise everything blends together. When life goes on unreflectively or prereflectively, he experiences a more intensified sense of consciousness-flowing-through-time. Acts of reflection interrupt this flow, and tend to lift up, extract, and hold up for individual examination, selected aspects of consciousness's natural continuity. Within Bergson's perspective, reflection is an activity of consciousness that freezes the flow of consciousness into segments, and (misleadingly) crystallizes the contents of consciousness into a set of static objects available for retrospective examination.

An act of reflection thus introduces a distance within consciousness that allows one to see, as if in a mirror, a solidified image of oneself, along with aspects of one's flow of consciousness, as things or objects. This capacity for self-consciousness is a profound feature of human beings, but according to Bergson, it has the distracting side-effect of obscuring the flowing temporal reality of consciousness. So instead of using reflection to discover the truth – a method which has been a procedure within the Western philosophical tradition since the time of Socrates – Bergson maintains that the intuition of consciousness's continuity, rather than self-conscious reflection, is the best way to apprehend oneself as one truly is, namely, as a being whose internal, lived, reality is characterized by an unbroken flow of rich temporal experience. He believes that in our essential depths, we are more like flowing water than like a tray of ice cubes, and more like fluctuating energy than like a constellation of static matter. In sum, Bergson recognizes our human being as a fundamentally down-to-earth being in smoothly changing, continuous time.

Comparison between intellect-based and intuition-based modes of apprehension

On the distinction between intuition and intellect, Bergson states the following:

> [T]o think intuitively is to think in duration [i.e., in real time]. Intelligence starts ordinarily from the immobile, and reconstructs movement as best it can with immobilities in juxtaposition. Intuition starts from movement, posits it, or rather perceives it as reality itself,

and sees in immobility only an abstract moment, a snapshot taken by the mind, of a mobility. Intelligence ordinarily concerns itself with things, meaning by that, with the static, and makes of change an accident which is supposedly superadded. For intuition the essential is change: as for the thing, as intelligence understands it, it is a cutting which has been made out of the becoming and set up by our mind as a substitute for the whole. Thought ordinarily pictures to itself the new as a new arrangement of pre-existing elements; nothing is ever lost for it, nothing is ever created. Intuition, bound up to a duration which is growth, perceives in it an uninterrupted continuity of unforeseeable novelty; it sees, it knows that the mind draws from itself more than it has, that spirituality consists in just that, and that reality, impregnated with spirit, is creation.[47]

An implication of Bergson's view is this: with the use of our intellectual, reflective, puzzle-solving, mathematical capacities alone, we cannot apprehend reality as it is in itself. He concludes that we must use some other means:

> *Our intelligence, when it follows its natural inclination, proceeds by solid perceptions on the one hand, and by stable conceptions on the other.* It starts from the immobile and conceives and expresses movement only in terms of immobility. It places itself in ready-made concepts and tries to catch in them, as in a net, something of the passing reality. It does not do so in order to obtain an internal and metaphysical knowledge of the real. It is simply to make use of them, each concept (like each sensation) being a *practical question* which our activity asks of reality and to which reality will answer, as is proper in things, by a yes or no. But in so doing it allows what is the very essence of the real to escape.[48]

To apprehend the absolute truth, we must go with the flow of time to apprehend, in an immediate, direct and intuitive manner, ourselves and the world as our experience continually moves us. In short, the doorway to truth is through the phenomenology of time-consciousness.[49] For Bergson, the primary reality is time, which he regards generally as the source of all creativity, and as the life-force in reality as a whole. Time gives birth to everything.[50] So when we arrive at an intuitive appreciation of ourselves as fundamentally temporal beings, we also come into contact with the force that drives all evolutionary and historical development. Self-knowledge consequently yields cosmic knowledge, for insofar as human beings themselves are a part of the cosmos, and are not outside of it, they have discoverable within themselves the absolute truth that inhabits each thing in the universe.

Schematic summary of oppositions within Bergson's outlook

A		B
Time-centered	vs.	Space-centered
Intuitive	vs.	Intellectual/Mathematical/Scientific
Absolute	vs.	Relative
Internal	vs.	External
Flux	vs.	Stability
Dynamic	vs.	Static
Non-symbolic	vs.	Symbolic
Immediate	vs.	Mediated/Reflective
Creative	vs.	Employs already-established results

The categories under 'A' represent the qualities which Bergson associates with metaphysical knowledge and the categories under 'B' represent the qualities he associates with practical, survival-related knowledge. Contrary to those who maintain that science potentially holds the answer to every important question, both physical and metaphysical, Bergson does not believe that the categories under 'B' can provide metaphysical, or absolute, knowledge, as a matter or principle.

Critical reflections

To evaluate Bergson's time-focused and intuition-focused standpoint, we can ask whether there can be absolute knowledge of any being other than oneself. Suppose we accept that absolute knowledge of oneself, as Bergson characterizes it, is attainable through empathic intuition. A problem arises once someone tries to have absolute knowledge of any human being other than himself or herself, for it is difficult, if not impossible, to know whether or not we have successfully put ourselves in the experiential place of another person. Even among close friends, there are limits to the degree of shared feelings (in any knowably exact sense) that are possible, since even the best of acquaintances are unlikely to apprehend the world and react emotionally in exactly the same ways. If there is any absolute knowledge to be gained in such cases, it will usually be of a more general sort.

The question becomes more complicated when we consider whether absolute knowledge is possible with respect to people who we do not know in our immediate surroundings, or people who live in another culture, or people who lived long ago. Since we are all human beings, there are likely to be some types of experience – certain pleasures, pains, satisfactions, hopes, and fears – that we can reasonably assume that all humans similarly have. But once we consider cultural, temporal, local, and individual variations, the differences between people multiply. As these variations become more pronounced, the kind of absolute knowledge we might be able to attain becomes more generalized, more superficial, and less informative.

With respect to other living non-human beings, the kind of absolute knowledge that might be attainable becomes even more vague and difficult to pin down. We might be able to empathize to some extent with other mammals, but it is difficult to imagine what it might be like to experience what an antelope tastes like to a lion, or what a worm tastes like to a bird, or what a fly tastes like to a frog. At the level of one-celled animals and plants, it is close to impossible to imagine what it is like to be such a being. Poetry and speculation might help us to grasp such realities, if there are any, but we could never be sure that our imagined experiences correspond to the actual experiences of living beings that are so distantly related to us. At an even greater distance from human experience, one might question, furthermore, whether it even makes sense to imagine 'what it would be like' to be a rock, or a waterfall, or a snowflake, or a cloud. This spectrum suggests that Bergson's method of intuition, which advises us to secure absolute knowledge through the attempt to empathize with other beings, is limited to the knowledge of living things, and more reasonably, limited to the knowledge of beings that have a consciousness or inner experience closely akin to human beings.

Let us return now to the initial hypothesis above, where we assumed with Bergson that one could have absolute knowledge of oneself. What kind of knowledge could this be? To what extent does the intuition of myself as a consciousness-flowing-through-time provide absolute knowledge of the person I know as 'me,' or as my specific personality? This question arises, because we usually imagine ourselves to be relatively constant characters, rather than as beings that flow and change from moment to moment. The flow and change in experience that Bergson identifies may capture the truth of how consciousness ultimately is, but this pure flow also has the effect of dissolving one's sense of unchanging personal identity.

Contrary to what Bergson suggests, it is typical to identify oneself as a specific someone who persists in quality through time; today, I feel as if I am the same person I was yesterday, because I sense something that has remained constant, despite the wide array of thoughts and changes of consciousness that have happened within me since yesterday. So one might conclude that

Bergson's view implies that one's ordinary sense of selfhood dissolves as absolute knowledge is approached, if we understand the selfhood to be a stylistic constancy-over-time that defines a specific personality. This leads us to question, not necessarily the truth of Bergson's view that the awareness of consciousness-flowing-through-time illuminates the reality of consciousness; rather, it leads us to wonder whether such an awareness reveals the true 'me' which underlies 'my' experience. His view suggests that there ultimately is no true 'me' at all, since, upon examination, 'I' turn out to be a flow of varied experiences that takes place within a consciousness of no necessarily constant personal quality. An adherent of Bergson's view, that is, will be led to question the idea of an enduring self with a definite character, or an enduring individual personality or 'ego,' as an ultimate constituent of human consciousness.[51]

Along a different critical line, we can also ask whether it is consistent for Bergson to claim that symbolic (e.g., scientific or mathematical) thinking is incapable of providing absolute knowledge, as he defines it. Bergson clearly accepts the validity of the scientific outlook insofar as he regards human reason as having emerged primarily as a way to cope with practical problems relating to survival. In this sense, he accepts the earthy spirit of evolutionary theory. However, Bergson's restriction of human reason to practical affairs combined with his general optimism that metaphysical problems can be resolved, leads him to believe that there must be an alternative to the purely intellectual approach towards the world; since the intellect seems to have evolved primarily in view of practical problems, and not for metaphysical inquiry, it appears to Bergson that there must be another mode of awareness that provides the metaphysical answers. Hence, he advocates intuition as way to absolute knowledge.

Bergson also claims, though, that the living flow of creative energy (*élan vital*) that is revealed in intuitive awareness, is also the source of creativity in the world in general. So this *élan vital* is the creative force that underlies evolutionary development as well. And if this is so, evolution is moved by a non-rational energy, which suggests that human rationality – a style of thought-processing generated by evolutionary pressures to enable humans to survive – should to some extent reflect the nature of the energy that generated it. That it does not on Bergson's view is a mystery, since one would expect that reason, if it is generated by the supposedly non-rational source, should somehow display, or embody, or be consistent with, its source. So Bergson claims that reason issues from this non-rational energy (since this living energy is the foundation for evolution) and yet he denies that reason has any power to express the energy from which it stems. It would be more natural to expect that both reason and intuition can reveal absolute truths.

If the above assessment is convincing, we can then ask whether personal introspection, if it is an avenue for understanding the nature of time, is the only available truth-embodying way to understand it. For if both reason and intuition can reveal absolute truths, then mathematically measured time, along with intuitively experienced time, may capture a truth about time as well. To render this position plausible, it is first necessary to question an aspect of Bergson's definition of absolute knowledge, namely, as a kind of knowledge that is supposedly inexpressible by means of symbols.

There is reason to believe that symbolically expressed knowledge is consistent with absolute knowledge, as Bergson understands it. If we admit that it is possible to write a sequence of words that replicates the internal flow of a person's inner thought-experience, for instance, then when someone else reads those words, that person could experience a flow of thought similar to the writer. If this occurs – and it might occur most effectively with a set of sharply defined, clear-cut, mostly non-ambiguous symbols, such as what is aspired to in the development of mathematical symbolism – we would have a straightforward case where the use of symbols allowed us to share the contents of another person's mind.

This suggests that symbolic sequences may be able to reflect an author's (or speaker's) inner experience, not by representing it with substitutes, but by causing an experience isomorphic to what the author had, in the person who comprehends the author's written or spoken symbolic sequences. If such a use of symbolic expression is compatible with Bergson's conception of absolute knowledge, then his reluctance to associate metaphysical truth with the meanings expressible through symbols is unwarranted. Upon reflection, his reservations appear not to be with symbolic expression *per se*, but with symbolic expression in connection with an external perspective on whatever it is one wishes to understand.[52]

The above point brings us a step closer to accepting that a mathematical description of time need not be ruled out from the start as being incompatible with all true understandings of time, at least insofar as true understandings could include those expressed by means of symbols. The more pressing diffi-culty resides in comprehending how a mathematical description of time could capture what it is like to be a being that flows through time. In view of this difficulty, the more accurate position for a Bergsonian would be to hold that mathematical descriptions of time do not represent time as it is in itself, not because they use symbols, but because they remain external to the flow of time. In sum, if we distinguish between a symbolic expression and a description of some phenomenon taken from a standpoint external to it,

Bergson's central idea that it is important to become what one wishes to understand, will generate less confusion.

The place of Henri Bergson in twentieth-century French philosophy

As suggested in the introduction, we can understand much about the cultural changes that took place at the end of the 1700s if we consider the modifications that occurred in the cultural experience of time. With a more concrete appreciation of lived time, abstractive rationalistic and religious styles of thought that located one's center of attention in an unchangeable, timeless dimension, started to diminish in persuasive power, and a stronger sense of history's passing emerged in turn. Hence developed organically inspired conceptions of progress, unfolding, and systematicity, all tuned into a global awareness that asked where we came from and where we were likely to be going as a civilization. And along with this time-awareness, as noted, were various attempts to grasp the nature of time, either by means of some form of rationality, or by non-rational, intuitive means.

Bergson is important as a thinker who brought the idea of temporal experience to the forefront of his philosophy, and who emphasized the centrality of lived experience, emotional life, subjectivity, empathy, and direct knowledge as the means to achieve traditional philosophical ends. By orienting his philosophizing towards temporal experience, Bergson was able to conceive of experience more forcefully – not to mention in a more existential and down-to-earth manner – as a kind of rationality-resistant flux and fluidity, as opposed to a segmented, atomized, and intellectually manageable sort of being. And with this, his thought falls into sympathy with romanticist energies and the accompanying anti-scientific undercurrent that had previously stretched across the nineteenth century. As much as he respected the products and practical power of scientific thought, Bergson's philosophy ran against the external-observation-oriented scientific grain, for he developed in connection with his metaphysical interests, a more subjective and phenomenological focus upon what it actually feels like to come into direct and vital contact with the temporal forces that shape history. His emphasis upon the experience of time, his questioning of the powers of reflection and object-centered styles of metaphysical speculation, along with his implicit challenge to equally solidified, elementary conceptions of the self, all had a powerful impact upon later twentieth-century French thought.

Selected works of Henri Bergson

1889 (age 30): *Essay sur les données immédiates de la conscience* [*Time and Free Will*][53]
1896 (age 37): *Matière et mémoire, Essai sur la relation du corps avec l'espirit* [*Matter and Memory, An Essay on the Relation of the Body with the Spirit*]
1900 (age 41): *Le rire, Essai sur la signification du comic* [*Laughter, an Essay on the Significance of the Comic*]
1903 (age 44): *Introduction à la métaphysique* [*Introduction to Metaphysics*]
1907 (age 48): *L'Évolution creátrice* [*Creative Evolution*]
1932 (age 73): *Les deux sources de la morale et de la religion* [*The Two Sources of Morality and Religion*]
1934 (age 75): *La pensée et le mouvant* [*Thought and Movement*]

3

Jean-Paul Sartre, Existentialist (1905–80)

Life and works

Jean-Paul-Charles-Aymard Sartre was, as he would have put it, 'thrown into the world,' on June 21, 1905 in Paris, into a family supportive of academic and intellectual values. Although Sartre's father died while Sartre was an infant,[54] his grandfather – a teacher of modern languages – was present along with Sartre's mother[55] to support his creative development. He attended various *lycées*, and at the age of nineteen, entered the École Normale Supérieure in 1924. In 1929, he met his lifelong companion, Simone de Beauvoir (1908–86), who would become a leading figure in French feminist thought. After a brief military service from 1929–31, Sartre obtained a position teaching philosophy at a *lycée* in Le Havre – an environment that inspired his early novel, *Nausea* (*La nausée*). During this period, Sartre took a research break (1933–34) to study in Berlin, where he became indelibly impressed with the phenomenology-centered theories of Edmund Husserl (1859–1938) and the existence-and-phenomenology-centered theories of Martin Heidegger (1889–1976).[56]

In 1939, Sartre was drafted into the French army and was taken prisoner by the Germans after the French surrendered. After his captivity, he returned to Paris in 1941, and taught philosophy at the Lycée Condorcet while continuing his work on what would be his most influential book, *Being and Nothingness* (1943). In 1944, he established the editorial board for the journal *Les Temps*

Modernes, the first issue of which appeared in 1945.[57] Sartre also wrote two plays which were performed at this time, *The Flies* (1943) and *No Exit* (1945).[58] By the end of the 1940s, Sartre's existentialist philosophy had become popular, and his own interests during the next decades became increasingly political.[59]

In the early 1950s, Sartre developed a strong interest in Marxism, and soon set his existentialist philosophy upon Marxist foundations in the *Critique of Dialectical Reason* (1960), continuing his political activity throughout this time, as well as during the 1960s and 1970s. In 1964, he was offered the Nobel Prize in Literature, which he declined.[60] His travels, either giving lectures, or participating in political committees, took him to Austria, China, Germany, the Soviet Union (where he met Nikita Khrushchev), Cuba (where he met Fidel Castro and Che Guevara), Yugoslavia (where he met Josip Tito), Poland, Czechoslovakia, Italy, Japan, Egypt, Israel, Greece, the United States, and Portugal. Sartre suffered heart attacks in 1971 and 1973, and though physically weakened and semi-blind by this time, continued his work through the use of tape recordings and appearances on television programs. He died on April 15, 1980 soon after being hospitalized for a lung ailment. Sartre's ashes are buried in Montparnasse cemetery in Paris.[61]

Husserl's phenomenology and Sartre's conception of consciousness

Sartre's predecessor in Germany, Edmund Husserl, hoped to establish the field of philosophy as a 'rigorous science' by grounding it upon indubitable foundations. To this end, Husserl reintroduced the word 'phenomenology' that had been used a century earlier by G. W. F. Hegel in reference to his own science of consciousness and experience, and Husserl appropriated Hegel's term as a name for a new philosophical science. His hope was to identify experientially, a level of pure consciousness that was infected with no presuppositions whatsoever, which would secure for him an absolute foundation for his philosophical inquiries.

In his search for an absolute philosophical grounding, Husserl followed consciously in René Descartes's footsteps, for the latter made the same kind of pronouncement almost two hundred and seventy-five years earlier, in 1641:

> It is now some years since I detected how many were the false beliefs that I had from my earliest youth admitted as true, and how doubtful was everything I had since constructed on this basis; and from that time I was convinced that I must once for all seriously undertake to rid myself of all the opinions which I had formerly accepted, and

commence to build anew from the foundation, if I wanted to establish any firm and permanent structure in the sciences.[62]

Descartes attempted to reach a secure and lasting philosophical foundation through a process of 'universal doubt' – a process where he actively set aside any doubtable proposition with the hope that some doubt-resisting proposition would eventually remain. Since our five senses sometimes deceive us, Descartes doubted the perceptual evidence presented by his senses; since we sometimes make mistakes in our reasoning, Descartes doubted any results arrived at through step-by-step logic and inference, and he therefore set all of these propositions aside in his initial quest for indubitable philosophical foundations. This left him with little to work with and little remaining, except for the immediate, indubitable awareness of himself, as he thought about himself engaged at that very moment in the act of thinking and doubting. This was, to him, a core awareness that has become known as the Cartesian *cogito* ('I think') – a state of mind which affirms that as much as anyone or any being might try to cause one to be deceived, it remains that as long as one is aware of oneself as the possible subject of such deception, one cannot doubt that one exists.

In the same spirit as Descartes's method of doubt, Husserl developed a method of setting aside (or 'bracketing') aspects of our perceptual experience that appear to involve presuppositions or interpretation. His procedure was to examine carefully what is presented to a person's consciousness as he or she experiences things, and imaginatively to peel off layer upon layer of interpretive overlay, as one might remove layers and layers of clothing to arrive at the naked body. The hope was to arrive at a set of uninterpreted presentations that would constitute the sought-after presuppositionless foundation for all human experience.[63]

Husserl focused upon the nature of consciousness in its simplicity, which when it is conceived of independently of the complications of individual personality, reveals itself to be a pure consciousness, or mere directedness towards some object of which consciousness is aware. Consciousness, Husserl maintained, is always a consciousness 'of' an object. Sartre remained in sympathy with this Husserlian notion of a pure consciousness, but he maintained carefully that this pure consciousness should nonetheless not be understood as a solid and definitive 'ego,' 'self,' or 'substance' of any kind. This Sartrean conception of a depersonalized and fluctuating consciousness, we can recall, was implicit in Bergson's view that consciousness is primarily a flowing movement through time.

Sartre's denial of a substantial, unchanging, nature of consciousness provides an alternative to what is arguably an entrenched notion in the history of Western philosophy, namely, that there is a clear distinction between a thing's essential, unchanging qualities, and a thing's non-essential, or accidental qualities. Plato (*c.* 375 B.C.E.), for instance, distinguished between perceivable, changeable, physical objects and the non-perceivable, and only conceivable, eternal and unchanging essences of those objects. To illustrate this distinction, one can draw many imperfect circles upon a piece of paper, erase the drawings, and yet notice throughout this exercise, that the abstract, mathematical definition of a circle remains elsewhere, untouched and unchanged. Similarly, one can change one's clothes, gain or lose weight, cut one's hair, but (on this view) one's constant, Platonic character and personality would remain the same throughout such superficial modifications. Sartre disputes these Platonic ideas and distinctions, however, claiming that there are no essences of things that remain constant behind the perceptual scenes:

> But if we once get away from what Nietzsche called 'the illusion of worlds-behind-the-scene,' and if we no longer believe in the being-behind-the-appearance, then the appearance becomes full positivity.[64]
>
> The appearances which manifest the existent are neither interior nor exterior; they are all equal, they all refer to other appearances, and none of them is privileged.[65]

Sartre thereby replaces the distinction between a perceptual object's perceivable 'exterior' as opposed to its hidden 'interior' with the distinction between the finite presentation of the object and the infinitely many, possible presentations that the object can have at other times and places. Sartre refers to this standing potentiality for other possible presentations as the 'transphenomenality' or 'transcendence' of the object. So instead of referring to an imperfect and changeable circle drawn on a piece of paper that contrasts with the essential and unchangeable definition of a circle, his conception of things recognizes only a set of drawings of circles that can appear in different ways.

To elaborate on the concept of transphenomenality, Sartre distinguishes a narrow sense of being, which he uses to refer to the immediate presence of something of which we are aware, from a wider sense of being. The former, immediate presence he calls the 'phenomenon of being,' since a presentation of this kind, such as when we look at a teacup, is the experiential way that the object reveals itself to us perceptually at that particular time. Even more importantly, in the experience of some object at some particular time, such as a teacup, the 'phenomenon of being' refers to our more extraordinary experience of the 'isness,' 'existentiality,' or 'raw physicality,' of the object. The wider being of the teacup, however, is different: the wider being of the teacup is not restricted to those moments when someone happens to be looking at it. The 'being of the phenomenon' includes the thing as it is perceived now, as well as the appearances it had, might have had, will have, and might have. This is how the being of a perceptual phenomenon, such as a teacup, is thereby 'transphenomenal,' since it is impossible for all of its possible perceptual aspects to appear at once within anyone's single experience. And yet, all of the possible appearances of the teacup are of the same general kind, namely, they are particular experiences in space and time. There is nothing otherworldly about Sartre's anti-Platonistic view.

The upshot of Sartre's position is that perceptual objects are not mysterious, and that there are no aspects of perceptual objects that remain, in principle, unavailable to perception. He maintains that such objects have nothing in their constitution that is, by nature, imperceivable. Everything concerning objects of perception is publicly presentable, and there is nothing private about them.

The pre-reflective *cogito*

In his *Meditations on First Philosophy* (1641), Descartes offers a line of reasoning whose plausibility never fails to be impressive:

> Am I so dependent on body and senses that I cannot exist without these? But I was persuaded that there was nothing in all the world, that there was no heaven, no earth, that there were no mind, nor any bodies: was I not then likewise persuaded that I did not exist? Not at all; of a surety I myself did exist since I persuaded myself of something [or merely because I thought of something]. But there is some deceiver or other, very powerful and very cunning, who ever employs his ingenuity in deceiving. Then without a doubt I exist also if he deceives me, and let him deceive me as much as he will, he can never cause me to be nothing so long as I think that I am something. So that after having reflected well and carefully examined things, we must come to the definite conclusion that this proposition: I am, I exist, is necessarily true each time that I pronounce it, or that I mentally conceive it.[66]

Descartes's reasoning is strong, but Sartre has two difficulties with Descartes's approach to truth. The first is that in the above Cartesian *cogito*, the self appears to itself in self-consciousness as an explicit object to itself. When Descartes says, 'I think [about myself],' he is explicitly self-conscious and he consciously and deliberately thinks about himself thinking. Sartre believes, though, that this idea of 'being an object for oneself' obscures a nest of problems, which we shall soon articulate. Second, Sartre has reservations about Descartes's subsequent definition of the self as a 'thinking substance:' Descartes maintains that the self is an individual entity that has a being and integrity of its own, quite independently of the physical world – a characterization which, if true, is consistent with the belief that the soul survives after bodily death. As alluded to above, however, Sartre maintains that consciousness is not a 'self,' 'object,' 'thing,' or 'substance' at all. It is better described as a dynamic field of impersonal awareness.

For Descartes, the *cogito* is the foundational, indubitable point from which all of his philosophizing is grounded. Within the realm of consciousness, there is nothing more steadfast, so it appears, than one's explicit awareness of oneself. But Sartre questions whether the explicit awareness of oneself represents the most fundamental level of consciousness, for he can discern aspects of our conscious awareness that we must presuppose – aspects which are even more basic – in order for Descartes's *cogito* to be thinkable to begin with. Sartre claims, in other words, that prior to anyone's having an explicit self-awareness, there must first be an implicit self-awareness. This, he refers to as a 'pre-reflective' *cogito*. Sartre maintains that consciousness exists in a fundamentally pre-reflective manner. He admits that human consciousness is a mode of self-awareness, but he adds that at the primordial level, human self-awareness is not the same as being explicitly aware of oneself. Explicit self-awareness – Descartes's *cogito* – comes afterwards.

Sartre arrives at this notion of the pre-reflective, yet self-aware consciousness, through an inspiration from Edmund Husserl's phenomenology. The following is an excerpt from Husserl's *Ideas – General Introduction to Pure Phenomenology* (1913), which informs Sartre's position. Husserl writes:

> In actual perception, when it is veridical, I am facing the object, for example, the piece of paper, and I apprehend it as this being here and now. The apprehension is a singling-out-for-attention, for every item that is so perceived has an experiential background. Around the paper lie books, pens, inkpot, etc., which in a certain way are also 'perceived' there in perception, in the 'field of intuition,' but during the attention to the paper, these are bypassed, and given not even a secondary attention and apprehension. They appeared, but were still not singled out for attention and set out for themselves. Every apprehension of a thing has in this way an entire region of *background-intuitions* ... and this is also a '*conscious experience*,' or in short, 'consciousness of' all indeed which was in fact present in the jointly-perceived objective 'background.'[67]

Husserl observes – and this insight is foundational for the history of twentieth-century French philosophy – that when we are aware of any object at all, we must also presuppose a *background* against which the object is highlighted. If we apply this principle to the experience of being explicitly aware of oneself as an object of one's own consciousness, then we must postulate within ourselves a wider, continuous field of consciousness in general, against which our specific awareness of ourselves at some moment or other is highlighted.[68]

Moreover, contrary to the common assumption that prior to acts of reflection we remain completely unaware of ourselves and are conscious only of things other than ourselves, Sartre shows that this is not the case, for he cites examples which lead him to conclude that the wider field of human consciousness is itself a special mode of self-awareness, namely, one that does not involve explicit reflection. He discerns that there is a sense in which we remain aware of ourselves, even though we may not be explicitly thinking about ourselves at the time:

> If I count the cigarettes which are in that case, I have the impression of disclosing an objective property of this collection of cigarettes: *they are a dozen.* This property appears to my consciousness as a property existing in the world. It is very possible that I have positional consciousness of counting them. Then I do not know myself as counting ... [But] if anyone questioned me, indeed, if anyone should ask, 'What are you doing there?' I should reply at once, 'I am counting.' This reply aims not only at the instantaneous consciousness which I can achieve by reflection but at those fleeting consciousnesses which have passed without being reflected-on, those which are forever not-reflected-on in my immediate past. [So] it is the non-reflective consciousness which renders reflection possible; there is a pre-reflective cogito which is the condition of the Cartesian cogito.[69]

With his introduction of a pre-reflective state of self awareness, or pre-reflective *cogito*, Sartre intends to advance beyond Descartes.[70] The foundation of philosophizing, rather than being focused upon an explicit, indubitable, self-awareness, is instead identified as a flow of awareness that is implicitly conscious of itself. It is difficult to speak of 'indubitability' here, since nothing can be explicitly defined, highlighted and isolated as an object of thought, without contradicting the implicit nature of this kind of self-awareness. What we have is a more phenomenological and existential foundation, which maintains that all philosophizing starts from an active consciousness that has not yet split itself into 'subject' (the thinker) and 'object' (that which is thought 'about') but which stands as fundamentally and intrinsically unified. We have, that is, a view close to (but not identical to) what we observed earlier in Bergson's account of consciousness, where the latter was conceived of as a constant flowing of awareness.

One of the difficulties with Sartre's notion of the pre-reflective *cogito* resides in evaluating his claim that if one is conscious of an object, then one must always be conscious of one's being conscious of that object, if only implicitly. There is a long tradition which asserts that human beings are essentially self-conscious beings, and Sartre follows directly in this tradition. His contribution is to argue that the primordial and constant quality of human self-awareness is a pre-reflective, rather than a reflective, self-awareness. Nonetheless, he regards self-consciousness as permeating the situation.

Sartre observes significantly, that 'reflection' and 'self-consciousness' are not coincident terms within the field of consciousness, and that 'self-consciousness' has a wider scope of application. Still, it is more likely that consciousness is only sometimes, rather than always, pre-reflectively aware of itself, just as it is only sometimes, rather than constantly, reflectively aware of itself. When initially waking up from a condition of sleep, for instance, there are bodily activities of which one might not even be prereflectively aware; also, in habitual actions, there might also be a lack of pre-reflective awareness of their performance, once the actions sink to the level of being virtually automatic. So although Sartre identifies a level of consciousness which needs to be philosophically recognized, it remains unclear whether this level of pre-reflective awareness is present throughout every act of human consciousness, as he claims.

Being in itself

Sartre draws a broader distinction between two realms of being, namely, the realm of consciousness, or subjectivity, or 'being-for-itself,' as opposed to the realm of objects, or what he calls 'being-in-itself.' This latter realm of objects is alien to pre-reflective consciousness and it stands as a source of consciousness's frustration. People want to become one with the external world – people want to be 'at home' in the world – but Sartre holds that they must either fail to do so, or they must completely annihilate themselves in the process.[71] For there is no middle ground where one can be a satisfied consciousness that has become identical with what is essentially alien to consciousness. Since a subject cannot fully become an object, the subject must always remain frustrated in its effort to apprehend itself in a purely objective fashion.

'Being-for-itself' is the being of consciousness and Sartre describes it as 'a being such that in its being, its being is in question in so far as this being implies a being other than itself.'[72] In contrast, 'being-in-itself' (to which Sartre often refers more shorthandedly as the 'in-itself') refers to the being of objects, or the world of 'things.' Here, we find the entrance of Sartre's belief that the world of daily experience is absurd, and intrinsically meaningless, for he describes being-in-itself – the physical worlds of rocks, stars, and trees – as: (1) uncreated, (2) massive, in the sense that it never reveals itself completely to consciousness, (3) something which cannot realize itself, since it cannot refer to itself and is solid, opaque, 'glued to itself' and 'filled with itself,' (4) something that 'has nothing secret,' and 'has no *within* which is opposed to a *without*;' (5) something that is superfluous (*de trop*), and which is completely contingent, lacking any reason for being.

In one of his early novels, *Nausea* (1938), Sartre describes an experience that reveals the existential significance of being-in-itself, as that which resists total comprehension. The world, as being-in-itself, is filled with accidental qualities which defy all efforts to grasp them fully with our intellect. This frustration of the effort to understand the world rationally, generates a feeling of nausea for Sartre's main character, Antoine Roquentin:[73]

[T]he world of explanations and reasons is not the world of existence. A circle is not absurd, it is clearly explained by the rotation of a straight segment around one of its extremities. But neither does a circle exist.[74] This [tree] root, on the other hand, existed in such a way that I could not explain it. Knotty, inert, nameless, it fascinated me, filled my eyes, brought me back unceasingly to its own existence. In vain to repeat: 'This is a root' – it didn't work any more. I saw clearly that you could not pass from its function as a root, as a breathing pump, *to that*, to this hard and compact skin of a sea lion, to this oily, callous, headstrong look. The function explained nothing: it allows you to understand generally that it was a root, but not *that one* at all. This root, with its colour, shape, its congealed movement, was … below all explanation.[75]

This moment was extraordinary. I was there, motionless and icy, plunged in a horrible ecstasy. But something fresh had just appeared in the very heart of this ecstasy; I understood the Nausea, I possessed it. To tell the truth, I did not formulate my discoveries to myself. But I think it would be easy for me to put them in words now. The essential thing is contingency. I mean that one cannot define existence as necessity. To exist is simply *to be there*; those who exist let themselves be encountered, but you can never deduce anything from them.[76]

Being-in-itself is the physical presence of things – a presence whose detail, complication, and sheer physicality, overwhelms and outstrips all efforts to capture its being in a network of concepts, in any system of thought, in any static scientific framework, in any set of rigid definitions, or in any style of intellectualization. In this respect, the physical world sublimely defies comprehension and philosophical reflection in an almost intimidating and debilitating way. It is an 'Other' to us all. It defies the extraordinary power of a theoretical mind such as Sartre's, and he recoils against this frustration, becoming sickened, weakened, and apprehensive by the human inability to gain intellectual control over the situation in which we find ourselves.[77] The manner in which individuality, contingency, accidentality, and unpredictability permeate the world, renders the world an absurd place to be. With this absurdity, however, comes a kind of personal freedom of choice.

Negation, freedom, and anguish

In addition to his notion of pre-reflective self-awareness, Sartre is important as a philosopher who attended to a family of philosophical concepts related to negativity, such as 'nothingness', 'negation', and 'lack'. One of his achievements was to link these concepts to an understanding of what it is to be human, insofar as humans are beings that are free, and are beings who ask questions.

In *Being and Nothingness*, Sartre examines what it means to 'ask a question' by attending specifically to the role of 'negation' in the act of questioning. He finds that for any (genuine, as opposed to merely rhetorical) question, there exists for the questioner 'the permanent objective possibility of a negative reply.'[78] He further describes the questioning situation as involving a relation between the questioner who does not know the answer to the question posed, along with a relation between the alternative answers to the question, one of which is a negative answer. Sartre points out that since each answer excludes the other, there is also a negation (i.e., an oppositional relationship) that obtains between the alternative answers. He thereby identifies a 'triple non-being' inherent in the act of posing a question. There is: (1) the uncertainty of the questioner; (2) the possible negative answer to the question; and (3) the opposition between the two possible answers themselves.

Sartre's discussion importantly highlights the various places where non-being permeates the questioning situation, and it foreshadows later themes in French post-modernism. His style of thought looks 'between the cracks' of a situation to identify the places where negation or non-being are present. If we were to consider any situation at all as having an articulated structure, like a skeleton, then we can understand Sartre as focusing his attention upon the joints, or spaces, or points of transformation or transition, between the bones, rather than attending to the positive structure of the bones themselves. His thought highlights the conditions for the articulation of any structure whatsoever, namely, the interstices, gaps, breaks, fissures, separations, ruptures, discontinuities, differences, and relationships, as opposed to the positive items that are themselves brought into structural relation at these various points of discontinuity. Later, we will see more of this style of gap-centered thought in Ferdinand de Saussure and in Jacques Derrida, as it is applied to the structures of words and texts.

Martin Heidegger also examined the nature of questioning at the beginning of his *Being and Time* and he is the inspiration for Sartre's own investigation into the nature of questions. Heidegger's investigation led to an understanding of the human being as a being which asks questions about other things and about itself. Heidegger writes:

This being, which each of us is, and which among other things, includes questioning within the possibility of its being, we will comprehend terminologically with the term *Dasein*.[79]

The *Dasein* is a being that does not merely occur among other beings. It is rather marked off ontically through the fact that to this being, its own being is a *concern* for it.[80]

Human beings are thrown into the world, in other words, with a dominating question mark inscribed into their being. Heidegger's characterization of human beings as those whose 'Being is a *concern* for it' closely relates to Descartes's idea that the quest for certainty begins with an effort to question everything, in the hope of finding something indubitable. Once one applies the process of 'doubting everything' to one's own being, however, human beings become understandable in general as self-doubting, self-questioning, beings. This Cartesian–Heideggerian idea that one can always subject oneself to question, is the keynote of Sartre's conception of authenticity.[81]

When the idea of self-questioning is put into practice, and we actively try to realize our human being as that which is 'always a concern' for us, unexpected emotional experiences arise. Questioning oneself involves recognizing the real possibility that what happened in the past, need not have happened, that our present dispositions need not determine us in the direction that they exert upon our psyche, and that the future is wide open to hitherto unimagined changes. The act of self-questioning helps put the past out of present play, it operates as a form of disengagement, and it undermines an assortment of stable assumptions that we use to lend security and predictability to our experience.

Sartre maintains that once we question ourselves seriously, and realize that nothing is permanent, we experience a kind of 'vertigo.' When coming face-to-face with the nothingness that emerges when we question ourselves, when we disengage from our self-definitions, the result is personal destabilization and anguish. Which is to say that when we actively realize ourselves as self-questioning beings, there is more pain, as opposed to when we remain entrenched in our self-conceptions and in the *status quo*. And when we question ourselves less, and minimize our realization of ourselves as self-questioning beings, there is less pain. Experiencing one's freedom, in other words, has a price.

The escape from freedom: bad faith and self-deception

If anguish results from a person's ability to question himself or herself, along with the rest of the world, then anguish is the direct expression of human freedom. If one is reluctant to experience pain, then it is likely that one will try to minimize one's anguish, and this will entail that one will minimize one's self-questioning. Such a strategy amounts to an attempt to negate oneself as a free, questioning being through a process that Sartre identifies as one of self-deception. It is self-deception, according to Sartre, because he maintains that it is an inescapable fact that one is fundamentally free, if one is a human being. One is condemned to be free, as he says, and he refers to the condition of self-deception and avoidance of freedom as a condition of 'bad faith' (*mauvais fois*) It is a contradictory state of being, because one is involved in the attempt to deny what cannot be denied. For Sartre, our objective surroundings provide no security, and to be free is to be fundamentally free-floating and non-secured.

Given that, in principle, one can constantly question oneself, Sartre's characterization of bad faith assumes a surprising and upsetting form. Since one can always question and undermine oneself, then the constancy, stability, solidity, or reliability of any solid characterization that one might construct for oneself is always under challenge, if only implicitly. Which is to say that one is being self-deceptive, if one defines oneself essentially and unchangeably as a 'waiter,' or 'businessperson,' or 'cook,' or 'employee.' These social definitions are changeable, and when they are taken to be rock-solid, then a kind of false security and false consistency enters into one's self-conception and into one's life.

A further implication of conceiving definitions of oneself as referring to an unchanging, essential self, is that the use of such definitions involves an avoidance of responsibility. If, for example, one defines oneself as an essentially 'evil' person, then one can use this definition as an excuse to do evil actions in the future, and use it as an excuse to avoid taking responsibility for evil actions done in the past. Similarly, if one defines oneself as an essentially 'good' person, then one can use this definition to avoid facing the possibility that one has done evil acts, or use it to avoid facing the possibility that one has the capacity to do evil acts in the future.

Bad faith can involve saying securely to oneself, for example, 'I am a grocer,' 'I am a tailor,' 'I am a courageous person,' 'I am a level-headed person,' or 'I am a sophisticated person,' when it is difficult to acknowledge the possibility of changing professions, acting cowardly, losing one's temper, or acting with embarrassing ignorance. It often involves the use of personal definitions to deny what one has done, when what one has done is difficult to accept, or it involves the use of such definitions to deny what one could do, if one is unable to face the disturbing kinds of actions in which one might engage. In all cases of bad faith, Sartre observes that there is an avoidance of personal responsibility as one hides behind a façade of false consistency.

The key process in bad faith is that of 'objectification:' we escape responsibility by objectifying ourselves as having a certain kind of permanent character or certain kind of secure social role. Such definitions can help us deceive ourselves into believing that we are incapable, by definition, of doing anything questionable, or outside of the definition's bounds. As in the examples above, one can similarly define oneself as an 'artist' or 'writer' (in the celebratory, rather than purely descriptive sense) to escape the responsibility for producing mediocre works in the future, or to escape the possibility of having produced them in the past; one can define oneself as a 'scientist,' to escape the responsibility as a citizen for using large amounts of money in research that might have been used better to feed starving people; one can define oneself as a 'businessperson' to escape the responsibility for taking excessively large profits; one can define oneself as an 'administrator' to escape the responsibility for denying jobs to people, and so on.

At first sight, it could be assumed that an effort to be sincere would help combat the tendency to be in bad faith. But being sincere has dangers of its own, for Sartre notes that if one consequently defines oneself as a sincere person, then one obscures the possibility that one might someday not be sincere. Saying definitionally that one is essentially sincere, and that one never lies to oneself, is itself a kind of lie, for it always remains possible to lie to oneself. Trying to be honest with oneself, then, is not the fail-safe path to being authentic. It could backfire: one could be honest with oneself, and conclude with yet another ossifying definition of oneself (e.g., 'yes, I am really selfish' or 'yes, I am really a good person,' etc.) that falsely implies that one's destiny must be such and such, and that it cannot be otherwise. Once again, by means of the static definition – and this act of consistency-imposing definition is the main source of difficulty – I have characterized myself as a kind of 'object' or 'thing.' This, however, involves denying my freedom and it involves obscuring my own recognition of the powers I have to change my behavior.

Dominance and submission: looking at oneself, looking at others, and being looked at by others

Being explicitly aware of oneself

In his discussions of explicit human self-awareness, Sartre draws on his distinction between 'being-for-itself' and 'being-in-itself' in conjunction with his focus upon gaps, negations, distances, separations, differences and discontinuities, as noted above. He refers to the experience of being explicitly self-aware as the experience of being 'present to oneself' and he describes it as follows:

> Presence to self … supposes that an impalpable fissure has slipped into being. If being is present to itself, it is because it is not wholly itself. Presence [to self] is an immediate deterioration of coincidence, for it supposes separation. But if we ask ourselves at this point what it is which separates the subject from himself, we are forced to admit that it is *nothing*.[82]
>
> The being of consciousness qua consciousness is to exist *at a distance from itself* as a presence to itself, and this empty distance which being carries in its being is Nothingness. Thus in order for a *self* to exist, it is necessary that the unity of this being include its own nothingness as the nihilation of identity.[83]

These excerpts describe how Sartre conceives of human consciousness as having a 'distance' within itself, to explain how we can be self-aware. Being aware of oneself presupposes a certain fissure or separation within consciousness that is characteristic of one's being. It is this very distance within oneself which allows one to take a perspective upon oneself in the act of self-awareness. At the same time, however, it is difficult to describe what this distance is, for there is, in a sense, literally nothing to identify. Sartre thus says that 'nothing' separates one from oneself. Despite this curiosity, it is clear that our human mode of being is different from that of a rock, since a rock (apparently) has no consciousness, no self-awareness and no 'separation' within itself at all.

Upon noticing this distancing within the human being, Sartre draws the consequence that the human being is divided against itself, and can never fully coincide with itself in its capacity as an explicitly reflective being. Explicit self-consciousness introduces internal division, conflict, and frustration, in other words. To be explicitly self-aware implies that one can never be what one aims to be, both in a narrow and broader sense. I cannot be what I aim to be in a basic act of explicit self-awareness, since there must always remain a distance between the aspect of consciousness that does the reflecting and the aspect of consciousness that is held up as an image or object to itself. Similarly, I cannot be what I aim to be in a broader sense, insofar as the 'self' that I project as a future, or ideal self, can never be identical with me as I presently am at this moment.

Sartre paradoxically describes the basic condition of explicit self-consciousness as that 'which is what it is not' and 'which is not what it is.' One is what one 'is not,' in the sense that one identifies with some projected object, which is either oneself as reflectively conceived, or is some other personal condition that one projects into the future or past. Conversely, one is not what 'one is,' because in the act of projecting and imagining and thereby, in the act of continually escaping from one's present condition, one loses sight of the very being that is actively doing the projecting and imagining, namely, the pre-reflective self that is never explicitly aware of itself. Insofar as consciousness is consciousness of something other than itself, it is always escaping from itself and distancing itself from the free and projecting being that it is.

One of the upshots of Sartre's discussion is that whenever one thinks explicitly about something, whether it is oneself, or something other than oneself, one is aware of it as an 'object' or aspect of 'being-in-itself' that is opposed to the unified pre-reflective consciousness that is doing the thinking. So when one thinks explicitly about oneself, or when one thinks explicitly about someone else, there is an act of objectification, and an act of alienation and opposition between consciousness and its object. Explicit attention to something introduces a 'distance,' and renders explicit an opposition between 'subject' and 'object' – one which Sartre believes is unbridgeable. In this condition, consciousness always experiences a 'lack' or kind of emptiness and frustration in being unable to coincide with the object of its thought. Which is to say that the human reality that emerges through explicit reflection is a world of solitude, disengagement, isolation, and alienation. It is a world of exile where something is always missing:

> The being of human reality is suffering because it rises in being as perpet-
> ually haunted by a totality which it is without being able to be it, precisely
> because it could not attain the in-itself [object] without losing itself as
> for-itself [subject]. Human reality therefore is by nature an unhappy
> consciousness with no possibility of surpassing its unhappy state.[84]

As beings which can never fully get what they aim for, human beings are in a condition of perpetual frustration. For once we get what we want (on a small scale), we automatically project into the future a new goal, and find ourselves striving to attain that new goal.[85] Referring to Hegel's description of a religious consciousness that tries to find God within itself, but which apprehends its own finitude as standing in the way of realizing this goal, Sartre describes the human being as an 'unhappy consciousness.'[86]

Being aware of other people

The philosophical 'problem of other minds' is usually formulated as a quandary arising in the theory of knowledge: 'How can I know that there are other minds in addition to my own?' Although I am directly acquainted with my own mind, can I reasonably infer from the consciousness that I experience within my own body, that there are other minds as well? I see a body like mine before me, but how can I be sure that this body has a mind, just as my body has a mind? What I see might only be a material thing that moves as if it had a mind; there might not be a person there, but simply a material thing that moves as if it had a mind. Worse yet, there might not even be a 'material world' which exists outside me, for it might be a dream or a figment of my imagination – a possibility which Descartes briefly entertained.

Descartes's philosophy is a paradigm of how the philosophical problem of other minds can quickly emerge, if one begins one's philosophizing from the first-person standpoint and the fact of one's immediate self-awareness. Through his 'method of doubt,' whereby he cast aside each of his beliefs that could be doubted, Descartes quickly generated the problem for himself:

> But I have convinced myself that nothing in the world exists – no sky, no earth, no minds, no bodies.[87]

Descartes found himself in the position to doubt the existence of other minds, because he regarded his knowledge of other minds as being on a par with his knowledge of everyday objects such as tables and chairs. And since his method of doubt allowed him to question whether he was even sitting in front of the fireplace (as he in fact was), he could further doubt that there were minds which inhabited the bodies of other people that he perceived. If we come to know other minds only through our knowledge of other bodies, then a solution to the problem of other minds requires that we must somehow bridge the gap between those bodies and the minds that inhabit them.

Descartes solved the problem of other minds by introducing God as the guarantor of his perceptions: he held that he was not hallucinating the existence of an external world inhabited by real people, after proving (so he believed) that God exists, and by reasoning that God (as all good) would not deceive him, or anyone else, in such an exquisitely evil manner. Descartes offered a theistic solution to the problem of other minds, but if one operates within an atheistic philosophy, as does Sartre, then this strategy of solving the problem is unavailable.

To appreciate Sartre's solution to the problem of other minds, we need to introduce his phenomenological description of 'my world' (or your world, etc.) as the set of things highlighted by my (or your) personal interests. Since I need to buy food, for example, the grocery store becomes part of my world; since I need to travel from my house to the store, the sidewalks and roads become part of my world; if I travel to a different city, the transportation system and the people within it become part of my world; if I have an interest in reading, certain authors become part of my world, etc. 'The world' (i.e., the world for me as I now live in it) is thus defined in relation to my interests; it spreads out before me in all directions as I contemplate what to do and how to do it. My interests define my center of interpretation, and my interpretation introduces value into my surroundings. My 'world' is thereby constructed in light of the set of values, or meanings, that I have projected as a consequence of my specific interests.

If there were no other people in the world, I might rarely experience the interruption of my world insofar as there would be no other interest that would conflict with mine.[88] For Sartre, it is a fact that my world does not retain this kind of solidity. What happens, rather, is that we eventually experience the rupture of our personal world:

> I am in a public park. Not far away there is a lawn and along the edge of that lawn there are benches. A man passes by those benches. I see this man; I apprehend him as an object and at the same time as a man. What does this signify? What do I mean when I assert that this object *is a man*?
>
> … Perceiving him as a man … is to register an organization *without distance* of the things in my universe around that privileged object … the distance *is unfolded starting from* the man whom I see and *extending up to* the lawn as the synthetic upsurge of a univocal relation. We are dealing with a relation which is without *parts*, given at one stroke, inside of which there unfolds a spatiality which is not *my* spatiality; for instead of a grouping *toward me* of objects, there is now an orientation *which flees from me*.[89]
>
> Thus suddenly an object has appeared which has stolen the world from me. Everything is in place; everything still exists for me; but everything is traversed by an invisible flight and fixed in the direction of a new object. The appearance of the Other in the world corresponds therefore to a fixed sliding of the whole universe, to a decentralization of the world which undermines the centralization which I am simultaneously effecting.[90]

Sartre describes the initial apprehension of other people ('the Other') in a negative way: other people are beings who undermine and threaten the stability of the world one has constructed for oneself. 'My' world centers around 'my' projects, but my recognition of another person implies a recognition of projects other than my own, and hence, of forces that compete with my personal interests. For Sartre, my initial apprehension of the Other is filled with conflict. He describes the situation once more, using memorable imagery:

> Rather it appears that the world has a kind of drain hole in the middle of its being and that it is perpetually flowing off through this hole.[91]
>
> The man is defined by his relation to the world and by his relation to myself. He is that object in the world which determines an internal flow of the universe, an internal haemorrhage.[92]

'The Other' is presented to me as being the focal point of a world other than my own – one which has a different center of interests, interpretations, and values. The person under consideration perhaps has not yet looked at me, but I can already apprehend a competitive presence other than my own. When the other person does look at me, the intensity of my feeling that the world is fleeing from me, Sartre believes, grows even more intense. To describe this phenomenon of the Other's look, he gives his (now famous) example of a person who is caught spying through a keyhole:

> Let us imagine that moved by jealousy, curiosity, or vice, I have just glued my ear to the door and looked through a keyhole. I am alone and on the level of a non-thetic consciousness. This means first of all that there is no self to inhabit my consciousness …
>
> But all of a sudden I hear footsteps in the hall. Someone is looking at me! What does this mean? It means that I am suddenly affected in my being and that essential modifications appear in my structure – modifications which I can apprehend and fix conceptually by means of the reflective *cogito*.[93]

When we realize that we are being looked at by another person, we become more self-aware: the other person's look causes us to reflect upon how we are being seen. In the example of being caught looking through a keyhole, we become self-conscious in both the emotional and the philosophic sense. Given Sartre's conception of the human being as a being that has interests and that introduces value into the world as a projection of those interests, being looked at involves becoming the object of someone else's judgment. We become an object in the other person's eyes, and in Sartrean terms, this is to say that the other person's look transforms me into an 'in-itself.' The other person's look is deadening, while it causes us to reflect and become more aware. Being looked at is a mixed experience, for as we are deadened and enslaved, we also receive recognition.

With regard to the philosophical problem of other minds, Sartre maintains that the experience of being-seen-by-another is an irreducible fact.[94] He claims that this look is immediately given to us, and that it is different in kind from our experience of inanimate things. Moreover, Sartre maintains that the objectifying force of another person's look upon us, always competes with the objectifying force of our own look which is directed at the person who is looking at us. The objectifying nature of the look thereby generates a social conflict:

> I should willingly say here: we can not perceive the world and at the same time apprehend a look fastened upon us; it must be either one or the other. This is because to perceive is to *look at*, and to apprehend a look … is to be conscious of being looked at … What I apprehend

immediately when I hear the branches crackling behind me is not that *there is someone there*; it is that I am vulnerable, that I have a body which can be hurt, that I occupy a place and that I can not in any case escape from the space in which I am without defense – in short, that I *am seen.*[95]

An important aspect of the act of looking, then, concerns its role as an objectifying force. The other person's look makes me conceive of myself, and hence makes me objectify myself as something of which I am aware; the other person's look projects an interpretation of me as it looks at me, and hence objectifies me in that it postulates a 'nature' for me. Two objects are thus generated by the look: the object which I generate for myself as I imagine how the other person sees me as an object, and the object that the other person actually perceives, which always remains a mystery for me (since I cannot become identical to the other person's perceiving consciousness).[96]

On Sartre's view, the other person's look is fundamentally negative: it is intimidating; it steals my world away from me; it upsets my field of constructed meaning; it projects a different set of values upon me; it makes me feel vulnerable; it makes me feel afraid; it makes me feel ashamed; it makes me feel as if my possibilities are restricted; it makes me feel like I am no longer the master of the situation. According to Sartre, as he states in his play, *No Exit*, 'hell is other people.'

Trying to achieve a community with others

According to Sartre's analysis of human interaction, we are either *looking at* others or we are *being looked at*. The one activity precludes the other, for we must either take the role of the subject (as looker) or the role of the object (as being looked at). This 'either/or' situation with respect to the act of looking is the logical basis for Sartre's examination of our concrete relationships with other people. As we can already sense, human relationships will be permeated by tension and impasse, since it is impossible to direct our will in looking at another person and at the same time accommodate ourselves to the will of another person directed at us, given that they are an alien personality.

Due to this 'subject versus object' opposition and asymmetry, Sartre believes that it is impossible to establish a perfectly harmonious relationship with other people, for we are either dominating them with our look and thereby taking away their freedom by objectifying them, or we are submitting ourselves to their look and allowing our own freedom to be taken away by being objectified. Either we turn other people into objects under our look, or we allow them to turn us into objects under their look. On this theory, human interrelationships are dominance–submission relationships at the core. One could say that on this view, 'to look, is to fight.'

This conflictual situation between people mirrors the conflictual situation that occurs within each individual consciousness: since 'human reality as for-itself is a lack and … what it lacks is a certain coincidence with itself,'[97] we find ourselves in a conflictual situation as isolated individuals. We cannot capture ourselves in reflection, since this very act of self-objectification robs us of our subjectivity. The objective image I create for myself is not identical to who I am as a concrete, prereflective, active consciousness.

Humans are nonetheless beings that, owing to their explicit acts of reflection and their physical separation from other things in the world, both of which involve a distance between pre-reflective consciousness and its objects, try to 'find themselves' by bridging the gap between pre-reflective consciousness and its objects by means of various methods. The 'other person' with whom we try to identify may be an idealized image of ourselves, or it may be another independent individual, with whose opinion of us we try to identify. The latter situation is the focal point of Sartre's discussion of interpersonal relationships. His discussion stems from his original position that human beings are beings that essentially fail to coincide with themselves, and are constantly driven to overcome this lack of self-coincidence and internal disharmony.

So the impossible project of a pre-reflective 'subject' (or 'for-itself') that tries to be an 'object' (or 'in-itself') is located on the interpersonal level as well, and this attempt to achieve unity defines our basic relationships with other people. Our being as an explicit self-consciousness entails that we project ourselves as an object to ourselves, and then attempt to reappropriate this object as a representation of who we are, when we say to ourselves, for instance, 'that is me.' Similarly, to gain a better understanding of who we are, we try to appropriate the interpretations of ourselves that other people formulate about us, as when we say to ourselves, for instance, 'that is how they see me.' Other people see us as an 'object,' and as we try to apprehend ourselves through other people's perspectives, we attempt to see ourselves more objectively and truthfully. Unfortunately, the complete adoption of another person's perspective is impossible to achieve.

As it follows from these Sartrean assumptions, human beings find themselves in a tension-filled situation with respect to their relationships with other people. On the one hand, other people represent a fearsome and threatening presence in one's world because they disturb our individual field of meanings, and challenge the world we have made for our particular selves. On the other hand, other people are an irresistible source of seductive attraction, because they can see us in a way in which we cannot see ourselves. To some extent, other people hold the keys to who we really are, so there is a natural desire to become one with other people, so we can learn the truth about ourselves. Sartre describes such opposing tendencies in our experience of others:

> Thus being-seen constitutes me as a defenseless being for a freedom which is not my freedom. It is in this sense that we can consider ourselves as 'slaves' in so far as we appear to the Other … In so far as I am the object of values which come to qualify me without my being able to act on this qualification or even to know it, I am enslaved.[98]
>
> [But] the Other *looks* at me and as such he holds the secret of my being, he knows what I *am*. Thus the profound meaning of my being is outside of me, imprisoned in an absence. The Other has the advantage over me.[99]

In light of this mixed-up situation, Sartre outlines various ways in which we try to incorporate other people's view of ourselves. One way is to try to be loved; a second way is to engage in sexual contact; a third way is to allow others to dominate and manipulate us; a fourth way is to try to dominate and manipulate others. These methods are love, sex, masochism, and sadism, or more generally described, total care for another person, physical intimacy with another, complete submission to another, or complete domination over another person. For Sartre, every one of these attempts to achieve intimacy fails.

Love, sex, masochism, and sadism

In trying to be loved, according to Sartre, one aims to become the center of another person's value system, and the center of another person's world. Once this happens, the alienness of the other person appears to be removed. For by identifying with the other person's loving view of oneself as the center of his or her world, one overcomes the alienness of the other person, insofar as they express their love. The goal is to see oneself objectively by seeing oneself through the lover's eyes, and to overcome the alienness of the other person in this process by identifying oneself with the person who gives their love. Moreover, being loved removes the feeling of being absurd, or being simply an accident in the world, since one's status as the unconditional center of another person's world makes one feel as if the meaning of one's being has an absolute quality.

Sartre maintains that the project of love backfires, because once one perceives distinctly that one's own being is the center of another person's life, then the difference between oneself and the other person is accentuated, rather than diminished. Not only does one become more aware of oneself as being the center of the other person's interests, one becomes more aware of oneself as being responsible for the other person's world-organization. Hence, the more a person experiences being loved, the more the person who is loved has a sense of his or her own individuality and distance from the person who is projecting the love.

A second way in which a person can attempt to absorb another's perspective of oneself into his or her own perspective is by engaging in sexual contact with the other person. In this situation, the other person's subjectivity is 'brought to the surface' as his or her skin surface is made available to the other person's touch, and in the mutual touching and pleasure that results, there is a blending of consciousnesses. Each person absorbs the other person's subjectivity through the pleasures of intimate bodily contact as they each physically stimulate the other in parallel fashions.

Sartre observes, however, that when one becomes fully absorbed in one's own sexual presence as a mode of pleasure, it becomes difficult to simultaneously appreciate the other person in their similar state of arousal. He believes this, because he assumes that the pleasure within the sexual experience is so intense, that it has the effect of diverting one's concentration away from the other person, by making one too-aware of one's own state. And if one's self-awareness reaches the point where one becomes reflective during the sexual activity, then one begins to lose one's pure sexual presence as one becomes distanced from the other person. So the greater the sexual pleasure, the less one is aware of the other person and the more one is absorbed into one's own awareness, according to Sartre.

A third way to absorb another person's view of oneself is to divest oneself of all personality as much as possible and to give oneself up completely to the other person. One allows the other person to have all means of control over oneself, and one thereby becomes directly acquainted with the other person's view of oneself. By turning oneself into an object to be manipulated by another person, one is able to experience oneself through the lens of the other person's perspective. This strategy of submission is the opposite of love: when one is the object of another person's love, one becomes 'everything' to the other person; when one allows oneself to become the object of another person's manipulation, one must become 'nothing' to the other person and offer no resistance, to give the other person the freedom to do the manipulating as he or she wills.

The problem with the masochistic strategy, Sartre claims, is that those who allow themselves to be manipulated in fact choose to locate themselves in this subordinate position. But insofar as the submissive person makes this active choice, the person assumes a contradictory position to the extent that the person has become a manipulator. So the submissive person who allows himself or herself to be manipulated, undermines the goal of being an object of manipulation by implicitly dominating and defining the situation at the outset, for he or she uses the dominating person to manipulate them. So it is not clear whether a person can be properly called an object of manipulation, if that very person has implicitly maneuvered other people into the dominating role.

A fourth way in which one can try to merge with another person is by explicitly assuming the manipulator's role in the attempt to dominate and manipulate another person. The aim here is to force the other person to conform to one's own desires. In the most extreme form of manipulation where the manipulation becomes sadistic, the privacy and feelings of the individual are unconditionally invaded and controlled. The sadist, in an attempt to see himself or herself objectively in another person, acts like a being with absolute power, and tries to shape the other person's body, along with the contents of the other person's psyche, as if these were putty.

Sartre claims that the practice of manipulating another person for the purposes of seeing one's own image reflected in the other person's behavior is doomed to failure: it is impossible to maintain control over another person completely, because people are fundamentally free. Even if the person were completely immobilized, their thinking consciousness would offer a form of resistance to manipulation. Which is to say that the attempt to turn another person into an object is impossible, if one intends to control a living person. Since consciousnesses are by nature subjects, and not objects, the project of sadism logically ends in the victim's death – which would turn the victim into a material object – and hence in self-defeat for the sadist owing to the loss of the victim's recognition of the sadist.

By surveying these various strategies that aim to achieve community with other people (which he believes exhausts the possibilities), Sartre concludes that every attempt to discover or create our reflection in other people, in any absolute way, is hopeless. Each person is fundamentally alone and insecure on Sartre's view, and each person's unique individuality cannot be relinquished, even by choice. Since he believes that the subject–object distinction is absolute and unbridgeable, so does he regard the distinction between each person.

One can ask nonetheless, whether Sartre's conclusions are too extreme. For example, it remains uncertain whether we must exclusively either objectify another person with our look, or be objectified by another person's look. When looking into another person's eyes during an animated and friendly conversation, the experience can be experienced as a fusion and balance between the two looks and respective outlooks, especially if the two people are acknowledging each other in thematic agreement. Sartre's analysis depends on the claim that people are each different from one another and are in a fundamentally conflictual relationship owing to their difference in individuality. This overlooks the general identity between people, insofar as they have the same types of consciousness and share a common language. One might conclude, then, that Sartre's pessimistic analysis depends upon the logical opposition between the terms 'subject' and 'object' (i.e., 'looker' and 'looked-at') and overlooks that in actual experience, the experience of friendly social and linguistic interactions can be described in more fusion-related, as opposed to oppositional, terms.

Freedom, responsibility, and authenticity

'Existence precedes essence'

The existentialist slogan, 'existence precedes essence,'[100] expresses Sartre's view that human beings 'make themselves' through their freedom, and are in no way predetermined to be any specific kind of being. He states that we are 'condemned' to freedom and 'are a freedom which chooses, but we do not choose to be free.'[101] When we emerge on the earthly scene, we are initially free, and if we are to have any further determination, then we later choose to adopt these qualities, according to Sartre.

Sartre is antagonistic towards 'essences,' along with all philosophical theories that recognize them (e.g., Platonism) because essences refer to definite characteristics which prescribe and circumscribe a being's possibilities. If the essence of a being is to be an 'oak tree,' for instance, then this being is not free to be anything else but an oak tree. Conceiving of the world in terms of essences is compartmentalizing, rigidifying, definitive, and restrictive.[102] Sartre maintains that human beings, as self-conscious beings, are radically different from other beings such as oak trees, for through their freedom, they have the capacity to determine the kinds of persons they will be. They need not be anything specific at all, in the sense that whatever specificity a person happens to have, is changeable.

Though humans need not be anything specific, this does not mean that a human being can make itself into anything at all in a concrete sense. No one, at present, can develop his or her body so that it can live for one-hundred thousand years. In his claim that humans do not have an essence, Sartre is mainly attempting to illuminate our ability to interpret ourselves and our surroundings freely, even though a certain givenness or 'facticity' restricts these surroundings and our practical possibilities. It is our power of interpretation and choice which, in principle, he regards as virtually unlimited.

How we interpret our surroundings depends significantly upon how we interpret ourselves, since our self-interpretation determines many of our interests, and since our interests play a role in determining our values, and what we subsequently recognize as our 'world.' With regard to the sphere of self-interpretation, Sartre's view is extreme: he claims that we are absolutely free. He argues for this claim in the following excerpt:

> If we start by conceiving of man as a plenum [i.e., as like a solid rock], it is absurd to try to find in him afterwards moments or psychic regions in which he would be free. As well look for emptiness in a container which one has filled beforehand up to the brim! Man can not be sometimes slave and sometimes free; he is wholly and forever free or he is not free at all.[103]

This excerpt expresses the radical character of Sartre's theory of freedom. Common opinion is that people, depending upon the context, are sometimes free and sometimes unfree to various degrees, but Sartre maintains that there is an important sense in which human beings are completely free. This view on freedom might, at first, seem strange or exaggerated, but there are some historical predecessors: both Descartes and the Stoic philosopher, Epictetus (60–117 C.E.) held related views. Each recognized the virtually unlimited power humans have in their powers of judgment or interpretation. For example, Descartes points out that in one respect, human judgment is 'infinite:' we may choose to assent to, or dissent from, any given proposition:

> It is free-will alone or liberty of choice which I find to be so great in me that I can conceive no other idea to be more great; it is indeed the case that it is for the most part this will that causes me to know that in some manner I bear the image and similitude of God ... for the faculty of will consists alone in our having the power of choosing to do a thing or choosing not to do it (that is, to affirm or deny, to pursue or to shun it).[104]

Sartre's theory of freedom is psychologically valuable in its suggestion that we can significantly modify our personality, if we were to will that end with sufficient strength. In practical terms, this implies that we could, at the very last second, choose to react differently than the way our past habits have led us to react. If we were to achieve this result within many different situations, it would not be long before we became a new person. With this, Sartre's theory encourages us to contemplate the possibility of reestablishing a new personality for ourselves and that of experiencing a personal transformation in contrast to our former style of behavior.

Responsibility, authenticity, and morality

Sartre states that a consequence of being condemned to be free is that one must 'carry the weight of the whole world' on one's shoulders. In being absolutely free, one has a corresponding 'absolute responsibility:'

Thus there are no *accidents* in a life; a community event which suddenly bursts forth and involves me in it does not come from the outside. If I am mobilized in a war, this war is *my* war; it is in my image and I deserve it. I deserve it first because I could always get out of it by suicide or by desertion; these ultimate possibles are those which must always be present for us when there is a question of envisaging a situation. For lack of getting out of it, I have *chosen* it. This can be due to inertia, to cowardice in the face of public opinion, or because I prefer certain other values to the value of the refusal to join in the war (the good opinion of my relatives, the honor of my family, etc.) Any way you look at it, it is a matter of choice.[105]

Sartre's theory of absolute freedom implies that human beings have no excuse for any self-deception they might bring upon themselves, and it implies that they are fully responsible for what they do. Sartre maximally extends this account of personal responsibility: he maintains that each of us (either implicitly or explicitly) chooses a general life project and through that very choice, chooses also to be a certain kind of person. Given this 'fundamental choice' which determines our 'fundamental project' – a choice which we are always free to change – Sartre maintains that we choose the kind of reactions we will have to situations, whether these reactions happen to be emotional or rational. By choosing to lead a certain kind of life, we have implicitly chosen to develop our personality in a certain direction.

As noted above in the discussion of bad faith, the awareness of our fundamental freedom can be overwhelming and disconcerting, and it can become all-too-easy to choose the path of self-deception as a way to escape the anguish of freedom. If this happens, then one can gravitate into interpretations of the world in terms of essential and determinate structures that say we cannot change, and which dictate that the world must be of a certain determinate and natural character. Once a person is self-deceptively convinced that the world must be a certain way, then the burden of choice with respect to changing the world is lifted.

On the other hand, Sartre believes that the recognition of our absolute freedom and responsibility sets us squarely along an authentic path. Being authentic entails admitting that we are responsible for what we have been, and it involves finding ourselves capable of making ourselves change. Being authentic involves recognizing that there is no escape from our power of choice, that there is no excuse for what we are, and that it is self-deceptive to blame others in an effort to relieve ourselves of responsibility. A question, then, concerns the moral implications of being authentic, for one can ask whether an authentic person must therefore be a good person.

It is clear that a Sartrean authentic person has some moral qualities: the person is responsible for his or her own actions, the person takes responsibility for the larger-scale situations within which he or she acts, and the person does not blame others. But if a properly moral consciousness also requires that complete selfishness is to be rejected in principle, then the question of whether an authentic person is thereby a moral person seems to have a negative answer in *Being and Nothingness*. This is because Sartre claims that freedom is primary and prior to the creation of all values, which include moral values.

Sartre claims that values arise from personal interests, and that personal interests arise from choice, which is an expression of one's freedom. If so, then we can choose whatever values we want, without constraint. In itself, Sartre's theory of freedom and authenticity provides no reason to choose to live one's life as a quest for pleasure, or as a quest for power, or as a quest to achieve self-realization, or as a quest to achieve what is commonly understood as the morally good. In terms of the expression of freedom, there is no determination to choose what is morally good over the selfish quest for power and domination over others. Sartre requires only that we live authentically in recognition of our absolute freedom, which means that we live in full acknowledgment of the path we choose, whatever path that happens to be. A person who is absolutely free to create whichever values she or he chooses stands, in effect, beyond good and evil. Such a person also, however, assumes full responsibility for whatever is done.

Selected works of Jean-Paul Sartre

1936 (age 31): (1) *La transcendance de l'ego, Esquisse d'une description phénomènologique* [*The Transcendence of the Ego. An Existentialist Theory of Consciousness*]
(2) *L'imagination* [*Imagination, a Psychological Critique*]
1938 (age 33): *La nausée* [*Nausea*, or *The Diary of Antoine Roquentin*]
1940 (age 35): *L'imaginaire: psychologie phénomènologique de l'imagination* [*The Psychology of Imagination*]
1943 (age 38): *L'être et le néant: Essai d'ontologie phénomènologique* [*Being and Nothingness – A Phenomenological Essay on Ontology*]
1943 (age 38): *Les mouches* [*The Flies*]
1945 (age 40): *Huis clos* [*No Exit*]
1946 (age 41): (1) *L'existentialisme est un humanisme* [*Existentialism as a Humanism*]
(2) *Réflexions sur la question juive* [trans. as *Portrait of the Anti-Semite* and also as *Anti-Semite and Jew*]

1947 (age 42): *Baudelaire*

1947–72 (ages 42–67) *Situations I* to *X*

1952 (age 47): *Saint Genet, comédien et martyr* [*Saint Genet, Actor and Martyr*]

1960 (age 55): *Critique de le raison dialectique (Vol. I)* [Critique of Dialectical Reason, Volume I]

1963 (age 58): *Les mots* [*The Words*]

1985 (posthumous): *Critique de le raison dialectique (Vol. II)* [Critique of Dialectical Reason, Volume II]

4

Albert Camus, Absurdist and Novelist (1913–60)

Life and works

Albert Camus was born in Mondovi, Algeria on November 7, 1913. As was also true in Jean-Paul Sartre's life, Camus's father died during military service while Camus was an infant. Camus's father's family had settled in Algeria in 1871, and Camus's father, Lucien Camus (1885–1914), worked as a laborer for a wine producer. While growing up in Algeria, Camus lived in poverty throughout his childhood with his older brother and his mother, Catherine Helene Sintes (1882–1960), who was of Spanish descent. With his outstanding natural intelligence, Camus became a scholarship student at the Lycée of Algiers, and later went on to study philosophy at the University of Algiers. To his misfortune, he suffered an attack of tuberculosis during this time, and it ended his preparations for a career in college teaching. Camus was married at age nineteen, but this ended sadly in divorce a year later.

While in his twenties, Camus was briefly a member of the Communist party, partially in response to the rise of fascism in Spain; he was also an actor–director–playwright in a theatre company which he founded. Camus received his *diplôme d'études supérieures* in philosophy, and then worked as a reporter for the socialist newspaper, *Alger Républicain*, where he wrote about the difficult circumstances facing the Algerian Muslim population. At age twenty-six, he married for a second time. During 1942, troubled by ill-health and an oppressive political situation in Algeria, Camus left North Africa for France, soon joining the French resistance movement as the editor of a clandestine newspaper, *Combat*. By the time Camus had reached his thirtieth year, he had written two of his most successful, and still widely-read, books, *The Stranger* (1942) and *The Myth of Sisyphus* (1942). During 1942–44, Camus suffered recurring difficulties with tuberculosis.

In the years that followed, Camus worked as an editor for the Gallimard Publishing house in Paris – a fateful position which he began in 1943 – and he continued as editor for *Combat*. He wrote, produced, and translated plays, wrote novels and short stories, went on lecture tours of the United States and South America, and received the Nobel Prize for Literature in 1957. He also spoke and wrote in defense of workers' rights in various parts of Europe, and he was a steadfast opponent of the death penalty. Camus's battle against the forces of time came to an end unexpectedly and prematurely at the age of forty-six, when he was involved in a car crash while returning to Paris from the small scenic village of Lourmarin (where he lived, and where his grave is now located) on January 4, 1960. The driver of the car was Michel Gallimard, Camus's friend and editor, and nephew of the publisher, Gaston Gallimard. The manuscript of Camus's unfinished autobiographical novel, *The First Man*, was recovered from the crash. Camus's briefcase also contained a copy of Nietzsche's *The Gay Science*.[106]

Is life worth living? The feeling of the absurd

Camus's essay, 'The Myth of Sisyphus,' begins with the following assertion:

> There is but one truly serious philosophical problem, and that is suicide. Judging whether life is or is not worth living amounts to answering the fundamental question of philosophy.[107]

In *Hamlet*, William Shakespeare wrote in a kindred spirit, 'To be, or not to be, that is the question.'[108] And as the above excerpt shows, Camus believes that the question Hamlet asked himself while contemplating suicide, is at the core of philosophical reflection. As tragic as suicide frequently is, the contemplation of suicide can have a philosophical dimension, for some people have killed themselves as a consequence of feeling that their life was incomprehensible, or that living was no longer worth the trouble. Often, but not always, the decision to commit suicide involves an apprehension of the absurdity or meaninglessness of life.[109] In light of such facts, Camus inquires into the sources of the feeling of the absurd, and into the question of whether suicide is the reasonable thing to do, if life is indeed meaningless.

The feeling of the absurd, Camus observes, can suddenly come upon a person 'at any streetcorner,' and he believes that the absurdity of life is perceivable everywhere, if one were only to look closely and honestly at the world. Usually we remain unaware of it, Camus believes, and only infrequently does the feeling of absurdity intrude upon our awareness. But when the feeling arrives, it is a shock: daily life takes on a mechanical and pointless quality, and one becomes alienated and disengaged from the ordinary, meaning-filled way of interpreting the world. In this state of disengagement, the scenes of daily life can appear as nothing more than episodes upon an extensive stage set, filled with actors in an endless play without a point. The experience can take the form of feeling that one is partici- pating in a relay-race without an ultimate goal, as one watches generation after generation passing the torch of its consciousness to the next, only to die even- tually of exhaustion. Upon seeing the world in this manner, 'the stage sets collapse' and one experiences life's absurdity. Camus describes the feeling:

> At certain moments of lucidity, the mechanical aspect of their gestures, their meaningless pantomime makes silly everything that surrounds them. A man is talking on the telephone behind a glass partition; you cannot hear him, but you see his incomprehensible dumb show: you wonder why he is alive. This discomfort in the face of man's own inhumanity, this incalcu- lable tumble before the image of what we are, this 'nausea,' as a writer of today calls it, is also the absurd.[110] Likewise the stranger who at certain seconds comes to meet us in a mirror, the familiar and yet alarming brother we encounter in our own photographs is also the absurd.[111]

Camus experiences life's absurdity in a 'moment of lucidity,' as he stands beside himself considering things objectively, and regarding this awareness as an expe- rience of insight. It reveals to him how the world of everyday life appears in the shadow of nothingness: it appears as a theatrical stage, complete with artificial scenery and people in costume who play their roles. As Camus further reflects upon how the products of human culture will eventually perish, the absurd enters further into his consideration. He concludes that there is no permanent meaning in life, even if one's personal achievement and contribution to humanity is at the very highest level. If one were a virtual superhuman, it would make no absolute difference, for global fame remains conditional:

> But all kinds of fame are ephemeral. From the point of view of Sirius [i.e., from the point of view of an entity that lasts millions of years], Goethe's works in ten thousand years will be dust and his name forgotten. Perhaps a handful of archaeologists will look for 'evidence' of our era. That idea has always contained a lesson.[112] Seriously meditated upon, it reduces our perturbations to the profound nobility that is

found in indifference. Above all, it directs our concerns toward what is most certain – that is, toward the immediate. Of all kinds of fame the least deceptive is the one that is lived.[113]

The key words here are 'nobility,' 'indifference,' and 'immediacy.' The Bible expresses similar, though somewhat less redeeming, sentiments regarding the temporary nature of life, as we can read in the Book of Ecclesiastes:[114]

Yet I perceived that the same fate befalls all of them. Then I said to myself, 'What happens to the fool will happen to me also; why then have I been so very wise?' And I said to myself that this also is vanity. For there is no enduring remembrance of the wise or of fools, seeing that in the days to come all will have been long forgotten. How can the wise die just like fools? So I hated life, because what is done under the sun was grievous to me; for all is vanity and a chasing after wind.[115]

Upon recognizing the earth's inevitable destruction and humanity's eventual oblivion, Camus concludes that in a metaphysical, extra-human sense, life is not grounded upon an absolute meaning. For him, no realm of godlike eternal values exists independently that confers absolute significance upon us as individuals and upon our civilizations as a whole. Camus distinctly envisions the day, whenever it might be, either tomorrow or in two hundred thousand years, when all monuments to the highest human achievement will no longer exist, such as, to name just a few, Shakespeare's plays, the Pyramids, the Taj Mahal, the Cathedral of Notre Dame, the Sistine Chapel Ceiling, the Parthenon, the music of Mozart and Beethoven, and Homer's *Iliad* and *Odyssey*. The day will come when there will be no one left to remember the greatest acts of heroism, self-sacrifice and contributions to humanity. Camus accordingly concludes that 'of all kinds of fame the least deceptive is the one that is lived.' Recognizing no everlasting future for anyone or anything in view, and with no appeal to superhuman divinities that he is willing to make, he turns his attention to the here and now in an effort to decide whether life is nonetheless worth living.

As the above excerpt from the book of Ecclesiastes shows, the awareness that life is, or might be, without absolute significance hardly received its first formulation with Camus. The idea appears later in Shakespeare's works, where his formulations often combine the awareness of absurdity with the thought that the world is a stage. We see this, for instance, in *Macbeth*, at the moment when Macbeth learns of his wife's death from Seyton, one of Macbeth's officers.[116] Though in the midst of preparing for battle, Macbeth takes a moment to reflect upon life's meaninglessness, for it appears to him then that life is a walking shadow – a tale told by an idiot who appears on stage, recites enthusiastically his insignificant lines, and who then disappears into oblivion.[117]

In passing reflections, most people have had such thoughts at one time or another, but it remains difficult to appreciate the implications of having a long-term experience of life's absurdity. Usually, the feeling of the absurd dissipates as one resumes one's daily activity, and it does not persist to become a general state of mind. But to appreciate Camus's absurdist outlook, it is necessary to imagine living (or actually live) with the belief that there is no hope for a life beyond what we have at present. One must live as if one knew that God does not exist, and as if one knew that there is no rebirth and no moral balance (e.g., no rewards in heaven; no punishments in hell); one must live as if one knew that after the death of the human body, there would be nothing but eternal oblivion, not only for oneself, but for everyone. It is to live with the knowledge that everything will be forgotten.

Such thoughts are easy to recite. They are harder to assimilate and practice as a way of life or as a general mentality, in a large part because the ideas of heaven, hell, reward, punishment, hope, faith, miracles, spirits – all sorts of otherworldly ideals – permeate most human cultures, and perhaps the natural tendencies of human imagination as well. It is also difficult to perpetuate such an extremely distanced standpoint within oneself, if only because one's immediate practical engagement in the world requires a more involved attitude. It is therefore a challenge to consider at length what it might be like to live continuously without acknowledging even the remote possibility of an absolutely meaningful and reliable foundation. It is a test and trial – and for Camus it is a philosophical test – to imagine what it might be like to live, day in and day out, without hope and without appeal, while also resisting the descent into psychological depression and alienation from the world that can accompany such an arguably realistic attitude.

Camus is certain that feelings of the absurd reveal the truth about our world. His effort is to acknowledge this truth, come to terms with the feeling of life's absurdity, and decide whether or not life is worth living in the face of it. This philosophical and practical effort, Camus believes, requires 'integrity:'[118]

> There can be no question of masking the evidence … It is essential to know whether one can live with it [viz., the absurd] or whether, on the other hand, logic commands one to die of it … Being able to remain on that dizzying crest – that is integrity and the rest is subterfuge.[119]

Weak-minded reactions to the absurd: suicide and hope

Prior to describing his way of encountering the absurd with integrity, Camus rejects two competing alternatives, namely, 'suicide' and 'hope.' One possible reaction to the absurd is to give up living, since there is no absolute meaning, and therefore no unconditional reason for remaining alive. The reasoning is that since one will be dead in the long run, and since all of our achievements during this life will become dust and be forgotten, then all suffering and all effort is ultimately worthless. Since there is no unshakeable reason to postpone the inevitable, one should therefore get things over with. By reflecting along such lines, a person might come to believe that life is pointless, and that suicide is the most courageous and honest thing to do in light of the disheartening facts.

Camus rejects this suicidal rationale, however, regarding it as escapist and weak-minded. Committing suicide does not nobly and courageously confront the absurd, he argues, but rather eliminates one's awareness of the world altogether; it does not solve the problem of how to live in the face of life's absurdity, but only dissolves the context within which the problem arises and persists. According to Camus's assumptions, one could grant that suicide would make sense, if the only good reason for living is to secure an absolute meaning for one's life. Suicide might be reasonable, if realizing a permanent and eternal goal were life's essential point, and if one knew that this goal is impossible to attain or even approach. Camus avoids this crushing conclusion by maintaining that there are other sources of value in life that do not require the recognition of absolute, unchanging meanings.

As we shall see, Camus highlights an immeasurably positive value in human temporal experience – one which he believes is worth preserving as long as possible. So his position is exactly opposed to suicide: instead of cutting life short as quickly as one can, Camus asserts that one ought to live as long as possible, providing that one is able to appreciate the infinite value of the present moment as it is experienced, no matter what is experienced. Before exploring this theme further, let us note the second alternative which Camus rejects, namely, that of 'hope' in the face of meaninglessness.

The strategy of hope is typically associated with religious beliefs that offer salvation in an otherworldly realm, such as heaven. An examination of traditional religion is not part of Camus's main discussion, and insofar as he recognizes that many traditional religious views issue from the standpoint of hope, he rejects them. His argumentative concern is with positions theoretically closer to his own, namely, those which present themselves as being absurdist, but which prove themselves to be religiously hopeful and escapist nonetheless. As such, they run contrary to the stronger-minded attitude Camus wishes to advocate – a view which paradoxically claims that life is indeed hopeless, but still of immeasurable value.

Specifically, Camus criticizes existentialist views which explicitly acknowledge the experience of the absurd, but which, in his mind, fail to appreciate the experience's shocking implications. He claims that they too, like traditional religion, fall back upon hope as a kind of escape from life's painful absurdity. Rather than invalidating or denying the experience of the absurd, these existentialist views esteem it. But this, according to Camus, characterizes the experience of the absurd as a mode of salvation, which he refers to as an objectionable 'nostalgia for the absurd.'

Søren Kierkegaard's outlook is the leading example that Camus has in mind.[120] As Camus himself experienced a century later, Kierkegaard (1813–1855) was also struck by a fundamentally absurd dimension to human experience. Unlike Camus, though, Kierkegaard understood the experience of the absurd as a stepping stone to the experience of absolute consciousness. By focusing upon a person's ability to make a completely free 'leap of faith' – a leap without rational foundation (i.e., a leap that is grounded in absurdity) – Kierkegaard discovered a revelation of divine consciousness in the very experience of freedom. A person who makes an absolutely free choice of his or her own, can be regarded as experiencing a quality of consciousness comparable to what God can be supposed to have had, when God created the world from a purely free choice.[121] As we have seen in the previous chapter, Jean-Paul Sartre acknowledges that human consciousness is based on this kind of absolute freedom, although he resists associating this infinite freedom with the concept of God.

Camus criticizes the quest for the divine experience of freedom as an escape from the absurd reality in which we live. Such a quest, he claims, glorifies the absurdity of life with a nostalgia for the absurd, and this reveals how the more telling implication of this absurdity – namely, that there is 'no future,' 'no appeal,' 'no hope,' and no living escape – has been avoided in these religious attitudes towards the absurd. He writes:

> My reasoning wants to be faithful to the evidence that aroused it. That evidence is the absurd. It is that divorce between the mind that desires and the world that disappoints, my nostalgia for unity, this fragmented universe and the contradiction that binds them together ... Any other position implies for the absurd mind deceit and the mind's retreat before what the mind itself has brought to light.[122]

Camus intends to live with life's absurdity, and he resists denying its incoherence through self-deception or bad faith. Outright suicide eliminates the absurdity, since suicide eliminates the mind, and for Camus 'there can be no absurd outside the human mind.' Religious existentialism also obscures life's absurdity by negating its force with a consoling covering of nostalgia, romanticism, and associations with the divine. Camus, rather, desires a more confrontational solution: 'if I attempt to solve a problem, at least I must not by that very solution conjure away one of the terms of the problem.'[123] With this commitment, he rejects suicide and tries squarely to face life's incomprehensibility, and resists the more comforting route of religious existentialism. This leads him to advocate 'revolt,' as it arises within the context of a lucid state of consciousness.

Strong-minded reactions to the absurd: revolt and lucidity

Upon recognizing how certain kinds of experiences can fill one's consciousness with a feeling of absurdity, and upon refusing to commit suicide or escape into a nostalgic celebration of this disturbing and alienating experience, Camus offers the option of 'revolt' as an authentic solution to the problem of living in a irrational world. To revolt is to maintain a defiant and confrontational attitude toward the world's absurdity; it is to adopt a martial attitude through which one fights against the painful incomprehensibility of things with all of one's strength. Revolt, he claims, is 'one of the only coherent philosophical positions,'[124] and it involves a constant acknowledgment of the feeling of the absurd, and a constant confrontation with the ultimate disappearance of one's consciousness from existence.

Just as Sartrean authenticity requires that we question ourselves continually in light of the instability of all conceptual constructions that we happen to devise, Camusian authenticity requires that we continually maintain ourselves defiantly against a world that contains no solid ground of meanings. Being authentic involves setting oneself sublimely against the far more powerful external universe which will eventually swallow the earth into oblivion. In other words, Camus's conception of authenticity celebrates the nobility of fighting a losing battle against an unbeatable enemy, namely, the passing of time.[125]

As concrete expressions of revolt, Camus describes various absurdist lifestyles which exemplify his ideal of a non-escapist attitude toward life. These he sharply contrasts with the lifestyle of the everyday person:

> Before encountering the absurd, the everyday man lives with aims, a concern for the future or for justification (with regard to whom or what is not the question). He weighs his chances, he counts on 'someday,' his retirement or the labor of his sons. He still thinks that something in his life can be directed. In truth, he acts as if he were free, even if all the facts make a point of contradicting that liberty.[126]

The everyday person exemplifies what is usually recognized as a normal, rational and healthy attitude towards life: there is hope and concern, and these hopes define personal projects that focus a significant part of one's attention upon future days when the hopes will be satisfied and happiness will be more completely realized. For someone who has apprehended the absurdity of life, however, this everyday lifestyle appears to be out of touch with the facts, for the absurdist person regards the everyday person as being directed by hopes which are mostly illusory, if only because death can happen at any time. When one takes the absurdity of life seriously, Camus believes, the everyday lifestyle reveals itself to be grounded on non-secure foundations, for the hopes which define the everyday person's life projects are attempts to secure a permanency in life where, in fact, there is none.

Camus, too, can be seen to be aiming traditionally for some permanency amidst the world's change. But upon realizing the uncertainties within experience, he can only apprehend this permanence as dwelling within the presence of the moment as it happens right now, and in nothing more. The pattern of his reasoning recalls Descartes, who, in his efforts to find a reliable foundation for knowledge, was led to narrow his focus more and more, until he arrived finally at the bare awareness of himself in the present moment as he, Descartes, immediately experienced it. This was his *cogito*.

In a surprisingly comparable manner, Camus's absurd person also attends closely and narrowly to the here and now, in an effort to experience life as it actually transpires, moment to moment, without looking too far ahead, and without reminiscing about the past. The absurd person does not postpone his or her appreciation of time's passing right now to some future day when hopes will finally be realized, because that day may never arrive. Neither does the absurd person constantly review bygone days. The focus is narrowed down upon the ever-present moment.

Camus is inspired by the experience of a person condemned to death, who, upon realizing that her, or his, life will soon be extinguished, reacts to a last-minute reprieve with overflowing exhilaration, clinging in appreciation to the breath of life that remains. Since fate condemns everyone to death, his message is philosophical and universal: each moment that we continue to live, is yet another exhilarating reprieve from the moment of death's final seal. For in a broad sense, we are all prisoners within space and time who await execution by the fateful hands of the clock. He writes:

> The divine availability of the condemned man before whom the prison doors open in a certain early dawn, that unbelievable disinterested-ness with regard to everything except for the pure flame of life – it is clear that death and the absurd are here the principles of the only reasonable freedom: that which a human heart can experience and live.[127,128]

By considering the appreciation that can issue from being granted a last-minute reprieve before an expected moment of death, and by reflecting upon the resulting surge of joy in being still alive, Camus concludes that within the present moment the 'pure flame of life' has immeasurable value. The over-whelming quality of one's appreciation for merely being alive right now, insofar as this is brought to light by apprehending the near loss of one's life, is a moment of enlightenment and awakening for Camus. The intensity of this awareness obscures everything but the experience and value of one's breath of life in the present moment, and in recognition of this heightened state of awareness, Camus asserts that 'the present and the succession of presents before a constantly conscious soul is the ideal of the absurd man.'[129] There is nothing better than being fully awake right now, there is nothing of value beyond such an enlightened awareness, and there is no point in life except staying awake in that condition as long as one can.

Such considerations lead Camus to draw his well-known conclusion that staying alive and maintaining one's consciousness at this hyper-aware level is sufficient to render life meaningful, and that under such conditions 'what counts is not the best living but the most living.'[130] Since every moment within a heightened awareness cognizant of life's overflowing value is itself of immea-surable worth, all considerations of comparative quality from moment to moment disappear. Camus concludes that under these conditions, the quantity of life is a more important consideration than the quality of life, because the maximum quality is presumed already to have been achieved in the enlightened appreciation that one is still alive right now, purely and simply. Within this perspective, every moment has infinite value, and there is no longer any scale of values that would imply that some moments are better than others.

In an effort to be consistent with the immeasurable value of the 'flame of life,' Camus proposes absurdist lifestyles that incorporate various ways to focus centrally upon the present moment. The particular examples he suggests are diverse, and it is debatable whether they are the best examples. But Camus does claim that absurdist lifestyles in general involve an 'indifference to the future,' an attempt to 'drain everything' from the present moment, and a tendency to have as many different kinds of experience as possible. His prescriptions thus aim to maximize the quantity of life's duration and variation. For him, the best life is the longest and most varied, assuming that one has already appreciated the immeasurable value of the breath of life.

Absurd lifestyles: the seducer, the actor, the conqueror

As examples of absurdist character types, Camus describes the lifestyles of seducers, actors, and conquerors of a certain kind, namely, those within whose

lifestyles 'quantity' rules over 'quality.' A seducer in the Camusian style is interested in the quantity of people he, or she, can seduce; the quality of the relationship does not matter. The Camusian actor is interested in the number of
roles he, or she, can play; the quality of the characters portrayed does not
matter. The Camusian conqueror is interested in the number of battles he, or
she, can engage in; the quality of the competing group remains unimportant.
From these reflections alone, we can see that these kinds of lifestyle minimize
success-seeking in that they do not strive for outstanding achievement in
terms of quality.

The character of the Camusian seducer is partially inspired by Søren
Kierkegaard's conception of the 'aesthetic' lifestyle – a lifestyle that aims to
derive pleasure from the sensory surface of experience and from the playful
manipulation of situations to reconstruct them into more entertaining ones.[131]
Camus projects the qualities of the Kierkegaardian aesthete into his character
of the seducer, who is interested in gratifying his every wish. In the sphere of
love, this kind of seducer aims for short-term relationships, rather than long-
term and committed ones, since short-term relationships ensure more variety
and less concern with the future. In being driven to gratify every wish, the
seducer–aesthete is an instinctual, imagination-centered type, who, in the
manner of a young child, remains unconcerned with moral reflection.

The actor in the Camusian style similarly displays an interest in quantity
and a disregard for quality. Camus locates this kind of actor among absurd
lifestyles, in part owing to his recognition that in general, the fame of most
actors is short-lived: new actors continually step into the spotlight to replace
the old, and past actors are quickly forgotten as fashions change. As someone
who wrote for the theatre, Camus witnessed this phenomenon first-hand.

The goal of the actor who is touched by life's absurdity, is to play as many
different characters as possible, of any kind. Unlike the traditionally motivated
actor who strives to realize theatrical roles of the highest quality and who aims
to reach the great moments that few can attain, the absurd actor prefers to play
as many roles as possible, regardless of the quality of the parts. In this respect,
Camus likens the absurd actor to the traveller whose project is to visit as many
different places as possible, simply for the sake of variety. Such an absurdist
traveller never chooses to revisit a place of quality, but prefers to find a new
destination, wherever it might be.

Consistent with his vital interests in rebellion, defiance, combat, and struggle,
and inspired by the historical events and personages of the Second World War
that surrounded him as he was writing *The Myth of Sisyphus*, Camus also reflects
upon the character of the conqueror or adventurer. Unlike traditional
conquerors who engage in territorial conquest for the purpose of restructuring

and creating a long-lasting social order, the absurdist conqueror believes that such efforts are futile. Rather, such a conqueror assumes an attitude of revolt and defiance, recognizing the eventuality of defeat at some future point. This conqueror knows that his or her victories will be eventually erased, but to the conqueror, this ultimate loss is unimportant. Of greater value is the experience of the fight itself, as opposed to the material results of the struggle.

So Camus respects the absurdist conqueror, not owing to his or her material conquests, but owing to the conqueror's strength of character, since he recognizes the conquest of territories as evidence of a more personal kind of self-overcoming – one that involves the overcoming of one's character limitations. Like Nietzsche, Camus celebrates ruling and dominating types in reference to their capacity to look down upon themselves and thereby grow beyond their former selves.[132] But as is true for the morally insensitive seducer–aesthete, the conqueror tramples upon those who he or she vanquishes, and both types disregard an assortment of traditional moral values.

If we now reflect upon Camus's three absurdist lifestyles, the question arises whether living in cognizance of life's absurdity necessitates a disregard for traditional morality. This same issue arises in connection with Sartre and Kierkegaard, since moral values, or the ethical lifestyle, take a back seat to the value of freedom in both of these latter thinkers as well. Camus's requirement that variation and duration should be maximized similarly entails that there are no moral barriers that need to be respected, if mere variation is the goal. Nonetheless, since all variations are quantitatively alike, and since there are so many variations to choose from, even within the constraints of a moral lifestyle, it remains possible to choose a moral life – if one adopts an appropriate absurdist attitude – and yet remain faithful to Camus's sense of revolt. As we can see from Camus's next example – the character of Sisyphus – it is possible to have a very narrowly circumscribed set of experiences, and still embody the idea of revolt.

The myth of Sisyphus

The fourth and most well-known of Camus's absurdist characters is the mythic Sisyphus, who was condemned by the gods to roll hopelessly a heavy rock to the top of a mountain, only to have its own weight cause it to roll back down the mountain once again, time after time. Camus recites the myth of Sisyphus as follows:

> It is said also that Sisyphus, being near to death, rashly wanted to test his wife's love. He ordered her to cast his unburied body into the middle of

the public square. Sisyphus woke up in the underworld. And there, annoyed by an obedience so contrary to human love, he obtained from Pluto permission to return to earth in order to chastise his wife. But when he had seen again the face of this world, enjoyed water and sun, warm stones and the sea, he no longer wanted to go back to the infernal darkness. Recalls, signs of anger, warnings were of no avail. Many years more he lived facing the curve of the gulf, the sparkling sea, and the smiles of earth. A decree of the gods was necessary. Mercury came and seized the impudent man by the collar and, snatching him from his joys, led him forcibly back to the underworld, where his rock was ready for him.

You have already grasped that Sisyphus is the absurd hero. He *is*, as much through his passions as through his torture. His scorn of the gods, his hatred of death, and his passion for life won him that unspeakable penalty in which the whole being is exerted toward accomplishing nothing.[133]

As for this myth, one sees merely the whole effort of a body straining to raise the huge stone, to roll it and push it up a slope a hundred times over; one sees the face screwed up, the cheek tight against the stone, the shoulder bracing the clay-covered mass, the foot wedging it, the fresh start with arms outstretched, the wholly human security of two earth-clotted hands. At the very end of his long effort measured by skyless space and time without depth, the purpose is achieved. Then Sisyphus watches the stone rush down in a few moments toward that lower world whence he will have to push it up again toward the summit. He goes back down to the plain.

It is during that return, that pause, that Sisyphus interests me. A face that toils so close to stones is already a stone itself! I see that man going back down with a heavy yet measured step toward the torment of which he will never know the end. That hour is like a breathing-space which returns as surely as his suffering, that is his hour of consciousness.[134]

[Sisyphus] concludes that all is well. This universe henceforth without a master seems to him neither sterile nor futile. Each atom of that stone, each mineral flake of that night-filled mountain, in itself forms a world. The struggle itself toward the heights is enough to fill a man's heart. One must imagine Sisyphus happy.[135]

As Camus describes him, Sisyphus reacts with a lucid mind to the absurdity of life. Sisyphus represents a person who, as if he were caged in a factory or prison, works without any hope for resolution or satisfaction in his labor, while yet having found peace of mind. Sisyphus's 'whole being is exerted towards accomplishing nothing,' and yet he remains happy in his imprisonment and frustration. He rolls the rock up to the top of the mountain, and as he watches it roll back down again in defeat, he realizes that his labor will be frustrated forever. Worse yet, for the eternal Sisyphus, there is no possibility of death as a final salvation and release from his torture, so he represents a standing condition of a world where nothing absolutely enduring and meaningful can be accomplished. As long as one lives, such are the frustrating conditions under which one will work. Insofar as life is portrayed as an essentially frustrating enterprise, Camus's vision recalls not only the world of the ancient Greeks, whose characterization of human experience included an assortment of images representing eternal dissatisfaction (e.g., Tantalus, the Danaids, Ixion), but those of classical Buddhism, Schopenhauer, and Sartre.

Sisyphus differs from Camus's other absurdist characters, however, because seducers, actors, and conquerors appear to enjoy more pleasure and freedom in their varied lives. Sisyphus more closely represents the conditions of proletarian labor, although in his love of sensory pleasure, he resembles the seducer–aesthete, and in his dedication to struggle, he resembles the conqueror. And yet, in contrast to the actor, seducer, and conqueror, Sisyphus's struggle is not a revolt against death, since he is an immortal; his struggle is against a set of frustrating living conditions that will not go away. In this respect, Sisyphus is the most philosophical and existential character in Camus's array, and in his symbolization of the factory worker, he is the most expressively socially critical among Camus's absurdist characters.

Critical discussion

Central to Camus's view is his prescription that we should live in the present, and appreciate the pure flame of life before it is annihilated by the passing of time. This appreciation can be realized, though, only with an extraordinary awareness of one's upcoming death: one requires a concrete idea of one's future non-existence and needs to feel distinctly what it might be like to face the prospect of being executed tomorrow. An abstract conception of one's death will not suffice. Appreciating the present moment thus requires a strong imaginative awareness of the reality of one's death at a later time: one needs to imagine one's lifeless body; envision one's tombstone; realize how one eventually will be forgotten; appreciate how life will continue on without one's presence, all in serious detail, just as in Charles Dicken's *A Christmas Carol* (1843), Ebenezer Scrooge was led to confront death directly by gazing upon his own tombstone. But such an act of imagination calls for a strong projection into the future, away from the present moment, not to mention a quality of imaginative awareness that is more determinate and realistic than is usual. So paradoxically, to appreciate the flame of life here and now, one's background orientation needs to be strongly directed towards the future, as one imagines the time when one will no longer exist.

Camus also strives to confront the absurd honestly, truthfully, authentically, and with integrity. Which is to say that in his reaction to life's absurdity, he adheres to familiar moral values such as truth and honesty. And yet, his absurdist characters of the seducer and the conqueror tend to behave selfishly, at a standpoint beyond good and evil. It is open to question, then, why Camus adheres to some traditional moral values, while he downplays values such as the respect for others. We can also question why the absurdity of life should be taken so seriously, and why we should attempt to live with integrity, if absolutely nothing matters.

As can be seen by comparing and contrasting the various absurdist types, Camus oscillates between aristocratic and plebian sympathies. The seducer–aesthete, the conqueror, and the actor, define roles that tend to be associated with the more privileged layers of society, whereas Sisyphus is more clearly aligned with workers and people in slavery. This is evident from Camus's description of the absurdist actor, to whom he addresses the luxurious recommendation to play as many roles as possible. Had Camus conceived of the absurdist actor in closer analogy to Sisyphus, he might have concluded that a more absurd actor would play the same small part every day, without variation, year after year. So Camus's prescription to maximize the variation of experiences is independent of his idea of appreciating the pure flame of life, since the example of Sisyphus reveals that even if the quality of that flame remains the same and life is monotonous, life can still be worth living.

Finally, we can question Camus's claim that certain lifestyles exemplify the absurdist approach to life better than others. For instance, the everyday person's lifestyle is supposedly not absurdist. But if Camus's leading claim is that the absurdist attitude involves a struggle against an overwhelming force, accompanied with an awareness that the battle is a losing one, then the everyday lifestyle can be easily interpreted in an absurdist light. One can 'fight a losing battle' by defiantly continuing in the impossible attempt to understand the world completely; one can fight a losing battle by defiantly continuing in the impossible and absurd attempt to establish a permanent meaning. If one judges from ordinary appearances, standard lifestyles might present themselves as being insensitive to life's absurdity. But if one believes that the attempt to establish a permanent meaning in a constantly changing world is absurd, then it remains possible to engage in the traditional attempt to establish a permanent meaning, while harboring an absurdist, defiant, rebellious attitude. Along comparable lines, one can engage in a life-project that appears to others to be one-sidedly goal-oriented and careerist, while enjoying one's activities as 'play,' letting the future take care of itself. In this case, the goal-orientation is only apparent, since the person's focus is upon the play of the present.

What matters, then, is not the specific kind of lifestyle one adopts, but one's attitude toward the activities within any particularly chosen lifestyle. Traditional lifestyles are open to absurdist interpretations, so whether or not a person is living defiantly and rebelliously, depends on how the person in question understands his or her activity, and not how the lifestyle appears to others. These reflections undermine Camus's celebration of the seducer, actor, and conqueror, but they also bring Camus's view closer to the Stoic solution for finding satisfaction amidst a frustrating and confining world, which was to prescribe a modification in one's interpretation and attitude. Every lifestyle is open to an absurdist interpretation, so changing one's behavior may not be necessary. Camus urges us to adjust our interpretations, so that the absurdity of human experience is brought into the foreground of our attention.

Camus emphasizes that one will always have burdens, and that the struggle against these burdens, the experience of resistance, and the test of oneself against a force greater than oneself, is what makes life worth living. Albert Camus was, however, more than a fighter who set himself against the odds; he waged a relentless battle against time, an unbeatable enemy, celebrating the nobility of inevitable failure, and celebrating the human condition thereby.

Selected works of Albert Camus

1937 (age 23): *L'Envers et l'endroit* [*Betwixt and Between*]
1938 (age 24): *Noces* [*Nuptuals*]
1942 (age 28): *L'Étranger* [trans. as *The Stranger* and also as *The Outsider*]
1942 (age 28): *Le Mythe de Sisyphe* [*The Myth of Sisyphus*]
1947 (age 33): *La Peste* [*The Plague*]
1951 (age 37): *L'Homme révolté* [*The Rebel*]
1956 (age 42): *La Chute* [*The Fall*]
1957 (age 43): *L'Exil et le royaume* [*Exile and the Kingdom*]

5

E. M. Cioran, Nihilist and Ecstatic (1911–95)

Life and works

In a brief autobiographical sketch, Emile Mihai Cioran described himself as follows:

> I was born on the 8th April 1911 in Rasinari, a village in the Carpathians, where my father was a Greek Orthodox priest. From 1920 to 1928 I attended the Sibiu grammar school.[136] From 1929 to 1931 I studied at the Faculty of Arts at Bucharest University.[137] Postgraduate studies in philosophy until 1936. In 1937 I came to Paris with a scholarship from the French Institute in Bucharest and have been living here ever since. I have no nationality – the best possible status for an intellectual. On the other hand, I have not disowned my Romanian origins; had I to choose a country, I would still choose my own. Before the war I published various essays in Romanian of a more or less philosophical nature. I only began writing in French in about 1947. It was the hardest experience I have ever undergone. This precise, highly disciplined, and highly exacting language seemed as restrictive as a straitjacket. Even now I must confess that I do not feel completely at ease with it. It is this feeling of uneasiness which has led me to ponder the problem of style and the very anomaly of writing. All my books are more or less autobiographical – a rather abstract form of autobiography, I admit.[138]

Among Romanian intellectuals who became known outside their native country – individuals such as Tristan Tzara (1896–1963),[139] Mircea Eliade (1907–86),[140] and Eugène Ionesco (1912–94)[141] – E. M. Cioran was among the least appreciated during his lifetime. And he wished things to be this way, intentionally avoiding notoriety and living quietly on the Left Bank in Paris. Unlike Camus, who believed that the only fame worth having is the fame that is lived, Cioran was uninterested in fame, either during his own life, or posthumously. Utterly convinced of the meaninglessness of existence, Cioran led an inconspicuous life, often in poverty, periodically living in inexpensive hotel rooms, suffering from insomnia, eating in cafeterias and eking out a meager and unpretentious existence. He worked part-time as a manuscript reader and translator, during which time he wrote articles – some of which appeared in the *Evergreen Review*[142] – and his collections of aphoristic books. Cioran died in Paris on June 20, 1995.

Irreconcilable perspectives within human consciousness

In *The Birth of Tragedy* (1872), Friedrich Nietzsche recalls the story of King Midas, who, in his quest to discover what is best and most desirable in human life, sought for the council of the wise and mythic Silenus. What Silenus had to say came as an unexpected surprise, for his 'wisdom' was to claim that what is best for the human being, is the impossible condition of not having come into existence to begin with. To be 'nothing,' Silenus awesomely laughed, is the best condition for the human being. The second best condition, he added, is 'to die soon.' He regarded life as an accursed condition.

Unlike Nietzsche, whose philosophy attempted to provide a positive value to life in the face of its horror, Cioran remains in sympathy with the nihilistic wisdom of Silenus. Like Albert Camus, Cioran philosophizes in recognition of the proposition that human life loses its value when it is seen from afar, either from the standpoint of distant space or distant time. Cioran, however, writes with greater scorn, less nostalgia for, and with less heroic celebration of, life's absurdity. His thinking leaves only the most minimalized room for salvation, and he faces the prospect of cosmic meaninglessness with a stark acknowledgment of how it diminishes the significance of moral evaluations:

> We should repeat to ourselves every day: I am one of the billions dragging himself across the earth's surface. One, and no more. This banality justifies any conclusion, any behavior or action: debauchery, chastity, suicide, work, crime, sloth, or rebellion ... Whence it follows that each man is right to do what he does.[143]

During the nineteenth century, Fyodor Dostoevski (1821–81) – through the voice of literary characters such as Ivan Karamazov in *The Brothers Karamazov* (1878–80) – also pondered whether everything is permissible, if there is no God to enforce, reinforce, and provide substance to moral prescriptions. Using a different line of reasoning, Cioran comparably concludes that everything is permissible, if only because each person is so numerically insignificant. For him, it makes no difference what one does in the larger scheme of things, whether or not one's behavior is moral or immoral, because one's existence ultimately makes no difference. According to the reasoning patterns of both Dostoevski's literary characters and Cioran, an amoral condition issues from a perceived lack of absolute and objectively grounded meaning.

We have also seen earlier, and in contrast, how in his recognition of the absurd, Albert Camus defends a more Nietzschean ethic of integrity, courage, and strength, insofar as he maintains that suicide and religious faith are escapist, and therefore condemnable, reactions to the absurdity of life. Cioran does not advocate suicide, but he is less concerned with evaluating alternative lifestyles: for him, every lifestyle diminishes in significance when seen from a wider and more objective perspective, and he believes that in the end, each person amounts to less than a water droplet in an infinite ocean. Cioran is less interested than Camus in evaluating alternative lifestyles in terms of their respective normative advantages, and he is not particularly concerned with what is morally good. He does, however, remain focused upon what is true, in the sense of living a life that is true to the hard facts. And central to this investigation of existential truth, is Cioran's interest in discovering ways to endure what he believes to be an agonizing human condition. In this respect, his philosophical and existential intentions are comparable to Nietzsche's.

When Cioran ascribes a positive value to human situations, this is usually in reference to those conditions under which we can experience insight into the nature of existence, and he attends to extraordinary states of mind that are comparable to what Camus describes as 'lucidity.' What is notable about Cioran's approach in general, is his more Romanticist–Bergsonian disinclination towards rationalistic philosophical efforts to capture the essence of things within a well-organized conceptual system, not to mention his distinctively Nietzschean emphasis on the proposition that the apprehension of truth involves pain. We encounter the former attitude in the following excerpt from *On the Heights of Despair* (1934), written when Cioran was twenty-two years old:

> I like thought which preserves a whiff of flesh and blood, and I prefer a thousand times an idea rising from sexual tension or nervous depression to an empty abstraction. Haven't people learned yet that the time of superficial intellectual games is over, that agony is infinitely more important

than syllogism, that a cry of despair is more revealing than the most subtle thought, and that tears always have deeper roots than smiles?[144]

We find here accentuated, the importance of being in touch with one's bodily energies and emotional experiences as a way to gain access to the more authentic dimensions of experience. This orientation locates Cioran's thought within a tradition of thinkers who emphasize the importance of non-rational forces at the basis of things – a tradition that extends through the German romanticism of the late eighteenth and early nineteenth century, through the works of Nietzsche, Henri Bergson, and the surrealists. In various ways, each of these theorists or cultural movements emphasizes, as does Cioran, feelings and instinctual energies over intellect and reflection.

Cioran's theorizing nonetheless precipitates some paradox. He repeatedly acknowledges that life is meaningless, and yet he maintains that one should experience one's deepest subjectivity in order to grasp what is true. This truth is not the recognition that life is meaningless; it is the truth associated with a rich spiritual life and with life's abundant inner glow:

> Those who write under the spell of inspiration, for whom thought is an expression of their organic nervous disposition, do not concern themselves with unity and systems. Such concerns, contradictions, and facile paradoxes indicate an impoverished and insipid personal life. Only great and dangerous contradictions betoken a rich spiritual life because only they constitute a mode of realization for life's abundant inner flow. People who know only a few spiritual states and never live on the edge do not have contradictions, because their limited resources cannot form oppositions. But how can those who violently experience hatred, despair, chaos, nothingness, or love, who burn with each passion and gradually die with each and in each, those who can only breathe on heights, who are always alone, especially when they are with others – how can they grow in linear fashion and crystallize into a system? All that is form, system, category, frame, or plan tends to make things absolute and springs from a lack of inner energy, from a sterile spiritual life. Life's great tensions verge on chaos and the madness of exaltation. Rich spiritual life must know chaos and the effervescent paroxysm of illness, because in them inspiration appears to be essential for creation and contradictions become expressions of high inner temperatures. Nobody who does not love chaos is a creator, and whoever is contemptuous of illness must not speak of the spirit. There is value only in that which bursts forth from inspiration, which springs up from the irrational depths of our being, from the secret center of our subjectivity.[145]

In Cioran, we encounter a markedly polarized consciousness that alternates in perspective between an extreme objective and an extreme subjective standpoint. Sometimes he stands outside of himself imaginatively, impersonally, and detatchedly, observing his activities from a long and very cool distance away in time or space. From this standpoint, he contemplates his personal meaninglessness in view of his being not more than a speck of dust in the wider scheme of things. And sometimes, in sharp contrast, Cioran becomes absorbed in his individual subjectivity, experiencing his personal agony, chaos, strong organic energies, violent emotions, and the irrational depths of his being.

From the latter standpoint, Cioran speaks of the value of having a rich spiritual life, of experiencing ecstasy, and experiencing how the (Bergsonian) flow of subjective life is absolute.[146] And, as he states above, if subjective life is absolute, then it is a source of value. More specifically, Cioran identifies the experience of suffering as an expression of what is absolute within subjective life:

> Is there an objective criterion for evaluating suffering? Who can say with precision that my neighbor suffers more than I do or that Jesus suffered more than all of us? There is no objective standard because suffering cannot be measured according to the external stimulation or local irritation of the organism, but only as it is felt and reflected in consciousness. Alas, from this point of view, any hierarchy is out of the question. Each person remains with his own suffering, which he believes absolute and unlimited. How much would we diminish our own personal suffering if we were to compare it to all the world's sufferings until now, to the most horrifying agonies and the most complicated tortures, the most cruel deaths and the most painful betrayals, all the lepers, all those burned alive or starved to death? ... Each subjective existence is absolute to itself. For this reason each man lives as if he were the center of the universe or the center of history. Then how could his suffering fail to be absolute? I cannot understand another's suffering in order to diminish my own. Comparisons in such cases are irrelevant, because suffering is an interior state, in which nothing external can help.[147]

Here, Cioran is reluctant to draw comparisons between his own suffering and the suffering of others, and this contrasts revealingly to the perspective he assumes when he takes a more objective or distanced standpoint upon himself. In this more objective mode, Cioran counts himself as only one among a few billion people, and as being virtually insignificant. When contemplating his experience of suffering, though, he refuses to measure his individual sufferings, even against the combined sufferings of humanity, and he does not conclude that his own suffering is a trivial matter. Rather, he maintains the opposite, stating that each subjective existence is absolute to itself and that with regard to the quality of anyone's individual suffering, comparisons are irrelevant.

Cioran explicitly recognizes this perspectival duality and tension within himself and within others, and he reflects upon his experience of suffering in the larger scheme of things:

> Although I feel that my tragedy is the greatest in history – greater than the fall of empires – I am nevertheless aware of my total insignificance. *I am absolutely persuaded that I am nothing in this universe; yet I feel that mine is the only real existence.* If I had to choose between the world and me, I would reject the world, its lights and laws, unafraid to glide alone in absolute nothingness.[148] Although life for me is torture, I cannot renounce it, because I do not believe in the absolute values in whose name I would sacrifice myself. If I were to be totally sincere, I would say that I do not know why I live and why I do not stop living. The answer probably lies in the irrational character of life which remains itself without reason.[149]

From the objective standpoint wherein one regards oneself from afar, experience loses its meaning;[150] from the subjective standpoint, wherein one identifies strongly with one's living presence, experience gains infinite meaning. Cioran acknowledges that both perspectives exist side-by-side within each person, and he observes that this co-presence of conflicting perspectives adds another dimension to the absurdity and incomprehensibility of human existence, for as the two perspectives work against each other, a person is led to experience himself or herself as a fundamentally divided and contradictory being. In Hegelian terms, one could refer to Cioran's position as that of the 'unhappy' or religious consciousness who is torn inwardly between identifying with a small, perishable, and trivial physical form, and identifying with a consciousness that can experience such ecstatic states of awareness that can be described as 'absolute' or as 'divine.'

In contrast to the respective ways in which Sartre and Camus understand the nature of life's absurdity, Cioran's thought locates absurdity within the very nature of human consciousness. For Sartre, absurdity resides in a material world (in the 'in itself') that resists all efforts to comprehend it fully. For Camus, absurdity resides in the conflict between a person's desires and a world that frustrates those desires. For Cioran, the absurdity of human existence does not issue mainly from the objective standpoint; it issues from the more penetrating fact that humans harbor both the objective and the subjective standpoints within themselves, and feel themselves to be contradictory beings to the extent that these two standpoints are experienced as being irreconcilable. The absurdity of human existence resides in how one realizes that, in a physical sense, one is only a miniscule and mechanical part of the material universe, while feeling at the same time, from the standpoint of one's living consciousness, that one is located at the conscious center of existence.

The value of sickness: Cioran, Nietzsche, and Buddhism

We have noted how Cioran and Nietzsche differ with respect to their evaluations of the value of life, and can see how Cioran is more akin to the more life-disconfirming Arthur Schopenhauer than to the life-confirming Nietzsche in this regard. So it is surprising to hear the American intellectual, Susan Sontag, claim that Nietzsche had already expressed Cioran's position, and that for the most part, Cioran is not an original thinker.[151] Although we clearly owe a debt to Sontag for having brought Cioran's work to wider English-speaking notice during the 1960s, it is important to reconsider her assessment. To appreciate Cioran's immediate differences from Nietzsche, we can briefly contrast his views with Nietzsche's concerning the value of sickness.

Nietzsche famously equated sickness with weakness and degeneration, and he accordingly developed a philosophy that highlighted maximal health. Such was the inspiration for his maximalized figure of the *Übermensch*, or Superhuman, who, like a mighty ocean that absorbs a muddy stream without becoming unclean itself, has the power to absorb and transcend any psychological difficulty, any poisonous and potentially debilitating force, to 'make good' from it and to come out stronger and more healthy as a result. In short, Nietzsche's philosophy is therapeutically aimed to combat various kinds of sickness, either physical, psychological, or social. In themselves, Nietzsche found minimal value in conditions of sickness and weakness.

Cioran takes an opposing stance on the matter, for he notes that when we are very ill and come close to experiencing death, we can also come closer to seeing the truth of our existential situation. When close to death, for example, we are in a position to experience the falling away of many previous illusions, to see how what seemed to be permanent is in fact transient, and to realize how our previous day-to-day feeling that we were going to live into the future for an indefinite period, was a false expectation. When one is near death, one can also come to believe that the ever-present moment is the only moment one has. In his doctrine of Eternal Recurrence, Nietzsche also expresses the importance of living in the moment, believing also that a Superhuman type would take death-defying risks and live dangerously. But he does not positively centralize the experience of sickness in this theorizing, insofar as he does not regard the very condition of being sick as one wherein an authentic awareness of human being can be experienced. Consider in contrast the following, non-Nietzschean excerpts where Cioran speaks of the positive value of sickness:

> Only sickness gives birth to serious and deep feelings. Whatever is not born out of sickness has only an aesthetic value. To be ill means to live, willingly or not, on the heights of despair. But such heights presuppose deep chasms, fearful precipices – to live on the heights means to live near the abyss. One must fall in order to reach the heights.[152]

> If illnesses have a philosophical mission in the world, then it can only be to prove how illusory is the feeling of life's eternity and how fragile its illusion of finality. In illness, death is always already in life. Genuine ailment links us to metaphysical realities which the healthy, average man cannot understand. Young people talk of death as external to life. But when an illness hits them with full power, all the illusions and seductions of youth disappear.[153]

Unlike Nietzsche, Cioran believes that conditions of excessive health perpetuate the illusion that death is far away. So whereas one can characterize Nietzsche as a philosopher of health and Eternal Recurrence, one can equally describe Cioran as a philosopher of sickness, decay, and death, and as someone who reaches a level of enlightenment about the human condition as a consequence of his continual contemplation of death. In this regard, Cioran is more Buddhistic than he is Nietzschean, although all three thinkers were struck by the transitoriness of existence and grounded much of their respective thought upon this apprehension.

Cioran's view also contrasts with Buddhistic outlooks, however, for neither is he convinced that we can secure any permanent peace of mind amidst the world's suffering, nor does he believe that this is desirable. For Cioran, there is no genuine salvation, either in this world or in another world. Some of this attitude can be traced to Cioran's own feelings of being continually out of place, forever looking for something else and forever trying to be someone else:

> In continual rebellion against my ancestry, I have spent my whole life wanting to be something else: Spanish, Russian, cannibal – anything, except what I was. It is an aberration to want to be different from what you are, to espouse in theory any and every other condition, except your own.[154]

> All my life, I have lived with the feeling that I have been kept from my true place. If the expression 'metaphysical exile' had no meaning, my existence alone would afford it one.[155]

In Buddhistic terms, Cioran can be described as a thinker who believed that, during life, there is no escape or redemption from the ever-turning wheel of life – the cycle of suffering that is based upon desire, upon the self-reinforcing cycle of violence and retribution, upon ignorance of the fact that all things are transitory and perishable, and upon the failure to appreciate that clinging to perishable things is a futile enterprise. Cioran recognizes the perishability of all things, and yet he cannot find any contentment, if only because his consciousness is permeated with dissatisfaction.

One can account for Cioran's dissatisfaction in reference to his personal feelings of homelessness and exile cited above, but one can also note that the feeling of harboring within oneself the contradiction of being both dust and divine, of being both objectively insignificant, and subjectively absolute, generates a perpetually uneasy and oscillating state of mind. We have seen how Sartre's theory of consciousness leads to a comparably unhappy conclusion. For Sartre, human consciousness is a kind of existence that projects beyond itself, is never coincident with itself, and is therefore essentially frustrated in its attempts to find itself. Cioran's own understanding of consciousness – one where human consciousness is constituted by opposing subjective and objective perspectives – resonates well with Sartre's account, for it has the same frustrating implications. In both, the subjective and objective perspectives cannot coincide, which yields an absurdity and impossibility for achieving peace of mind. Which is to say that for Sartre and for Cioran, a Buddhistic and Schopenhauerian tranquillity is out of the question, and human beings are condemned to be eternal wanderers who are lost in a futile search for themselves.

The place of Emil Cioran in twentieth-century French thought

Cioran develops absurdist themes from Sartre and Camus to a greater extreme, and he agrees with Sartre's existentialist view that our presence in the world is an incomprehensible, meaningless, and contingent matter, and that human existence is fundamentally unsatisfactory. Cioran also intensifies the Sartrean theme that 'hell is other people' by rendering it into a virtue: he asserts that 'we are here to make each other wretched, and that to rebel against this state of affairs is to undermine the very foundations of communal life.'[156] And in sympathy with Camus, Cioran philosophizes frequently from the standpoint of considering the world from afar, from the position where the entirety of human existence is reduced to an infinitesimal moment in endless time.

In a number of ways, though, Cioran is more intensely nihilistic and hopeless than either Sartre or Camus, since as modes of existential relief, Sartre offers us the godlike awareness of our unbounded freedom and Albert Camus, almost like a samurai warrior, offers us the glory of fighting a heroic, albeit losing, battle against time and death. Cioran recognizes states of intense ecstasy, but these are always short-lived, and are counterbalanced by each of us being nonetheless only one person amidst several billion. Cioran is also less moralistic than either of the other two, and he says straightforwardly that if he followed his natural inclination, he 'should blow up the world.'[157] Cioran also does not refrain from referring to himself as someone who is torn between violence and disillusionment, and who seems to himself to be 'a terrorist who, going out in the street to perpetuate some outrage, stops on the way to consult Ecclesiastes or Epictetus.'[158] In offensive and outrageous attitude, he compares with how Nietzsche was during his own time, for Cioran intends to please no one.

Moreover, there are stylistic differences between Sartre, Camus, and Cioran, for the latter employs an abundance of religious imagery and phraseology to express his strong nihilistic tendencies. Cioran, in the spirit of Schopenhauer, who was yet another Unhappy Consciousness, is an atheist who nonetheless refers to the Upanishads, the Bhagavad-Gita, Buddhism, Christian mysticism, Hasidism, the Kabbala, the Zohar, the Talmud, and the Bible, along with a series of contemporary writers. He embodies a religious sentiment that survives his nihilism, and he continues to search for meaning, while being almost completely convinced that the search is hopeless.

Once again, we can appreciate this dual sentiment by recalling Cioran's polarized characterization of human consciousness cited above: '*I am absolutely persuaded that I am nothing in this universe; yet I feel that mine is the only real existence.*' The bulk of Cioran's remarks are expressed from the standpoint that when measured in physical terms, he is virtually nothing, even though there is a residual undercurrent of religiosity and mysticism that appears in many of the writers he chooses to contemplate. Which is to say that according to Cioran's view, as long as one is alive, there remains this mystery of how such a tiny speck of dust – the conscious and reflective human being – has the capacity to reflect within itself the infinite universe, as it gazes upon the stars and surveys the expanse of time. This fact alone offers an ineradicable glimmer of hope against the nihilism that tends to predominate within Cioran's reflections.

We can thus approach Cioran as someone who appreciated the human existential condition, and who was captivated by the nihilistic side of human awareness. We can also regard him as a kind of 'existential mystic' in less frequent moments – someone more in league with the angst-ridden Kierkegaard, than with either the Nietzsche of joyful wisdom or the compassionate Buddha – who introduced into twentieth-century French thought, a more intense appreciation of the Bergsonian flow of time through one's consciousness. He stands in the tradition of thinkers who focus upon the phenomenology of time-consciousness, as he elevated his experience of the present moment into a kind of religious ecstatic agony, reminiscent of the experiences of St. Theresa of Avila (1515–82) – one of the two women with whom Cioran felt the greatest spiritual kinship.[159]

Selected works of E. M. Cioran

1934 (age 23): *Pe culmile disperării* [*On the Heights of Despair*]
1937 (age 26): *Lacrimişi Sfinţi* [*Tears and Saints*]
1949 (age 38): *Précis de décomposition* [*A Short History of Decay*]
1956 (age 45): *La tentation d'exister* [*The Temptation to Exist*]
1960 (age 49): *Histoire et utopie* [*History and Utopia*]
1971 (age 60): *Ecartèlement* [*Drawn and Quartered*]
1973 (age 62): *De l'inconvénient d'être né* [*The Trouble With Being Born*]
1986 (age 75): *Exercices d'admiracion/aveux et anathémes* [*Anathemas and Admirations*]

6

Pierre Teilhard de Chardin, Priest and Paleontologist (1881–1955)

Life and works

Pierre Teilhard de Chardin was born on May 1, 1881 in central France, into a family rooted in the French aristocracy.[160] He was the fourth of eleven children, and his mother was a descendent of the philosopher Voltaire (1694–1778).[161] Teilhard had a pleasant life at home when he was young, and he grew to be especially impressed with the extinct volcanoes that were located in the part of France where he was raised. These geological formations inspired him to reflect seriously about the earth's age, and this helped stimulate his later interest in palaeontology. As an adult, Teilhard subsequently devoted a good portion of his life to the study of the earliest human beings.

At the age of eleven, Teilhard entered a Jesuit school, and at the age of nineteen, he entered the Jesuit order as a novice in training for the priesthood. This training lasted fourteen years, from 1899 (age nineteen) to 1914 (age thirty-three). Thereafter, he was called immediately to serve in the First World War as stretcher bearer – an activity for which he received numerous decorations for bravery. After serving as a stretcher-bearer on the front lines from 1914–17, Teilhard took his solemn vows in 1918 (age thirty-seven). The details of his Jesuit training are as follows:[162]

1. novice (two years), leading to the taking of simple vows;
2. humane studies or juniorate (two years);
3. scholastic philosophy and science (three years);
4. teaching, in Egypt, 1905–08 (two to three years);
5. theology studies, preparatory to ordination (three years);
6. tertian, culminating in the taking of solemn vows (one year).

As a stretcher bearer during the First World War, Teilhard witnessed some of the most intense and saddening forms of human suffering, and he risked his life often for the sake of others. Two of his brothers were killed during the war, and being amidst this kind of suffering had a profound effect upon Teilhard's thought, for his view became realistic while yet remaining optimistic. He retained his faith in God, as he tried to understand how God could allow the sufferings and tragedies that humans are often fatefully led to endure.

After the First World War, Teilhard visited China for the first time (1923), traveling through Egypt, Sri Lanka, Sumatra, and Hong Kong. Throughout the rest of his life he returned periodically to China (sometimes remaining there for years at a time) conducting his researches into geology and palaeontology. His work in China brought him significant professional recognition as a palaeontologist, in which capacity he published over 150 scientific articles.[163] Teilhard also wrote significantly on philosophical and religious subjects, but most of these writings were censored by the Jesuit authorities (his main religious and philosophical works were published only after his death in 1955).[164] Teilhard's daily life was that of a scientist out in the field, and it was for him a time of study and inquiry which he conceived of as an investigation into the way God created human beings through the process of evolution.

There are alternative ways to focus upon Teilhard's thought: as he was as a palaeontologist and evolutionary theorist; as he was as a model for the religious life; as he was as a representative of the Jesuit religious lifestyle in particular; as he was as a human being in general, who comes to psychological grips with the evil in the world. Since the problem of evil is a serious question for anyone who considers the reasons for believing in the existence of an all-good, all-powerful, and all-knowing God (whether or not one ultimately believes in the existence of such a God), it is worthwhile to consider how Teilhard's thought addresses the problem of evil. This consideration will highlight his position as a priest and religious thinker, and also as a philosopher and human being in general. To do this, I will first outline his perspective on the world with respect to human evolution and God. Teilhard writes primarily as a theologian who also accepts the scientific evidence of evolution. Our philosophically oriented question will be whether he is able to render plausibly compatible, the concept of evolution and the concept of an omnibenevolent, omniscient, and omnipotent deity.

Teilhard and evolutionary theory

Like Henri Bergson, who also had a great respect for evolutionary theory, Teilhard accepts that human beings have evolved from other preexisting forms of life, and that our ancestors were ape-like beings which did not have highly developed capacities for personal reflection or reasoning. Teilhard does not accept the literally worded biblical account that God created humans and the rest of the animal kingdom within the span of a week. He understands living things as having evolved from inorganic matter, and understands the various complicated modes of inorganic matter as having developed from more basic forms of energy. Within Teilhard's writings, there is no extensive account of these basic forms of energy, and he speaks generally of the basis of all things as 'energy' in general. Presumably, he would accept whatever the prevailing scientific account of fundamental particles, etc., happened to be at the time, and would interpret this as our best knowledge to date, of what God had created.

In reference to the fundamental principles that appear to be governing the universe, Teilhard offers some speculations based on his synoptic observations. He notes that within the global process that ranges from raw matter to more and more complex forms of life, there is a gradual increase in complexity with time. This increase in complexity is coordinated with a corresponding increase in the unity of those things' diverse parts. Later, as the evolution of life emerges and continues, he observes an increase in both the complexity and the unity of the structures:

> First the molecules of carbon compounds with their thousands of atoms symmetrically grouped; next the cell which, at the very smallest, contains thousands of molecules linked in a complicated system; then the metazoa in which the cell is no more than an almost infinitesimal element; and later the manifold attempts made by the metazoa to enter into symbiosis and raise themselves to a higher biological condition.[165]

Teilhard also observes that the evolutionary process involves emergent properties – properties which, although they are grounded upon preexisting structures, come into existence with new qualities of their own. A typical example would be the emergent chemical properties of salt (sodium chloride), which differ from the properties of either sodium or chlorine taken in isolation. Teilhard describes the idea of emergent properties in the following:

> [M]odern thought is at last getting acclimatised once more to the idea of the creative value of synthesis in the evolutionary sense. It is beginning to see that there is definitely *more* in the molecule than in that atom, *more* in the cell than in the molecule, *more* in society than in

the individual, and *more* in mathematical construction than in calculations and theorems. We are now inclined to admit that at each further degree of combination *something* which is irreducible to isolated elements *emerges* in a new order.[166]

With the emergence of human beings onto the world scene, Teilhard also observes that 'interiorization', or the emergence of self-conscious awareness, is a further dimension along which evolution appears to be directed. He refers to this as an intensification of the 'within', as opposed to the 'without' of things, maintaining that the entire universe, and each of its parts, has an inner aspect.[167] In conjunction with this, he adopts the traditional opinion that this inner aspect only becomes explicit and self-conscious to itself within human beings. Teilhard makes the former point in the following:

It is impossible to deny that, deep within ourselves, an 'interior' appears at the heart of things, as it were seen through a rent. This is enough to ensure that, in one degree or another, this 'interior' should obtrude itself as existing everywhere in nature from all time. Since the stuff of the universe has an inner aspect at one point of itself, there is necessarily a *double aspect to its structure*, that is to say in every region of space and time – in the same way, for instance, as it is granular: *coextensive with their Without, there is a Within to things.*[168]

The emergence of self-conscious reflection in the human being is of profound significance for Teilhard, for he links this emergence with the meaning of the evolutionary process in general. For him, the evolutionary process has been progressing toward the human being for the express purpose of becoming self-aware. He speaks of 'evolution' as if it were a being of its own, with intentions and goals that transcend the existence of any particular human individual:

The consciousness of each of us is evolution looking at itself and reflecting.[169]

We are not only concerned with thought as participating in evolution as an anomaly or as an epiphenomenon; but evolution as so reducible to and identifiable with a progress towards thought that the movement of our souls expresses and measures the very stages of progress of evolution itself. Man discovers that *he is nothing else than evolution become conscious of itself* ...[170]

By interpreting the emergence of human self-consciousness (and with it, the emergence of thought in general) as indicative of evolution's overall path, Teilhard postulates the development of another kind of organism – an organism constituted by human thought itself – which will develop according to the evolutionary principles of increasing complexity and unity. This, he claims, is what we witness in the development of culture. Teilhard refers to this new layer of life – which he conceives of as a sphere of thought that covers the earth with increasing intensity – as the 'noosphere.'[171]

> And now, as a germination of planetary dimensions, comes the thinking layer [noosphere] which to its full extent develops and inter-twines its fibres, not to confuse and neutralise them but to reinforce them in the living unity of a single tissue.
>
> Really I can see no coherent, and therefore scientific, way of grouping this immense succession of facts but as a gigantic psychobio-logical operation, a sort of *mega-synthesis*, the 'super-arrangement' to which all the thinking elements of the earth find themselves today indi-vidually and collectively subject.[172]

Given his evolutionary principles of increasing complexity, increasing unity and increasing interiorization, we can anticipate how Teilhard imagines the future of evolutionary development. This development will occur within the global sphere of thought and culture, and it will lead to a worldwide inte-gration wherein people will operate together for the sake of the society as a whole, just as the cells and organs of the body operate for the sake of the entire body. He describes this phenomenon of humanity as follows:

> In spite of its organic links, whose existence has everywhere become apparent to us, the biosphere has so far been no more than a network of divergent lines, free at their extremities. By effect of reflection and the recoils it involves, the loose ends have been tied up, and the noosphere [i.e., the sphere of thought on earth] tends to constitute a single closed system in which each element sees, feels, desires and suffers for itself the same things as all the others at the same time.
>
> We are faced with a harmonised collectivity of consciousnesses equiv-alent to a sort of super-consciousness. The idea is that of the earth not only becoming enclosed in a single thinking envelope so as to form, func-tionally, no more than a single vast grain of thought on the sidereal scale, the plurality of individual reflections grouping themselves together and reinforcing one another in the act of a single unanimous reflection.
>
> This is the general form in which, by analogy and in symmetry with the past, we are led scientifically to envisage the future of mankind, without whom no terrestrial issue is open to the terrestrial demands of our action.[173]

With this, Teilhard coordinates the theory of evolution with key Christian themes. If we interpret the perfectly organized society as a 'heaven on earth,' then evolutionary tendencies coincide with a common religious image of human destiny. In connection with this, Teilhard introduces one of the central Christian virtues – love – as the means by which the purposes of evolution are achieved. Teilhard recognizes love as the main force of unification and reconciliation between people, and hence, as a principle of unity within the noosphere:[174]

> Love alone is capable of uniting living things in such a way as to complete and fulfil them, for it alone takes them and joins them by what is deepest in themselves. This is a fact of daily experience. At what moment do lovers come into the most complete possession of themselves if not when they say they are lost in each other? In truth, does not love every instant achieve all around us, in the couple or the team, the magic feat, the feat reputed to be contradictory, of 'personalising' by totalising? And if that is what it can achieve daily on a small scale, why should it not repeat this one day on worldwide dimensions?[175]

According to this vision, evolution is divinely directing itself towards a fully harmonized unity-amidst-diversity within the sphere of thought, and the emotional and not-purely-rational experience of love is the means by which evolution is working its way toward this complete unity. To act lovingly is to act in accord with the greater forces of evolution. It is also to act in accord with forces that transcend finite human nature, and it is to act in accord with the ultimate goal of humanity as this goal stands, according to Teilhard, as the very goal of evolution. This gives love a positive and universal significance. Teilhard thereby introduces the virtue of love into his overall account of human beings as having emerged through evolutionary processes.

Teilhard refers to the goal of the evolutionary process as 'Omega' (which is the last letter of the Greek alphabet) in an attempt to conceive of the terminal point of evolution in close relationship to the traditional conception of God as an infinite, self-conscious being. Specifically, he defines an overlap and infusion between the consciousness that is God, and the totally unified consciousness of the perfect human society, speculating that the communal consciousness characteristic of the perfect human society could transcend time and space (which would bring it closer to God, as traditionally conceived). The following is one of Teilhard's descriptions of the Omega point, which refers to the human consciousness as a perfectly integrated social consciousness that has reached a point of self-realization and awareness:[176]

> Now when sufficient elements have sufficiently agglomerated, this essentially convergent movement will attain such intensity and such quality that mankind, *taken as a whole*, will be obliged – as happened to the individual forces of instinct – to reflect upon itself at a single point;[177]

that is to say, in this case, to abandon its organo-planetary foothold so as to pivot itself on the transcendent centre of its increasing concentration. This will be the end and the fulfilment of the spirit of the earth.

The end [goal] of the world: the wholesale internal introversion upon itself of the noosphere, which has simultaneously reached the uppermost limit of complexity and its centrality.[178]

In a majestic glorification of humanity, Teilhard adds that the world-consciousness is not merely the fulfillment of the human being; it is the fulfillment of life and of existence in general. Conceiving of the human being as an ultimate expression of cosmic evolutionary forces and as the crown of creation, he infers that the fulfillment of the human being coincides with the meaning of the universe as well.

Man is not the centre of the universe as once we thought in our simplicity, but something much more wonderful – the arrow pointing the way to the final unification of the world in terms of life. Man alone constitutes the last-born, the freshest, the most complicated, the most subtle of all the successive layers of life.

This is nothing else than the fundamental vision and I shall leave it at that.[179]

In light of Teilhard's magnificent vision of the cosmos, we can consider what sort of response he gives to the problem of evil. If God is the creator of the universe and is the creator of the laws of nature along with the processes of evolution, then how are these propositions compatible with a conception of God as an all-good, all-powerful, and all-knowing being? An abundance of suffering accompanies evolutionary processes, so the problem of evil immediately presents itself. To understand Teilhard's view within the overall problem of evil, let us first consider the traditional formulation of the problem, along with some of the traditional answers. This will locate Teilhard's answer to the problem of evil among an array of frequently encountered responses.

The problem of evil

As classically formulated, the problem of evil is expressed as an argument that challenges the belief in an infinitely good, knowing, and powerful God. For if God is all-good, all-knowing, and all-powerful, then God would want to abolish evil, God would know how to abolish evil, and God would have the power to abolish evil. But evil exists. This generates the temptation to conclude that God must be either not all-good, or not all-knowing, or not all-powerful.

Which is to say that if evil exists, it is difficult to understand how the traditionally defined infinite God could also exist. The problem of evil thus presents the challenge reasonably to explain how evil can coexist with an infinitely good, knowing, and powerful God. With respect to the intellectual style of Teilhard's view, we can formulate the situation as follows: if God created evolutionary processes that involve tremendous suffering, then God is either not all-good, or not all-knowing, or not all-powerful, since suffering is evil.

Given this formulation, it will not suffice to offer one of the standard answers to the problem of evil, namely, that human beings are responsible. Humans are responsible for much evil in the world, but the free choices of human beings that cause so much suffering are mostly independent of the suffering caused by the 'dog-eat-dog' evolutionary processes, since much of this suffering occurred long before humans appeared on the world-scene. To resolve the problem of evil, one needs to explain primarily the presence of natural evil (e.g., tornadoes, earthquakes, disease, violence within the animal kingdom), rather than the moral evil that results from people's misuse of their free will.

In terms of Teilhard's view, neither will it help to resolve the problem of evil by denying the presence of evil, stating that evil is an illusion. For if evil is an illusion, one would need to explain why God created such a painful illusion, which returns us to the original problem.[180] Also, this way of accounting for evil is inconsistent with the realistic world-outlook expressed in the Bible, in both the Hebrew scriptures and the New Testament. The sufferings described in the Bible (e.g., of people in slavery and in poverty; of individuals who are put to death; of animals that are sacrificed) are assumed to be real. So if one intends to resolve the problem of evil within the Judeo-Christian outlook to which Teilhard subscribed, it will not help to maintain that evil is an illusion.

Sometimes it is suggested that if there were no evil at all, then concepts of goodness, courage, fortitude, virtue, generosity, and kindness would have no meaning, since the world would then be perfect. Since these concepts are central to our consciousness of morality, and to our understanding of God, evil must exist. This may help explain why some evil is necessary, but it does not explain why the amount of evil that exists is necessary. Nor does it explain the presence of any natural evil that existed prior to human existence.

Teilhard's response to the problem of evil implicitly embodies the philosophical position that evil is compatible with God's existence only if evil makes the world a better place than it otherwise would have been, or prevents it from being a worse place. Evil is conceived of as either necessary to create a future good or necessary to prevent an even greater evil. For instance, young children receive momentarily painful vaccination injections to prevent greater sufferings from disease in the future. Or some young children receive momentary painful injections (e.g., to alleviate a chemical deficiency or imbalance) in order to allow for the realization of their natural potentials. Such is the type of rationale that explains the need for some evil, and which aims to justify the amount of evil that exists.

If God created the evolutionary process, then this process must have a divine end. Teilhard conceives of this end as the formation of a global consciousness where love permeates throughout. Evil is justified because the value of the final condition ('heaven on earth') is believed to outweigh the pains taken to achieve this goal. In reaction to this position, one can ask the difficult question of why God created an evolutionary process that involves so much violence and suffering.

Ultimately, Teilhard offers a theological and faith-grounded, rather than philosophical, resolution to the problem of evil: if one assumes that God exists, then the world is in fact the world God chose to make, so for some reason or other, God chose not to make, or could not make, a better world. On the face of things, the very assumption of God's existence generates a justification for the world's evil.

The natural response to this theological position is to reassert that the violence inherent in evolution is too extreme, that God's reasons for allowing it are inscrutable, and that the very extremity of the violence is evidence that it could not have had a divine source. And one can reply to this objection by saying that a more accurate understanding of the overall human situation would arise if the universe could be understood more comprehensively, in a manner that more closely approaches the way God understands things. This brings us to an intellectual stalemate between those who maintain the faith that evolution is God's way of creating a totally positive world, and those who believe that evolution is evidence that God is either not all-good, all-powerful, or all-knowing.

A defender of the latter view can argue further that it is difficult to imagine why God could not have shortened the length or intensity of suffering for any of the earthquake victims in human history, or for some animal victim in the rain forest or desert, for at least a few seconds. In every one of these cases, Teilhard is required to maintain that God has some moral justification for having allowed the existence of every moment of human and animal suffering, even to the microsecond. Moreover, Teilhard's view entails that easily imagined worlds that are less pain-filled than the one within which we in fact exist are impossible and contradictory worlds. Which is to say that in agreement with the philosopher Gottfried Wilhelm Leibniz (1646–1716), Teilhard must claim that our world is the best of all possible worlds. It is a position that remains open to the question of how any future condition – whether it be a heaven on earth, or some cosmic consciousness, or any perfect condition one might imagine – can justify the suffering of innocent beings. The greater the magnitude of the suffering one recognizes in the world, the greater the difficulty in imagining the future conditions that could count as a redeeming compensation.[181]

Teilhard remains an optimist nonetheless, and he offers an argument against those who suggest that life if meaningless:

> All pessimistic representations of the earth's last days – whether in terms of cosmic catastrophe, biological disruptions or simply arrested growth or senility – have this in common: that they take the characteristics and conditions of our individual and elemental ends and extend them *without correction* to life as a whole. Accident, disease and decrepitude spell the death of men; and therefore the same applies to mankind.[182]

Teilhard shows effectively that some forms of pessimism rest upon the logical fallacy of composition: if every member of a set 'S' has some property 'P,' then it is fallacious to infer that the set of 'Ss' also has 'P.' For example, it does not follow that if every ingredient in a cake tastes good, then the cake as a whole must taste good; it does not follow that if every human being has a single brain and a stomach, then humanity as a whole has a single brain and stomach; it does not follow that if every item in the universe has a cause, then the universe as a whole has a cause. Similarly, it does not follow that if every individual human life is meaningless, that humanity as a whole is meaningless; it does not follow that if every human being is of a finite consciousness, then humanity as a whole (as a world spirit) must have a finite consciousness; it does not follow that if every human being must at some point die, that humanity itself must someday cease to exist (since, in principle, there might always be new people born to replace those who die).

Teilhard's reasoning against some forms of pessimism is valid, but unfortunately, one can employ the same reasoning to formulate corresponding concerns about Teilhard's own view. For example, if each human being has a conscious awareness, it does not follow that society as a whole has, or must develop, a conscious awareness.[183] One must assume this social consciousness, however, to understand Teilhard's concept of the noosphere and of the perfect society of Jesus-like people – the human beings whom he envisions as evolving naturally out of universal energies to populate the earth, and who will bring into being a more loving social situation. So just as we encounter a stalemate between those who believe, along with Teilhard, that evil and God are compatible, and those who believe the opposite, we find a comparable stalemate between those who believe that the universe has an ultimate meaning, and atheistic existentialists such as Camus, Sartre, and Cioran, who believe that the universe is ultimately meaningless.

Selected works of Pierre Teilhard de Chardin (philosophical and religious, published posthumously)

1955 *Le phénomène humain* [*The Phenomenon of Man*]
1956 *L'apparition de l'homme* [*The Appearance of Man*]
1957 *La vision du passé* [*The Vision of the Past*]
1957 *Le milieu divin* [*The Divine Milieu*]
1959 *L'avenir de l'homme* [*The Future of Man*]
1962 *L'energie humaine* [*Human Energy*]
1963 *L'activation de l'energie* [*Activation of Energy*]
1965 *La place de l'homme dans la nature* [*Man's Place in Nature*]
1965 *Science et Christ* [*Science and Christ*]
1969 *Comment je crois* [*How I Believe*]
1973 *Les directions de l'avenir* [*Toward the Future*]
1975 *Ecrits du temps de la guerre* [*Writings in Time of War*]
1976 *Le coeur de la matière* [*The Heart of the Matter*]

PART 2

STRUCTURALISM

7

Ferdinand de Saussure, Linguist (1857–1913)

Life and works

Ferdinand de Saussure was born in Geneva, Switzerland on November 26, 1857. His grandfather, Horace-Bénédict de Saussure (1740–99), was a geologist and mountaineer who was among the first groups of adventurers who climbed the highest mountain in Western Europe, Mont Blanc, in the late 1780s.[184] Saussure's father, Henri de Saussure, was a biologist. At an early age, Ferdinand developed an interest in languages, and at age eighteen, he joined the Société Linguistique de Paris. A year later, he gave an impressive lecture on Indo-European vowels which issued in his groundbreaking 1878 publication, *Mémoire sur le système primitif des voyelles dans les langues indo-européennes* (*Mémoire on the Primitive System of Vowels in the Indo-European Languages*). Saussure was soon teaching historical linguistics in Paris, and was studying Sanskrit and comparative languages. In 1889, he gave an important lecture on Lithuanian accent before the Société Linguistique de Paris, and in 1901, at age forty-three, he became professor of Indo-European Languages and Sanskrit at the University of Geneva, where he taught until the end of his life. Saussure died on February 22, 1913, at the age of fifty-five.

De Saussure's *Course in General Linguistics*

Published posthumously in 1916 as *Course in General Linguistics*, Saussure's linguistic theory – a theory in the field of descriptive linguistics expressed in lectures he gave at the University of Geneva from 1907–11 – was instrumental in inspiring French structuralist thought of the 1950s. By adopting Saussure's view on language, and operating under what became a leading structuralist assumption that all social phenomena are understandable as languages, theorists such as Claude Lévi-Strauss (in anthropology), Jacques Lacan (in psychoanalysis), and Roland Barthes (in literary theory), used 'structuralist' methods to understand human social practices and psychological conditions. They interpreted these broadly ranging phenomena as having structures comparable to languages, and they tried to discern in them elements which serve as a 'vocabulary,' and which, in turn, could be organized according to a 'syntax,' or set of definite rules. To appreciate the structuralist intellectual movement of the 1950s, we can begin by considering the general features of Saussure's linguistic theory, since it contains principles that were adopted by those who were later referred to as French structuralists.

With regard to structuralism in general, Saussure's linguistics contains a number of influential conceptual distinctions and themes, which we will consider in turn: (1) the view that the linguistic sign is constituted by two aspects, namely, the 'signifier' and the 'signified;' (2) the thought that the linguistic sign is 'arbitrary,' and its accompanying suggestions of linguistic relativism; (3) the analysis of linguistic phenomena into sets of binary relationships; (4) the almost exclusive interest in the relationships between linguistic signs, as opposed to a concern with either the internal nature of the signs themselves, or with any external objects to which they refer; (5) the emphasis upon a holistic (as opposed to an atomistic) style of inquiry, which continually keeps in mind the entire network of linguistic signs; (6) the emphasis upon 'synchronic' (happening at the same time) as opposed to 'diachronic' (happening across time) relationships; (7) the attention to language in general (*langue*) as opposed to particular acts of speaking (*parole*); and (8) the attention to more abstract and generalized, or 'deep,' structures as opposed to particular and transitory 'surface' phenomena.

The linguistic 'sign' as composed of the 'signifier' and the 'signified'

Prior to Saussure's linguistics, a prevailing view of language was that words serve primarily as labels for the things in the world. The assumption was that the daily world is divided naturally into sets of objects and properties – the earth, the sun, the moon, trees, rocks, colors, sounds, tastes, textures, animals, people, etc. – and that as these items are perceived, people use language to assign labels to them. Language is here understood to be grounded in the process of assigning labels to preexisting things and properties. Our words refer to these things and our accumulated vocabulary serves our interests in communication, as handy reminders of the 'furniture' of the world.

Saussure offers an alternative view of words, or what he calls 'linguistic signs.' Rather than understanding words as sounds or as inscriptions that immediately refer our attention to things in the daily world, he considers the nature of the signs themselves, maintaining that each linguistic sign has a dual aspect, and that this dual aspect is central to understanding the sign's meaning. The first aspect of the linguistic sign is materially based, and is a 'sound image;' the second aspect is thought-based, and is a 'concept.' Every linguistic sign is thus regarded as a sound-image fused together with a concept. Saussure refers to the sound-image as the 'signifier,' and he refers to the associated concept as the 'signified.' He famously compares the sound-image which signifies, along with the concept which is in turn signified by the sound-image, to the two sides of a piece of paper, holding that neither sound-image nor concept can exist independently from one other:

> Language [whose basis resides in the linguistic sign] can also be compared with a sheet of paper: thought is the front and the sound the back; one cannot cut the front without cutting the back at the same time; likewise in language, one can neither divide sound from thought nor thought from sound; the division could be accomplished only abstractedly, and the result would be either pure psychology or pure phonology.[185]
>
> Our definition of the linguistic sign poses an important question of terminology. I call the combination of a concept and a sound-image a *sign*, but in current usage the term generally designates only a sound-image, a word, for example (*arbor*, etc.). One tends to forget that *arbor* is called a sign only because it carries the concept 'tree,' with the result that the idea of the sensory part implies the idea of the whole.[186]

The proposition that sound-images and concepts are fundamentally inseparable (i.e., they are separable only by means of an act of imaginative abstraction, but are not separable in the actual operation of language) has a wide-ranging implication: language is necessary for any determinate thought. Each of the concepts that we think about, is given its contours and its definition only because that concept has been fused together with a particular sound-image (or inscription). According to Saussure, without language and its articulated network of various linguistic signs, we could not even conceive of a complicated world of objects. This importantly suggests that our very awareness of the world depends upon, and is structured by, the language we acquire:

> Psychologically our thought – apart from its expression in words – is only a shapeless and indistinct mass. Philosophers and linguists have always agreed in recognizing that without the help of signs we would be unable to make a clear-cut, consistent distinction between two ideas. Without language, thought is a vague, uncharted nebula. There are no preexisting ideas and nothing is distinct before the appearance of language.[187]

According to this theory, the articulation of consciousness results from a person's having incorporated an articulated language. With his claim that the linguistic sign is constituted by the fusion of a sound-image and a concept, along with his assumption that the articulation amongst our concepts is possible only by means of their connection to a network of linguistic signs, Saussure develops an interdependency between thought and language. 'Without language,' he states, 'thought is a vague, uncharted nebula.' Given this, a question arises about how we are to understand the differences in thought between people, once we recognize that there are many different languages in the world, many different ways to incorporate the same language amongst a population, and hence, many different ways of articulating a network of concepts that organize the things in our experience.

The 'sign is arbitrary'

As noted above, according to an age-old view of the relationship between language and the world, the world exists as an already-articulated entity that is independent of us, and our languages serve mainly to mirror this already-articulated world. Each word is believed to match a preexisting segment of the world as this or that segment exists in itself. A given natural order is reflected in the linguistic order, and in the ideal situation, a parallelism and structural congruency would exist between the structure of the world and the structure of the language. Aristotle, for instance, believed that the 'subject plus predicate' grammatical form of the declarative sentence mirrored the 'substance plus quality' form of things in the world.[188]

Saussure maintains that this traditional picture fails to appreciate the significantly diverse and contrasting structures of the many languages in the world. If the above picture were true, he claims, it would be easier to translate one language into another than it actually is. Rather, Saussure observes that different languages divide the world into different kinds of objects, and that there is a noticeable degree of arbitrariness in how these divisions are made.

For example (and there are many), English has a single word, 'know,' whereas French distinguishes between 'knowing people' (*connaître*) and 'knowing facts' (*savoir*). French has a single word for the verb 'to rent' (*louer*), whereas German has a word for 'to rent out to someone' (*vermieten*) and a word for 'to rent from someone' (*mieten*). Also, English refers to dark blue and light blue as two different shades of blue, whereas Russian refers to these as two different colors. In the way languages draw distinctions within the world, there is often arbitrariness and significant differences between languages. This is partly because people in different environments evaluate their surroundings differently: those who live in lush, jungle environments tend to draw subtle distinctions between shades of green; those who live in cold, snowy surroundings tend to draw subtle distinctions between shades of white, simply for survival-related purposes. So there is much variation between languages in terms of their respective vocabularies and articulations of human experience.

In reference to the relationship between sound-images and the concepts these sound-images signify, moreover, there is almost complete arbitrariness. That the English language uses the sound-image 'cup' to designate the idea of a certain kind of object from which we drink, is not necessarily related to the content of the idea, 'something from which we drink.' Any other sound would do, once we stipulate that the sound designates the idea in question. With regard to the intrinsic constitution of the sign (i.e., the aspects of sound-image and signified concept), there is no necessity that any particular sound be used to signify any particular concept. This is a conventional matter, even though there are a few onomatopoeic sound-images such as 'buzz,' 'gurgle,' 'pop,' 'meow,' and 'click' that exemplify their respective concepts to variable degrees.

Saussure's view that 'the sign is arbitrary' implies, for him, that 'the social fact alone can create a linguistic system.' This invites linguistic relativist positions which maintain that this or that society, through the language it happens to create, largely determines what counts as 'the world' (and also, by implication, what counts as 'true,' as 'right,' as 'objective,' etc.). This is a debatable view, if only because there is a strong natural tendency to believe that there is one true 'way the world is,' independently of what any society might think. It remains uncertain whether Saussure himself advocated an extreme linguistic relativism, but his theory can be developed such as to suggest that there is no single, objective way the world is. Saussure did, however, write the following:

> The arbitrary nature of the sign explains in turn why the social fact alone can create a linguistic system. The community is necessary if values [i.e., meanings] that owe their existence solely to usage and general acceptance are to be set up; by himself the individual is incapable of fixing a single value.[189]

In questions regarding who is the 'master' of the linguistic situation, the individual or society, Saussure maintains that the thoughts of individuals are fundamentally grounded upon the existing language that is spoken by those who raise the individual from birth. One is thrown into the world at birth, but more importantly, one is thrown into a specific linguistic world that expresses a specific way of organizing the world with a specific set of values. Whether anyone can completely escape the influence of the language which they initially learn, such as to see the world independently of that language, is a matter that Saussure's linguistic theory renders impossible.

Binary relationships define basic structure

Saussure develops his idea that 'the sign is arbitrary' by defining each sign in relation to other signs, and by establishing each sign's identity through its contrast with other signs. He is led to conceive of signs in this way, in part, because he does not recognize a sufficient number of sharply defined aspects of the world in reference to which signs can obtain and preserve their determinate identity. Consider words that refer to colors. To define the term 'red,' it is not sufficient to point out 'red' objects, because the limits of the concept 'red' will still remain unclear. One person, for instance, could group together only bright red objects, while another could include reddish-orange or reddish-violet objects under the concept as well. Without an implicitly defined contrast between 'red' and 'not-red,' and more determinately, a specified contrast between 'red' and 'orange,' and between 'red' and 'violet,' and between 'red' and 'green,' etc. there would be no way in which a person could come to understand the concept which the sound-image 'red' signifies in the language in question.

Since each of the above-mentioned contrasts to the sound-image 'red' is an oppositional one, Saussure holds that the basic relationships within a linguistic structure are binary. The structuralists of the 1950s, along with many poststructuralists, accept this assumption as well. If a concept has definite boundaries, then these boundaries form an opposition between the concept and what the concept is 'not.' So the establishment of a concept's definition creates an oppositional relationship between that concept and what is outside its definition.

Relationships between signs are fundamental

From the proposition that the sign is arbitrary, and the observation that we can understand the meaning of a linguistic sign only by means of contrasting that sign to a set of other signs, Saussure concludes that what is fundamentally operative in the determination of meaning is the place of the sign within a system of linguistic oppositions. As noted, the sense-quality that we might call 'redness' is not what fundamentally determines the meaning of the sign 'red,' according to Saussure. What determines the meaning is the place of the sign 'red' in the linguistic system within which it is opposed to other signs such as 'not-colored,' 'not-red,' 'orange,' 'violet,' 'green,' 'pink,' etc. The systematic network of opposing signs determines the boundaries of the concept signified, and it is this inter-systematic set of relationships that Saussure believes is what fundamentally determines a sign's precise meaning. He describes this in the following:

> Everything that has been said up to this point boils down to this: in language there are only differences. Even more important: a difference generally implies positive terms between which the difference is set up; but in language there are only differences without positive terms. Whether we take the signified or the signifier, language has neither ideas nor sounds that existed before the linguistic system, but only conceptual and phonic differences that have issued from the system.[190]

We can understand Saussure's point more clearly if we consider how different people can write the letter 't' (or any other letter) in many different ways, and yet have it still count as a 't' within their style of script. What is important in perceiving the letter as such, is not exactly how it is written, but whether, as written, it is distinguishable from the other letters within the script. Saussure states, 'the only requirement is that the sign for *t* not be confused in his script with the signs for *l*, *d*, etc.'[191] The way the letter 't' is distinguished, then, is not through any intrinsic feature of the way it is written; it is distinguished in contrast to the way other letters are written. Through this contrast to the other letters, the letter 't,' as written, obtains its identity.

Similarly, if we recall that in the Cyrillic and in the Greek script, the letter 'P' stands for the sound that in English would be symbolized by the letter 'R,' we can see how the wider context of the network of symbols is essential for understanding an inscription's meaning. For instance, if someone were to write 'P' on a blank sheet of paper, and if one did not know the language intended, one would be unable to tell from the shape of the inscription alone whether the person was beginning a word in Greek, Russian, or English, and how the word would initially sound. The background context and systematic framework are essential, for they define the contours of the foreground linguistic presentations.

A holistic and 'internalistic' perspective is necessary

As we can see, Saussure understands the meaning of linguistic signs from a consideration of the full linguistic network, whenever a question of an individual sign's meaning arises. He considers the part in relation to the whole, and he resists appealing to elements external to the linguistic system to explain the meaning of any particular sign. Saussure does not believe that the meaning of a linguistic sign is fundamentally determined by the referent of the sign, understood (typically) as some physical object(s) or property(s) in the world. This is because, as noted, he believes that one requires the background system of linguistic signs to determine what the referent of the sign happens to be.

As a result of his emphasis upon the linguistic system, Saussure focuses upon the system of signs, which he calls 'language.' More generally and influentially, he adds that a sign need not be defined in reference to a typically spoken language having letters and a script, and that the idea of a 'linguistic sign' can be understood in a generalized sense: signs can take the form of 'symbolic rites, polite formulas, military signals,' and, as later structuralists pointed out, styles of dress, cooking, and family patterning. Saussure refers generally, and with some historical impact, to a 'science of signs' that would include all of these disciplines, as the science of 'semiology.' The global idea that all kinds of social phenomena can be understood along linguistic lines, as mentioned above, is central to much of the subsequent French thought of the 1950s that later would be called 'structuralist.' Saussure defines semiology in the following excerpt:

> Language is a system of signs that express ideas, and is therefore comparable to a system of writing, the alphabet of deaf-mutes, symbolic rites, polite formulas, military signals, etc. But it is the most important of these systems.
>
> *A science that studies the life of signs within society* is conceivable; it would be a part of social psychology and consequently of general psychology; I shall call it semiology (from Greek *semeion* 'sign'). Semiology would show what constitutes signs, what laws govern them. Since the science does not yet exist, no one can say what it would be; but it has a right to existence, a place staked out in advance. Linguistics is only a part of the general science of semiology; the laws discovered by semiology will be applicable to linguistics, and the latter will circumscribe a well-defined area within the mass of anthropological facts.[192]

'Synchronic' relationships emphasized over 'diachronic' ones

Since Saussure is interested in how binary oppositions between signs determine their meaning, he attends primarily to the structure of the linguistic system in its 'cross-section,' independently of the subtle changes it may undergo through time. To understand any of the particular historical changes within a language, he believes that one must first have an idea of the overall structure of the oppositions between the terms within the linguistic system. Hence Saussure emphasizes 'synchronic' (i.e., happening at the same time) as opposed to 'diachronic' (i.e., happening across time) relationships. This colors his analyses with a more non-historical character, as remains true for those thinkers who adhere to structuralist principles in general.

The interest in revealing the more general structure of oppositions between linguistic signs leads Saussure to consider language in general, as opposed to the particular instances of speech that occur at definite moments in time. His way of distinguishing these two aspects of language – the structural versus the actually spoken aspects – is to refer to the former as 'language' (*langue*) and the latter as 'speaking' (*parole*), maintaining that language is the more fundamental object of study, as opposed to speaking:

> In setting up the science of language within the overall study of speech, I have also outlined the whole of linguistics. All other elements of speech – those that constitute speaking – freely subordinate themselves to the first science, and it is by virtue of this subordination that the parts of linguistics find their natural place.
>
> Consider, for example, the production of sounds necessary for speaking. The vocal organs are as external to language as are the electrical devices used in transmitting the Morse code to the code itself; and phonation, i.e., the execution of sound-images, in no way affects the system itself. Language is comparable to a symphony in that what the symphony actually is stands completely apart from how it is performed; the mistakes that musicians make in playing the symphony do not compromise this fact.[193]

The implication of Saussure's emphasis upon 'language' as opposed to 'speaking' is that his methodology leads him to distinguish what can be called 'deep structures' – those that persist independently of the actions of individual speakers – as opposed to 'surface phenomena.' The style of inquiry compares to what we encounter in natural science, and this affinity establishes a methodological affinity between structuralism and scientific thinking. A physicist, for example, does not investigate the mere appearance of this or that particular piece of matter, but attempts to understand the basic laws that govern matter in general (or the kind of matter in general). Physics attempts to look beneath the surface of the changes we ordinarily experience in an effort to understand the constant principles that determine the perceptual appearance. The same is true in other sciences as well. Linguistics, understood as a science, is understandable in these terms as the investigation into those constancies which underlie our modes of communication by means of (primarily) phonetic symbols.

Criticisms of Saussure's linguistic theory

Saussure maintains that the meaning of a linguistic sign (e.g., 'red') does not depend upon any intrinsic sensory quality to which the sign refers (or which causes a particular kind of sensation that supposedly gives meaning to the sign). He holds that the meaning of any linguistic sign is, at bottom, determined through its contrast to other signs within the linguistic system. The fundamental meaning of the sign 'red' is determined through its contrast to other signs, such as 'not-red,' 'non-red,' 'green,' 'orange,' 'crimson,' 'pink,' 'rose,' etc.[194]

Now although we may need a linguistic sign that contrasts with 'red' to understand its precise meaning, this does not imply that there are no clear boundaries within the world to be perceived, and that these perceivable boundaries play no significant role in giving the linguistic sign 'red' a meaning. There are many differences between languages, but there are also many similarities between languages, as there are also similarities in human experience. Translation between languages may sometimes be difficult, but it is not impossible, and this is because the various languages mark out mutually understandable territories in the world. What appears to be the case, is that some basic sets of signs in various languages are correspondingly formulated to capture some of the more obvious perceptual and natural distinctions within human experience (e.g., 'cold' vs. 'hot,' or 'pleasure' vs. 'pain,' or 'sweet' vs. 'sour,' etc.). If so, then it would be mistaken to assume that the entire meaning of a linguistic sign is constituted by the sign's oppositional situation within the linguistic field. There are also qualities of common human experience which play a role in the linguistic articulation of the world.

If the meanings of linguistic signs derive, at least in part, from independent conditions in the world outside the linguistic system, then although the sounds we use to designate particular concepts are arbitrary, the things to which the concepts themselves refer are not arbitrarily defined. The meanings of the linguistic signs are not arbitrary insofar as there are some shared and discernible distinctions within our common experience that, to a significant extent, remain 'thinkable' independently of this or that language. Children can perceive specific kinds of pleasures and pains, long before they acquire language, for example. Moreover, animals which do not have language can perceive subtle perceptual differences; otherwise they would be unable to survive. So if we recognize these perceptual distinctions as originating from actual distinctions among things and qualities in the world, we can question Saussure's claim that language is necessary for the articulation of consciousness, and can question his claim that the meaning of a word rests fundamentally in the differences between linguistic signs.

If the above is true, then the 'objects' in the world, as designated by the linguistic signs, would not be definable exclusively in terms of oppositions between linguistic signs. What counts as the 'world' would be, to a large extent, understandable as being independent of any linguistic system. This would imply that linguistic relativism – the view that people with different languages live in different experiential worlds – is not completely true, even if we assume that thought is linguistically structured to a great extent, and that linguistic systems vary.

Second, although Saussure's holistic approach is reasonable to a great extent, it remains unclear how much of the linguistic system is necessary for understanding the meaning of any particular word. It is not necessary to understand the entire dictionary to understand the meaning of this or that particular word, even though the word cannot be understood in complete isolation from the linguistic system. Since an extreme holism is not required to understand meanings, then it becomes a matter of judgment where one ought to draw the boundaries on Saussure's suggested holistic approach. But if certain lines are drawn, as they must be, then it becomes difficult to understand how binary relationships can extend throughout the linguistic system, such that they conjointly determine the meaning of a linguistic sign. We can appreciate this difficulty upon noticing that if we change the meaning of one linguistic sign, then the meanings of the rest of the signs within the system need not all change as well. Although some may change, others will remain constant, depending upon the centrality of the word's place within the linguistic system.

Third, the structuralist emphasis upon synchronic, non-historical relationships is in danger of overemphasis within Saussure's linguistic theory. According to the structuralist method of inquiry, as this can be generalized from Saussure's view, it is essential to focus mainly upon the constant and unchanging relationships that characterize a language (or any other social phenomenon). Sometimes, however, such an exclusively directed inquiry is not sufficiently informative. It is conceivable that any given synchronic description of a linguistic system would never quite conform to that system in its concrete reality, since all languages undergo change (and sometimes they change rapidly, especially in contemporary life). So it is important to remain sensitive not only to the synchronic structures, but also to the diachronic or developmental aspects of the linguistic system. In short, it is unreasonable largely to ignore historical conditions and the developmental aspects of social phenomena.

Fourth, it remains dubious that binary oppositions are the overriding relationships within social phenomena. Within a contrasting, historically based view, causal relationships also prove to be important. If there is an exclusive emphasis upon binary oppositions, this can have the effect of imposing false, distorting categories upon the world. For example, if one focuses upon the structure of the present situation as it stands today, and ignores the details of how it originated, much meaning will be lost. In the linguistic situation, Saussure argues that the etymology of a word often has little to do with its present meaning, and this is frequently true; relatively few people appreciate how the meaning of the word 'understand' is historically related to the history of the word 'substance.' But at the same time, it makes sense to say that the meaning of the present cultural situation stems not merely from present-day interrelationships, but from a long series of historical predecessors, influences, and cultural developments.

Fifth, and in a similar vein, it is questionable whether all patterns of social phenomena are 'codes' that have vocabularies and a syntax. For we can doubt whether any paradigm derived from the nature of language is sufficient to understand all aspects of social phenomena. For there is also a subjective or phenomenological quality of social or psychological experience, and a different feeling or overall atmosphere that is associated with the experience of this or that culture. This should not be overlooked. Some cultural environments are more alive, free, creative, and innovative, whereas other cultural environments are more oppressive and rooted in the past. Such lived-qualities are difficult to express by means of purely linguistic and structuralist models, despite the insights the social-phenomena-as-languages model can provide.

The place of Ferdinand de Saussure in twentieth-century French philosophy

The specific influences of Saussure upon thinkers such as Claude Lévi-Strauss, Jacques Lacan, Roland Barthes, and Jacques Derrida will be examined in the next several chapters. Saussure was influential in French thought owing to his claims that (1) linguistic formulations are extraordinarily arbitrary in their construction; (2) what appears to have a 'positive' presence, is actually the result of systematic and background considerations.

The first idea motivated later theorists to question the legitimacy of what we happen to inherit as being 'natural.' As Friedrich Nietzsche noted in the early 1870s, much of what we accept as 'true' has in fact been artificially constructed, and much of what we accept as literal, is in fact metaphorical and figurative. Saussure's linguistic theory reinforces this Nietzschean observation by locating it within a more general conception of the nature of linguistic signs. Upon accepting Saussure's linguistic theory, many of the Nietzschean observations about the largely artificial construction of our daily-experienced world follow by implication.

Second, and perhaps more influentially, Saussure's linguistic theory helped reinforce the phenomenological views of Edmund Husserl, who observed that the perceptual objects in our immediate foreground, derive their salient perceptual qualities from the nature of the perceptual background field within which they are situated. Saussure said much the same thing with regard – not to the perceptual items before us *per se* – but to the words we use. And once we acknowledge Saussure's claim that the field of perceptual experience is articulated as a direct reflection of the articulation that language lends to consciousness, then we arrive at a momentous blending and mutual overlay of the perceptual and semantic fields. The objects that we perceive become amenable to linguistic analysis thereby, for the perceptual field is transformed into a field of linguistic meaning. This amalgamation between the perceptual and linguistic-semantic fields allows one to interpret not only immediate perceptual presentations, but larger-scale social fields, within the framework of Saussurean linguistic analysis.

We can generalize this observation by saying that both Saussure and Husserl developed a methodology that urges us to consider the nature of the *background* in connection to whatever phenomena we wish to study. In the perceptual field, we would then consider what lies at the perceptual periphery; in the semantic field, we would then consider those words which are, upon reflection, oppositionally associated with the subject at hand, but which are not brought into explicit consideration; in the field of a textual interpretation, we would then consider what the author does not say, but which reveals the hidden interests that define the author's underlying agenda. In the field of psychoanalysis, we would then consider what the patient represses and will not discuss. In the field of social critique, we would then consider not the central social figures and the people in political control, but the outsiders, the oppressed, the powerless, the people who are rejected, and those who are silenced. This general style of looking towards the periphery, looking towards the background, and looking towards the underemphasized, is a deep-seated theme in twentieth-century French thought, appearing in writers from an assortment of disciplines who followed in Ferdinand de Saussure's, Edmund Husserl's, and also Jean-Paul Sartre's footsteps. As we shall see, they include figures such as Jacques Lacan, Jacques Derrida, Luce Irigaray, and Michel Foucault.

Selected works of Ferdinand de Saussure

1879 (age 22): *Mémoire sur le système primitif des voyelles dans les langues indo-européennes* [*On the primitive system of vowels in the Indo-European languages*]
1916 (posthumous) *Cours de linguistique générale* [*Course in General Linguistics*]

8

Claude Lévi-Strauss, Anthropologist (1908–)

Life and works

Claude Lévi-Strauss was born in Brussels, Belgium, on November 28, 1908 to Emma Lévy and Raymond Lévi-Strauss, an artist. When Claude Lévi-Strauss was five years old, his family moved to France, where he lived with his grandfather, who was a rabbi. In later years, Lévi-Strauss studied philosophy at the University of Paris,[195] and among his classmates were Simone de Beauvoir and Maurice Merleau-Ponty. At this time, he read works by French sociological thinkers such as Henri de Saint-Simon (1760–1825), Auguste Comte (1798–1857), Èmile Durkheim (1858–1917), and Marcel Mauss (1872–1950). When Lévi-Strauss was twenty-three he graduated in the fields of philosophy and law, and a year later he married. In his twenty-sixth year (1934), Lévi-Strauss obtained a position as professor of sociology at the University of São Paolo, Brazil, where he worked until 1937. He decided to focus upon ethnology – a branch of anthropology that considers the racial divisions of humanity, along with human origins – and was soon working with tribal groups in Brazil. These studies later resulted in one of Lévi-Strauss's most popular books, *Tristes Tropiques* (1955).

After leaving Brazil, Lévi-Strauss briefly returned to France and soon emigrated (1941) to the United States, where he remarried, and where he first worked at the New School for Social Research in New York, and then briefly at the French Embassy in Washington as a Cultural Attaché. While in New York, Lévi-Strauss met the principal founder of the Prague school of structural linguistics, Roman Jakobson (1896–1982), while the latter was working at the École Libre des Hautes Études, a school hosted by the New School. In 1947, Lévi-Strauss returned to France, received his doctorate, and soon became adjuct director of the Musée de l'Homme in Paris. In 1950, at age forty-two, Lévi-Strauss became Director of Studies (Social Anthropology Laboratory) at École Pratique des Hautes Études. Four years later (1954), he married for the third time, and in 1960, at age fifty-two, Lévi-Strauss became Chair of Social Anthropology, Collège de France, where he continued to teach and write for the next two decades, and during which time he became one of the world's most well-known anthropologists. Lévi-Strauss retired from the Collège de France in 1982, at age seventy-four.

Lévi-Strauss's structuralist methodology

Claude Lévi-Strauss is among the first theorists to apply structuralist methods within the field of anthropology. In his inquiry into the myths and kinship patterns of diverse peoples, he adopts the general structuralist position that social phenomena are structured in a manner similar to natural languages. Moreover, he is interested in discovering through anthropological research a single, linguistically structured patterning of human cultures in general – a pattern that he believes is expressive of an essential 'human nature.' It is towards the discovery of this essential, linguistically related structure that he directs his extensive anthropological studies on myth and kinship. In what follows, we shall consider Lévi-Strauss's structuralist methodology by focusing specifically upon his analysis of mythology, concluding with some criticisms of his view from both anthropological and philosophical standpoints.

One of Lévi-Strauss's central aims is to discover whether there is a common human nature that we all share as members of the same species, despite the obvious diversity of cultural differences. If there is such a human nature, then it is a constant factor in human experience, and it should be discernible in all cultures, whatever their manifest differences happen to be. In search of this human essence, Lévi-Strauss adopts a methodology that does not significantly recognize the influence of historical change. Indeed, such historical contingencies, such as the change in human culture stimulated by the development of writing (*c.* 4000–3000 B.C.E.),[196] or the change caused by the eighteenth-century industrial revolution, he regards as having had the effect of obscuring, rather than illuminating, that which contemporary peoples share with the rest of humanity. To perceive the essence of humanity more clearly, Lévi-Strauss consequently focuses his attention upon peoples who do not have a strong sense of historical change – those who have a more 'timeless' existence – and this leads him to study tribal groups whose lifestyle has not changed significantly over many centuries. In these efforts to understand human nature, he investigates what he believes to be the human mind in its more natural or 'wild' (*sauvage*) state.[197]

Rather than attend to aspects of historical change within a culture, Lévi-Strauss tries to discern the synchronic structure (i.e., the structure constituted by elements which occur simultaneously) of anthropologically prominent cultural features. Specifically, through a detailed study of these cultural phenomena, such as the specific myths of a wide number of different tribes, along with their diverse kinship patterns, he hopes to discern basic organizational concepts – usually expressed through pairs of concepts – which appear to be at the basis of all the cultural phenomena under consideration. These constitute what can be called the 'linguistic structure' of the phenomena in question, and it is a structure that Lévi-Strauss believes can be generally applied to other cultural situations as well.

The following is an elementary example that illustrates how the idea of 'structure' operates in Lévi-Strauss's methodology.[198] Consider the two colors, red and green, which in terms of color theory, are complementary or opposite colors.[199] If we introduce the natural association between 'red' and 'blood,' then 'red' easily becomes a signal for danger.[200] Correspondingly, since 'green' is the opposite of red on the color spectrum, then 'green' becomes a signal for safety (this is also in light of the association between 'green' and plants/life). If we encounter ambiguous situations that are not expressible through the use of either red or green, then an intermediary color between red and green – yellow – is used to signal a transitional state between danger and safety.

This style of thinking generates two kinds of sequence, namely, a natural sequence and a cultural sequence. In the above example, the natural sequence, 'red, yellow, green' matches the cultural sequence, 'danger, caution, safety.' Lévi-Strauss observes correspondences of this general kind in hundreds of examples within tribal cultures, some instances of which are exceedingly complex. With regard to understanding his structural anthropological method in general, we need at present only note that the natural and the cultural sequences have parallel structures.

Another example (from Lévi-Strauss himself, though simplified here) reveals a structural similarity between the way animals are often classified, and the way people are often classified:

Animal (natural) classification	People (cultural) classification
Wild Animals	Strangers
Pets	Companions
Vermin	Criminals

A further example can be taken from Lévi-Strauss's analysis of totemism. In many tribal organizations, different sub-groups within the tribe distinguish themselves according to clans, and each clan adopts a particular animal as its symbol or 'totem'. The totem animal is usually an object of religious worship as well. Some earlier theories of totemism maintained that such worship of animals is evidence of the allegedly childish way of thinking that is typical of primitive peoples; other, more sophisticated, functionalist theories of totemism, maintain that the animals chosen as totems are ones which the society needs to preserve (hence they are made sacred and are thereby religiously protected). Lévi-Strauss points out that there is more to totemism than is captured by either of these theories, and he especially denies that totemism is evidence of a childish mentality. He believes that the selection of the animals has much to do with a metaphorical connection between the animals' respective styles of behavior and the characteristic traits that distinguish the clans from one other. The following passage makes this apparent, where Lévi-Strauss describes the totem animals of the Chickasaw tribe.[201] Note the relationships between the behaviors of the totem animals and the specific behavior of the respective clan:

> The Racoon people ... live on fish and wild fruit, those of the Puma lived in the mountains ... and lived principally on game. The Wild Cat clan slept in the daytime and hunted at night ... Members of the Bird clan were up before daybreak ... the people of the Red Fox clan were professional thieves ... the Redskunk lived in dugouts underground.[202]

In the above examples, the parallel between the classification of animals in terms of their distinctive behaviors, and the classification of clans in terms of their distinctive behaviors is clear. What is important for Lévi-Strauss, is not the exact contents of each correspondence between animal and clan, but the more global idea that we can discern a structural similarity between the different kinds of classification. In the present case, as in the two examples mentioned above, the natural classifications are isomorphically transferred into the cultural realm through the employment of metaphor-based thinking. This suggests that metaphor-based thinking is a central feature of the more 'natural' or 'wild' state of the human mind.

Structuralist analysis of myth

To appreciate Lévi-Strauss's approach to myths, it is helpful to recall Sigmund Freud's method of dream interpretation. According to Freud, a dream has a manifest content and a latent content; the former is what the dream appears to mean according to its immediately presented imagery, and the latent content expresses what the dream means at more probing levels of interpretation. Freud draws this distinction between the manifest and latent dream content as a consequence of his view that dreams express wishes that, as a rule, are socially or personally unacceptable. For this reason, their true content needs to be disguised to the conscious self. One might have a wish to kill a parent, for instance, or a wish to have a sexual relationship with a close relative. Since such wishes conflict with what society says is morally appropriate, any dream which expresses these taboos will usually express them in a disguised form, so as to be less psychologically upsetting. So instead of dreaming of killing one's parent, one dreams that one causes one's mother or father to go on a very long trip – a trip that symbolizes the death of the parent.

Or, perhaps, rather than dreaming explicitly that one has a sexual relationship with a close relative, one dreams that the relative puts some food in one's mouth, or that one puts food in the relative's mouth (or, using the example below, that one lights a fire with the person, etc.). Within Freud's theory these are straightforward examples based on his understanding of typical dream symbolism, but the connections between the manifest content and the latent content of a dream can become complicated and obscured from immediate interpretive access. The core idea is that certain elements within a dream's manifest content symbolically stand for elements in the latent content. Here are some examples from Freud, taken from his *Introductory Lectures on Psychoanalysis*:

> Birth is regularly expressed in dreams through a relationship with water; one falls into the water or comes out of the water, which means: one gives birth or one is born.[203]
>
> In a dream, going away means dying. It is also customary in children's upbringing, when the child asks about the whereabouts of a dead person who he misses, to say to him that the person *has gone away on a trip.*[204]
>
> Preparing a fire, and everything connected with it, is permeated with sexual symbolism. The flame is always a male genital, and the fireplace, the hearth, a woman's womb.[205]

Lévi-Strauss interprets myths as if they are part of the collective dream of a culture, and at the most general level, as if they are part of the collective dream of humanity.[206] According to Lévi-Strauss, the general content of this collective dream expresses the wish to resolve fundamental life-and-survival-related conflicts. Sometimes these are general conflicts that every person must face; sometimes they are specific conflicts that concern the specific cultural group. Since Lévi-Strauss claims that 'the purpose of myth is to provide a logical model capable of overcoming a contradiction,'[207] we can consider an example of a myth, to illustrate how he analyzes it, and to show how the myth resolves a fundamental conflict within the culture's collective psyche.

Before considering a particular myth, it is important to describe Lévi-Strauss's structuralist method for analyzing any myth whatsoever. His method is inspired by structuralist linguistics insofar as he is most interested in the contrasts between the elements of a myth. This approach differs, for instance, from Carl Jung's characterization of myths as being constituted by a constant set of 'archetypes' (e.g., the mandala, the great mother, the trickster), all of which serve as the basic psychic themes for all cultural thought. The contrast between Lévi-Strauss and Jung is instructive, for it highlights the former's structuralist approach. Lévi-Strauss distinguishes his method from Jung's in the following excerpt:

Ancient philosophers reasoned about language the way we do about mythology. On the one hand, they did notice that in a given language certain sequences of sounds were associated with definite meanings, and they earnestly aimed at discovering a reason for the linkage between those *sounds* and that *meaning*. Their attempt, however, was thwarted from the very beginning by the fact that the same sounds were equally present in other languages although the meaning they conveyed was entirely different. The contradiction was surmounted only by the discovery that it is the combination of sounds, not the sounds themselves, which provide the significant data.

It is easy to see, moreover, that some of the more recent interpretations of mythological thought originated from the same kind of misconception under which those early linguists were laboring. Let us consider, for instance, Jung's idea that a given mythological pattern – the so-called archetype – possesses a certain meaning. This is comparable to the long-supported error that a sound may possess a certain affinity with a meaning: for instance, the 'liquid' semi-vowels with water, the open vowels with things that are big, large, loud, or heavy, etc. – a theory which still has its supporters. Whatever emendations the original formulation may now call for, everybody will agree that the Saussurean principle of the arbitrary character of linguistic signs was a prerequisite for the accession of linguistics to the scientific model.[208]

Lévi-Strauss does not, then, believe that any of the specific elements within a myth have a constant meaning from culture to culture. His alternative approach attempts to examine the elements within a myth in their association with other surrounding elements, with the aim of showing how the entire mythic-linguistic context determines the meanings within the myth as a whole. This is not to say that Lévi-Strauss denies a common essence to myths. It is only that the essence he finds within myth is structural, and is based on a kind of abstractive and literary thinking style upon which all myths are grounded.

At this juncture, the concept of 'transformation' becomes important in Lévi-Strauss's methodology. Since different cultures arise within different environments, different kinds of items will occur within the respective myths. A tribe living near the North Pole might use polar bears as characters in a myth, whereas a tribe living near the equator might use parrots. What counts at the structural level for the purposes of understanding human beings in general, however, is not the presence of either polar bears or parrots in particular, but how these animals are used to express universal oppositions which arise in every human social grouping, such as 'life vs. death,' or 'nature vs. culture.' Noting how myths from widely diverse sources often address the same fundamental issues, Lévi-Strauss shows how we can substitute one character for another within a set of individual myths, and arrive at a common structure to the style of myth in question. As an example of this kind of transformation of elements between myths, we can consider Lévi-Strauss's example of a set of terms, all of which serve as 'mediators' between opposing forces (recall the red, yellow, and green color example above), and which are structurally interchangeable in many contexts:

> Coyote (a carrion-eater) is intermediary between herbivorous and carnivorous just as mist between Sky and Earth; as scalp between war and agriculture (scalp is a war crop); as corn smut between wild and cultivated plants; as garments between 'nature' and 'culture;' as refuse between village and outside; and as ashes (or soot) between roof (sky vault) and hearth (in the ground). This chain of mediators, if one may call them so, not only throws light on entire parts of North American mythology – why the Dew-God may be at the same time the Game-Master and the giver of raiments and be personified as an 'Ash-Boy;' or why scalps are mist-producing; or why the Game-Mother is associated with corn smut; etc. – but it also probably corresponds to a universal way of organizing daily experience.[209]

By reading through many different myths, and by drawing linkages of opposition and mediation on the 'red-yellow-green' model as described earlier,

Lévi-Strauss shows how terms that first appear to be unrelated, can be structurally linked. In the above, for example, we have an unexpected association between coyotes, mist, scalp, corn smut, garments, refuse, and ashes – one that allows us to discern similarities and common purposes between myths from diverse parts of the world.

When Lévi-Strauss examines individual myths, he reads them in a novel way, much as one might read an orchestral score.[210] Reading a score involves a simultaneous interpretation from both 'left to right' and from 'top to bottom.' For example:

```
[time –>]    t1     t2     t3     t4     t5     t6     t7     t8---->
Flutes      |----- |----- |----- |----- |----- |----- |----- |----->
Clarinets   |----- |----- |----- |----- |----- |----- |----- |----->
Trumpets    |----- |----- |----- |----- |----- |----- |----- |----->
Violins     |----- |----- |----- |----- |----- |----- |----- |----->
Violas      |----- |----- |----- |----- |----- |----- |----- |----->
Bass        |----- |----- |----- |----- |----- |----- |----- |----->
etc.
```

To understand the sequence of notes as they occur sequentially in time, we read the score from left to right; to understand which notes are being played simultaneously, we read the score from top to bottom. The former provides the diachronic structure; the latter provides the synchronic structure. When analyzing myth, Lévi-Strauss initially sets each version of the myth in the places that would correspond to each musical instrument in the above chart, and he then isolates the myth's various crucial episodes (e.g., Oedipus answers the Sphinx's riddle; Oedipus marries his mother; Oedipus's father's identity is revealed, etc.) along the diachronic line. Some versions of the myth will omit certain episodes and while other versions will include others, so the total arrangement of all the different versions of the myth is intended to provide a representation of the 'myth' as a whole. The 'myth' is taken to be the sum of all of its versions. In the following, for instance, each number represents a crucial episode in a version of the myth:

Version one	1	2		4			7	8
Version two		2	3	4		6		8
Version three	1			4	5		7	8
Version four	1	2			5		7	
Version five			3	4	5	6		8

After this arrangement is set, Lévi-Strauss rearranges the elemental episodes of the myth (which he calls the 'mythemes,' upon analogy to the 'phonemes' in linguistics) into thematic groups. For example, he might group all of the episodes where monsters are killed into one column, or all of the episodes where relations between relatives are too close (e.g., as in an incestuous relationship) in another column, and all of the episodes where the relations between relatives are too far (e.g., as in patricide or fratricide) in still another column. In this way, he gradually constructs an abstract structure that reduces and coalesces the myth into basic oppositional themes, for Lévi-Strauss contends that 'mythical thought always progresses from the awareness of oppositions toward their resolution.'[211]

Through this structural analysis of myth, Lévi-Strauss shows how myths can be analyzed to reveal common themes that at first sight seem to be unrelated. Here, we can once again recall the example, cited above, of the transition from the opposition between 'red' (danger) and 'green' (safety), to the slightly more complicated 'red, yellow, green' sequence which introduces 'yellow' (caution) as the intermediary between the opposition between red and green. In mythological thought, we find the same process of initial opposition accompanied by the subsequent interposition of an intermediary, except that the elements which take the place of 'red' and 'green' in the actual myth examples have more cultural content, such as the opposition between 'death' and 'life,' or the opposition between 'nature' and 'culture.'

Using this basic 'logic' – one which Lévi-Strauss believes is characteristic of mythological (and by implication, human) thinking – he is able, for instance, to explain the hitherto mysterious connection between the character of the 'trickster,' which appears in many North American myths, and the images of the 'coyote' and the 'raven.' His explanation is that the trickster – an ambiguous character – serves as a mediator between 'life' and 'death.' Since 'life' is associated with agriculture, and 'death' is associated with warfare, there is an initial association between 'life, agriculture and (peaceful) herbivorous animals,' and a corresponding association between 'death, warfare and carnivorous beast of prey.'

Why, then, is the trickster, who is an ambiguous figure, so frequently associated with the coyote and the raven? Lévi-Strauss uses the above oppositions, and the need for a reconciliation between them, to explain the connection. Coyotes and ravens symbolize an intermediary position between the two opposing triads. Coyotes eat meat, but it is usually meat that has been killed by other animals. Their food is thus similar to the plants that are simply found and eaten by the herbivorous animals, while it is also similar to the meat of animals that are actively killed by the carnivorous predators. Hence the coyote and the raven can be associated with an ambiguous figure like the trickster, since all three are ambiguous. Through associations such as these, Lévi-Strauss is able to explain the meaningful structural relationships between myths from cultures that are located in different parts of the world, and which have had no contact with one another.

On the difference between 'primitive' vs. 'civilized' cultures

One of the results of Lévi-Strauss's investigations of myth is the judgment that there is no major difference between so-called 'primitive' and 'civilized' cultures with regard to the complexity of thought that stands behind the culture. Lévi-Strauss denies that people in more contemporary cultures are more intelligent, more insightful or more mature than people in so-called primitive cultures. He finds that human thought is comparable across all cultures with respect to these considerations, and that the main difference between primitive and modern cultures resides in the way the basic complexity of human thought is applied.

In so-called primitive cultures, the natural complexity of human thought is applied in a more pronounced metaphorical and symbolic mode, whereby natural sequences (consider the aforementioned example of totemism) are applied to cultural sequences; in modern cultures, the natural complexity of human thought is applied in a more literalistic mode, whereby attention is given to the process of categorizing objects with respect to their literally shared features. Whereas a more early tribal style of mind will more readily see a metaphorical relationship between a raccoon and the behaviors of a clan, the more mass-civilized mind will more readily see a literalistic relationship between raccoons, bears, and pandas, and wonder whether pandas ought to be classified as large raccoons or small bears. The latter focus of thought is geared toward literal properties, and is more attentive to the possibilities of empirical generalization and prediction. Lévi-Strauss regards this difference only as a matter of style, not as one of complexity or intellectual maturity. It is akin to asserting that the greatest scientists are not more intelligent than the greatest novelists.

With regard to the alleged differences between primitive and modern cultures, he writes the following:

> [T]he kind of logic in mythical thought is as rigorous as that of modern science, and that the difference lies, not in the quality of the intellectual process, but in the nature of the things to which it is applied. This is well in agreement with the situation known to prevail in the field of technology: What makes a steel ax superior to a stone ax is not that the first one is better made than the second. They are equally well made, but steel is quite different from stone. In the same way we may be able to show that

the same logical processes operate in myth as in science, and that humans have always been thinking equally well; the improvement lies, not in an alleged progress of the human mind, but in the discovery of new areas to which it may apply its unchanged and unchanging powers.[212]

Criticisms of Lévi-Strauss

Lévi-Strauss did not spend extensive amounts of time with the tribal groups he investigated, nor did he live with any particular tribe sufficiently long enough to learn the language fluently, speak at length to the people first-hand, and observe long-term subtleties in the culture. For this reason, questions arise regarding his analyses of the cultural groups, and he is sometimes unsympathetically categorized as an 'armchair' anthropologist.

In defense of Lévi-Strauss, it is clear that it is impossible to investigate a very large number of cultural groups, if one is required to live with each group for seven or eight years each, before one can speak with any anthropological authority. Since Lévi-Strauss's aim is to determine whether there are large-scale commonalities among human cultures, the nature of his project precludes the extensive immersion in each of the cultures to which he must refer. The nature of his anthropological, and specifically ethnological, project necessitates that he rely upon other people's first-hand accounts and ethnographical summaries of the various cultural groups' practices.

Since Lévi-Strauss's method is a structuralist one, however, he does take a predominantly external perspective on cultural groups, as he tries to abstract away from their differences for the purposes of discerning their similarities. Since he hopes to reveal cross-cultural resemblances, it is inevitable that he disregards many of the differences between cultural groups. Among these differences, though, it is important not to overlook those that bear on the subjective experience of the members of the group. That is, as was noted above in the criticism of Saussure's linguistic theory, Lévi-Strauss's structuralist method leads him to bypass the experiential aspect of what it feels like to be a member of a particular cultural group 'from the inside.'

Also, there is the danger of arbitrariness in Lévi-Strauss's style of analyzing myths. Literary and interpretive decisions need to be made regarding which are the proper parts or crucial episodes of each myth. There are also questions about how to group the various parts of the myth together, none of which have precise answers upon which all interpreters will agree. Since Lévi-Strauss assumes that the purpose of myth is to reconcile contradictions, there can arise the temptation to interpret and structure a myth in view of this presupposed end, almost in the manner of a self-fulfilled prophecy. So Lévi-Strauss's method of analyzing myths involves the potential problem of begging the question about whether myths actually do serve the purpose of conflict resolution.

At a fundamental level, moreover, there remains the philosophical question about whether or not there is a human nature. Sartre, for example, denies that there is any essential, or positively defining characteristic, to human beings. When Lévi-Strauss acknowledges that there are specific differences between the myths (and other cultural practices) among various cultures, one could alternatively begin to believe that this is evidence for the view that values, and perhaps even basic thinking processes, vary from culture to culture. Yet Lévi-Strauss draws the opposite conclusion by formulating his inquiry at a highly theoretical level that abstracts from individual cultural differences. He then attempts to discern the presence of human nature at this highly abstract, structural level. So one can ask whether he supposes uncritically that there is a human nature to be discovered at the level of basic structure.

In response to the above worry, we can modify the criticism by saying that Lévi-Strauss's structuralist method, more temperately considered, is only tentative in principle: if there is a human nature to be found, then it is more likely to reside at the abstract level of structure, given the wide diversity of cultural forms. So we can more sympathetically understand Lévi-Strauss as attempting to find out whether there is such a human nature to be discovered, and as amassing evidence for its existence, rather than assuming that there is one, and reading the data in light of that assumption. Given, however, the arbitrariness that is inherent in the structuralist interpretation of myth, it becomes difficult to determine whether the similarities noted amongst the various myths are objectively present, or are attributable to the projections made by the interpreter of the myth.

Selected works of Claude Lévi-Strauss:

1948 (age 40): *La Vie familiale et sociale des indiens Nambikwara* [*The Family and Social Life of the Nambikwara Indians*]

1949 (age 41): *Les Structures élémentaires de la parenté* [*The Elementary Structures of Kinship*]

1952 (age 44): *Race et histoire* [*Race and History*]

1955 (age 47): *Tristes tropiques* [*A World on the Wane*]

1958 (age 50): *Anthropologie structurale* [*Structural Anthropology*]

1962 (age 54): *La pensée sauvage* [*The Savage Mind*]

1962 (age 54): *Le totémisme aujourd'hui* [*Totemism*]

1964 (age 56): *Mythologiques I: Le cru et le cuit* [*The Raw and the Cooked*]

1967 (age 59): *Mythologiques II: Du miel aux cendres* [*From Honey to Ashes*]

1968 (age 60): *Mythologiques III: L'origine des manières table* [*The Origin of Table Manners*]

1971 (age 63): *Mythologiques IV: L'homme nu* [*The Naked Man*]

1983 (age 75): *Le regard éloigné* [*The View from Afar*]

1985 (age 77): *La potière jalouse* [*The Jealous Potter*]

1991 (age 83): *Histoire de lynx* [*The Story of Lynx*]

9

Jacques Lacan, Psychoanalyst (1901–81)

Life and works

Jacques-Marie Emile Lacan was born in Paris on April 13, 1901. He attended a Jesuit school, the Collège Stanislas, during his early years, and as a young adult, he studied medicine at the University of Paris, and later, psychiatry. At age twenty-six, Lacan began his clinical training as a psychiatrist, and at age thirty-one, he published his doctoral dissertation, *On Paranoiac Psychosis in its Relations to the Personality* (1932) – a copy of which he sent to Sigmund Freud, who was then in his seventy-sixth year. Owing to its attention to fantasy and language, Lacan's dissertation drew some interest from the surrealists.

In 1933, along with other intellectuals who were living in Paris, such as Maurice Merleau-Ponty and Georges Bataille, Lacan began attending Alexander Kojève's lectures on G. W. F. Hegel's *Phenomenology* – lectures that inspired Lacan to assimilate Hegelian ideas into his already-formed Freudian psychoanalytic perspective.[213] A few years later, at age thirty-five, Lacan presented one of his most influential papers – 'The Mirror-Stage' – at the International Psychoanalytical Conference in Marienbad, Czechoslovakia (1936).[214] During the Second World War, when the Nazis suppressed French psychoanalysis, Lacan worked in a military hospital, the Val-de-Grâce. He also studied the Chinese language at this time. After the war, he continued his participation in the Psychoanalytic Society of Paris (*Société Psychanalytique de Paris* [SPP]) and eventually became its director in 1953. Internal disputes within the society led to Lacan's resignation and the establishment of an alternative psychoanalytic group, the French Society of Psychoanalysis (*Société Française de Psychanalyse* [SFP]). During the same year (1953), Lacan gave an important lecture in Rome entitled 'The Function and Field of Speech and Language in Psychoanalysis' – a paper which articulated his view that the speaking subject is at the center of psychoanalysis.

Beginning in 1954, Lacan offered a series of seminars on topics in psychoanalysis that continued yearly until his death in 1981. In 1964, at the age of sixty-three, Lacan founded his own school of psychoanalysis – the Freudian School of Paris (*L'École Freudienne de Paris* [EFP]) – and soon had among his audience, not only psychoanalysts and psychiatrists, but linguists, anthropologists, philosophers, mathematicians and literary critics. He continued to offer his seminars for the rest of his life, while often giving guest lectures at other universities. Selections from these seminars were published in 1966 under the title *Écrits*, and they were translated into English eleven years later in 1977. Lacan died in Paris on September 9, 1981, at the age of eighty.

Lacan's theory of the subject

Sartre's theory

To appreciate Lacan's understanding of human subjectivity, it is useful to compare Jean-Paul Sartre's account of how consciousness as an active subject (i.e., as a 'for-itself') unsuccessfully attempts to identify completely with itself as an object (i.e., as an 'in-itself'). According to Sartre, to recall, this project of identifying 'subject' with 'object' is impossible to achieve, owing to the irreducible tension between consciousness as (1) that which thinks about things and regards them as objects, and consciousness as (2) that which is thought about, as it stands as one of the very objects of the active consciousness's attention. In the former instance, the subject is an active and projective awareness; in the latter instance, the 'subject' is an object that the active consciousness thinks about.

Sartre refers to this object-like projection of the actively thinking subject as the 'ego' and he characterizes it as an entity which emerges as a construction of consciousness-as-subject, and which stands on a par with all of the other objects in the world. This ego is consciousness in a deadened and frozen form, and Sartre maintains that it cannot coincide with the active, thinking subject, and that these two aspects of consciousness stand in perpetual tension throughout the duration of human existence. Sartre maintains that subjects and objects are two incompatible kinds of being, and that the human being is an internally tension-ridden host of both kinds of being.

Since Sartre believes that the opposition between subjectivity and objectivity is unbridgeable, he concludes that the human being is characteristically involved in a fruitless attempt to surmount this gap within itself, as it suffers from this perpetual division between consciousness as a thinking activity and consciousness as a being which is thought about. As Sartre describes it, the permanent project of consciousness is to strive for the impossible goal of becoming a 'for-itself-in-itself' – a satisfactory state of being that is both subject and object at once, coincident and at home with itself, and which Sartre equates with God.

The continuing effort to be at home, both with oneself and with the objective world, generates attempts to apprehend oneself as an object by means of trying to identify with the viewpoints others take upon us. In our personal relationships, for instance, we attempt to merge with the viewpoints of other people, so as to see ourselves as they see us. The inevitable failure of this project of trying to find oneself in other people, owing to the opposition between subject and object, is the source of Sartre's discouraging view of romantic and sexual relationships. For him, as we have seen, all such relationships are necessarily disappointing and frustrating. Lacan employs psychoanalytic terms to develop the same general idea that we can never fully merge with 'the other.'

Lacan's theory and the 'decentered' subject

Lacan's understanding of human subjectivity also compares with Sartre's in connection with the claim that we can never get into full, explicit, touch with ourselves as active, thinking subjects. When Lacan considers the situation of human consciousness, he regards our representations of other people, not to mention the language we speak – in short, all of our objectifications of things in our experience – as impediments to achieving a complete self-apprehension and sense of personal authenticity. When we interact with other people, for example, Lacan maintains that we interact with only 'shadows,' since ordinary language and daily contexts place a veil over everyone's inner psychological complexity. We therefore cannot achieve much more than an unsatisfying and superficial sort of social interaction with each other, if only because we cannot experience what directly happens in other people's minds, but can only experience other people's bodily expressions. Which is to say that we are mostly invisible to one another. To the extent that each subject of experience is always a step removed from the objective world of ordinary language and the daily experience of the world, each of us is 'decentered' insofar as we remain at a distance away from, and alienated from, the world of daily society.

In a second sense as well, the Lacanian subject is decentered in a manner that is understandable in reference to Sartre's theory. According to Sartre, consciousness has no permanently definitive qualities, and each person is free to choose his or her style of being: according to Sartre, a person can transform herself or himself into radically different kinds of personality by making a different fundamental choice about who she or he wants to be, or about whether she or he even wants to be. Although Lacan questions the degree of human freedom that is possible, he shares Sartre's view that there is no essential substance that can be called a 'self' which is fully determined prior to experience.[215]

So Sartre and Lacan reject the Cartesian view of the self as a solid, integrated, individual entity that has an unchanging essence of its own. Loosely following Sartre, Lacan sometimes refers to the subject as a 'nothing,' but he regards this locution as signifying that the subject, with respect to the content of its consciousness, is largely at the mercy of external forces such as language.[216] There is consequently an important difference between Sartre and Lacan with respect to how they construe the decentered subject: Sartre associates decentered subjectivity with absolute freedom; Lacan significantly associates it with the social determination of the individual.

Another important distinction between Sartre's and Lacan's respective understandings of human subjectivity, is that Lacan recognizes the existence of an unconscious side to the human psyche, whereas Sartre denies such a sphere. For Sartre, the thinking subject is itself grounded upon a more fundamental acting subject, which he conceives of as a free, fundamentally contentless nothingness. It is free precisely because it has nothing within it to determine or restrict it. Lacan believes that the reflectively inaccessible subject nonetheless has a diverse set of mental contents – contents that remain hidden, insofar as a person cannot easily access them by merely reflecting upon his or her mental states. These contents remain unconscious with respect to their relative inaccessibility: it is a difficulty in accessibility arising from the nature of consciousness as a being that must objectify things to bring its mental contents into explicit awareness.[217]

This restriction, however, does not prevent us from becoming aware of the unconscious contents of our minds, according to Lacan. It indicates only that if we are to become aware of these contents, we must do so in an indirect way, just as we interpret as implicit or as tacit the underlying or implied meanings that can reside within a person's explicit utterances. Developing this analogy between the unconscious and implicitly stated linguistic meanings, Lacan analyzes the rhetorical aspects of conscious utterances in an effort to reveal what remains latent and overlooked within the meanings of what people say explicitly. To do his psychoanalytic work, Lacan discovers the applicability of techniques that are usually employed by literary critics.

With respect to the practice of psychoanalysis, Lacan's understanding of the reflectively inaccessible, decentered subject implies the following: since the thinking subject cannot be fully characterized in purely 'objective' terms (viz., the terms of 'scientific' clinical psychology), it is a mistake to understand the subject exclusively and exhaustively as a set of objectively describable functions, as if it were an inanimate mechanism of some sort. Indeed, this motivates Lacan's resistance to the American psychoanalytic establishment of his time, which, in his opinion, operated with a far more scientistic and objectifying understanding of the mind.

It also explains some of Lacan's objections to the more materialistic and mechanistic aspects of Freud's own theory. Lacan rejects the view that the human mind is completely understandable in mechanistic, causal terms, because the mental life of a living consciousness is composed of 'meanings' which are not consistent with the kinds of analyses used in natural science. This consideration also motivates Lacan to employ methods that, as noted, are more akin to the rhetorical analysis of literary texts (i.e., where one looks for underlying, implicit, or indirectly expressed meanings) in his attempt to understand the nature of the mind, and of mental illness. To be an effective Lacanian psychiatrist, it is necessary to develop a sensitivity to poetic, literary, and fictive styles of thinking. In this respect, Lacan shares sympathies with Lévi-Strauss, who also emphasized the fundamentally poetic nature of the human mind.

In connection with psychoanalytic practice, the theory of the decentered subject also bears upon the ideal role of the analyst. Lacan resists the idea that the goal of analysis is to have the subject identify with the analyst's ego or socially explicit persona, since the analyst's own desires often distort the psychoanalytic exchange, and since the analyst's ego is itself a product of society's norms, and is thereby an alienating 'object' as well. Rather, he believes that the goal of analysis is to have the patient acknowledge the idiosyncrasy of his or her own psychological desires, and to come to authentic terms with himself or herself. This sort of self-awareness requires a realistic assessment of the person's place in the world, as the person stands in relation to others.

Lacan states illustratively, that when analysis begins, the situation is one-sided: the patient is either talking about himself (or herself) and is not talking to the analyst, or the patient is talking to the analyst and not talking about himself. In the former case, the patient evades treatment by resisting the analyst's questions and comments; in the latter case, the patient evades treatment by not revealing his or her deeper feelings and thoughts. When the person is finally listening openly to the analyst and talking about himself openly as well, then, Lacan maintains, the analysis will be over.[218] Which is to say that he believes that psychoanalysis is largely a process of overcoming the one-sided perspectives that can stand in the way of developing a more complete, realistic, and multi-aspected view of oneself. In effect, he follows the Freudian tradition that associates mental health with self-knowledge.

Hegel's influence on Lacan

Although the philosophy of G. W. F. Hegel had a world-historical impact upon nineteenth-century German and European culture, particularly in connection with its influence upon Karl Marx's communism and dialectical style of thought, Hegel was not a central figure within French thought until the early twentieth century. As mentioned above, the introduction of Hegel's thought into France was assisted by the lectures on Hegel's *Phenomenology of Spirit* offered by Alexandre Kojève during the 1930s. Especially influential to twentieth-century French thought, were Kojève's lectures on a section of Hegel's *Phenomenology* that concerns asymmetrical human relationships – those relationships where one person in the relationship has clearly more power than the other. The relevant section of the *Phenomenology* is entitled 'Self-Consciousness,' and it contains a historically important and widely discussed segment on the relationship between 'Masters' and the 'Servants.'

On Hegel's view, the most primitive, wild, and uncultured mental condition of the human being is one of exclusive psychological self-centeredness and extreme defensiveness. In this vicious condition of pure self-interest – a condition that Hegel describes as a theoretical abstraction and as an idealization – everything other than the self-centered consciousness is regarded as a threat. To defend and preserve itself, this 'natural' consciousness becomes immersed in the project of eliminating whatever appears to it as an alien being, as it tries to remove the threatening alien presence by various means: it attempts either to destroy it, to consume it, or to control it. Hegel's discussion proceeds by showing how this project of destruction and domination leads the self-centered consciousness, in a backfiring of its initial intentions, to become slowly attached to, and dependent upon, the alien presence that it aims to eliminate. Self-defeatingly, as the self-centered consciousness acts to secure greater freedom for itself, it gravitates into a condition of greater bondage.

Hegel postulates that when two of these self-centered consciousnesses come into initial social relationship with each other, their first impulse is to try to kill one another.[219] This locates a life-and-death struggle at the foundation of human social interaction. Hegel maintains that once this struggle reaches a conclusion where one consciousness absolutely dominates, the dominant self-consciousness realizes upon reflection, that with regard to its own interests, it is more beneficial to preserve the defeated consciousness as a slave or servant, than it is to take its life. Specifically, the dominating self-consciousness realizes the benefit in experiencing the defeated consciousness's recognition, for the dominating master anticipates the satisfaction of seeing itself reflected in the perceptions of the dominated slave. The very project that Sartre maintained was impossible – the project of finding oneself in another person – is, in fact, the project of the 'master.' It is the project of the servant as well, who tries to find him or herself reflected in the master's recognition of its work.

For the purposes of appreciating Hegel's influence upon Lacan, we need only add that according to Hegel, and also consistent with Sartre's view, neither the master nor the servant can ever be psychologically satisfied by such an asymmetrical social arrangement.[220] The servant gives recognition to the dominant master, but the master ambivalently realizes that this recognition is offered by a person whom the master does not respect. Although the recognition of a mere servant is better than no recognition at all, it remains of low value to the master.

In a parallel way, although the master recognizes the servant by preserving the servant's life, the master recognizes the servant merely as a thing to be manipulated. So the master's recognition of the servant is not fully satisfying for the servant. For the servant is recognized ambivalently by someone whom the servant respects, but who, in turn, does not respect the servant. So asymmetrical power relationships are psychologically frustrating and ambivalent, and necessarily so. The only way to achieve a mutually satisfying relationship, according to Hegel, is for individuals of equal power to respect and recognize each other as equals.

Asymmetrical power relationships have an internal tendency to balance themselves out in the long run, but Hegel's analysis of the master–servant relationship, along with Lacan's view and Sartre's view, suggest that it is impossible to reach a full identity or equality between a subject and an object. The specific argument Lacan offers for this necessary incongruence between subject and object (ego) we will see in a moment, in his discussion of the 'mirror-stage' of consciousness. But as we can now note, Lacan's idealized characterization of the relationship between psychoanalyst and patient, which begins as an asymmetrical power relationship and ends with a more balanced relationship between analyst and patient, is inspired by Hegel's influential ideal of subject–object coincidence and the overcoming of the master–servant opposition.

Lacan: the imaginary, the symbolic and the real

The 'imaginary,' the 'symbolic,' and the 'real' are three spheres in reference to which Lacan conceptualizes the human psychological landscape. The imaginary is the most primitive condition, associated with the close physical and mental relationship between an infant and its mother; the symbolic is the realm of language, both as language operates within us to structure our consciousness and as it operates independently of us within society at large; the real is the 'objective' realm that remains outside the sphere of symbolization altogether.

Lacan differs noticeably from Hegel insofar as Lacan's realm of 'the imaginary' – what he considers to be a primitive realm of the human psyche – is not described as a condition of alienation, division, and violence. Rather, somewhat more in the tradition of Jean-Jacques Rousseau (1712–78) and Claude Lévi-Strauss, it involves a feeling of identity and harmony. Only later, with the introduction of language and the introduction of persons other than the nurturing and supportive mother, does Lacan recognize the entrance of a (male) principle that divides the psyche, both from itself, and from other people.

The imaginary

One of Lacan's earlier psychoanalytic essays, 'The Mirror Stage as Formative of the Function of the I,' argues that the ego is a fictitious, self-constructed entity. According to Lacan, when a child is between the ages of six and eighteen months, it develops an ability to react to its image in the mirror, or to other comparable behavioral reflections, with the belief that the image represents itself. Upon perceiving its own image, the child experiences a feeling of pleasure and entertainment: it looks at its reflection and smiles or laughs with contentment. Lacan believes that this point of self-awareness coincides with the time when the child is beginning to form an explicit awareness of itself, and to form an 'ego.' He adds importantly that this self-image is idealized and misrepresentative, for it presents to the child an image of itself which is more solid, integrated, and coherent, than the child in fact is, both in reference to its physical motor capacities, and in reference to its internal psychological constitution. The perceptually articulated and well-defined mirror image represents to the child the mental permanence and integrity of the 'I,' but this sense of permanence and integrity is mostly an illusion.

In Lacan's later writings, he generalizes his account of the misrepresentative mirror-stage by defining a basic mental function called 'the imaginary.' This mental function identifies the subject primarily with its various self-images and underscores an identity between subject and ego (i.e., between subject and object), while denying their actual difference. The imaginary is thus a mode of representation that involves a surprising degree of misrepresentation: in an imaginary mental function, the subject represents what is actually different from itself as being exactly the same as itself, and overlooks, ignores, or denies the difference. In Sartrean terms, the imaginary state of mind is a kind of bad faith that permeates the human psyche from the very start. It is a kind of psychologically grounded 'original sin,' one could say from one angle, upon emphasizing the imaginary image's falsity; from another angle, one could describe it as a form of 'ignorance in bliss,' upon emphasizing how the imaginary image generates a feeling of being very much at home in the world. In general, imaginary states of mind implicitly involve being dominated by idealizations.

To obtain a more realistic sense of the world, however, it is also necessary to appreciate the difference between oneself as a field of fluctuating mental energy, as opposed to solidified ego-images of oneself and, by implication, the difference between oneself as an active subjectivity and the external world at large. So, for psychological health and especially for smooth social functioning, it is necessary to move beyond the imaginary condition by appreciating more and more differences within one's surroundings, and to develop a greater sense of discrimination between self and world. Lacan maintains that the development of language is central to this process of mental discrimination and socialization. These linguistic developments he associates with what he calls the 'symbolic' mode of thought, which he associates with the father-image.

The symbolic

Language as a dynamic system of differences between signifiers

During the 1950s, Lacan was influenced by Lévi-Strauss's structuralist anthropology, and he incorporated Saussure's linguistic theory into his reflections on psychoanalysis.[221] Although Lacan did not agree with Saussure that the possibility of articulated consciousness depends fully upon, and issues fundamentally from, linguistic awareness,[222] he did believe that whenever language was present, it had the Saussurean linguistic form. Specifically, Lacan adopted Saussure's view that the 'sign is arbitrary,' along with the view that linguistic structures are organized into binary oppositions. With this structuralist conception of language, Lacan distinguished the symbolic mode of thought from the imaginary mode, and also from the realm of the 'real,' or what is completely 'other.'[223]

The symbolic realm incorporates both the inner subjective sphere of experience in addition to the outer spatial–temporal world, and it partially determines the structures of both. To this extent, Lacan can be understood as a structuralist who believes that social phenomena are language-like. For Lacan, accordingly, this Saussurean realm of language is composed of signifiers (what Saussure calls a 'system of signs'), each of which refers to other signifiers and each of which is itself referred to by still other signifiers. To recall a simple example, 'sweet' can refer to 'sour' as its opposite, and 'sweet' can be referred to by the term 'sour' itself, as the latter's opposite. The pair of these is associated with the term 'tongue,' which is contrasted with the terms 'ears,' 'nose,' 'eyes,' and perhaps 'hands' (all in reference to the distinction between the five senses), which are themselves contrasted with each other. There are oppositions, and then associations to other oppositions, and so on. The central idea, as we have seen above in the discussion of Saussure's linguistics, is that the meaning of a term (signifier; symbol) is determined within an entire system of oppositional and contrastive relationships, wherein each term plays both roles of signifier and signified.

Once each term in the language is regarded as a signifier whose meaning is defined in reference to other signifiers, then the meaning of any signifier reveals itself as being figurative in an important sense: although the term appears to have a positive significance, it stands at a specific location within a network of other associated signifiers whose oppositional relations to it actually constitute the signifier's meaning. Within the Saussurean linguistic framework, each signifier obtains its meaning, not from any intrinsic qualities it has, but from the network of relationships within which it is situated with respect to other signifiers.[224]

Hence, when we regard any word as having a positive meaning of its own, we misrecognize the signifier as such. The signifier is empty in itself, and it has a 'positive' significance only in a figurative sense, as the condensation (to use Freud's term) of the complexity of the surrounding network of signifiers. In this sense, we arrive at the surprising result that all positively definitive and literalistic language reveals itself to be figurative language. Insofar as the meaning of the background completely determines the meaning of the foreground on this view, it is illusory to locate the foreground's meaning among the features of the foreground itself, as if this meaning were a positive presence that stood self-sufficiently alone.

This structuralist theory of language – and by implication, the Lacanian realm of the symbolic – thereby presents a picture that is diametrically opposed to the productions of the imaginary mode of consciousness. Within the imaginary mode, a person constructs an image that is solid, integrated, coherent, whole, etc., identifies with this image, and uses it to construct a sense of solid personality, or ego.[225] The imaginary mode of consciousness introduces stability into the self by means of identification with stable perceptual objects. In contrast, since language is composed of signifiers whose meanings are determined in endless reference to other signifiers, the symbolic sphere remains open-ended and without any final closure. Signifiers refer to signifiers that refer to yet other signifiers, without end. So when language becomes incorporated into consciousness, it serves as a disruptive force that is antagonistic to the permanent, bounded, and 'totalized' self that is generated by the imagination. In sum, within the more global 'self' there are two opposing tendencies: there is a tendency toward permanence that is introduced by the imaginary mode of consciousness, and there is a tendency toward disruption and division, which is introduced by the symbolic or linguistic mode of consciousness.

The 'phallus:' the transition from the imaginary to the symbolic

Lacan uses the term 'phallus' to refer to the principle through which a basic capacity needed for language – the ability to draw a distinction between signifier and signified – enters into consciousness. This principle functions analogously to a pencil that draws a dividing line on a piece of paper, or to a scissor that cuts the paper in two, or to the hand of a karate expert, that breaks a board into two pieces. There is a degree of violence involved in the process of division. Within this context, it might seem idiosyncratic for Lacan to use the term 'phallus' – one which refers to the male genital in its ordinary, and not necessarily violent, usage – but from a psychoanalytic standpoint, the focus upon sexual energies and sexual presences is pivotal to human development. So it is not altogether surprising to find Lacan using sexual imagery to express fundamental psychological principles.

Influenced by the style of Freudian theorizing where episodes from a person's childhood are considered to be psychologically determinative, Lacan focuses upon an idealized and elementary episode within a child's life that introduces this linguistic principle into the child's mind. Specifically, he identifies the introduction of the idea of the phallus into a child's consciousness at a point when the imaginary unity of the child's mind – represented by the unity of the child with its mother – is disrupted by a figure that opposes the mother. Lacan associates the initial fundamental imaginary unity between the child and its mother as a consequence of the natural bond between the two: the mother typically maintains the child's life through nourishment and care/love. On this view, the child sees itself as the object of the mother's desire and initially identifies with the mother. Imagination is associated with the motherly relationships; symbolization is opposingly associated, in terms of traditional imagery, with language and fatherly relationships.

Once a young child perceives that there is an 'other' who receives the mother's attention as well, and stands as competing object for the mother's desire, Lacan postulates the formation of a psychic disruption within the child and a sense of distance from the mother. This other is symbolically the father, which Lacan represents by the general, male-designating term 'phallus.'

According to Lacan, the 'father' introduces the 'law' (i.e., the principles of language, and hence, of societal norms) into the child's consciousness. Since the father-presence functions as the symbol of language, or the symbol of signification itself, Lacan refers to this principle as the 'name-of-the-father' (*Nom-du-Père*) that is impressed upon the child's mind.

The father-phallus-language thus introduces a sense of distance between the child and its mother, and by implication, a sense of distance between the child and other people in general. This distance generates a desire for reunification with others, and an overall feeling that this unity with others is lacking. Insofar as the child perceives the father-figure as being interruptive of a sense of unity, the latter appears as the 'other.' But at the same time, this 'other,' understood in a general sense, is the very being with which the child seeks to reunify itself. So in Lacanian phraseology, the result is that everyone lacks the phallus, and that everyone seeks to become the phallus, simply as a consequence of having their sense of personal identity solidified in a manner that distinguishes them from other people. Since at such a point of personal development the full merging with another person becomes impossible, Lacan maintains that it is impossible for anyone to become the phallus. The situation is not unlike Sartre's view that a subject cannot become an object, and the phallus closely compares to Sartre's notion of being-in-itself, or full positivity.

Since Lacan appears to give a central function to the phallus as the source of language, and since language is so crucial to the continuation of human life and civilization, it might be thought that Lacan is celebrating male imagery in his theory of the phallus. If language had a completely affirmative value within his view, such an interpretation might be justified. This, however, does not seem to be the case, for Lacan states – foreshadowing Barthes – that our language is imposed upon us, and that speech is a 'parasite' and 'form of cancer' in which people are afflicted.[226]

It is also important to note that Lacan's discussion of the phallus in connection with the social intrusion of the father-figure, refers to an idealized, theoretical episode. Lacan is clear about the status of his discussion, and he points out that the 'father,' insofar as it is a functional principle that explains the transition from the imaginary to the symbolic phase, is not an actual person operating at a particular place and time. He explicitly states that he has constructed a myth, and that there is no exact moment when a male figure enters a room, and when language is thereby introduced into the child's consciousness. A person enters the domain of discourse and develops a sense of having a distinctive self gradually, implicitly, and with subtlety, rather than abruptly and explicitly.[227]

Psychoanalytic practice: the unconscious as a language

Freud and the unconscious: condensation and displacement as basic processes within the unconscious

According to both Freud and Lacan, we can understand the way people behave – and especially understand the behaviors that depart from society's conception of what counts as standardized behavior – by considering the structure of the energies that characterize the unconscious part of the mind. For example, Freud explains slips of the tongue (*parapraxes*), structures of interpersonal attachments and antagonisms (to one's father, to one's mother, to people who resemble them), and symptoms in mental illness (obsessions, compulsions, other sorts of non-standard behavior) all in reference to the way unconscious energies are structured, and in terms of the ways these energies achieve an observable social expression.

When Freud explains the processes within the unconscious – those which lead to the structures of dreams, external behaviors manifested by neuroses, psychoses, etc. – he refers to two basic psychological processes. These are 'condensation' and 'displacement,' which he believes operate in everyone. Freud describes the two processes as they occur in dream formation in the following excerpts:

> The first achievement of the dream-work [the process of dream formation] is *condensation* [*Verdichtung*]. We understand by this the fact that the manifest dream is of more narrow content than the latent, and is therefore a kind of abridged translation of the latter. Condensation may sometimes be lacking; as a rule it is there, and very often it is enormous. It is never turned around in the opposite way, i.e., it does not happen, that the manifest dream is richer in content or wider in range than the latent dream. Condensation arises through the conditions when (1) certain latent elements are completely left out, (2) a broken-off part of some complexes in the latent dream is carried over into the manifest dream, (3) that latent elements having something in common, are set together in the manifest dream, and melted into a unity.[228]
>
> The second achievement of the dream-work is *displacement* [*Verschiebung*]. For this we have the good fortune of having already done some preparatory work; we know that it is completely the work of the dream-censorship. Its two manifestations are first, that a latent element is replaced, not by one of its own components, but by something more distant, that is, by an allusion; and second, that the psychical

accent upon an important element is transferred over to an unimportant element, so that the dream is centered in a different way and appears strange.[229]

With regard to the formation of mental symptoms, Freud maintains that the same processes that create dreams are responsible for creating symptoms (e.g., phobias, peculiar behaviors, etc.):

> We must remember further, that in the formation of symptoms, as with the formation of dreams, the same processes of the unconscious are involved: condensation and displacement. The symptom, like the dream, represents something as being fulfilled, a satisfaction in the style of the infant; but through extreme condensation, this satisfaction can be packed into a single sensation of innervation, and through extreme displacement it can be narrowed down to a small detail of the entire libidinal complex. It is no wonder, then, when we too have difficulties recognizing in the symptom, the libidinal satisfaction that is suspected and every-time confirmed.[230]

Through the above examples, it is clear that Freud regards the processes of condensation and displacement as central to the workings of the unconscious in general, and that they provide us with some keys to understanding the meaning of dreams, along with all sorts of mental disturbances.

Lacan: metonymy and metaphor

What strikes Lacan is how the psychological processes of the unconscious are mirrored in linguistic devices such as metonymy and metaphor.[231] Metonymy – a linguistic/literary/rhetorical device where one uses a part of an object to represent the object itself[232] – is the linguistic analogue to the process of condensation. Metaphor – a linguistic/literary/rhetorical device where one substitutes an object similar to the object in question as a representation of the object – is the linguistic analogue to the process of displacement.

Lacan's observation that linguistic devices can express the processes of the unconscious described by Freud, opens up a field of new possibilities for understanding the nature of the unconscious. It implies, for example, that techniques used in rhetorical analysis (the analysis of texts in reference to their techniques of persuasion) are useful for understanding people's behaviors, their dreams, and for understanding social phenomena generally. Lacan's observation reveals that psychological phenomena can be regarded as 'texts' to be interpreted in accord with literary techniques. Rather than using scientific (i.e., mathematical; causal) models to understand the workings of the mind, Lacan moves toward the humanities, and in particular, in the direction of literary theory and rhetorical analysis. This brings us to a major historical intersection and transformation, through Lacan's thought, between psychoanalysis, the earlier structuralist approach to human phenomena as a 'science of signs' – semiology – as prescribed by Saussure in his linguistic theory, and literary theory.

Literary models are also useful in understanding the nature of psychological repression, for we can understand repression as often resulting in symptoms that are interpretable in reference to the formation of metaphors. Freud defines repression in the following:

> [F]or its precondition, the existence of the symptom is that some psychological process was not brought to an end in a normal way, so that it could become conscious. The symptom is a substitute for what did not happen there. Now we know at which point we must locate the suspected force's operation. An intense struggle must have been advanced against bringing the questionable psychological process to consciousness; owing to that, it remained unconscious. As being unconscious, it has the power to form a symptom. During the analytic cure, this very same struggle once again opposes the efforts to bring into consciousness, what is unconscious. We become conscious of this opposition as [the patient's] resistance. The pathogenic process, which the resistance makes evident, is to be given the name *repression* [*Verdrängung*].[233]

Repression is a psychic process closely associated with displacement, and it can be illustrated linguistically in the structure of a metaphor. As a basic example, we can cite Freud's claim that 'water' tends to be a metaphor for 'birth.' Whenever 'water' appears in a dream, the unconscious and repressed meaning of that part of the dream is what the water refers to in the unconscious, which is likely to be 'birth.' So when Lacan states accordingly that 'the symptom is a metaphor,' this indicates that he reads a person's symptoms as if he were interpreting a dream (which, for him, is like interpreting a text). Just as 'water' metaphorically signifies 'birth' in a dream, a person's manifest 'symptoms' metaphorically signify a hidden, or repressed, unconscious content.

If one makes the structuralist assumption that social phenomena are understandable as linguistic phenomena, and if one then interprets the world with an eye toward looking for linguistic phenomena that assume the form of metaphor, then it is a short step to the point where we find ourselves 'psychoanalyzing' the world at large, or 'psychoanalyzing' the social consciousness. This is one way to understand the intellectual projects of structuralist cultural theorists such as Roland Barthes, who do semiological analyses of cultural phenomena. If the manifest social phenomena are regarded as metaphors, then one can reveal the unconscious contents of society by discerning the hidden meaning of the metaphors.

To return to individual cases, we can illustrate Lacan's claim that 'the symptom is a metaphor' through a fairly straightforward Freudian case from the experience of the analyst Masud Khan. This is the case of a woman who entered into analysis as a result of a phobia about seeing people vomit or encountering vomit in the subways.[234] The fear of vomit is the symptom, which we read as a metaphor. The interpretive task – as expressed in literary-critical terms – is thus to understand the meaning of the metaphor. During analysis, it was revealed that the woman had borne an illegitimate child and (due to pressure by her own mother) had abandoned the child in a subway when the child was seven weeks old.[235] With this information, the fear of vomit was interpretable as a metaphor for the fear of encountering the dead and decayed child in the subway.

In the above connection we can discern in the structure of the woman's psychological processes a metaphoric displacement of the image of the womb to the image of the stomach, and a metaphoric displacement of the image of the child to image of the vomit. The woman felt guilty about having abandoned her child and this was eating her up inside. The subway recalled the scene of the moral offense, so she kept thinking about the subway in her guilt. Since the thought of what she had done was so painful, however, her mind formed a metaphor of the child as the image of vomit – as something issuing from the body that is discarded or refused. Hence the woman expressed a fear of vomit in subways as a hidden, or disguised, expression of her fear of facing what she had done to her child.

This phobia, and the formation of the symptom-as-metaphor, resolved the inner dilemma: the woman could not explicitly think about what she had done, because it was so terrible, and the woman could not stop thinking about what he had done, because it was so terrible. So she needed to think about what she has done, and she needed to avoid thinking about what she had done. The psychological resolution of this tension was to constantly think *indirectly* about what she had done – and this was achieved by thinking about a metaphor for what she had done, rather than thinking explicitly about what she had done – which led her to become obsessed by the thought of encountering vomit in the subway. The phobia resolved her psychological dilemma, but it did so with a price, for it translated her guilt into a sense of fear that not only made her suffer, but also inhibited her ability to travel on the subways. Following Lacan's phrase, 'the symptom is a metaphor,' we can see how psychological tensions can be resolved in symptomatic behaviors that carry a metaphorical meaning. By means of their metaphorical meanings, the symptoms reconcile psychological tensions, and these meanings become understandable if we interpretively 'read' a person's behavior, just as we interpret the underlying meaning of a literary text.

Critical reflections on Lacan's psychoanalysis

Aspects of Lacan's view have been subject to numerous criticisms over the years, as have aspects of Freud's outlook. But unlike Freud, Lacan has sometimes suffered the charge of presenting sheer nonsense, or of being thoroughly confused.[236] Although Lacan can be confusing, a method to his madness is discernable, if we associate Lacan's mode of expression with Freud, with the surrealist movement, and with the existentialist interest in being authentic.

Just as surrealist poets were reluctant to polish or rewrite the words that emerged into their explicit consciousness from the intuitive and unconscious depths of their minds, Lacan can also be regarded as someone who tried to embody the voice of the unconscious in his writings and in his lectures. When reading Lacan, one often encounters contradictions, free plays of association, metaphors, and phrases that do not mean what they seem to mean (as in a dream-formation), all set alongside rationally constructed insights regarding the nature of psychoanalysis and human mental functioning. One encounters a complicated, multidimensional amalgam of linguistic styles, where the purely theoretical component – the component that usually appears in isolation in traditional theorizing – is mixed in with the assorted mental contents that generated it.

Or, alternatively described, we find Lacan offering his stream of consciousness which includes not only his theory proper, but the rest of his mind at the time, as well. In this respect, we can understand Lacan to be one of the first theorists (we will also see this acknowledgment in Barthes and in Derrida) to appreciate how literalistic, theoretical verbiage is embedded within the rich context of a multidimensional linguistic structure, and within the similarly complicated mental states of any person who uses language to express an abstract theory.

For anyone who expects to encounter a purely literalistic, traditionally well-formed, organized, systematic presentation of theory, Lacan will appear to be confused. But among his aims, is to display a richer and truer presentation of the human psyche than is typical. Usually and traditionally, we are presented with polished, often heavily censored, morally non-objectionable, mostly depersonalised and objective, expressions of theoretical speculation. His argument – but one that he tends to exemplify rather than present in abstraction – is that such traditional forms of expression are imaginary and false abstractions, because they neglect, silence, and do not represent, the richly aspected linguistic ground (the unconscious) from which they issue. Traditional theorizing is comparable to a leaping dancer who, carried away by imagination, forgets that there is gravity, or to a theoretician, similarly carried away, who aspires to express transcendent and timeless truths, who forgets that he or she is a finite human being;[237] it is comparable to a traditionally minded theoretician of knowledge who disregards that acts of knowledge are always instantiated by a person who unavoidably lives within a historically conditioned social network that involves power relationships.

So if one is to evaluate Lacan's writings, it is necessary to be aware of how he appreciates that traditional theoretical statements are always enmeshed within the rich web of language as whole. Without this appreciation, he will appear to engage in distracting digressions or irrelevancies. But Lacan's side-comments, jokes, not to mention confusing inconsistencies, are included to present the theoretical ideas as an authentic and truth-revealing product of an actual, living, and functioning human mind.[238] His psychoanalytic theory, when considered abstractly and in isolation from its mental sources, might be questionable on logical and psychological grounds, but such criticisms ought not to be grounded on the claim that Lacan's intentionally confusing and multidimensional presentations are somehow indecipherable, and are therefore not worth one's extended intellectual attention. This would be to overlook how Lacan, in his lectures and writings, is attempting to embody the authentic voice of the unconscious, and thereby, to express a dimension of psychological truth, not unlike the surrealist poets of a generation earlier.

Selected works of Jacques Lacan

1936 (age 35): 'Le stade du miroir. Théorie d'un moment structurant et génétique de la constitution de la réalité, conçu en relation avec l'expérience et la doctrine psychanalytique' [*The Mirror Stage*]

1947 (age 46): 'La psychiatrique anglaise et la guerre' ['English Psychiatry and the War']

1953 (age 52): 'Fonction et champ de la parole et du language en psychanalyse' ['The Function and Field of Speech and Language in Psychoanalysis']

1953–54 (ages 52–53): *Le séminaire. Livre I: Les ecrits techniques de Freud* [published 1975] [*Seminar, Book I: Freud's Papers on Technique*]

1954–55 (ages 53–54): *Le séminaire. Livre II: Le moi dans la théorie de Freud et dans la technique de la psychanalyse* [published 1978] [*Seminar, Book II: The Ego in Freud's Theory and in the Technique of Psychoanalysis*]

1955–56 (ages 54–55): *Le séminaire. Livre III: Les psychoses* [published 1981] [*Seminar, Book III: The Psychoses*]

1956 (age 55): 'Fetishism: The Symbolic, the Real and the Imaginary' [with Wladmir Granoff]

1957 (age 56): 'L'instance de la lettre dans l'inconscient ou la raison depuis Freud' ['The Agency of the Letter in the Unconscious, or Reason Since Freud']

1958 (age 57): 'Die bedeutung des phallus' ['La signification du phallus'] ['The Signification of the Phallus']

1960 (age 59): *Le séminaire. Livre VII: L'ethique de la psychanalyse* [published 1986] [*The Ethics of Psychoanalysis*]

1964 (age 63): *Le séminaire. Livre XI: Les quatre concepts fondamentaux de la psychanalyse* [published 1973] [*Seminar, Book XI: The Four Fundamental Concepts of Psychoanalysis*]

1966 (age 65): *Écrits*

1973 (age 72): *Le séminaire. Livre XX: Encore* [published 1998] [*On Feminine Sexuality and the Limits of Love and Knowledge*]

10

Roland Barthes, Literary Critic (1915–80) Structuralist Views: 1950s–67

Life and works

Roland Barthes was born on November 12, 1915 in Cherbourg, on the northwest seacoast of France. As was true for Sartre and for Camus, Barthes's father was in the military – he was a Naval Lieutenant – and similarly, he died when Barthes was an infant. Like Camus as well, Barthes lived in poverty with his mother while he was young. Also, as was experienced by Camus, Barthes contracted tuberculosis in his late teens, and had several relapses during his lifetime. He attended the University of Paris in his early twenties, studied Greek and Latin, and became involved in a theatre group. Two years after receiving a degree in Classical Letters from the University of Paris in 1939 (age twenty-four) at the outset of the Second World War, Barthes had a relapse of tuberculosis at age twenty-six, which led him to spend an extended time recuperating in a sanitarium. He received a degree in Grammar and Philosophy from the University of Paris in 1943 (age twenty-eight).

Finding a job was difficult in the 1945 aftermath, but Barthes was appointed to various teaching positions in Turkey and in Egypt, where he experienced colonialist attitudes first-hand, and where he also developed a revulsion towards them. In the 1950s he came into contact with Saussure's linguistic theory, and this inspired him to write on subjects in the field of semiology, specifically in connection with contemporary myths and fashion. Barthes modified his views during the late 1960s, and argued for the primacy of literature over science – a position akin to Jacques Lacan in this respect – and he began developing what, in retrospect, was a more poststructuralist outlook. Barthes's assorted writings soon brought him significant social recognition, not to mention helpful friends and intellectual influences such as Michel Foucault. Near the end of his career, in 1976, Barthes was appointed to the Collège de France as Professor of Literary Semiology, where he continued to lecture until his death four years later. Tragically, Barthes suffered a fate similar to Camus, for he also died as a result of traffic accident: after having lunch with a group of friends, among whom was the future leader of France, François Mitterand, Barthes was hit accidentally by a passing laundry truck. He died a month later from his injuries, on March 26, 1980, at age sixty-five.

Barthes's semiological cultural analyses: contemporary 'mythologies'

In our inquiry into French structuralism, we first considered Ferdinand de Saussure's linguistic theory, along with some of the structuralist thematics that derive from it. Among these were the 'arbitrary nature of the sign,' and its implication that meaning is fundamentally defined in reference to the internal relationships among the terms of a language. This developed into the more specific claim that these relationships have the form of binary oppositions. We also noted Saussure's emphasis upon 'synchronic' as opposed to 'diachronic' aspects of language. Then, after discussing Saussure's linguistics, we considered how Lévi-Strauss applied structuralist methods in anthropology in his studies of myth, and next, how Lacan applied structuralist principles within the field of psychoanalysis.

In Lacan's view, we encountered the position that psychological phenomena such as dreams and the various symptoms of mental illness, are understandable as being interpretable linguistic forms. In particular, Lacan's understanding of dreams and symptoms as metaphors were among the specific ways he applied Saussure's linguistic theory to psychoanalysis. But Lacan's view can be generalized: if we can interpret dreams and psychological symptoms as linguistically structured phenomena (e.g., as kinds of metaphor and metonymy), and if cultural phenomena are also linguistically structured phenomena, then we can understand a variety of cultural phenomena as if we were interpreting literary texts; we can 'read' cultural phenomena with a view toward discerning underlying, or unconscious, meanings, as if we were inter- preting a dream. According to this method, we can uncover what might be called the unconscious meaning of the cultural forms, which is to say that structural analysis can reveal aspects of our culture which were previously unrecognized in any explicit or conscious way. This is the sort of project typical of Roland Barthes's semiology – a version of the 'science of signs' as defined by Saussure – as it applies to cultural signs such as clothing and media icons of contemporary culture.

Barthes extends the structuralist method to cover a diverse range of cultural phenomena. Each of these (e.g., the system of fashion; the system of cultural icons; the system of food; the system of architecture) he understands as a semiological system composed of particular signifiers and signifieds that are arrangeable into a system of relationships analogous to the sentences of a language. As an example of Barthes's structuralist analysis and culture critique, we will consider his contemporary way of understanding mythology – a phenomenon which is ordinarily thought of in reference to ancient or tribal groups, as we saw in Lévi-Strauss's anthropological studies – which focuses upon present-day myths. His book, *Mythologies* (1957) – a book which is also inspired by Marxist ideas and which employs Marxist terminology – focuses on myths within our society, providing an analysis that reveals mythic expression to be an ideological tool of the prevailing bourgeois capitalist system. Assuming that social phenomena have a linguistic basis, he claims that 'myth is a type of speech' (cf. Lacan's 'the symptom is a metaphor') where what counts as speech is construed broadly:

> [Speech] can consist of modes of writing or of representations; not only written discourse, but also photography, cinema, reporting, sport, shows, publicity, all these can serve as a support to mythical speech. Myth can be defined neither by its object nor by its material, for any material can arbitrarily be endowed with meaning: the arrow which is brought in order to signify a challenge is also a kind of speech.[239]

In Barthes's semiological analysis of contemporary mythic thought, he accepts Saussure's linguistic theory, but he gives it a particular enhancement: Barthes claims that contemporary myth is constructed from already- existing signifiers (e.g., an arrow, a hunter, a movie-star, a mathematical equation, a guide-book, a soldier, a drink, a sport, etc.) and he maintains that the mythic results thereby constitute a 'second-order' semiological system. For instance, we may have the word-image 'wine' (signifier) which signifies the concept 'wine' (signified) in the ordinary, first-order language. In the second-order mythological language, the previously signified concept 'wine' becomes the signifier for a 'drink with transformative power.' Barthes's analysis of mythological meaning into a relationship between a first-order 'signifier' and a second-order 'signified' is analogous to Freud's and Lacan's understanding of dreams as having a 'manifest' (first-order) content and a 'latent' (second-order) content.

Barthes's numerous and entertaining analyses are fairly straightforward and they do not exhibit the structural complexities which attend, for instance, some of Lévi-Strauss's analyses of tribal myths. This is a consequence of Barthes's political and commonsensical, as opposed to theoretically anthropological, interest in focusing on mythic thought. His aim is to identify some negative features of everyday myths that we can easily recognize, uncover their implicit or subliminal message, and use these revelations as a basis to criticize political conservatism.

To begin, Barthes points out that 'myth' – as he understands the term in reference to contemporary myths – is a mode of speech which robs the first-order signifier of its meaning. When a signifier such as the famous mathematical formula '$E=mc^2$' – a formula which is rich in meaning within the context of theoretical physics – becomes a contemporary mythological image for 'the secret of the world,' it immediately becomes superficial, and suitable for cartoon-like representations:

> The historic equation $E=mc^2$, by its unexpected simplicity, almost embodies the pure idea of the key, bare, linear, made of one metal, opening with a wholly magical ease a door which had resisted the desperate efforts of centuries. Popular imagery faithfully expresses this: *photographs* of Einstein show him standing next to a blackboard covered with mathematical signs of obvious complexity; but *cartoons* of Einstein (the sign that he has become a legend) show him chalk still in hand, and having just written on an empty blackboard, as if without preparation, the magic formula of the world.[240]

In the following example, Barthes criticizes the superficial mentality that underlies popular tour guides, as they mythologically characterize a variety of social groups:

> For the *Blue Guide*, men exist only as 'types.' In Spain, for instance, the Basque is an adventurous sailor, the Levantine a light-hearted gardener, the Catalan a clever tradesman and the Cantabrian a sentimental highlander. We find again here this disease of thinking in essences, which is at the bottom of every bourgeois mythology of man (which is why we come across it so often). The ethnic reality of Spain is thus reduced to a vast classical ballet, a nice neat commedia

dell'arte, whose improbable typology serves to mask the real spectacle of conditions, classes and professions.[241]

By using the term 'robbery' in his characterization of myth, Barthes suggests that the process of myth-making objectionably reduces complicated themes and people to abstract and superficial presentations. He claims further that deception is involved, and he introduces the concept of an 'alibi' to express this idea. In an alibi, a person who is accused of a crime asserts that he or she was in some other place during the time of the crime. When myth is used for political purposes – for instance, when a political leader is shown shaking the hands of an ordinary citizen – the 'shaking hand' is the political leader's 'alibi.' The leader is suspected of being corrupt, but the shaking of hands represents the leader's honesty, or even-handedness. Barthes illustrates this in his analysis of the meanings of children's toys:

> The fact that French toys *literally* prefigure the world of adult functions obviously cannot but prepare the child to accept them all, by constituting for him, even before he can think about it, the alibi of a Nature which has at all times created soldiers, postmen, and Vespas.[242] Toys here reveal the list of all the things the adult does not find unusual: war, bureaucracy, ugliness, Martians, etc.[243]

In conjunction with his conceptions of myth as 'robbery' and as 'alibi,' Barthes makes a generalized claim that myth works generally in favor of the bourgeois class that holds political power, mainly because he regards myth as a force of conservatism. Barthes observes generally, though, how myth can be an effective form of propaganda which can work for anyone who employs its techniques. Since myth shows itself as an immediate 'fact,' it misleadingly suggests a natural, and not arbitrary, connection between the signifier and the signified. Barthes notes how this 'natural' connection between signifier and signified is often used by socially powerful classes to perpetuate through myth, an ideology that functions to sustain their power. Since the myth's constellation of meanings that support the established government is portrayed as 'natural' or 'eternally true,' the rhetorical effect is to lead people to believe that these meanings have been written into the very fabric of things:

> What the world supplies to myth is an historical reality, defined, even if this goes back quite a while, by the way in which men have produced or used it; and what myth gives in return is a natural image of this reality. And just as bourgeois ideology is defined by the abandonment of the name 'bourgeois,' myth is constituted by the loss of the historical

quality of things: in it, things lose the memory that they once were made. The world enters language as a dialectical relation between activities, between human actions; it comes out of myth as a harmonious display of essences. A conjuring trick has taken place; it has turned reality inside out, it has emptied it of history and has filled it with nature, it has removed from things their human meaning so as to make them signify a human insignificance. The function of myth is to empty reality: it is, literally, a ceaseless flowing out, a haemorrhage, or perhaps an evaporation, in short a perceptible absence.[244]

In the following excerpt, Barthes is even more explicit:

Statistically, myth is on the right. There, it is essential; well-fed, sleek, expansive, garrulous, it invents itself ceaselessly. It takes hold of everything, all aspects of the law, of morality, of aesthetics, of diplomacy, of household equipment, of Literature, of entertainment ... The oppressed makes the world, he has only an active, transitive (political) language; the oppressor conserves it, his language is plenary, intransitive, gestural, theatrical: it is Myth. The language of the former aims at transforming, of the latter at eternalizing.[245]

In his description of wine as a mythological image of transformation, Barthes does not hesitate to add that the contents of modern myths frequently support the established capitalistic system:

The mythology of wine can in fact help us to understand the usual ambiguity of our daily life. For it is true that wine is a good and fine substance, but it is no less true that its production is deeply involved in French capitalism, whether it is that of the private distillers or that of the big settlers in Algeria who impose on the Muslims, on the very land of which they have been dispossessed, a crop of which they have no need, while they lack even bread. There are thus very engaging myths which are however not innocent. And the characteristic of our current alienation is precisely that wine cannot be an unalloyedly blissful substance, except if we wrongfully forget that it is also the product of an expropriation.[246]

In *Mythologies*, Barthes spoke both entertainingly and soberly about the mythologies of wine and milk, along with steak and chips, plastics, and soap detergent. If he had been writing fifty years later, he no doubt would have included a section on the mythology of popular drinks such as tea and coffee, the sociological and economic contours of which are comparable to the wine described above.

The transition from 'structuralism' to 'post-structuralism': Barthes on the distinction between 'literature' and 'science'

In his essay, 'Science Versus Literature' (1967), Barthes writes the following:

> French university departments keep an official list of the social and human sciences recognized as being taught, and are thus restricted to awarding degrees in specific subjects; it is possible to become a doctor of aesthetics, psychology or sociology, but not of heraldry, semantics or victimology. It is thus the institution which directly determines the nature of human knowledge, by imposing its own modes of division and classification on it, in exactly the same way that a language, with its 'compulsory headings' (and not only its exclusions), obliges us to think in a certain way.[247]

Barthes compares the set of concepts that define university curricula – and hence, the set of concepts that partially determine accepted categories of 'knowledge' – with the set of concepts embodied within any language in general. His claim is that both sets of concepts impose their modes of division and classification upon us, and thereby determine us to think in certain ways. By its very structure, any specific language includes certain possibilities for thought while it excludes others.

Through his use of the term 'imposes,' Barthes expresses an extreme view that derives from his adherence to Saussurean linguistics. For it suggests that the categories of the language are mostly arbitrary, that they could be different from what they are, and that the categories we have are thereby 'imposed' upon us by social entities such as university institutions. Although the imposition of arbitrary categories often occurs, there is less flexibility than Barthes suggests, when we consider the categories of language as a whole. In theory, perhaps, there could be a language that distinguishes, for example, only two 'colors' (e.g., 'light' and 'dark'), but people might have a difficult time surviving with such an abstract and limited mode of discrimination. It is imaginable, similarly, that we attend only to color values and ignore differences in hue, but it seems unlikely as a matter of practice. Although Barthes extends to the general sphere of language, and its own supposedly analogous imposition of categories, his observations about the institutional impositions of linguistic categories – impositions that he claims are arbitrary – we can wonder whether some of the more physiologically grounded and survival-relevant categories that we use are less open to modification in response to mere institutional or linguistic decisions.

Moreover, in reference to the categories that Barthes claims are imposed upon us by the social institutions, we can ask how, and why, an institution would make such an imposition. In some cases, this might involve a matter of one group exercising power over another, but in other cases, it might be a response to a prevailing social demand. An example of the former might be a conception of 'worker' which is embodied in a taxation code and imposed upon a general population in the interest of a powerful subset of the population; an example of the latter might be the creation of a new university department called 'women's studies,' established in communal response to an increasing social recognition of women's rights. In both kinds of case, though, Barthes suggests that categories of this type are imposed upon us by the social institutions. If, however, one is a participating member of the institution itself and is involved in legislating new rules and modes of conceptualization, the term 'imposition' becomes inappropriate. Language is not always oppressive, in short.

At this time (1967), Barthes's more extreme mode of expression reveals his interest in challenging the social legitimacy of the sciences, for he believes that literary studies had been accorded a subordinate status by the then prevailing social institutions. He wishes to overturn this mode of social valuation – to revalue the standing values, as Nietzsche would say – by arguing that literature is a more fundamental field of study than science.[248] His first move in this project was to challenge the institutional status of science as a superior mode of inquiry, for he believes that literature has exactly the same intellectual properties that the defenders of science use to justify the respected social status of science. According to Barthes, literature addresses the same topics, tries to formulate a total picture of things, has research methods, and has an ethic. Since it parallels science in these fundamental ways, Barthes claims that literature deserves at least an equal social status.

An opponent might argue that the crucial difference between science and literature is that science is objective, neutral, and universal in its style of inquiry, whereas literature is subjective, and frequently attends to the unique perspective of the individual. With such variable interests, literature cannot be a discipline capable of revealing practical and universal knowledge of the kind obtained, for instance, in the field of atomic physics.

Barthes addresses this objection in a way that sets the tone of much poststructuralist thought: he challenges the universal legitimacy of the concepts of neutrality and objectivity. Barthes begins his argument by distinguishing between science and literature in reference to a difference in their respective attitudes towards language: in science, language 'is simply an instrument, which it profits to make as transparent and neutral as possible;' in literature, language cannot be regarded as peripheral or as merely an instrument, since 'language is literature's Being, its very world.'[249]

Barthes's point is that science regards language as an accidental feature of its inquiry into the objective nature of things, whereas literature must, almost as a matter of definition, regard language as constitutive of any literary inquiry. He perceives that the scientific mentality, as he understands it, implicitly assumes that its proper objects of inquiry exist independently of language. Since Barthes operates with the Saussurean linguistic assumption that language and thought are inseparable, and hence that language and what counts as 'the world,' are inseparable, he denies that there are any objects that exist in complete independence from the contours of language. So to the extent that Saussure's linguistics is questionable, Barthes will have one less reason to question the legitimacy of scientific inquiry, as opposed to what literary theory provides. At this point in time, one can say that Barthes remains a general adherent of structuralist presuppositions.

Supposing with Saussure that thought and language must go hand in hand, Barthes asks a discerning question: what does the amalgamation of thought and language imply for our understanding of the structuralist method itself, which had hitherto been conceived of as a science. Saussure defined a new 'science,' which he called 'semiology,' the 'science of signs.' And at the beginnings of the structuralist movement, Lévi-Strauss applied this 'science of signs' to topics within the field of anthropology, offering analyses of mythology and kinship in terms of linguistic structures. And as we have seen, Lacan also applied quasi-structuralist methods to Freud's psychoanalytic theory, and was thereby able to analyze all cultural phenomena in terms of processes analogous to those in dream formation and psychological symptom formation (viz., metaphor and metonymy).

Similarly, Barthes himself applied structuralist methods to contemporary cultural phenomena such as styles of fashion and modern mythological images and social icons. In each of these instances, the prevailing assumption was that the proper analysis of the phenomena in question should be scientific, and that the appropriate style of scientific inquiry is provided by Saussure's science of signs. It was assumed that the proper study of social phenomena is informed by linguistics, conceived of as a science, at least the cases of Lévi-Strauss and Barthes's work in *Mythologies*. Although Lacan adhered to a Saussurean conception of language, he foreshadowed the questions Barthes asked explicitly in 1967 by questioning the assumption that the human mind can be understood exclusively in scientific terms.

In his inquiry into the distinction between science and literature, Barthes notes that all sciences (including linguistics, the foundation of structuralist method) require a view of language as detached, neutral, and objective. With respect to linguistics, conceived of as a science, we arrive at the view that the very language linguistics uses to describe language must also be detached and neutral. This is to say, as noted, that the language of linguistics must be conceived of as a mere instrument to get at the heart of language. The essence of language that the science of linguistics seeks thus turns out to be a language-independent entity – a conclusion that is paradoxical, if not contradictory.

Barthes argues that language, when it is considered to be an object of scientific inquiry, cannot be regarded as being on a par with the traditional objects of scientific inquiry, such as rocks, electrons, or plants. For in linguistic inquiry, we must use language itself to investigate language.[250] If the structure of language revealed by linguistics can only be language itself, then we cannot regard the language we use as being independent of, and as being a mere instrument within, our inquiry. Barthes concludes from these reflections that structuralism cannot consistently conceive of itself as a science. He claims, rather, that it must conceive of itself as literature and as discourse:

> In short, structuralism will be just one more 'science' (several are born each century, some of them only ephemeral) if it does not manage to place the actual subversion of scientific language at the centre of its programme, that is, to 'write itself.' How could it fail to question the very language it uses in order to know language? The logical continuation of structuralism can only be to rejoin literature, no longer as an 'object' of analysis but as the activity of writing, to do away with the distinction derived from logic which turns the work itself into a language-object and science into a meta-language, and thus to forgo that illusory privilege which science attaches to the possession of a captive language.
>
> It remains therefore for the structuralist to turn himself into a 'writer,' certainly not in order to profess or practise 'fine style,' but in order to rediscover the crucial problems involved in every utterance, once it is no longer wrapped in the beneficent cloud of strictly *realist* illusions, which see language simply as the medium of thought.[251]

Barthes's questioning of structuralism's status as a science has widespread implications: if structuralism itself is assimilated into literature, then so will our understanding of the social institutions which are analyzed according to structuralist principles. Since all social phenomena are regarded as linguistically grounded within the structuralist framework, and since structuralist methods are transformed into literature through Barthes's argument, we arrive at the view that social phenomena can be understood as modes of literature. This suggests a view where it makes some sense to speak of human life itself as a kind of literature – a position that undermines purely scientific attempts to understand people and the nature of human society, and that renders the term 'social science,' a contradiction in terms.

In support of his claim that, as a discipline, science is subordinate to literature, Barthes asserts that there is always a grammatical subject in any mode of discourse, and that – invoking Lacan – this subject is itself constituted within the discourse in any number of imaginary ways:

> Every utterance implies its own subject, whether this subject be expressed in an apparently direct fashion, by the use of 'I,' or indirectly, by being referred to as 'he,' or avoided altogether by means of impersonal constructions. These are purely grammatical decoys, which do no more than vary the way in which the subject is constituted within the discourse, that is, the way he gives himself to others, theatrically or as a phantasm; they all refer therefore to forms of the imaginary. The most specious of these forms is the privative, the very one normally practised in scientific discourse, from which the scientist excludes himself because of his concern for objectivity. What is excluded, however, is always only the 'person,' psychological, emotional or biographical, certainly not the subject. It could be said moreover that this subject is heavy with the spectacular exclusion it has imposed on its person, so that, on the discursive level – one, be it remembered, which cannot be avoided – objectivity is as imaginary as anything else.[252]
>
> The notion of 'writing' implies indeed that language is a vast system, none of whose codes is privileged or, if one prefers, central, and whose various departments are related in a 'fluctuating hierarchy.' Scientific discourse believes itself to be a superior code; writing aims at being a total code, including its own forces of destruction. It follows that writing alone can smash the theological idol set up by a paternalistic science, refuse to be terror-stricken by what is wrongly thought of as the 'truth' of the content and of reasoning, and open up all three dimensions of language to research, with its subversions of logic, its mixing of codes, its shifts of meaning, dialogues and parodies.[253]

Barthes's extraordinary argument is that when we write or speak, we have available to us an entire spectrum of stylistic presentations. We can write in the first-person, second-person, third-person, with irony, with seriousness, with comedy, with objectivity, with strong emotion, with detachment, etc. None of these styles of presentation, he asserts, is privileged or superior to any other. He adds that there is a sense in which all of the styles are fictitious or 'imaginary.' There is always a grammatical subject or writer or speaker, but that – echoing

Sartre's claim twenty-five years earlier that consciousness has no essence – the constitution of this subject is an open-ended matter. Moreover, Barthes observes that language contains its own 'forces of destruction,' which serve to prohibit the permanent ascendancy of one way of writing over another. Since this variability of stylistic expression is a basic feature of discourse, and since we cannot avoid these multiple aspects, Barthes concludes that the scientific mode of discourse has no legitimate claim to superiority over other modes.

Barthes thereby questions the linguistic status of scientific inquiry, and argues that literary forms of discourse are equally, if not more, legitimate, if only because they are more comprehensive: they include the scientific mode of speech along with many other forms.[254] In this vein, Barthes observes that the intellectual pleasures of discourse have been overlooked as a consequence of the prevailing emphasis upon objectivity and neutrality in scientific discourse. If literary forms of discourse are, as they ought to be, given a status comparable, if not superior, to scientific forms, he believes that neglected and marginalized aspects of discourse – the merely pleasurable, the stylistic, the erotic – will regain the importance they deserve. He develops this theme a few years later in his book, *The Pleasure of the Text* (1973).

In sum, in connection with Barthes's reflection on the differences between science and literature, we can express the distinction between structuralism and post-structuralism in reference to how linguistics – the foundational inspiration of the structuralist method – is first conceived of as a science, and later regarded as being more akin to literary theory. Lévi-Strauss and Barthes (1950s) all worked in close sympathy with Saussure's understanding of semiology as the 'science of signs,' and throughout their structuralist investigations they believed that they were revealing social structures that were as objective as those discerned by natural scientists. Once we enter the 1960s, however, and once the scientific status of linguistics as a science is questioned at the end of that decade, literary methods begin to replace the typical structuralist, 1950s methods of Lévi-Strauss and the early Barthes. Once the aims of linguistics and the structuralist approach which stem from it are explicitly transformed from a scientific formulation into modes of literary analysis, we enter the post-structuralist phase of French thought.

Selected works of Roland Barthes (to 1967)

1953 (age 38): *Le degré zéro de l'écriture* [*Writing Degree Zero*]
1957 (age 42): *Mythologies*
1964 (age 49): *Eléments de sémiologie* [*Elements of Semiology*]
1967 (age 52): *Système de la mode* [*The Fashion System*]

PART 3

POSTSTRUCTURALISM AND POSTMODERNISM

11

Roland Barthes, Literary Critic (1915–80)
Poststructuralist Views: 1968–80

The year 1968 was a dramatic, tragic, and revolutionary one. On January 30, with the onset of the Tet Offensive, the war in Vietnam began to boil over;[255] on April 4, the African–American civil rights leader, Dr. Martin Luther King Jr. was assassinated; in mid-April, an inspiring, forward-looking, reformist government assumed control in Czechoslovakia; during the entire month of May, student protests in France quickly expanded into a nation-paralyzing, potentially revolutionary, general strike; on June 5, Senator Robert F. Kennedy was assassinated after having won the California primary election for the U.S. Presidency; on August 20–21, Warsaw Pact tanks, led by the Soviet Union, rolled into Czechoslovakia, crushing the hopes for the continuation of the liberal-minded government that had emerged only months earlier; on August 28, riots broke out during the Democratic National Convention in Chicago.

Within the wider context, 1968 was a year still haunted by the nationally traumatic and disheartening 1963 assassination of President John F. Kennedy, and it was more immediately framed by the 1967 Summer of Love in San Francisco, and the 1969 Woodstock Music Festival, the youthful atmospheres of which gave a sharply reactive voice against the confusing and controversial Vietnam war that had been pulsing in the social background throughout most of the decade. Compounding the intensity of the world-scene, the Cultural Revolution in China was also taking place during 1966–69.

The events of May 1968 in Paris issued in a large part from a standing French population that was frustrated and angered by repressive government policies – policies that were leading to increased poverty and unemployment – as it was repeatedly kept in check through the strong-arm tactics of the police. At the beginning of May, approximately five hundred students at the Sorbonne gathered in protest against the arrest of demonstrators at the Nanterre campus the day before, and, when the police heavy-handedly overreacted to the Sorbonne protest with an attempt at mass arrests, they were interrupted by the hostile reaction of yet more students. With the immediate closure of the university that followed, the situation mushroomed: virtually overnight, outraged students, lecturers, and their supporters took to the Parisian streets in the thousands, which precipitated yet even more violent confrontations with the police in the days and weeks to follow.

Within a short time, leaders of the major French trade unions joined in the social resistance, calling for a general strike, and by May 20, with approximately ten million workers on strike, the country came to virtual economic standstill. For a brief time, the people succeeded in rendering the government powerless. Order was eventually restored, elections were held in June, and social improvements were gradually put into effect. Overall, the events of May 1968 were an inspiration to those who believed in the power of the people, and these general conditions reverberated to inform the distinctive revolutionary spirit within French philosophical thought that emerged during 1968 and thereafter, as we will see here initially in the poststructuralist views of Roland Barthes.

'The death of the author' (1968)

Barthes and the critique of capitalism

In Roland Barthes's estimation, 'the author' has been the focal point for literary criticism during the past several hundred years: interpretations of texts have been directed traditionally toward the recovery of the author's intended meaning – a meaning assumed to be embodied within the text, and to be recoverable through the process of proper interpretation. Barthes also finds that as a consequence of this emphasis upon the recovery of the author's intentions, the text itself has been overlooked to the point where the author's personality and inner psychic workings have become the primary object of critical inquiry. He therefore regards the traditional emphasis as misdirected, and his primary concern is to refocus critical and interpretive interests to where he believes they rightly belong, namely, upon what the author wrote (i.e., the text itself) and upon the reader of that text. According to Barthes, the text and the reader, and not the person who wrote the text, should be the primary loci of interpretation. And among the two of these, Barthes believes that the text should take precedence:

> The image of literature to be found in ordinary culture is tyrannically centered on the author, his person, his life, his tastes, his passions, while criticism still consists for the most part in saying that Baudelaire's work is the failure of Baudelaire the man, Van Gogh's his madness, Tchaikovsky's his vice. The *explanation* of a work is always sought in the man who produced it, as if it were always in the end, through the more or less transparent allegory of the fiction, the voice of a single person, the *author*, 'confiding' in us.[256]

Barthes argues that during the early 1960s and before, the prevailing interpretive practice reflected an ideology of individualism – an ideology coincident with the emergence of capitalism and the modernist consideration of each person as an autonomous being. So underlying his prescription for a change of focus within literary criticism is a critique of modern capitalist society. He calls for a democratization within critical practice which challenges the authority of the author within literary criticism. Just as authoritarian rulers tend to prohibit the balanced participation of the citizens in the processes of government, Barthes believes that an attitude of slavish respect for a text's author likewise prohibits the balanced participation of the text's interpreters in the processes of interpretation.

Given Barthes's association of traditional literary criticism with capitalist ideology, his project in 'The Death of the Author' continues the themes he advanced in *Mythologies*, a decade earlier. In this earlier work, as we have seen, Barthes showed how many of the 'myths' which prevail in our society serve capitalistic interests – interests that often involve the objectionable exploitation of human life. For Barthes, the 'author' – insofar as this figure has appeared in traditional literary criticism – is yet another one of these myths. He draws the explicit parallel:

> Classic criticism has never paid any attention to the reader; for it, the writer is the only person in literature. We are now beginning to let ourselves be fooled no longer by the arrogant antiphrastical recriminations of good society in favor of the very thing it sets aside, ignores, smothers, or destroys; we know that to give writing its future, it is necessary to overthrow the myth: the birth of the reader must be at the cost of the death of the Author.[257]

Barthes associates capitalism with authoritarianism, and he writes with an imagery that derives from Karl Marx, invoking memories of how workers can be dominated, oppressed, and exploited by those relatively few capitalists who own the basic means of production. This connection allows Barthes to draw an analogy between the 'death of the author' in literary criticism and Marx's call for the overthrow of the factory owners. Barthes's proposed ideal within literary criticism is comparable to the communist model, wherein the instruments of oppression are taken over by those who were formerly oppressed. By analogy, the readers who were formerly oppressed by the author's authority – the authority as embodied within the text's alleged meaning – are urged to become the authorities of the text's meaning themselves. The birth of the reader is comparable to the communist liberation of the oppressed worker.

Just as Marx described the Protestant Reformation by saying that Martin Luther changed the priests into laymen by changing the laymen into priests, and just as Marx allowed us to understand the workers' revolution as a situation where factory-owners are turned into workers by turning workers into factory-owners, we can appreciate Barthes's proposed revolution in literary criticism as a situation where, by analogy, authors are turned into readers through the act of turning readers into authors. In this respect, Barthes intends to stimulate a revolution in literary criticism.

In its analogy to the Marxist critique of capitalism, Barthes's proposal to overthrow the authority of the author is psychologically attractive. We should, however, consider what standards of literary interpretation arise from such a proposal. If the author's authority is undermined, then we must ask whether the text itself imposes restrictions upon what can count as a legitimate or plausible interpretation. Continuing with the social–political comparisons introduced by Barthes, we might ask whether his alternative to a capitalist style of literary criticism suggests less of a communist style, and more of an anarchic style that imposes very few constraints upon the interpreter.

The author as a myth

Along with Sartre and Lacan, Barthes denies that the Cartesian conception of the self (viz., as an individual thinking substance) accurately characterizes human subjectivity. Within Barthes's particular perspective, he expresses this denial within the sphere of literary criticism and within his associated conceptions of language, writing, texts, and interpretation. Similar to Sartre and Lacan, he imagines the subject as a diffuse and only vaguely specifiable energy which has no precise borders. His way of describing this subjectivity, moreover, has a specifically linguistic emphasis:

Did he wish to *express himself*, he ought at least to know that the inner 'thing' he thinks to 'translate' is itself only a ready-formed dictionary, its words only explainable through other words, and so on indefinitely.[258]

From this excerpt, we can see how Barthes understands human subjectivity as a linguistic field – a field which is both ready-formed, insofar as language permeates and informs the contents of consciousness, and which is potentially endless in signification, insofar as the meaning of each word is perpetually deferred through its association with other words, and so on. What is commonly called 'expressing oneself,' becomes reinterpreted by Barthes as a process of mixing and recycling the terms and structures of the already-given language. He speaks at times as if this process is mostly mechanical and relatively non-creative; to express oneself amounts to not much more than mixing and matching previous writings, whereby one segment of writing is 'countered' by another:

Similar to Bouvard and Pécuchet, those eternal copyists, at once sublime and comic and whose profound ridiculousness indicates precisely the truth of writing, the writer can only imitate a gesture that is always anterior, never original. His only power is to mix writings, to counter the ones with the others, in such a way as never to rest on any one of them.[259]

According to Barthes, the process of writing issues from a subject – a subject whose articulated consciousness is, as Saussure would have it, thoroughly constituted by language – which has within itself a swirling array of textual segments. These segments are mixed and matched against other segments in an endless process of countering and counter-countering the segments that have already been written, and which are repeatedly instantiated in daily conversation. As they are read, written texts reverberate and rebound off the storehouse of texts both within and without the subject. Writing and 'expressing' are thereby conceived as a product of the interplay and counterplay of the texts both within and outside consciousness.

Within this model of writing, there is no need to postulate a 'self' or 'ego' that is uniquely responsible for the contents of what is written. In its own dynamic interplay of signs and textual segments, the properties of the language itself do most of the work. Barthes thus rejects the model of the individual author who composes a text and to whom we assign primary responsibility; instead he claims that 'language' itself does the writing, describing it as almost a transpersonal force operating through the writer's subjectivity:

In France, Mallarmé was doubtless the first to see and to foresee in its full extent the necessity to substitute language itself for the person who until then has been supposed to be its owner. For him, for us too, it is

language which speaks, not the author; to write, is, through a prerequisite impersonality (not at all to be confused with the castrating objectivity of the realist novelist), to reach that point, where only language
acts, 'performs' and not 'me.'[260]

The author as an individual – a being who is now rendered ineffectual in a
literary–critical sense – is replaced by another, far more expansive and intangible author, namely, language itself conceived as a force that operates through
human subjects. If we conceive of language as an impersonal 'author' that
transcends human individuality, many of Barthes's descriptions of writing –
ones which at first sight seem strange – begin to make sense. For example, his
positive reference to the surrealist's practice of automatic writing is consistent
with his view that a force more powerful than human individuality is at the
center of literary creativity. For the surrealists, it was the instinctual and over-
powering Freudian unconscious that was this generative force; for Barthes it is
language (recall how Lacan stated that the unconscious is a language),
conceived of as an infinite and multidimensional semantic energy. Also,
Barthes's dissolution of the 'author-who-expresses-previously-formulated-
meanings' into the 'scriptor-who-inscribes' is understandable once we recall
how he acknowledges only a vaguely defined, rhetorical subject which can be
'voiced' in linguistically alternative ways. That writing has very little to do with
an author's intentions, we find expressed in the following:

> Linguistically, the author is never more than the instance writing, just as
> *I* is nothing other than the instance saying *I*: language knows a 'subject,'
> not as a 'person,' and this subject, empty outside of the every enunci-
> ation which defines it, suffices to make language 'hold together,' suffices,
> that is to say, to exhaust it.[261]

Barthes expresses his conception of the death of the author not only through
his sympathy with Sartre's and Lacan's denial of the individual ego, along with
his claim that language rather than the individual author is the true voice of
the text, but also through his conception of writing. According to Barthes,
writing is a process that entails the author's demise in literary–critical significance, for it is supposedly a process that destroys every individual voice and
operates in a neutral zone where a multitude of interpretive perspectives are
possible.[262] The death of the author dissolves the traditional quest for a single,
true interpretation of the text:

> Succeeding the Author, the scriptor no longer bears within him
> passions, humours, feelings, impressions, but rather this immense
> dictionary from which he draws a writing that can know no halt: life

never does more than imitate the book, and the book itself is only a tissue of signs, an imitation that is lost, infinitely deferred.[263]

We know now that a text is not a line of words releasing a single 'theological' meaning (the 'message' of the Author–God) but a multi-dimensional space in which a variety of writings, none of them original, blend and clash. The text is a tissue of quotations drawn from the innumerable centers of culture.[264]

Here, the producers of literary works are 'scriptors' who write 'texts', all instances of which lack a single, determinate meaning. The subjects who write are not 'authors' who use language to 'express' their specific intentions and ideas; rather, language itself speaks through these subjects and does the writing. However, since language is infinitely complicated, there is a sense in which the writings of 'language' are endlessly complex, multidimensional, multi-interpretable, and open-ended:

Once the Author is removed, the claim to decipher a text becomes quite futile. To give a text an Author is to impose a limit on that text, to furnish it with a final signified, to close the writing. Such a conception suits criticism very well, the latter then allotting itself the important task of discovering the Author (or its hypostases: society, history, psyche, liberty) beneath the work: when the Author has been found, the text is 'explained' – victory to the critic.[265]

In precisely this way literature (it would be better from now on to say *writing*), by refusing to assign a 'secret', an ultimate meaning, to the text (and to the world as text), liberates what may be called an anti-theological activity, an activity that is truly revolutionary since to refuse to fix meaning is, in the end, to refuse God and his hypostases – reason, science, law.[266]

Similar to Jean-Paul Sartre's claim that consciousness is only a surface without any unconscious depths, Barthes claims that there is no depth to texts insofar as there is no single, underlying set of meanings that a text expresses.[267] Just as Sartre rejects the Freudian project of dream analysis – a process that aims to reveal the underlying meaning and unconscious intentions of dreams – Barthes rejects the idea of a literary criticism that aims to reveal the underlying meaning and (conscious or unconscious) intentions that supposedly inform texts. Barthes accordingly rejects the view that a text's meaning is antecedent to the formation of the text, just as a dream's meaning is antecedent to the dream. Although he conceives of language on a par with the unconscious, and speaks of writing almost as the surrealists described 'automatic writing' and the creation of poetry, Barthes does not ascribe any specifically intended meanings to texts, especially underlying or substantially permanent meanings.

Barthes's rejection of the traditional approach to the interpretation of texts thus introduces a new conception of textual interpretation. First, as mentioned above, he maintains that there is no closure in the process of interpretation; every text is inherently multidimensional, and there is consequently no final interpretation or authoritative reading. With this advocacy of this open-endedness of texts, Barthes sets forth a stance that entails a rejection of the tradi-tional endpoints of interpretation – ones which are typically grounded in concepts such as God, reason, science, or law. Barthes's denial of closure in textual interpretation, in effect, aims to undermine the authority of the concepts that have served to stabilize the practice of interpretation for centuries.

Once we reject the project of looking beneath the linguistic surface for a text's inner, hidden, or substantial meaning, we are left to extend our attention across that surface in diverging and intersecting directions. And this intro-duces a different attitude toward texts. No longer are we to decipher them, as if they contained a secret message; we are to disentangle them, in an effort to appreciate aesthetically the text's semantic tensions, complications, segmenta-tions, overlays, etc. We are to disentangle texts to acknowledge their structure, but without the aim of revealing some underlying meaning(s) they are presumed to express in any finalistic or permanent manner.

The 'birth of the reader'

Barthes concludes his famous essay by stating that the birth of the reader must be at the cost of the death of the author. One of the arguments he offers for the change of focus from author to reader considers how a reader – and presumably only a reader – can be aware of the variety of alternative meanings a text may embody. He claims that only the reader is in a position to integrate and organize a text's meanings. This is a questionable claim, as we shall see momentarily. The argument is as follows:

> Another – very precise – example will help to make this clear: recent research (J.-P. Vernant) has demonstrated the constitutively ambiguous nature of Greek tragedy, its texts being woven from words with double meanings that each character understands unilaterally (this perpetual misunderstanding is exactly the 'tragic'); there is, however, someone who understands each word in its duplicity and who, in addition, hears the very deafness of the characters speaking in front of him – this someone being precisely the reader (or here, the listener). Thus is revealed the total existence of writing: a text is made of multiple writings, drawn from

many cultures and entering into mutual relations of dialogue, parody, contestation, but there is one place where this multiplicity is focused and that place is the reader, not, as was hitherto said, the author.[268]

Barthes's argument is that a text is more properly focused upon the reader, as opposed to the author, because only the reader is in a position to discern the multiplicity of meanings that are present within a text. After providing what he believes is a convincing example, Barthes concludes his argument by comparing the reader's advantage, to the author's disadvantage. When we look at Barthes's argument, however, the contrast he actually draws is not between the reader and the author, but between the reader and the perspective of the characters within the text, for he compares the reader's awareness to the 'deafness,' not of the author, but of the characters, who are themselves unaware of the double-meanings they voice.

The argument does not show that the author was, or must have been, unaware of the double meanings that attend the character's words – and there is good reason to doubt this, since individual authors typically write the texts that we read. Relatively few texts (although there are some culturally important ones that fit this description) arrive in our hands via an untraceable oral tradition, and stand as an amalgamation of mostly unknown authors. And if single authors can be aware of the resonance of meanings in the texts they compose, just as the reader can, then the author and the reader are in a parallel position. With the more insightful and talented authors, one can reasonably speculate that such authors frequently embody more multiple-meanings within the text than most people are able to discern. (This is what can be meant, upon occasion, by characterizing someone, such as James Joyce, as a great writer.) So Barthes's argument is not persuasive in the version he offers.

A more convincing argument would illustrate how certain double, triple, quadruple meanings which are inherent in a text were not, in principle, accessible to the author. We might, for example, consider the set of Freudian, Marxist, and Feminist interpretations of Shakespeare's *Hamlet* that were presumably never within Shakespeare's awareness. Given that in such cases the author could not have imagined the text's meaning as construed according to one of the above styles of interpretation, we must refer to the reader as the focal point of textual meaning. This example shows that although Barthes's own argument is not altogether convincing, his point concerning the importance of the reader is not without plausibility.[269]

Suppose we follow Barthes for the moment, and hold that interpretation should be primarily reader-focused rather than author-focused. How are we to understand the nature of this reader? Since Barthes follows Sartre and Lacan in denying that there is any ego in general, who is it that does the interpreting of a text? Barthes explains:

> The reader is the space on which all the quotations that make up a writing are inscribed without any of them being lost; a text's unity lies not in its origin but in its destination. Yet this destination cannot any longer be personal: the reader is without history, biography, psychology; he is simply the *someone* who holds together in a single field all the traces by which the written text is constituted.[270]

We can question Barthes's claim that the reader is simply a linguistic space without personality, without history, without psychology, and without any individual identity. In its high degree of abstraction, the notion is problematic, for there are no provisions that distinguish different readers from one another – Barthes speaks as if 'the reader' exists on a level of abstraction that has no historical dimensions. Since 'the reader' amounts to a severe abstraction from actual circumstances, it is difficult to discuss in concrete terms how such an entity could understand or disentangle a text. For it is the very historical context of a particular reader that allows language to take a certain embodied form, and that allows particular readers to disentangle texts in accord with a specific knowledge of words, textual segments, etc. So when Barthes describes the reader as being without history and without biography, he removes some of the key features (e.g., historical hindsight; a knowledge of diverse texts) that place the reader in a more advantageous position in comparison to the author.

Barthes would like to advocate the birth of the reader, but the kind of reader he describes is, unfortunately, disembodied and detached from concrete, historical life. As he characterizes 'the reader,' such a being cannot be an actual, living person who does any actual reading at some time and place. It is possible, then, to wonder whether Barthes has unintentionally brought about the death of the reader in his efforts to precipitate the death of the author. By dissolving the ego, the biography and the intentions of the author, he appears to have been led – owing to his general rejection of the ego in general – to dissolve those very aspects of the reader as well.

Barthes's conception of writing

According to one widespread view, the act of writing is fundamentally an act of transcription or recording: when we write, we allegedly take our previously formed thoughts, and fit them into written words for the purpose of preserving those thoughts, either for ourselves or for others. This view has prevailed, not only as an account of writing, but more generally as an account of artistic creation. Mozart, for instance, stated that he composed some of his music entirely within his imagination, without the aid of either a musical instrument or a pen and paper, and only later recorded the thoughts in musical notation for the purposes of performance and future preservation.[271] According to this imagination-centered conception of writing and artistic creation, thinking comes first, and the material embodiment of that thought – for example, as a piece of writing – comes afterwards as a recording device. The thinking or imaginative process creates a thought-product, and writing then functions to preserve the product within a publicly accessible and reproducible format. Thought comes first, and the written word comes later.

This conception of writing, and its accompanying supposition that there is an author who has definite intentions which are expressed through writing, is connected closely to Barthes's criticism of the scientific conception of language. On this scientific conception, language operates as an instrument for the investigation of a language-independent reality. Just as the contents of an author's creative imagination are believed to be independent of writing, the reality investigated by the scientist is believed to remain independent of language. Just as the author uses writing as an instrument merely to record his or her intentions, the natural scientist uses language as an instrument merely to record his or her insights about the physical world. In both cases, writing and language are not essential to creative processes or to moments of scientific insight.

We have seen Barthes argue against the idea that language and science can be separated from each other, as he claimed that the voice of scientific neutrality is only one of many possible voices through which a subject can be linguistically constituted. Similarly, Barthes argues further that the author cannot be removed from language: by claiming that every author is actually a linguistically constituted subject, following Saussure's linguistic theory, Barthes maintains that it is impossible to conceive of the author as being independent of language, and hence, as being independent of written language, if the author is a writer. With his assertion that the subject is itself a 'dictionary' composed of textual fragments, Barthes rejects the idea that authorship and artistic creativity in general can be detached from their modes of expression, all of which are linguistic to a significant extent. This brings us to a set of interrelated theoretical moves in Barthes's thought: (1) 'language-as-mere-instrument' and 'language-as-mere-accessory' are replaced by 'language-as-omnipresent' and 'language-as-inescapable;' (2) 'author-as-ego' is replaced by 'language-as-speaker;' (3) 'author-as-authority' is replaced by 'reader-as-authority;' (4) 'the author's work' is replaced by 'the text;' (5) 'author' is replaced by 'scriptor.'

We can appreciate Barthes's reworking of the traditional understanding of writing by reflecting upon an analogy – one which he believes is representative of the traditional view. Barthes claims that the author's work is analogous to a parent's child, and that society itself conceives of the relationship between author and work in this very manner:

> The author is the respected father and owner of his work: literary science therefore teaches *respect* for the manuscript and the author's declared intentions, while society asserts the legality of the relation of author to work (the '*droit d'auteur*' or 'copyright,' in fact of recent date since it was only really legalized at the time of the French Revolution).[272]

Barthes's conception of the death of the author thereby challenges the prevailing conceptions of authors, their works, the legal system which protects such works, the process of artistic creation, and the nature of the subject itself, conceived of as an individual ego. It also challenges what it means to interpret some piece of writing, along with the idea of science and its alleged neutrality. To illustrate the kind of systematic change that Barthes urges, we can note how he describes the transition in the conception of writing:

> The removal of the Author ... utterly transforms the modern text ... The temporality is different. The Author, when believed in, is always conceived of as the past of his own book, which is to say that he exists before it, thinks, suffers, lives for it, is in the same relation of antecedence to his work as a father to his child. In complete contrast, the modern scriptor is born simultaneously with the text, is in no way equipped with a being preceding or exceeding the writing, is not the subject with the book as predicate; there is no other time than that of the enunciation and every text is eternally written *here and now*.[273]

By rejecting the idea that writing is only a tool that we use to convey our thoughts, Barthes is led to postulate an intrinsic value for writing. This involves a different conception of the temporality of writing – one that dispenses with the concept of some previously existing author who later uses language as an instrument. One way to conceive of writing as being valuable for its own sake, is to dissolve the idea of an independent author. Barthes consequently locates writing in the here and now and refers no longer to an author *per se*, but to a 'scriptor' born simultaneously with the text.

It is worth pausing for a moment upon Barthes's supposition that an author is related to his or her textual work, as a father is related to his child. Since Barthes speaks of the death of the author in parallel with the death of the father, and thereby urges us to eliminate the author/father in our practice of literary interpretation, it is easy to draw a connection between the death of the author/father and Freud's Oedipus Complex (viz., to the basic psychological tensions grounded in a male child's perceived rivalry between himself and his father for his mother's attention). In his analogy between 'work' and 'child,' Barthes does not specify that the child is a male child, but neither is it necessary for him to conceive of the author as a father as opposed to a mother (which would be a more natural association). Since Barthes has chosen the father-image as opposed to the mother-image to represent the author, and speaks of the death of this author/father, we can draw the psychoanalytic analogy without too much difficulty.

The import of this psychoanalytic connection coheres with the revolutionary intentions that inspire Barthes's overall view. Within Freudian psychoanalysis, resolving the conflict between oneself and one's same-sex parent marks an important point on the road to maturity and independence. The rhetoric of Barthes's discussion of the death of the author similarly suggests the theme of achieving independence, establishing one's freedom, and making a mark of one's own upon the world. Moreover, we find this death of the author/death of the father/death of the parental authority theme reinforced once more in Barthes's association of the death of the author with the rejection of single-meaning interpretations of the Bible – interpretations that he regards as 'theological' and as essentially authoritarian. By questioning this style of theological interpretation which alleges to provide the true interpretation of texts such as the Bible, Barthes rhetorically invokes associations between his view and forces which have been traditionally antagonistic to God's authority, namely, demonic forces:

> Against the work, therefore, the text could well take as its motto the words of the man possessed by demons (*Mark* 5:9): 'My name is Legion: for we are many.' The plural of demoniacal texture which opposes text to work can bring with it fundamental changes in reading, and precisely in areas where monologism appears to be the Law: certain of the 'texts' of Holy Scripture traditionally recuperated by theological monism (historical or analogical) will perhaps offer themselves to a diffraction of meanings.[274]

Barthes's rhetorical connection between the multidimensional, multi-interpretable text and what is demonic, has also a philosophic and literary resonance with Friedrich Nietzsche's proclamation of the death of God.[275] For Nietzsche, the single, true interpretation of all things allegedly issues from God's absolute perspective, and if God is conceived of as being 'dead,' then there is no longer recognized any single, absolute interpretation. Nietzsche's atheism is designed to urge people to accept their ability, and their freedom, to construct their own perspectives on the world.

It is revealing that Nietzsche's death of God proposal compares with Martin Luther's protest against Roman Church authority in the latter's reformist claim that scripture alone should be the final authority in all matters of faith and doctrine.[276] In Nietzsche's case, the principle is the same, except that in place of the Roman Church's authority, we encounter God's authority itself under attack. In Barthes's conception of the death of the author, the theme of defying authority is present once more. For once we associate 'author' with 'creator,' Barthes's anti-theological spirit becomes apparent.

Theological overtones in Barthes's account of language, writing, and texts

Barthes conceives of the death of the author as a revolutionary principle, and insofar as he associates the author with forces of oppression, he invites comparisons between his view and Marx's critique of capitalism. As we have seen, just as Marx called for the overthrow of the oppressive capitalists, Barthes calls for the overthrow of the oppressive authors. From what we have noted in the above associations between Barthes and Nietzsche, in conjunction with Barthes's own descriptions of his view in terms of the demonic motto, 'We are Legion,' the distinctly anti-theological tone to Barthes's outlook should be evident. If we look more closely, however, it is surprising to discover some parallels between Barthes's poststructuralist conceptions of language and texts, and some traditional theistic conceptions.

Consider the following features of Barthes's view: (1) the subordination of the individual to language itself (i.e., the idea that the author's ego or individuality is a fiction, and that there is only a linguistically constituted subject); (2) the idea that the author, as ego, does not speak or write, but that language itself speaks or writes through the subject; (3) the idea that language is infinite and multidimensional and that there is no single, finite interpretation for any given text; and (4) the conception of writing as being a spontaneous activity, comparable to the surrealist's intuitively generated automatic writing.

Although many aspects of Barthes's thought run counter to traditional theism, it is intriguing how closely Barthes's central claims regarding language, the subject, writing, and texts, match some traditional theistic conceptions. First, Barthes describes the subject as a complex linguistic field, or as a 'dictionary' that overshadows and puts into question any finite and definitely contoured integrity that the subject might have as an independent ego or self. Due to its constitution by language, the subject cannot determine any precise boundaries to its individuality and it regards itself as absorbed by, and as part of, a power far greater than itself. One connection to traditional theology, then, is the way in which the individual is here conceived of as part of a larger, infinite power. In Barthes's case, this power is language, and not God. Yet both are infinite beings that overwhelm and absorb the individual.

Note further how Barthes eliminates the voice of the author and replaces this with the voice of language itself. It is language – a power that transcends the author's individuality – that speaks through the author.[277] The author-as-individual does not create a literary work; it is language that inscribes a multi-dimensional text by means of a scriptor. Once we are presented with this trans-individual power which speaks through individual people, it is difficult to resist the analogy between this linguistic power and the voice of God who allegedly speaks through inspired people such as, in past times, the prophets, and similarly, artistic geniuses. Such inspired people can be regarded as God's appointed scribes. Although Barthes rejects the conception of the author as a distinct, authoritative individual, so does the age-old conception of the artist as being divinely inspired: artists who are divinely inspired do not attribute their works to their own making, but regard them as the creations of a higher power that works through them.

Third, Barthes's conception of the text as infinitely interpretable and multi-dimensional is consistent with, if not suggestive of, the text as having originated from a source that transcends the finite powers of human individuality. An endlessly interpretable, multidimensional text is exactly the kind of product we would expect to find if God were the voice behind the text. Since God is infinite, it would make sense to expect God's message to be infinitely complex and multidimensional. This, of course, is not to maintain that Barthes believed that language is the way God communicates with us. Barthes was an atheist. It is to show that Barthes's atheistic conception of language has features that theists have also attributed to God, namely, infinity and multidimensionality. Perhaps one could say that at this point in his career, Barthes venerated language itself, even though his attitude towards language would grow more unfavorable as time went on.

Fourth, Barthes's characterization of writing in connection with the surrealist's practice of automatic writing reveals his conception of the writing process as operating without the formulation of prior intentions or reflections. There is a spontaneity and intuitiveness associated with Barthes's conception of writing which, given this linkage to the surrealists, recalls the romantic conception of artistic genius, wherein the artist is mysteriously, spontaneously and intuitively inspired by transcendent powers.

These connections to traditional theism, romanticism and surrealism lead to general speculations about whether there is an implicitly religious aspect within Barthes's poststructuralist theory of language. According to his theory, there is a distinct submission of the individual to the powers of language, and a celebration of language's infinity and multidimensionality – both of which lend support to an analogy between linguistic qualities and divine qualities. Side by side with these theological resonances, it must be added, we encounter distinctly anti-theological themes: a Marxist and Nietzschean call for freedom from oppressive authorities, an existential focus on the here and now, a centeredness within history and the changes upon language which history perpetuates, and an implicit rejection of all views which allege to determine a specific meaning for human life. So Barthes is still far from being a theist in literary disguise. To appreciate some of the psychological appeal of poststructuralist conceptions of language, however, we can nonetheless attend to the theological parallels. The thought of language's infinity and overwhelmingness is close to the mystical image of God as an infinite ocean into which we, as droplets of water, rise out of, embody in microcosm, and inevitably return.

The pleasure of the text

Barthes's revolutionary conception of the text has another theoretically important and psychologically attractive dimension. This is a more existential association, traceable to Albert Camus, between reading and seduction – an association which Barthes characterizes as 'the pleasure of the text.' Having dissolved the traditional quest for the single correct or true interpretation of the work, along with the cluster of classical aesthetic values such as unity and coherence which accompany such an interest, Barthes introduces an alternative set of aesthetic values which are consistent with the idea of a text's multidimensionality and infinite interpretability. Among these is the value of pleasure, which he opposes to the 'nausea' of the traditional literary structures. The pleasure is predominantly sensuous and erotic. Barthes's aesthetic thus opposes both the classical Aristotelian values of unity, limitation, coherence, structure, and the necessary unfolding of the plot, as well as displeasureable existential nausea that can sometimes permeate human experience.[278] In place of the Aristotelian values and displeasureable experiences of nausea, Barthes retains an existential dimension, but as inspired by Camus, insofar as Camus celebrated erotic, pleasure-centered seducers such as Don Juan. Barthes writes as follows:

> The text you write must prove to me that it desires me. This proof exists: it is writing. Writing is: the science of the various blisses of language, its Kama Sutra (this science has but one treatise: writing itself).[279]

The distrust of the stereotype (linked to the bliss of the new word or the untenable discourse) is a principle of absolute instability which respects nothing (no content, no choice). Nausea occurs whenever the liaison of two important words follows of itself. And when something follows of itself, I abandon it: that is bliss.[280]

The above excerpts recall some of the existential themes and concepts from Camus and Sartre. Just as Camus imagined the seducer as an instance of the absurd person, we find Barthes's scriptor and text both assuming the attitude of the seducer. The association to the existential theme of absurdity is operative not only in the concept of a seducer; it is present in Barthes's claim that the text never allows a final, coherent, and fully rational interpretation. In this sense, Barthes's text is as rationality resistant as Camus's seducer, actor, and conqueror, and as rationality resistant as the ultimately meaningless world of daily experience within Sartre's outlook. Barthes's characterization of the text is also sublime, insofar as what is sublime defies all efforts to comprehend it fully.

We also find specifically Sartrean themes in Barthes's conception of the pleasure of the text. We have already heard Barthes maintain that there is no exit from language, and hence, from texts. What further parallels Sartre's view is Barthes's resistance to make any final or circumscribed adventure – an experience with a beginning, middle, and end – out of the text. This amounts to a reluctance on Barthes's part to extract an essence or static meaning from the text. For Sartre, as for Barthes, such strategies amount to a mode of self-deception and bad faith, as Sartre would describe it.

An interesting twist that Barthes makes in contrast to Sartre is his positive characterization of the more down-to-earth aspects of life – ones which Sartre would describe as nauseating. Barthes, however, speaks most positively of the fleshiness of the lips, of the 'presence of the human muzzle,' and of the 'grain of the voice,' when he refers to the aesthetic value of the pleasure of the text. In the following excerpt, this positive attitude toward the existential nuances of bodily presence is clear:

Due allowance being made for the sounds of the language, *writing aloud* is not phonological but phonetic; its aim is not the clarity of messages, the theater of emotions; what it searches for (in a perspective of bliss) are the pulsional incidents, the language lined with flesh, a text where we can hear the grain of the throat, the patina of consonants, the voluptuousness of vowels, a whole carnal stereophony: the articulation of the body, of the tongue, not that of meaning, of language. A certain art of singing can give an idea of this vocal writing; but since melody is dead, we may find it more easily today at the cinema. In fact, it suffices that the cinema capture the sound of speech *close up* (this is, in fact, the generalized definition of the 'grain' of writing) and make us hear in their materiality, their sensuality, the breath, the gutturals, the fleshiness of the lips, a whole presence of the human muzzle (that the voice, that writing, be as fresh, supple, lubricated, delicately granular and vibrant as an animal's muzzle), to succeed in shifting the signified a great distance and in throwing, so to speak, the anonymous body of the actor into my ear: it granulates, it crackles, it caresses, it grates, it cuts, it comes: that is bliss.[281]

One way to interpret Barthes's positive interpretation of pleasure, and its existential manifestations, is in reference to his overall revolutionary and socially critical interests. We have seen above that Barthes contrasts nausea with pleasure. In the same excerpt, more revealingly, Barthes associates nausea with stereotypes – that style of thinking he located at the heart of contemporary capitalist mythology, and which Sartre identified with essentialism and 'bad faith.' If we consider these themes in conjunction with what we have seen so far, we can form two clusters of terms within Barthes's thinking: (1) Text-Scriptor-Pleasure-Play-Multidimensionality-Freedom, as opposed to, (2) Work-Author-Nausea-Boredom-Onedimensionality-Oppression. The former cluster is positively valued; the latter cluster is negatively valued.

Barthes's 'inaugural lecture, Collège de France' (January 7, 1977)

In 1977, Barthes was elected to the prestigious Collège de France and chose as the title for his position, Chair of Literary Semiology. In his inaugural lecture, he forecasted the style of his prospective teaching and research, summarizing many of his previous intellectual interests and situating them within a new idiom. This, specifically, was the theme of 'power' and its embodiment in language – an emphasis that Barthes adopted from his friend, Michel Foucault. The following excerpts from Barthes's inaugural lecture illustrate Foucault's major influence at this point in Barthes's theorizing:

And yet, what if power were plural, like demons? 'My name is Legion,' it could say; everywhere, on all sides, leaders, massive or minute organizations, pressure groups or oppression groups, everywhere 'authorized' voices which authorize themselves to utter the discourse of all power: the discourse of arrogance. We discover then that power is present in the most delicate mechanism of social exchange: not only in the State, in classes, in groups, but even in fashion, public opinion, entertainment, sports, news, family and private relations, and even in the liberating impulses which attempt to counteract it. I call the discourse of power any discourse which engenders blame, hence guilt, in its recipient.[282]

For if it [power] is plural in a social sense, power is, symmetrically, perpetual in historical time. Exhausted, defeated here, it reappears there; it never disappears. Make a revolution to destroy it, power will immediately revive and flourish again in the new state of affairs. The reason for this endurance and this ubiquity is that power is the parasite of a trans-social organism, linked to the whole of man's history and not only to his political, historical history. This object in which power is inscribed, for all of human eternity, is language, or to be more precise, its necessary expression: the language we speak and write.[283]

Language is legislation, speech is its code. We do not see the power which is in speech because we forget that all speech is a classification, and that all classifications are oppressive: *ordo* means both distribution and commination.[284]

In his essay 'From Work to Text' (1971), we have seen Barthes use the same biblical excerpt, 'We are Legion,' to refer to how texts embody a multiplicity of meanings. The demonic and multiple associations attached to the phrase epitomized one of his central insights. In the 1977 inaugural lecture he reintroduces this phrase, not to describe a text's multiplicity of meaning, but to describe the multiple manifestations of power as they appear within a text. With this, Barthes integrates the themes of power and language, and conceives of them as comparable modes of being: just as language is always there and offers us no exit, and just as language permeates our consciousness and the structures of our society, power never disappears and is ever-present within our consciousnesses, society, and language.

Rather than fully identifying power with language, Barthes refers to power as a perpetual 'parasite' within language – a parasite that is allegedly arrogant, oppressive, alienating, as well as guilt-generating and blame-engendering. Revealing his structuralist background and recalling his earlier essays, Barthes adds that power resides within the structure of language, insofar as language cannot but draw distinctions and oppositions. For him, all classifications are oppressive, as they demarcate oppositions between things and people and thereby create opposing forces within society. A person must speak in accord with established – and oppressive – distinctions: one must posit oneself before others as a subject, as either masculine or feminine (e.g., as in French or Spanish), and speak either in a familiar or in a formal voice. In Lacanian terms, one could say that Barthes believes that the symbolic register oppresses the imaginary register; in Freudian terms, one could say that Barthes believes that the reality principle oppresses the pleasure principle.

In view of the depths to which power permeates linguistic structure, Barthes defines an overall intellectual program which continues and broadens his earlier interest in criticizing the ideological stereotypes embodied in capitalist myths: his goal is to unmask the structures of power which reside within language, and to undermine these structures as much as possible. In the following excerpts, Barthes describes language as an enemy, and as generally 'fascist,' insofar as it compels people to employ oppressive terminology in their thinking and speech. Since we have no choice but to use the language at hand, we have no choice but to perpetuate the oppressiveness which language embodies:

> But language – the performance of a language system – is neither reactionary nor progressive; it is quite simply fascist; for fascism does not prevent speech, it compels speech.[285]
>
> The sign is a follower, gregarious; in each sign sleeps that monster: a stereotype. I can speak only by picking up what *loiters* around in speech. Once I speak, these two categories unite in me; I am both master and slave. I am not competent to repeat what has been said, to settle comfortably in the servitude of signs: I speak, I affirm, I assert *tellingly* what I repeat.[286]

Although he recognizes that language itself is oppressive, Barthes offers a method to oppose the constellations of power inherent in linguistic structure. This combines his aesthetic of 'the pleasure of the text' with an emphasis upon constant change or shifting of one's position. Barthes believes that the solidification of meaning as it is embodied in entrenched linguistic distinctions is the foundation of oppression, and he consequently resists all meaning-construction (i.e., he rejects the aims of traditional interpretation) insofar as this construction is intended to stand as an enduring linguistic force. His prescription is to emphasize the immediately creative, playful, and pleasurable aspects of writing and reading, lest we will fall prey to the oppressive forces of socially structured power – a power which always manipulates the products of pleasure for its own purposes:

> For power seizes upon the pleasure of writing as it seizes upon all pleasure, to manipulate it and to make of it a product that is gregarious, nonperverse, in the same way that it seizes upon the genetic product of love's pleasure, to turn it into soldiers and fighters to its own advantage. *To shift ground*, then, can mean: to go where you are not expected, or, more radically, to *abjure* what you have written (but not necessarily what you have thought), when gregarious power uses and subjugates it.[287]

With his emphasis upon text, pleasure, and the shifting of one's ground, as these stand against the forces of meaning-solidification, institutionalization, and oppression, Barthes proposes a program of instruction that, as the Chair of Literary Semiology, he intends to institute:

> What I hope to be able to renew, each of the years it is given me to teach here, is the manner of presentation of the course or seminar, in short of 'presenting' a discourse without imposing it: that would be the methodological stake, the *quaestio*, the point to be debated. For what can be oppressive in our teaching is not, finally, the knowledge or the culture it conveys, but the discursive forms through which we propose them. Since, as I have tried to suggest, this teaching has as its object discourse taken in the inevitability of power, method can really bear only on the means of loosening, baffling, or at the very least, of lightening this power. And I am increasingly convinced, both in writing and in teaching, that the fundamental operation of this loosening method is, if one writes, fragmentation, and, if one teaches, digression, or, to put it in a preciously ambiguous word, *excursion*. I should therefore like the speaking and the listening that will be interwoven here to resemble the comings and goings of a child playing beside his mother, leaving her, returning to bring her a pebble, a piece of string, and thereby tracing around a calm center a whole locus of play within which the pebble, the string come to matter less than the enthusiastic giving of them.[288]

Barthes's discourse against power, oppressive language and social institutions does harbor some self-referential paradox. After all, his emphasis upon textuality, pleasure, and play constitutes yet another form of power, despite the intention to oppose the structures of solidified institutional power. By the year 1977, Barthes himself stood as a member of one of the most prestigious French institutions of learning, and, as the bearer of a prestigious professorial title, he further emphasized his own participation in the established institutions of power. Moreover, in the years to come, the subsequent institutionalization and social legitimation of poststructuralist thought as an academic power-structure should also lead us to reflect upon the effectiveness of Barthes's revolutionary program. In this respect, Barthes observed himself that what is at first revolutionary can soon become oppressive. Barthes, in reference to his own high-profile institutionalization and in reference to the consequent social legitimation of his intellectual enterprise, might appear to have contradicted his theory with his practice.

One way to relieve the tension between Barthes's position as critic of institutional power and his position as a leading figure within the French academic institution, is to suggest that he took a distanced and ironic, and perhaps even fatalistic, view toward his position at the Collège de France. Throughout his intellectual life, he remained aware that there can be no absolute distancing from one's subject matter: we cannot avoid investigating language with language, we cannot but be a member of a social institution, and we cannot but be involved in power relations while attempting to dissolve them.[289] With this self-awareness, Barthes offers us a thought-provoking analogy through which we can appreciate his ambiguous position as being both a revolutionary and as an institutionalized and well-known intellectual:

> [W]hat I am led to assume, in speaking of signs with signs, is the very spectacle of this bizarre coincidence, of that strange squint which relates me to the Chinese shadow-casters when they show both their hands and the rabbit, the duck, and the wolf whose silhouettes they simulate.[290]

Selected works of Roland Barthes (1968–80)

1968 (age 53): 'La mort de l'auteur' ['The Death of the Author']
1970 (age 55): *S/Z*
1973 (age 58): *Le plasir de texte* [*The Pleasure of the Text*]
1980 (age 65): *La chambre claire* [*Camera Lucida*]

12

Jacques Derrida, Linguist and Literary Theorist (1930–)

Life and works

Jacques Derrida was born in El-Biar, Algeria, in the suburbs of Algiers, on July 15, 1930. His family was of Sephardic Jewish heritage, and he attended schools in El-Biar until the age of nineteen. His interests in philosophy and literature were stimulated in his early teens by his readings of Andre Gide, Friedrich Nietzsche, and Jean-Jacques Rousseau, and this was soon supplemented by an awareness of the French surrealist movement, which was complemented by his reading of Bergson, Camus, Sartre, Kierkegaard, and Heidegger during his last two years in Algeria.

In 1949, Derrida left El-Biar to continue his education in France, attending the Lycée Louis-le-Grand (1949–52) and the École Normale Supérieure (1952–56), where he studied Hegel, Husserl, Heidegger, Bataille, and Blanchot, among others. From 1957–59, Derrida fulfilled his military service in Koléa, near Algiers, teaching at a school for soldiers' children. He then returned to Paris, where from 1960–64 (ages 30–34) he was Assistant de Philosophie Générale at the University of Paris. Derrida then taught the history of philosophy from 1965–84 at the École Normale Supérieure, later becoming Directeur d'Études at the École des Hautes Études en Science Sociales in Paris.

1967 was a notable year for Derrida, for he published three major books that established his scholarly reputation for the years to come: *Speech and*

Phenomena, Of Grammatology, and *Writing and Difference*. In the thirty years that followed, Derrida advanced a 'deconstructive' approach to interpreting texts, authoring a series of influential books on a variety of topics related to the thought of Hegel, Nietzsche, Freud, Lacan, Marx, along with themes in political and moral thought. His extensive popularity in the intellectual world has been marked by numerous visiting appointments and scholarly honors from universities throughout the world, particularly in the United States, where he has had regular visiting appointments at Johns Hopkins, Yale, and the University of California at Irvine, which houses an extensive collection of Derrida's original manuscripts.

'Différance' (1968)

Derrida and Saussure

As is true for Lévi-Strauss, Lacan and Barthes, Jacques Derrida is also impressed by Ferdinand de Saussure's linguistic theory. Indeed, we can understand Derrida to have extended Saussure's theory by drawing forth its implications more explicitly and consistently. In this sense, at least, the distinction which is often drawn generally between structuralist views of the 1950s (as represented, for instance, by Lévi-Strauss, Lacan, and the early Barthes) and poststructuralist views of the late 1960s and 1970s (as represented typically by the later Barthes, Derrida, and Foucault) can be seen as less of a change in overall view, and more of a continuous thematic development. In the structuralist outlook, there is an effort to discern all social phenomena as linguistic systems, and an accompanying effort to articulate the synchronic structure of those systems on the model of a literalistic scientific system; in the poststructuralist views, there is a more historically sensitive effort to investigate the nature of systematic thought in general, by regarding it – with widespread implications – through the strongly reinterpreting lens of literary thought. The latter effort, especially as it appears in Derrida's writings, leads to a critical examination of the most fundamental presuppositions of literalistic philosophical speculation, considered in general. This renders Derrida's view important not only to literary theory, but to the study of philosophy.

In his essay, 'Différance,'[291] Derrida summarizes a core idea within Saussure's linguistic theory and highlights those aspects that are of particular interest to him:

> Now Saussure first of all is the thinker who put the *arbitrary character of the sign* and the *differential character* of the sign at the very foundation

of general semiology, particularly linguistics. And, as we know, these two motifs – arbitrary and differential – are inseparable in his view. There can be arbitrariness only because the system of signs is constituted solely by the differences in terms, and not by their plenitude. The elements of signification function not through the compact force of their nuclei but rather through the network of opposition that distinguishes them, and then relates them to one another. 'Arbitrary and differential,' says Saussure, 'are two correlative characteristics.'[292]

With this Saussurean linguistic backdrop, Derrida draws some conclusions, and provides some explanation of what he intends by the term '*différance*' – a term which, in the years to come, he would describe as his main historical contribution. In French, the ordinary word for 'difference' is *différence*, similar to the English spelling, but Derrida's homophonic technical term, '*différance*' substitutes for the seventh letter of the word, an 'a' for the usual 'e.' The word '*différance*' derives its initial meaning through the written contrast with the word '*différence*,' for the difference between these two words amounts to no difference at all when the two words are spoken; whatever difference there is between them is a silent difference, since this difference appears explicitly only when the words are written.

Derrida's serious-minded word-play and letter-play represents his attempt to express the idea that the word '*différance*' alludes to the silent and intangible point of distinction between the two words, '*différance*' and '*différence*' rather than to either of the words taken positively. The problem with which Derrida grapples, compares well with the need to take precautions when using the word 'nothing,' lest there be a misunderstanding that 'nothing' is a 'something' of some kind. It is no surprise, then, that the paradoxes that emerge in Derrida's view recall the ancient problems inherent in trying to talk about nothing, or about nothingness, or about non-being, which are found in Eleatic philosophers, Parmenides, and Zeno.

According to Saussure, any system of signs is constituted by the differences between the terms that constitute the system, which implies that the meaning of any word cannot be comprehended independently of the network of concepts within which the word is located. The meaning of any word, as we have seen in the discussion of Saussure, is constituted by its network of relationships to other words in the system. Given this view, we can see how the idea of 'differentiation' is central to Saussure's conception of meaning, and we can appreciate immediately that Derrida's term '*différance*' is closely related to the differentiation within a network of linguistic signs as Saussure describes it. In the following excerpt, Derrida explains what he takes to be some of the important implications of Saussure's understanding of linguistic meaning:

> The first consequence to be drawn from this [view of Saussure] is that the signified concept is never present in and of itself, in a sufficient presence that would refer only to itself. Essentially and lawfully, every concept is inscribed in a chain or in a system within which it refers to the other, to other concepts, by means of the systematic play of differences. Such a play, *différance*, which is not a concept, is not simply a word, that is, what is generally represented as the calm, present, and self-referential unity of concept and phonic material.[293]

To understand Derrida's claim regarding the way any signified concept is never present in and of itself, we can recall how Saussure's linguistic theory departs from what Derrida calls (pre-Saussurean) classical semiology. Derrida describes the classical view as follows:

> Let us start, since we are already there, from the problematic of the sign and of writing. The sign is usually said to be put in the place of the thing itself, the present thing, 'thing' here standing equally for meaning or referent. The sign represents the present in its absence. It takes the place of the referent. When we cannot grasp or show the thing, state the present, the being-present, when the present cannot be presented, we signify, we go through the detour of the sign. We take or give signs. We signal. The sign, in this sense, is deferred presence. Whether we are concerned with the verbal or the written sign, with the momentary sign, or with electoral delegation and political representation, the circulation of signs defers the moment in which we can encounter the thing itself, make it ours, consume or expend it, touch it, see it, intuit its presence.[294]

This excerpt illustrates – in Derridean terms – how we may describe the classical view as one which assumes that words are the substitutes or 'deferred presences' of actual things or 'presences.' For instance, when I apprehend the absence in the room of my friend, Pierre, I can say to myself his name, 'Pierre' to recall, and to stand for, his presence. This understanding of language has a long history, and appears in Aristotle's writings.[295] On Aristotle's view, the primary entities in the world are ordinary things such as tables, chairs, rocks, people, etc. (which he called 'primary substances') that impress themselves upon our minds when we perceive our surroundings. Spoken language, Aristotle believed, represents states of mind, and written language represents spoken language. For him, the 'primary substances' are the fundamental 'presences' and written language is several steps removed from the most basic things.

Derrida inverts the above Aristotelian picture by establishing writing as the central meaning-related discipline. He thus challenges the idea that the perceptually intuited presences of ordinary experience and Aristotelian metaphysics are fundamental. This is done by appealing, in a structuralist manner, to the qualities of the Saussurean linguistic field as a way to characterize the qualities of the perceptual field, relying upon the Saussurean assumption that the general field of consciousness derives its articulation from the articulation of language. On Derrida's view, consequently, the traditional focus upon presences in general (whether these are taken to be perceptual objects, or abstract ideas) is regarded as antagonistic to the primacy and legitimacy of language, and especially to written language.

We have already encountered this language-centered theme in Barthes's critique of scientific thinking. In Barthes's case, he regarded the scientific use of language as one which diminished the importance of language in general, since science regards language as a mere instrument. He argued that this scientific use ignores how language itself constitutes consciousness, and hence, how *a fortiori* it constitutes the consciousness of the scientist. With this established, Barthes argued that since language constitutes consciousness, subjectivity itself can assume a number of differing voices, of which the objective voice of science happens to be only one among several.

Derrida employs the same strategy when he argues against the classical view of linguistic reference – one which is consistent with the scientific view. Specifically, he claims that we cannot escape language, and that the basic features of language must be presupposed in order for there to be any higher-level reflections, or references to things at all. Unlike Barthes, however, Derrida grounds his argument upon the idea of the underlying differentiations within language, noting how these are themselves responsible for there to be anything which could be called a 'presence.' Derrida thus seeks to indicate that there is something which inhabits language – he calls this *différance* – which is prior to the apprehension of any particular thing's positive presence.

To grasp this notion of presence more clearly, we can remember that according to Saussure, the words in a language have no intrinsic or positive content exclusively of their own, and derive their exact meanings through their relationships to other words. If we attend to each (nominal) word in a language as if it designates some thing or positive presence in isolation, following Saussure, we can see how we are attending to an illusion of sorts, because these positive presences fail to express the underlying foundation of that word's meaning. Since the exact meaning of any word is held to depend upon its distinction from other words, Derrida concludes that the very idea of distinction itself is more fundamental than anything which some specific word could designate as a positive presence. To capture this notion of 'differentiation itself,' Derrida uses the term *'différance.'* We will return to this theme shortly. First, however, we must consider another related aspect of Derrida's view of language – one that introduces the idea of language as being unavoidably metaphorical.

Derrida's conception of language as being unavoidably metaphorical

At the outset of his address, Derrida is careful to express the kind of enterprise in which he is engaged:

> And I must state here and now that today's discourse will be less a justification of, and even less an apology for, this silent lapse in spelling, than a kind of insistent intensification of its play.[296]

Derrida refers here to the title of the essay, *'différance,'* which, as noted above, is a word he has coined in contrast to the ordinary French word, *'différence.'* Expecting that his audience will anticipate a justification or explanation for his introduction of the word as a technical term in his new theory, Derrida immediately interrupts this expectation. He makes it clear that he is not especially interested in the traditional ways of presenting new ideas to a scientifically minded or philosophically minded audience; he does not intend to offer justifications, explanations or proofs in the ordinary sense. He is neither a supporter of traditional scientific method, nor is he an advocate of the conceptual presuppositions of this method (e.g., that the concepts proposed are clearly formulated, and that proofs proceed in a logical and orderly fashion). As a consequence of his conception of language, he finds it instructive to characterize the dynamics of linguistic meaning in terms of metaphors such as 'weaving' and sonic 'resonance.' The former metaphor appears in the following:

> [T]he assemblage [of previous thoughts/writings on *différance*] to the proposed has the complex structure of a weaving, an interlacing which permits the different threads and different lines of meaning – or of force – to go off again in different directions, just as it is always ready to tie itself up with others.[297]

Derrida often regards language as having a structure analogous to a complex weaving, where threads can be traced in various directions, where patterns are reiterated in various places within the textile, where each thread holds the other threads together, where the edges are sometimes rough, and where reweaving of torn parts sometimes occurs. His metaphor is designed to reveal the underlying dynamic of language as not merely logically constituted, but as operating along associative and metaphorical lines as well.

Derrida reflectively exemplifies his conception of linguistic meaning in his own style of writing.[298] For example, he often brings the associative aspect of language to the surface by introducing a word, then continuing his thought, not by means of drawing a straightforward logical connection, but by means of an associative, metaphorical, or literary connection. In a single sentence, we can encounter a wealth of associations and semantic reverberations, almost – but not exactly, since these associations are more tied to objectively grounded chains of meaning – like Freudian free-association or surrealist automatic writing. For instance, in the following excerpt, Derrida describes his notion of *différance* in reference to things that are mysterious, such as the Egyptian pyramids and tombs in general. He does not offer an explicit account of the term *'différance,'* but provides comparisons and metaphors which constitute part of the network of meanings he associates with that term:

> Now it happens, I would say in effect, that this graphic difference (*a* instead of *e*), this marked difference between two apparently vocal nota- tions, between two vowels, remains purely graphic: it is read, or it is written, but it cannot be heard. It cannot be apprehended in speech, and we will see why it also bypasses the order of apprehension in general. It is offered by a mute mark, by a tacit monument, I would even say by a pyramid, thinking not only of the form of the letter when it is printed in a capital, but also of the text in Hegel's *Encyclopedia* in which the body of the sign is compared to the Egyptian Pyramid. The *a* of *différance*, thus, is not heard; it remains silent, secret and discreet as a tomb: *oikesis*. And thereby let us anticipate the delineation of a site, the familial residence and tomb of the proper in which is produced, by *différance*, the economy of death. The stone – provided that one knows how to decipher its inscription – is not far from announcing the death of the tyrant.[299]

The above excerpt is written with an attention to the metaphorical resonance that attends the term, *'différance.'* Derrida draws associations to mystery, tombs, Hegel, pyramids, the death of tyrants, the death of authority, the death of the author, economy, speculation (of both the economic and philosophical sort), and so on.[300] He provides us with a network of resonating meanings to convey the meaning of the word *'différance,'* and thereby illustrates how the foundations of meaning are metaphorical and associative, and not exclusively logical or referential. Derrida also displays the influence of Saussure, insofar as we are given the meaning of a new sign, by means of being presented with the network of its associated terms.

With this, we encounter another metaphor that Derrida uses, namely that of 'resonance.' To communicate is to make meanings resonate. We might, then, conceive of any word, or any sentence within a language as analogous to the sounding of a bell that has a deep and continuous echo, or to the sounding of a tuning fork, or perhaps to the dropping of a pebble in a pond, which causes ripples of reverberations along the water's surface. Whichever analogy we choose, what is central is that Derrida is unsympathetic with the idea of language (or of some linguistic ideal, as we might encounter in symbolic logic) as being predominantly a static, crystallized, precisely articulated, literal, logical system of crisply defined terms. This logically centered conception of language is antagonistic to Derrida's style of understanding, if only because he recognizes that the dynamically resonant aspect of language is paramount, and that logical crystallizations are seen to arise only later as abstract and incomplete representations of an initially complicated and multidimensional linguistic reality. The existential richness of language insofar as language includes metaphorical, associative, and logical dimensions, thus takes precedence over any abstract conception where, for instance, only literalistic language is highlighted as being true or objective.

The difficulties in talking about *différance*

Before addressing the explicit difficulties Derrida encounters in communicating his notion of *différance*, we can consider one avenue Derrida uses to give expression to this notion. He does this through an analogy that involves the 'silent' aspects of written language, such as punctuation marks and spacing. Calling his experience as a linguist into play, he points out that it is a mistake to regard all of the marks within written language as mere transcriptions of vocalizations, or to believe that the written language could ever be formulated with such a simple transcription.

The spacings and punctuation marks within a written language are not vocalized, and yet they are essential to the positive articulation of what would be spoken, for example, if a section of written text were read aloud. To express the thought of *différance*, Derrida extends this analogy by giving priority to written language: just as the spacings and punctuation marks of written language are 'silent' with respect to the spoken language, and yet are essential for distinguishing the positively spoken features of the language, *différance* is 'silent' with respect to written language (and to language and thought in general), and yet is essential for distinguishing the positively written (or spoken) features of the language. '*Différance*' designates the notion of 'difference' pure and simple; it refers to the very point of distinction, difference, or differentiation, within any given distinction. Whatever distinction we might imagine (e.g., between 'plus' and 'minus;' 'inside' and 'outside;' 'here' and 'there;' 'I' and 'you;' 'before' and 'after;' etc.), it is *différance* which is essential to drawing the distinction. *Différance* is the very force of distinction, one could say. It is like the distance that arises within consciousness when one reflects, to which Sartre referred to as 'nothing.'

We have also already encountered this idea in Jean-Paul Sartre's Heidegger-inspired analysis of the situation in which questions are asked, where Sartre referred to the 'triple-negation' involved in asking any question. Sartre, like Derrida, draws our attention to the 'joints,' 'spaces,' 'interstices,' 'gaps,' etc. It is also important to add that for Derrida, *différance* also expresses a dynamic force of disruption, and conveys time's creative and destructive passing, whereby old distinctions are dissolved and transformed into new distinctions via the process of interpretation. *Différance* is a sort of cut, or interruption, and in this respect, we can refer to Derrida's outlook as a 'philosophy of the caesura,' as it emphasizes silent pauses and semantic breaks.

The attempt to designate the meaning of the term '*différance*' thus generates a paradox for Derrida. If the term '*différance*' refers to whatever distinguishes any two items within a given distinction, then the use of any word must fail to express the direct meaning Derrida has in mind. Since words themselves are opposed to other words, they always remain the positive elements within any distinction, and cannot themselves stand for the point of distinction itself. To say the very words 'the point of distinction itself' is to suggest that what is designated by the term '*différance*' is a point, or a thing, or an entity of some sort. Similarly, in the preceding sentence, the phrase, 'what is designated ...' suggests that the term '*différance*' designates a 'what' of some sort. This is problematic, for although Derrida realizes that '*différance*' inhabits language, he also realizes that it defies being expressed through any specific word (and once again, the term 'it' in the preceding phrase, introduces a falsification of what '*différence*' designates). Derrida is aware of this, and says that he cannot adequately convey the meaning of the term '*différance*:'

> And it is a tomb which cannot even be made to resonate. In effect, I cannot let you know through my discourse, through the speech being addressed at this moment to the French Society of Philosophy, what difference I am talking about.[301]

Derrida maintains that the situation in which he finds himself with respect to the difficulty in expressing the notion of *différance*, compares to that of theologians who represent what has been labeled 'negative theology.' These theologians maintain that God is beyond words, and that whatever words we use to express the nature of God, we will necessarily miss the point. The following excerpt gives a clear description of negative theology:

> According to this doctrine [of negative theology], nothing positive can be known about God, who has nothing in common with any other being. No predicate or descriptive term can legitimately be applied to him unless it is given a meaning which is wholly different from the one the term has in common usage and is purely negative. All statements concerning God considered in himself should, if they are to be regarded as true, be interpreted as providing an indication of what God is *not*. This applies even to the statement that God exists. Maimonides [1135–1204] maintains that progress in this kind of negative knowledge is of considerable value, for it does away with false ideas concerning God.[302]

For reasons which we shall see, Derrida dissociates himself from negative theology, although both deconstruction and negative theology agree that the main subject under consideration in their respective views (viz., *différance*; God) is of an order different from any positive designations which can be expressed through language. If language is to assist us in communicating what is meant by the term '*différance*', it will not – without being in some sense misleading – be through any straightforward definition. The truth of *différence* thus can only be deduced from, alluded to, and indirectly captured in the forms of positive linguistic expression. With this in mind, we can consider one of Derrida's remarks concerning the literal inexpressibility of *différence* and his attempt to communicate its meaning nonetheless.

> [T]he difference marked in the 'differ( )nce' between the *e* and the *a* eludes both vision and hearing perhaps happily suggests that here we must be permitted to refer to an order which no longer belongs to sensibility. But neither can it belong to intelligibility, to the ideality which is not fortuitously affiliated with the objectivity of *theorein* or understanding. Here, therefore, we must let ourselves refer to an order that resists the opposition, one of the founding oppositions of philosophy, between the sensible and the intelligible. The order which resists this opposition, and resists it because it transports it, is announced in a movement of *différance* (with an *a*) between two differences or two letters, a *différance* which belongs neither to the voice nor to writing in the usual sense, and which is located, as the strange space that will keep us together here for an hour, between speech and writing, and beyond the tranquil familiarity which links us to one and the other, occasionally reassuring us in our illusion that they are two.[303]

Here, Derrida maintains that our reflections upon the meaning of *différance* lead us to postulate an order which is neither sensible nor intelligible, and which belongs to neither speech nor writing. *Différance*, as such, is somehow beyond ordinary perceptual experience and reflective thought – and there are even difficulties speaking of it at all, since this suggests that *différance* designates an entity or a quality (i.e., a 'suchness') of some sort. Derrida is explicit about the difficulty:

> What am I to do in order to speak of the *a* of *différance*? It goes without saying that it cannot be *exposed*. One can expose only that which at a certain moment can become *present*, manifest, that which can be shown, presented as something present, a being-present in its truth, in the truth of a present or the presence of the present. Now if *différance* is (and I also cross out the 'is') what makes possible the presentation of the being-present, it is never presented as such.[304] It is never offered to the present.[305]

Différance thus appears to remain implicit behind whatever is present, or whatever presents or discloses itself to us. It is the absolute background and absolute presupposition, but it is also a non-entity. There are positive beings which appear to us as presences, and these presences keep *différance* hidden from us. At the same time, however, Derrida resists this straightforward way of describing the situation, and he does so for the same reason he wishes to disengage himself from the standpoint of negative theology. When we conceive of *différance* as something which is hidden and which stands behind the appearances of things which are present, it is easy to conclude that *différance* simply designates another order of being, or mode of metaphysical presence – one which we can designate as reality, or as the way the world is in-itself, or at least as our basic psychological, epistemological, or phenomeno-logical reality. Derrida, however, claims that this misrepresents *différance*:

> 'Older' than Being itself, such a *différance* has no name in our language. But we 'already know' that if it is unnamable, it is not provisionally so, not because our language has not yet formed or received this *name*, or because we would have to seek it in another language, outside the finite system of our own. It is rather because there is no *name* for it at all, not even the name of essence or of Being, not even that of '*différance*,' which is not a name, which is not a pure nominal unity, and unceasingly dislocates itself in a chain of differing and deferring substitutions.
>
> 'There is no name for it:' a proposition to be read in its *platitude*. This unnamable is not an ineffable Being which no name could approach: God, for example. This unnamable is the play which makes possible nominal effects, the relatively unitary and atomic structures that are called names,

the chains of substitutions of names in which, for example, the nominal effect *différance* is itself *enmeshed*, carried off, reinscribed, just as a false entry or a false exit is still part of the game, a function of the system.[306]

With the above excerpts we come closer to what Derrida has in mind with his use of the term '*différance*.' It designates an unceasing dislocation or play which is the necessary condition for the experience of 'presences.' To understand *différance*, then, we need to consider the dynamic aspect of language, which would include the way in which every linguistic expression resonates with association and metaphor, the way language changes over time, the way in which segments of text constantly overlap and refer to each other, and, in general, the way in which language continually resists a static and final formulation.

One important reason for Derrida's introduction of the term *différance* into his account of language, is to illustrate how any part of language leads us into a 'bottomless chessboard' with respect to interpretive possibilities.[307] If we look deeply enough, we will soon discover that simplicity and clarity are mostly illusory, since linguistic meaning is fundamentally complicated, continually resonant and multidimensional. Since even the most elementary word resonates in its meaning in an endless associative complexity, we always speak, write and think within a realm of semantic inexhaustibility. Derrida refers to the source of this inexhaustibility as the 'play of differences' or as the effects of *différance*. Words are less like a large set of opaque marbles, which can be rearranged without each affecting one other; they are more like prismatically cut diamonds, each of which mirrors and reflects upon the others in a different way, as they are rearranged.

In light of the above account of language and interpretation, we can introduce yet another metaphor that perhaps comes even closer to capturing the dynamic of language as Derrida describes it. Any word, or piece of text, is like an open-ended conversation among a group of people. As the conversation continues over time, there is an unpredictable interaction among the meanings at play, there is change in meaning as time progresses, and as open-ended, there is a potentially inexhaustible articulation of meaning over time. One might say that on Derrida's view, written texts, and language in general, have the structure of an endless interplay of multilayered dialogue.

Heidegger on the distinction between 'Being' and 'beings' ('entities')

At the beginning of *Being and Time* (1927), Martin Heidegger draws an important distinction between 'Being' and 'beings' ('entities'):

'Being' does not define the highest region of beings, insofar as this region is conceptually articulated according to genus and species ... The 'universality' of Being '*goes beyond*' [*übersteigt*] all universalities defined in terms of genus.[308]

'Being' is not the same as how beings are. That is why the justified way (within certain limits) of determining entities – 'definition' in traditional logic, which itself has its foundations in ancient ontology – is not applicable to Being.[309]

The Being of beings 'is' not itself a being. The first philosophical step in understanding of the problem of Being consists then ... 'not in telling a history', i.e., by defining beings as such by looking back to other beings in their heritage, as if Being had its character in some possible individual being. Being, as that which is being asked about, requires its own manner of display which is distinguished from the manner of discovering beings. Accordingly, that which is questioned about, the meaning of Being, requires its own conceptualization, which is again essentially different from the concepts in which beings acquire their meaningful determination.[310]

The above remarks concerning the difference between 'Being' and 'beings' issue from Heidegger's interest in a fundamental, if not the most fundamental, philosophical question: 'What is the meaning of Being?' He realizes that this Being is not identical to any particular thing or entity, but is that which is present in them all as that which makes them 'be' as such. To describe Heidegger's focus upon Being in another way, we can say that he is not imme-diately interested in 'what-ness' or essence of any individual thing, but is inter-ested in the 'that-ness' or 'is-ness' or existential quality of anything which is said to be or to have being.[311] Like Derrida, Heidegger too is inspired by Husserl, and he is interested in uncovering the absolute background (a small aspect of which always projects into the foreground and constitutes the fore-ground), which he identifies as 'Being.'

As Heidegger investigates the question of the meaning of Being, he realizes that most Western philosophical thought from the time of Plato up until the late nineteenth century has focused its attention elsewhere, namely, upon the what-ness or essence of individual things, or of types of things, as opposed to their Being *per se*. It appears to him that most traditional metaphysical thought – in part owing to the emphasis upon reflection, which both Bergson and Sartre have pointed out has the result of ossifying the world into a set of static objects – has been directed reflectively toward the understanding of entities as such, and not toward the Being, or existential quality which every entity embodies. He characterizes this failure to focus upon the meaning of Being itself as the 'forgottenness' or 'forgetfulness' (*Seinsvergessenheit*)[312] of Being in Western philosophical thought.

A further reason for this oversight, Heidegger believes, is that Being is so phenomenologically 'close' to us in our experience – as is every background – that it is constantly overlooked. It is close, in the way one can feel one's heartbeat or feel one's breathing in the distant background of one's awareness, or how one can wear eyeglasses or clothing without directing any reflective attention toward those items at all. One might become aware of one's eyeglasses, perhaps, when they break, or when they become fogged, but otherwise they remain phenomenologically invisible, in the background, and constantly overlooked. The awareness of gravity – the recognition that everything is always being drawn toward the ground – is another example of a phenomenon that is so close that it usually goes by unnoticed.

In this phenomenological respect, such close phenomena are actually very 'far away' in the sense that they resist being brought into explicit awareness. It is Heidegger's task in *Being and Time* to bring Being into a more distinct awareness, for it is so close to us that it tends to remain overlooked and forgotten-about within our day-to-day experience. This is not to say that all of Being will ever come into our perceptual foreground as one's eyeglasses might become present upon being broken; it is to say that the question of Being needs to be brought into our reflective foreground, to more effectively appreciate the ever-present and infinitely extensive background to all experience.

We can now see a similarity between Heidegger's 'Being' and Derrida's '*différance*.' As is also true of Heidegger's Being, Derrida describes *différance* as of a different order in comparison to ordinary objects or presences. Just as Heidegger claims that Being is not an entity, Derrida claims that *différance* is not an entity. Moreover, just as Heidegger claims that Being is the condition for the existence of any specific being or entity, Derrida claims that *différance* is the condition for the precisely articulated presence of any specific being or entity. And just as Being remains mostly in the background of our daily awareness, so does *différance* remain in the background.

In view of the above kinships, we can ask whether there are any significant differences between Derrida's notion of *différance* and Heidegger's conception of Being. Before addressing this issue, however, we can take a further look at some similarities in Heidegger's and Derrida's attitudes toward the Western philosophical tradition – a tradition that has tended to focus reflectively upon the nature of individual entities or presences.

Heidegger's 'destruction of the history of Western metaphysics'

In Heidegger's thought, the term 'metaphysics' is ambiguous. In the general sense, he uses the term to designate any approach that attempts to illuminate the human being's relationship to Being. In this respect, Heidegger himself is a metaphysician who develops a metaphysical outlook on the world. In the more restricted sense – and also the sense that has become more popular within the Heideggerian/Derridean context – the term 'metaphysics' refers to a particular, and allegedly unfruitful, way of illuminating the human being's relationship to Being, namely, that which employs categories that designate or highlight individual entities or presences. This is considered to be the main style of Western metaphysics, and is the object of criticism for both Heidegger and Derrida. The central problem, as far as Heidegger is concerned, is that in its construal of Being as yet another kind of individual entity, the tendency of Western metaphysics has been to obscure Being by employing categories that are appropriate only for the understanding of individual entities – categories such as 'thing,' 'substance,' 'quality,' 'presence,' etc. In sum, Heidegger believes that Western metaphysics has mostly failed to recognize that Being is of a different order than individual beings or entities; it has failed to recognize that the Being or 'is-ness' of individual beings is different in kind from any particular being.

One of the consequences of the entity-focused style of Western metaphysics, is to understand truth – that conception which is the standard for all inquiry – as the correspondence between a judgment and some condition of individuals. This, according to Heidegger, is a mistake. Once the idea of truth is defined in reference to individuals, it becomes inevitable that one will understand the truth associated with Being in a manner which assumes that Being is just another entity. From a Heideggerian standpoint, this implies that the conception of truth that is central to Western metaphysics has lost sight of the proper investigation of Being.

To remedy this situation, Heidegger proposes an alternative conception of truth – one which he believes is more suitable for an inquiry into Being. This is an ancient conception of truth as the revealing or uncovering of that which has remained hidden. He describes this in the following, and claims that this conception of truth is what the Presocratic Greeks originally had in mind:

> The statement *is true*, means: it uncovers [*entdeckt*] the being in itself. It testifies, it indicates, it 'allows to be seen' … the being in its uncoveredness. The statement's *being-true* (*truth*) must be understood as *being-uncovered*. Therefore, truth has by no means the structure of a

correspondence between knowing and object in the sense of an alignment between one being (subject) and another being (object).[313]

However, the seemingly capricious definition only contains the *necessary* interpretation which, what the oldest tradition of ancient philosophy originally suspected and also pre-phenomenologically understood ... . And is it an accident, that in the fragments of Heracleitus, the oldest philosophical pieces which *expressly* concern the *logos*, the phenomenon of truth in the sense of uncoveredness (unhiddenness) shines through as it has been set forth here?[314]

Since Heidegger's conception of truth might seem mysterious or vague, we can consider a brief example as an illustration. With regard to the conception of one's own death, Heidegger points out that the public conception of death – the conception forced upon us by the public at large, or by 'them,' or 'the They' [*das Man*] – tends to hide the reality of our own death from us. In an obvious sense, the public conception is misleading, for it conveys the message that death always happens to someone else; death appears as a well-known event in the mass media, and as something which, at present, does not have much to do with those who are still living. Heidegger says that the public conception 'provides a *continual comforting about death*' and '*does not allow to arise, the courage for anxiety in the face of death*.'[315] In short, the way the public, or 'the they,' obscures the reality of our eventual death from us, precludes a proper contemplation of it, and it provides us with a false understanding of death.[316] In light of these reflections on truth-as-disclosure, we can see how *différance*, since it can never be positively disclosed, escapes formulation even within Heidegger's more ancient and primordial conception of truth.

Derrida's critique of metaphysics as a 'metaphysics of presence'

Derrida is well-known for his critique of Western metaphysics as a 'metaphysics of presence.' The sense in which the term 'metaphysics' is used here, is the wider sense described above, viz., the human being's attempt to understand Being or reality in general. His critique of metaphysics is thus applicable to Heidegger's metaphysics as well. Now given the similar features of Heidegger's conception of Being and Derrida's notion of *différance*, we need to examine how Derrida's notion of *différance* can serve nonetheless as the basis for a critique of Heidegger's conception of Being. At first sight, it would seem that the two terms express roughly the same notion. But to distinguish between Heidegger's and Derrida's views, we can consider the following excerpt, where Derrida suggests that *différance* transcends Heidegger's distinction between Being [*Sein*] and individual beings [*Seindes*]:

> Which is to say the ontology of beings and beingness. It is the domination of beings that *différance* everywhere comes to solicit, in the sense that *sollicitare*, in old Latin, means to shake as a whole, to make tremble in entirety. Therefore, it is the determination of Being as presence or as beingness that is interrogated by the thought of *différance*. Such a question could not emerge and be understood unless the difference between Being and beings were somewhat to be broached. First consequence: *différence* is not. It is not a present being, however excellent, unique, principle, or transcendent. It governs nothing, reigns over nothing, and nowhere exercises any authority. It is not announced by any capital letter. Not only is there no kingdom of *différance*, but *différance* instigates the subversion of every kingdom. Which makes it obviously threatening and infallibly dreaded by everything within us that desires a kingdom, the past or future presence of a kingdom. It is always in the name of a kingdom that one may reproach *différance* with wishing to reign, believing that one sees it aggrandize itself with a capital letter.[317]

In the above excerpt, Derrida describes *différance* as that which 'makes tremble' or 'shake as a whole' and in this respect he characterizes it as the source of change or instability. It is a form of intellectual dynamite. So Derrida's *différance* expresses a view sympathetic with philosophies that emphasize flux, change (as either destruction or as creation), transitoriness and temporality as opposed to those that express permanency, stability, solidity, and eternity.[318] As it applies to Heidegger's distinction between Being and individual beings, it may be true that Derrida characterizes *différance* in a manner comparable to the way Heidegger discusses Being, but we can see that *différance* itself is a precondition for the very distinction between Being and individual beings. Without *différance*, no distinction could be made at all. In this respect, *différance* transcends Heidegger's central distinction between Being and beings, since it is included within neither, and yet stands as a precondition for the very distinction.

Derrida also associates *différance* with a challenge to all final authorities. Since Heidegger's Being is expressed with a capital letter – one that rhetorically emphasizes its centrality or primordiality (as Heidegger would say) within his view – Being appears to be the absolute authority within Heideggerianism.[319] Heidegger's account of how one can become 'authentic' as a person by means of achieving a true awareness of Being emphasizes the connection between the authority of Being and authentic experience. Although his view is carefully expressed in terms designed to avoid the Western metaphysics of entities and of individuals, Heidegger's view nonetheless exhibits aspects of authority that Derrida finds objectionable. For Heidegger, Being is the foundation of all things, the absolute background and the constitution of the specific and variable foreground, revealing itself as a presence or existential positivity. In this respect, Being is something tangible, universal and transcendent of finite individuality; Being is the ultimate ground to our existence. As such, Heidegger's view is not altogether different from other philosophies that offer us an unshakeable metaphysical foundation.

When Derrida claims that *différance* is 'not announced by any capital letter,' that 'there is no kingdom of *différance*,' and that '*différance* instigates the subversion of every kingdom,' he echoes the anti-authorial, anti-theological, anti-authoritarian, and revolutionary themes that we saw in Barthes's discussion of the death of the author. Similarly, Derrida's '*différance*' expresses the associated death of God theme developed earlier by Nietzsche, insofar as God is conceived as the ultimate authority and source of the one, true interpretation of things.

From the above reflections, *différance* is to be distinguished from the conception of God found in negative theology, for this latter conception offers us an authority once more, albeit an unnameable and unsayable one. And unlike Heidegger's conception of Being, and unlike the infinitely transcendent God of negative theology, Derrida's '*différance*' has no positive content, either expressible or inexpressible. As such, it stands as no authority as it nonetheless challenges all authority. To accept the primacy of *différance* is to accept a principle of perpetual revolution that denies all final grounds or final resolutions.

Deconstruction

Derrida's critique of Heidegger's differentiation and hierarchicalization between Being and individual beings is an example of the critical approach Derrida takes toward all systems of philosophy, and indeed, toward all interpretive presentations which exhibit themselves as being systematic and complete. His strategy is to reveal how all allegedly systematic conceptual formulations rely upon a provably arbitrary differentiation and hierarchicalization – a hierarchicalization which, at minimum, can always be conceived in reverse, and hence as an inversion or subversion of the initial hierarchical preference.

For example, with regard to the traditional philosophical distinction between 'intelligibility' (concepts; thought; universals; forms, essences, etc.) and 'sensibility' (perceivable individuals; sensations; matter; etc.), Derrida observes how such pairs of opposites permeate systematic thought, how *différance* is always implicit within the system, and how the preferred opposition can always be reconsidered:

> [P]hilosophy lives *in* and *on différance*, thereby blinding itself to the *same*, which is not the identical. The same, precisely, is *différance* (with an *a*) as the displaced and equivocal passage of one different thing to another, from one term of an opposition to the other. Thus one could reconsider all the pairs of opposites on which philosophy is constructed and on which our discourse lives, not in order to see opposition erase itself but to see what indicates that each of the terms must appear as the *différance* of the other.[320]

The above excerpt provides an elementary and schematic description of what it means to 'deconstruct' some philosophical theory or systematic interpretation. Within any systematic structure, it is inevitable that some terms become the focal points around which other, subordinate terms derive their meaning. There are many examples. In Heidegger's conceptual system, key terms include 'Being' and 'beings;' in Plato's conceptual system, key terms include 'the Good' and 'Idea;' in Aristotle's conceptual system, key terms include 'Form' and 'Matter;' in Hume's conceptual system, key terms include 'Impressions' and 'Ideas;' in Kant's conceptual system, key terms include 'Concept' and 'Intuition;' in Hegel's conceptual system, key terms include 'Concept' and 'Spirit;' in Marx's conceptual system, key terms include 'Capitalism' and 'Socialism;' in Sartre's conceptual system, key terms include 'Being' and 'Nothingness;' and so on. Every conceptual system has its focal points and implicit hierarchies among the cluster of terms within its respective linguistic field, just as within the perceptual field, as Husserl pointed out, typical acts of perception involve highlighting a selected foreground of attention against an implied set of background objects that renders that very foreground possible. In his development of textual deconstruction, Derrida can be understood as having transported into the linguistic field, and as having derived a general principle of textual interpretation thereby, Husserl's phenomenological observation that the perceptual field is constituted by an interdependency between foreground and background.

In an elementary and superficial sense, to deconstruct a system or theory involves identifying the system's focal terms for the purposes of articulating the theory's mirror image, or photographic negative image, such as to illustrate that the theory does not offer an absolute or completely comprehensive interpretation.[321] Since any system must operate according to hierarchies of terms, and since one can always structurally and structuralistically invert the terms to generate an alternative systematic array, it follows that no system can present itself as the total or absolute system, if only because its global meaning significantly derives from the contrast to its mirror image. In a sense, the deconstructive process amounts to an argument against totalization and absolutism in interpretation. This deconstructive process also has the useful effect of revealing what the system suppresses and does not allow one either to say explicitly or to value highly. Deconstruction poses a threat to established authorities who do not wish to see their strategies of oppression revealed.[322]

Derrida's understanding of deconstruction, however, is more complicated than the above characterization. To appreciate this, we need to recall the Saussurean idea that the meaning of a word is provided through the word's network of associations and contrasts to other words within the language. This implies that it is a mistake to believe in the idea of a final, definitive, and clear-cut meaning for any word. Every word carries a richness of meaning that is virtually inexhaustible. Every text, by extension, is a multidimensional network of meanings, where no particular dimension – literal, metaphorical, associative, etc. – has any *a priori* primacy over the others. This idea of a multi-dimensional network of resonating meanings is the more fundamental principle that underlies the project of deconstruction, in comparison to that of binary opposition and inversion.

If we acknowledge that meanings are complex, and that the meaning of a word extends into metaphorical and associative dimensions as well as literalistic ones, then we must regard any text as an interweaving which embodies an assortment of literary dimensions. These dimensions (e.g., the literal vs. the metaphorical) are in perpetual conflict and opposition, so any view that denies or suppresses this conflict – viz., those which understand a text as being a consistent, tension-free, integrated network of concepts – is based on an illusion. Due to the multidimensional nature of linguistic meaning, all texts are intrinsically opposition-ridden and therefore semantically dynamic. Deconstruction is the active demonstration of this fact about texts, especially in relation to those texts that present themselves as supposing a more static conception of linguistic meaning.

Suppose, for instance, one is engaged in a theoretical enterprise which elevates one of the dimensions (usually this is the literalistic dimension)[323] over the others. Philosophical and scientific theorizing, as a rule, try to operate exclusively within the literalistic realm, and these styles of theorizing attempt to remove all non-literalistic connections (viz., associative; metaphorical) from their theoretical structures. In any such theoretical construction, one thereby encounters an inevitable suppression and a denial of the metaphorical content of the literalistic terms. This, however, produces an imaginative abstraction from the richer meanings of those terms, and a failure to acknowledge (or a failure to appreciate) that an abstraction, and a draining, of meaning has been performed. Moreover, such theorizing implicitly asserts that the abstract product is truer than the concrete, complex, and rich field from which the abstraction was derived.[324]

When one deconstructs such a text, however, one shows how the suppressed, and often metaphorical, meanings operate to constitute the literalistic meanings of the terms, and, thereby, how the text – insofar as it one-dimensionally presents itself and neglects their constitutive meanings – is semantically inconsistent and therefore self-defeating. The problem for all theories is that each tries to be exclusively literalistic, but such theories can achieve this condition only by falsely denying the metaphorical resonance of meaning that constitutes their textual expression in a kind of bad faith, as a Sartrean would say.[325]

In the fuller sense of 'deconstruction,' then, we encounter a Saussure-inspired acceptance of the multidimensional meanings of texts, and an associated project of revealing how texts which present themselves as being exclusively literalistic, systematic, coherent, rational, and integrated, are uniformly self-deceptive. If textual meaning is always multidimensional, complicated, and tension-ridden, then complete coherence and systematicity are impossible, for the very idea of multidimensionality implies that every text will embody tensions among its various dimensions of meaning.

We can conceive of the inherent difficulties of literalistic, metaphysical, totalizing thought in a further way – one that brings Derrida's views about deconstruction closer to Nietzsche and to existentialists such as Sartre and Camus. All four thinkers share the view that human rationality cannot provide a total and final interpretation of reality. For Nietzsche, 'there are no facts, only interpretations,' and he regards the Apollonian, rationalizing drive toward coherence and system as a way to help us feel more at home in an irrational and terrifying world; for Sartre, the 'in-itself' is absurd, and it resists all adventurous attempts to turn it into an organic whole; for Camus, what is absurd is our continual attempt to make sense of a world which has no sense to it. For Derrida, the situation is comparable: language – as the medium through which we experience anything at all – is not a coherent, systematized, univocal, totalizable whole; it is conflictual and multidimensional, and it resists all attempts to use it for the purposes of perfect systematization.

The deconstructive perspective, then, is comparable to those of Nietzsche, Sartre and Camus, according to which the world we live in is not a fully rational place. Nietzsche used psychologistic methods to indicate the relativity of philosophical constructions; Sartre introduced the experience of nausea as a way to break up the conception of the everyday, normal, coherent world; Camus introduced the experience of absurdity in a manner similar to Sartre. More linguistically oriented than any of these thinkers, Derrida introduces the idea of deconstruction within the contexts of language and texts. It serves a similar purpose, however, namely as a significantly non-rational force which reveals the arbitrariness of our rational constructs, and the non-rational nature of things.

In this respect, Derrida can be understood as having developed an existentialist-inspired conception of language, where the deconstruction of a text expresses one's authentic awareness of (what is a strongly Saussurean) linguistic reality. Just as Lacan can be seen as having tried to speak authentically from the unconscious-as-linguistically-constituted, and as having therefore incorporated literalistic, metaphorical, and associative dimensions of the unconscious into his verbal and written expressions, Derrida can be seen as adhering to a comparably multidimensional view of language, and as having developed a method of deconstructive textual interpretation that illustrates the instability and expansive semantic power inherent in all textual expressions. He can be referred to as a 'linguo–existentialist,' although his writings are mostly silent about this implicit historical connection to earlier French existentialist philosophy.

Derrida's deconstruction of Lévi-Strauss's anthropological theory

In his essay, 'Structure, Sign and Play in the Discourse of the Human Sciences' (1966), Derrida shows one way to deconstruct a theory in his critique of Claude Lévi-Strauss. For example, Derrida indicates the following tensions that are inherent in Lévi-Strauss's theoretical perspective:

> If Lévi-Strauss, better than any other, has brought to light the play of repetition and the repetition of play, one no less perceives in his work a sort of ethic of presence, an ethic of nostalgia for origins, an ethic of archaic and natural innocence, of a purity of presence and self-presence in speech – an ethic, nostalgia, and even remorse, which he often presents as the motivation of the ethnological project when he moves toward the archaic societies which are exemplary societies in his eyes.[326]

Derrida reveals an inconsistency within Lévi-Strauss's view, namely, between advocating a view that acknowledges, on the one hand, that there is no hidden unity to be grasped,[327] and on the other, that the study of myths can reveal a universal human nature. In this respect, Lévi-Strauss inconsistently combines a Saussurean linguistic theory – one that leads to the acknowledgment of 'play' and open-endedness – with the traditional philosophic goal of discovering an unchanging human nature.

Derrida's critique of Lévi-Strauss is an 'internal' critique: he does not intend to import a theory of his own into the critique, but wishes to consider Lévi-Strauss's thought structure on its own terms. This method differs from that of an 'external' critique, whereby one introduces an alternative theory (in this context an alternative anthropological or linguistic) theory, and shows why the view under criticism is inferior, relative to that alternative theory. Derrida aims to show how any given purely literalistic theory self-destructs on account of its own internal conflicts. He does not explicitly offer a positive theory in place of the theory that he deconstructs.

Since Derrida does not offer any theory, the project of deconstruction could be interpreted, quite unsympathetically, in merely negative terms: one takes any given viewpoint, and indicates how it cannot stand as a consistent theory according to its own dictates. The process is negative in that no new theory is offered as a constructive improvement. The deconstructionist, on this interpretation, would be comparable to the revolutionary who tears down the existing social structure, but who has no vision upon which positively to reconstruct the society. In reply to this criticism, we can note initially that some insight can be provided by showing merely how a theory is internally inconsistent. In the case of Lévi-Strauss, for example, we discover how his high esteem of archaic societies might have to be rejected, if we are to construct a more consistent Saussure-based anthropological theory in light of the resultant idea that there is no universal human nature.

We can also shed light on the process of deconstruction by comparing it to Lacan's linguistic reinterpretation of Freud's method of interpreting dreams and psychological symptoms. As discussed above, Lacan explores the metaphorical and metonymic meanings of dream images and psychological symptoms in an effort to reveal the patient's unconscious mental processes. Usually, such analysis reveals how the patient's manifest symptoms conceal (while also metaphorically revealing) some psychological fact from the patient's explicit awareness. If we draw an analogy between the conscious mind and the literal or superficial meaning of a text, then a corresponding analogy can be formed between the unconscious mind and the more complex metaphorical meaning of a text (i.e., its existential depth). With this, we can regard deconstruction as a revelatory process akin to psychoanalysis.[328] To the extent that both bring forth the meanings that the surface structure tends to hide, subordinate and suppress, the process of deconstruction can be understood as one of liberation and revelation, even though it aims to offer no positive theory.

The problem of polarities and hierarchies within Derrida's view

Derrida characterizes *différance* as the point of distinction between any two words or 'presences', and he maintains that this point of distinction is the condition for our awareness of those presences. He argues that without distinction or *différance*, there can be no articulation at all, and hence, nothing specific to think about. Since distinction is at the basis of all opposition, and since meaning itself issues from opposition and contrast (following Saussure), then all meaning depends upon *différance*. This is fundamental to Derrida's deconstructionist perspective, and is what Derrida himself acknowledges as his most important contribution. *Différance* is very peculiar, for it even makes possible the distinction between 'presence' and 'absence', and can therefore not be equated with sheer absence or nothingness. It has a character more like a relation that connects things, and remains of a different kind than whatever the relationship serves to connect.

When we verbally articulate the deconstructionist perspective – the perspective that issues when *différance* is acknowledged as foundational, it is curious that a network of conceptual polarities and priorities emerges. It is the very kind of network that Derrida claims is unable to describe any final truth. The situation is a theoretically paradoxical, if not a dangerous one, because the occurrence of this conceptual structure suggests that the deconstructionist perspective is subject to its own destructive principles. For if we express the deconstructionist perspective in terms of a conceptual network constituted by polar opposites and priorities, then the perspective becomes positively formulable, and thereby subject to deconstruction insofar as it can be contrasted to, and limited by, its opposite mirror-image within the realm of theoretical constructions.

If this is the case, then the deconstructionist may be left in the uneasy position of acknowledging finalistically a system of thought that says that there is no final system, thereby exposing the theory to a self-critique. The situation is comparable to that of a person (recall the Dada manifestos) who makes self-defeating assertions such as, 'all is relative,' 'nothing is true,' 'everything is meaningless,' etc. For if everything is relative, then the very claim 'everything is relative' cannot be absolutely true. Similarly, if nothing is true, then the very claim, 'nothing is true' must be false along with everything else.

The deconstructionist perspective maintains that every network of concepts is internally tension-ridden and unstable, and this implies that the deconstructionist perspective is also tension-ridden and unstable. Whether this should be worrisome to the deconstructionist is unclear. The problem is classic, and although the perspective of traditional philosophy (which is committed to the value of logical consistency) has always regarded the occurrence of a self-referential inconsistency as an indication of intellectual defeat, there are a few philosophers who have questioned this conclusion.[329] Before coming to a more specific decision regarding the appropriate way to evaluate the self-referential inconsistency that appears to accompany the deconstructionist perspective, we should first outline some of the bipolar oppositions and priorities within Derrida's view. This will illustrate how deconstruction can be seen as having a theoretical structure comparable to the other theories that it attempts to undermine.

First, there is the distinction between positively valued 'writing,' as opposed to 'speech,' which is subordinated to writing. Derrida is aware that people speak before they can write, and that human beings had spoken language long before they had written language. But he claims that writing is 'prior' to speech. With this, however, he does not assert that actual written language precedes, or ever preceded, actual spoken language in a temporal sense. Also, his understanding of the term 'writing' in this context is more abstract than is usual.

The claim that writing is prior to speech reflects his view that *différance* precedes any 'presences' as the condition for their very being. One could say that *différance* must be assumed *a priori*, as a condition for the possibility for speech.[330] Spoken words manifestly designate the presence of the speaker and the presence of the speaker's thought, but Derrida wants to indicate that these presences depend upon a prior *différance*. This priority is embodied in the system of symbols that exists prior to any speaking. It is this (silent) system of symbols that Derrida means by 'writing' in this context. The system of symbols as a whole precedes any specific use of that system. This is the sense in which his view prioritizes writing over speech.

Second, there is the distinction between positively valued 'complex metaphorical and associative resonance,' as opposed to 'straightforward literal meanings,' which are subordinated to metaphor and association. As discussed, Derrida regards any text (or any word) as involving a rich network of metaphorical, literal, and associative relationships to other texts and other words. He emphasizes this linguistic reality of the text (which we might call the text's 'existential depth'), and he regards as involving a false abstraction any view that tends to isolate from this concrete whole only a single strand of meanings. (Usually the abstraction is in favor of 'literal' meanings and 'clear' expression.) So literalistic thought is given a subordinate position within the Derridean linguistic vision.[331]

Third, there is the distinction between positively valued 'play,' as opposed to 'literalistic truth,' which is subordinated to play. For Derrida, 'truth' is a term that positively operates within those perspectives that acknowledge the possibility of a single, totally comprehensive, non-distorting, outlook, if only as an idealization and goal toward which we aspire in our quest for knowledge. The term 'truth,' that is, here signifies a commitment to a final, closed interpretation. Derrida maintains that since the resonances of meaning within a text are impossible to articulate completely, and since language itself is continually changing and altering those resonances of meaning, what we call 'interpretation' is, most importantly, a tracing through the play of these resonances of meaning. Moreover, since we are involved in an inexhaustible and changing network of meanings when we encounter a text, it makes no sense to regard the process of interpretation as a finite one that aims to reveal the 'true' and 'closed' meaning of the text.

Also, two associated polarities are linked to the above opposition between 'play' and 'truth.' The first is Derrida's positive advocacy of 'multiple-interpretation' as opposed to 'single-interpretation.' This follows from his recognition that every text is a multidimensional network of historically changing meanings. The second is Derrida's positive advocacy of 'historical transitoriness' as opposed to 'ahistorical stability.' Recognizing that language changes over time, Derrida resists the traditional structuralist approach whereby the synchronic structures of language are explored. Rather, he defines *différance* as the movement according to which language, or any system of reference in general, is constituted historically as a weave of differences.

Fourth, there is the distinction between positively valued 'meaning as internally determined,' as opposed to 'meaning which is referentially determined,' where the latter is subordinated to the internal determination of meaning. As we have seen, Derrida accepts Saussure's theory of meaning as involving opposition among the terms of the language, and as being defined exclusively within the linguistic system. He does not advocate theories of meaning which claim that the meaning of a term is fundamentally derived from the (language-independent) object to which it refers.

And similarly, associated with the above polarity is yet another opposition between conceiving of language as the primary reality, as opposed to conceiving of a language-independent, fully articulated physical world as the primary reality. Associated with his acceptance of Saussure's view, is Derrida's rejection of a conception of a sharply articulated world that is language-independent. For Derrida, as for Saussure, it makes no sense to refer precisely to 'objects' in the world that exist independently of language. This is because both believe that it is none other than the specifics of language itself that determine what exactly counts as a socially recognized 'object.'

Fifth, there is the paradoxical distinction between positively valued '*différance*,' as opposed to the lesser-valued 'presence' which is subordinated to *différance.* This is the paramount distinction within Derrida's perspective.[332] From the standpoint of philosophical valuations, negativity (*différance*) is positively valued, and positivity (presence) is negatively valued. He maintains that *différance* precedes all 'presence,' and that the latter depends upon the former. For Derrida, *différance* is more fundamental than ordinary objects, or words, or thoughts, and is even more fundamental than the all-embracing conception of 'Being' which we encounter in Heidegger's philosophy. Although Derrida resists referring to *différance* as a 'metaphysical' principle, this is because he does not recognize the discipline of 'metaphysics' – which he conceives as the study of presences – as foundational. It remains, however, that *différance* has the philosophical role of being beyond any postulated fundamental entity, or beyond any pairs of positive items that are defined in relation to one another. In this sense of being beyond these items, *différance* operates within the overall framework of providing a final vision of reality (viz., reality as flux; reality as an endless play of meanings).

'Deconstructing' the perspective of deconstruction

Given the above, rather weighty, network of polarities and priorities, the deconstructionist perspective appears to present the structure of a 'theory.' What would it mean, then, to deconstruct this perspective, and to illustrate its internal inconsistencies? One option would be to follow the pattern of Derrida's deconstruction of Lévi-Strauss's view, where he showed that the ethics embodied within the latter's view (e.g., nostalgia for archaic tribes, the quest for a human nature) contradicts a Saussurean linguistic principle that recognizes the endless play of signifiers, since the latter implies that there can be no final interpretation or determination of human nature. If we were to follow this example, then we might look for an inconsistency within the deconstructionist perspective that arises between some of its primary polar oppositions and their respective priorities.

Let us consider the main opposition between '*différance*' and 'presence.' *Différance* signifies what renders contrast, differentiation, and redifferentiation possible, and Derrida's advocacy of multiple interpretation and of the endless play of signifiers is consistent with this emphasis upon differentiation and contrast. If we were to deconstruct the deconstructionist perspective, then, we could look for any aspect of this view which involves a commitment to unity, or synthesis, or non-differentiation, for this could contradict the meaning of *différance*.

One place where unity or foundation is of vital importance within Derrida's view, is in the idea that *différance* cannot be surpassed. For there is a sense in which *différance* is more fundamental than any metaphysics of presence, especially since in view of recognizing the destabilizing play of *différance*, no particular metaphysics of presence can provide us with a final interpretation of the world. Derrida also shows that *différance* is beyond Heidegger's conception of Being, which itself aims to surpass all metaphysical views that focus upon entities as the fundamental modes of Being. We thus have the traditional metaphysicians, who, in their limited attention to individual entities and specific properties, are surpassed by Heidegger's conception of Being, and then Heidegger, who, in his attention to the distinction between Being and beings, is surpassed by Derrida, who indicates that *différance* is even more fundamental than any particular distinctions one might wish to draw. *Différance* is more fundamental than the distinction between Being and beings, because *différance* designates (in terms of the present Kantian interpretation of Derrida) the formal *a priori* condition for drawing any distinction whatsoever.

Since *différance* is the necessary condition for drawing any distinction, the deconstructionist perspective – given its relationship to traditional metaphysics and Heidegger's metaphysics – seems to offer us a final perspective. If we acknowledge that the deconstructionist perspective has surpassed both traditional metaphysics and Heidegger's metaphysics, there appear to be no further perspectives beyond the deconstructionist perspective. This is to acknowledge a final perspective on the world, and to adopt a view which provides some unity to experience. The unity is admittedly a peculiar one: we can know *a priori* that our interpretations – wherever and whenever they will take place – will take a certain form, namely, as involving play and multiplicity. Despite this eccentricity, this alleged universality and necessity of the deconstructionist perspective suggests that it is itself susceptible to being deconstructed. For the deconstructionist perspective claims on linguistic grounds that there is no final perspective, and yet it stands philosophically as a final perspective.

A more immediate way to deconstruct the deconstructionist perspective is to show an inconsistency between the 'writing vs. speech' polarity and the 'historical change vs. ahistorical stability' polarity. Derrida prioritizes writing over speech, and also prioritizes change, *différance*, transition, and flux, over all modes which have a static, unchanging aspect to them. The inconsistency here is that writing presents a far more stable image of language than does speech, so Derrida is inconsistent in his use of metaphors. If change and flux are to be given priority, then transient and constantly changing speech should operate as the more salient metaphor, and not writing (which in some instances, retains its stable form on the printed page for centuries). Since Derrida cannot reject the priority of writing without rejecting the priority of *différance*, and since *différance* suggests a principle of flux that contradicts the stability of writing, the deconstructionist perspective thereby expresses itself with fundamentally inconsistent metaphors.

How should we interpret such tensions within the perspective of deconstruction – tensions which suggest that the deconstructionist perspective can be itself deconstructed? The answer is not clear. There are at least two possibilities. The first is that when we show that the perspective of deconstruction is itself unstable (i.e., that it can itself be deconstructed), we show that the perspective is self-referentially inconsistent, and hence that it cannot provide us with the final truth about language and the nature of interpretation. By deconstructing the deconstructionist perspective, we show that this perspective is implausible.

On the other hand, the second possibility is that when we show that the deconstructionist perspective is self-defeating (i.e., that it can itself be deconstructed), we thereby display the paradoxical truth of the deconstructionist perspective. Since the deconstructionist perspective claims that all perspectives are semantically unstable and are subject to deconstruction, then if some perspective cannot be deconstructed, then this would be a counterexample to the view. By deconstructing the deconstructionist perspective, we thereby show to the contrary, that the deconstructionist perspective applies to all perspectives, including itself, and is thereby self-referentially consistent. So one can argue paradoxically, and claim that by showing that the deconstructionist perspective is self-referentially inconsistent with respect to its internal construction, we show that that very perspective is self-referentially consistent with respect to the general claim that it makes about the non-absolute nature of any given theory.

On a more foundational level, we can note that the paradox inherent in the deconstructionist perspective closely resembles the structure of a well-known, much-discussed and still perplexing logical paradox known in various versions as the Liar paradox, the Epimenides paradox, or the Eubulides paradox. One of the most succinct forms of this paradox is represented by the sentence, 'This sentence is not true,' which, if true, is false, and if false, is true. The paradox is of interest to philosophers of knowledge and truth, because this Liar sentence appears to be a counterexample to most theories of truth, and especially to most common-sense, realistic theories of truth. So extensive efforts have been made to resolve the paradox with various degrees of success. Showing that some theory or other either implies the Liar paradox or reduces to the Liar paradox, amounts to casting doubt upon the theory's logical integrity or plausibility, as conceived in the traditional Aristotelian logic and in most mathematical logics.

To see the parallel in the case of deconstruction, we can start with the premise 'all meaning is unstable' which implies 'the meaning of this sentence is unstable.' This latter sentence resolves into a structure that approximates the Liar paradox, for if 'the meaning of this sentence is unstable' has a stable meaning, then the sentence, assuming its truth, has an unstable meaning. And if 'the meaning of this sentence is unstable' has an unstable meaning, then the sentence, assuming its truth, has a stable meaning. This association between deconstruction and the Liar paradox is intellectually resonant on a number of levels, but for the purposes of the present survey, we will relate this association to earlier discussions of skepticism, as we saw in the chapter on Dada and Surrealism.

In thematic augmentation here in relation to the Liar paradox, we can add that the phrase 'God is dead' made popular by Nietzsche, philosophically translates and transforms into the more abstract sentence 'Absolute truth is non-existent' (or 'Everything is false'), which implies 'This sentence is not absolutely true.' If one further holds traditionally that the phrase 'absolutely true' is redundant, and that 'absolutely true' simply means 'true,' then this would reduce 'This sentence is not absolutely true' into 'This sentence is not true,' which is the paradoxical Liar statement. So the statement 'God is dead,' under certain interpretations and presuppositions, can also lead us directly to the Liar paradox. Hence may derive some of the popularity of Nietzsche's iconoclasm with deconstructionists, since we have seen the corresponding linkage between deconstruction and the Liar paradox.

Hegel's characterization of skepticism was found to be especially useful for understanding Dadaistic claims as being actively skeptical, rather than passively nihilistic. To recall, Hegel stated that a skeptical consciousness is a negating and contrary consciousness which, when presented with 'A' asserts 'not-A,' and when presented with 'not-A' asserts 'A.' Which is to say that a skeptical consciousness is an oscillating consciousness, which first says 'true,' when someone else says 'false,' and then says 'false' when someone else says 'true,' much like the oscillating logic of the Liar sentence. What is slightly different in the paradigmatic Liar sentence, 'This sentence is not true,' however, is that the sentence's alternating truth values are not established in reaction to other sentences, but are generated from within the semantics of the single sentence, as it refers to itself.[333]

Interestingly enough, Hegel develops his account of skepticism in *The Phenomenology of Spirit* to a point where he hypothesizes the two opposing aspects of the skeptical dialogue as inhabiting single consciousness – a consciousness which is consequently divided against itself, and is continually frustrated in its attempts to reconcile itself with itself. This state of mind, he calls 'the unhappy consciousness,' to which we referred to earlier in the discussion of Jean-Paul Sartre's view of consciousness as perpetually frustrated in its efforts to become fully both subject and object at once, and in the discussion of Cioran's view of consciousness as being conflicted with respect to its finite and infinite aspects. With regard to the oscillation that occurs within this kind of conflicted consciousness, Hegel writes:

> This unhappy, *inwardly divided* consciousness, because this contradiction within its being is nonetheless for it a *single* consciousness, where each [divided side of] consciousness always has the other [divided side of] consciousness within it, must always immediately be driven out of each in turn, upon thinking that it has succeeded in having arrived at a peaceful unity with the other.[334]

The unhappy religious consciousness, upon introspectively contemplating the infinity of the universe, and upon becoming one with this expansive content to a satisfying extent, soon reflects and recalls its own finite condition as being in a frail and limited bodily form, but in the midst of experiencing such physical limits, it then inevitably tends to return to its prior condition of introspective and expansive contemplation, only then to reflect and return to an awareness of its limited bodily form, continually oscillating and never reconciled.

Through these comparisons between the Liar paradox, skepticism, the deconstructive perspective and the unhappy religious consciousness, we can discern a common structure that involves an internal oscillation and resistance to stabilization. Within a psychological context, perhaps revealingly, there are related structures that involve a comparable internal oscillation, such as 'I am content, only when I am frustrated,' which characterize unsettling states of mind, either cognitive or emotional, that involve mixed emotions, confusion, oscillation, instability, and being of two minds.[335] From these accumulated associations, one can venture the proposition that the general tone of deconstruction – towards texts, theories, truth, metaphysics, traditional philosophy, logic, univocality, and science – is one of emotional ambivalence. In sum, one could say that philosophically, deconstruction expresses an ambivalence toward strict and exclusionary bivalence, wherein one adopts one side of an opposition, and consistently retains that position in a predictable manner.

Further tensions within deconstructive practice

We can now consider whether there are any practical, phenomenological or hermeneutic difficulties inherent in deconstructive practice, in light of our association between deconstruction and Hegel's account of skepticism and the unhappy consciousness. Given that the Liar paradox is still unresolved after centuries of reflection, we can suspend the question of whether the theory of deconstruction is logically coherent, and consider more concretely whether, if one is an advocate of deconstruction, the practical attitudes one must assume make general sense.

Suppose one approaches as a deconstructionist, a traditional philosophical text in metaphysical theory. One knows beforehand that the text will specify some entities as the fundamental centers of reality; one also knows that the text will be constituted by oppositions clustered around, and emanating from, these centers; one also knows that there will be priorities within the theory's conceptual structure, where certain concepts will be elevated, and where others will be subordinated and suppressed, if not altogether hidden. This is the universal form of all such theories, and one knows exactly what to look for.

As a deconstructionist, one will then search for tensions within the theory, and, for example, will discern ways in which the core of the theory depends upon concepts that have been subordinated, and that are not explicitly central. One will discern ways in which the metaphorical content of the central concepts perhaps conflicts with their literal content; one will show that the underlying message of the text opposes the surface meaning. In short, one will dissect the text along literal, metaphorical, and associative lines (i.e., along rhetorical lines) for the purposes of showing how it is fundamentally tension-ridden and inconsistent, merely owing to the multidimensional nature of the language within which the theory is formulated. After showing how the text is inconsistent, one will conclude that the theory's pretensions to finality, closure, and truth, are misguided. One will, in effect, show how the text undermines itself and is thereby false to itself.

To achieve this deconstruction, there is presumably no need to import anything into the text; the text is assumed to embody its own tensions, and these tensions alone are taken to be sufficient to destabilize the text. The assumption is that all texts self-destruct, and that they need not be refuted from the outside. This implies that the deconstructionist should ideally bring no positive position of his or her own into the text. The ideal position of the deconstructionist is neutral and theory free. 'There is no kingdom of *différance,*' as Derrida states. In this respect, we might characterize the deconstructionist as a free agent with no theoretical attachments or commitments. Ideally, the deconstructionist is nothing more than the embodiment of *différance,* which is merely the force of distinction, change, and transformation.

From this description, the activity of deconstruction reveals itself to be primarily an activity of refutation: through the activity of deconstruction, the pretensions of any theory to truth and comprehensiveness can be shown, at least in principle, to be self-undermining in every possible case. The deconstructionist is thereby a universal refuter or gadfly, who admits to no positive position of his or her own, and who acts as a destructive force in reference to any given positive position. Let us consider then more closely, this free activity of the deconstructor.

In the act of deconstructing a text, the deconstructor turns out to be a force of domination over the text: the text stands as a theory which asserts its truth and authority against the deconstructor, and the deconstructor confronts this text, refutes it, dissolves its authority, and thereby dominates it. Like a guillotine, deconstruction decapitates the once-authoritative author of a text, rendering all texts *adespotis*, without a master. The deconstructor asserts his or her own 'negative truth' (viz., that there is no truth; that there is no authority) against the theory, and neutralizes the text's claim to positive truth. Refutation, as ordinarily understood, is an act of domination; the person who refutes wins, and the person who is refuted, loses.

Upon this construal, the deconstructor fully operates within the standard intellectual practice of theorizing and refutation, but has adopted a novel way to achieve the refutation of any given positive viewpoint. In this way, the deconstructor dominates over other views by refuting them (i.e., by deconstructing them), and, most ingeniously, achieves this from a perspective which itself appears to be immune to the traditional modes of refutation. From the standpoint of traditional modes of logical refutation, the deconstructor – since the deconstructor has no position – is invincible, while also having the power to refute or deconstruct any positive position whatsoever. Hence derives the impressive power of deconstruction. It seems almost intellectually godlike, as if one were an invisible warrior, like a ninja.

Given the apparent intellectual power of the deconstructionist perspective, one might easily be tempted to become a deconstructionist. It appears to offer not only power, but total freedom. One can choose any text one wishes, deconstruct it, and thereby display one's dominance over the text. One is in the position of being able to conquer any intellectual territory one wishes, while presenting oneself as a revolutionary thinker who supports freedom and who fights oppression. In connection with such exercise of freedom, there is indeed a more positive aspect of deconstruction which relates to Sartre's theory of freedom, for this links Derrida revealingly with not only Sartre, but with the patron-saint of Western philosophy, namely, Socrates.

For Sartre, one is in bad faith when one fails to recognize that one is absolutely free, and when contrary to this irrevocable freedom, one submits to the temptation to form ossified and unrevisable definitions of oneself. In therapeutic opposition to this tendency, the Sartrean–Heideggerian practice of constant self-questioning serves to undermine bad faith by undermining one's solidified self-definitions. Analogously, most texts can be compared to people who are in a condition of bad faith, for those texts that purport to express unchangeable and absolute truths, compare well to people who rigidly and absolutely define themselves. Deconstructing a text, then, amounts to undermining a text's pretensions to absoluteness; to deconstruct a text is to help realize the text's freedom to mean something else, and to show how the text can always question itself, if only because it contains inner tensions that undermine its manifest meaning. So Derrida can be appreciated as a kind of midwife, or 'linguo-Socrates,' who accosts truth-asserting texts in the intellectual agora, and who stimulates them to question themselves in an attempt to show how these texts 'do not know.'[336] This also leads us to appreciate the deconstructionist as an implicit advocate of Sartrean authenticity, if we expand Sartre's notion of authenticity to include 'authentically expressive, self-questioning texts.'

If we consider this freedom more carefully, however, we must ask whether or not it presents merely the appearance of freedom. The deconstructor seems to be free in being able to concentrate upon any text whatsoever, but since the deconstructor purportedly has no positive theory of his or her own, and acts only as a midwife, the activity of deconstruction is dependent upon the presence of existing theories. Otherwise, there would be nothing to expose and illuminate as being in a condition of textual bad faith. That is, the deconstructor is a slave to the existing theories and existing pretensions to truth, since without their presence, deconstructions cannot take place. The possibility of intellectual self-sufficiency – the idea of formulating one's own positive theory – is thereby precluded for the deconstructionist. If we were to take the deconstructionist project to the limit, and suppose that all positive theories were deconstructed, the deconstructionist will have ended up eliminating the possibility of his or her own activity through its own process, if only because the very idea of not having a position makes sense only against the background presence of positive theories.

Reformulating the deconstructionist perspective

As the activity of deconstruction is frequently understood, the deconstructionist operates with no positive theory, and takes any given theory to show how that theory undermines itself as a consequence of its inner semantic tensions. On this model, the deconstructionist's consciousness is blank, neutral, positionless, and without presence, as far as positive theoretical presuppositions are concerned, and it merely acts as the operative force of *différance*. This suggests that we should expect a certain amount of objectivity in the results of deconstruction: if every theory has a set of conceptual centers which are discernible upon reflective examination, and if the deconstructionist's action is only to point out impartially and disinterestedly the tensions within the theory itself, then there should be a noticeable similarity in the results of various deconstructionists who address the same text. The supposition is that the tensions within the theory are objectively present, and that a competent deconstructionist will be able to discern these deconstructor-independent tensions. The tensions are presumably in the text, and not in the deconstructor.

We can see immediately that the above model is questionable. If we consider examples of Derrida's own deconstructions, for instance, we notice that they are impressively imaginative, and are unlikely to have been duplicated by anyone who might have been independently deconstructing the same text. This is due, significantly, to Derrida's own wealth of knowledge – of foreign languages, and of both literary and philosophical texts. The deconstructor is thus very far from acting as the objective force of *différance* when approaching a text. The deconstructor always operates with a wealth of background presuppositions, and unavoidably brings these to bear on the activity of discerning the text's tensions and internal conflicts. Any particular deconstruction, then, will carry the mark of the deconstructor.

The deconstructor must always, therefore, operate with a background theory in the practical activity of deconstruction. Much depends upon what we mean by the term 'theory' here, but even if we set aside the 'theory' of deconstruction outlined earlier, it remains that the deconstructor is a finite being and is linguistically constituted. So it is reasonable to hold that the deconstructor must always assume some basic theory (in the broad sense), if only the assumptions of common-sense (i.e., that there are tables, chairs, books, letters, as opposed to molecules, energy-packets, etc.). The deconstructor may be aware of the metaphorical resonance of language, but this does not imply that the finite consciousness of the deconstructor operates within the world without a determinate perspective. This perspective constitutes a background theory, as the deconstructionist understands the term, if only in the rudimentary sense of containing basic distinctions and priorities – distinctions and priorities such as that between physical objects and hallucinations, mirages, afterimages, etc. The deconstructor's consciousness (and everyone's consciousness) is thus constituted by a 'theory' in fusion with the metaphorical resonance that attends the terms of that theory.

The upshot of these observations is that every deconstructionist consciousness – and every interpreter whatsoever – operates with a background theory in the act of interpretation. Everyone has a theoretical projection; everyone is pregnant with their own positive meaning; everyone has a position. The deconstructor's background theory (or 'interpretive horizon') that is brought to the text, is thus liable to deconstruction as well as the theory that the deconstructor explicitly deconstructs. Indeed, we might even be able to examine the style of some particular textual deconstruction and discern the theory that is implicit in the deconstructor. This shows (1) that the deconstructor's actively interpretive consciousness, since it embodies a distinctive theoretical background or horizon, and hence a positive position and theoretical 'presence,' is itself inconsistent with the Socratic deconstructionist-as-midwife perspective, which supposedly presupposes no prior position and subordinates the notion of 'presence;' (2) that it is thereby possible to deconstruct the deconstructor's implicit background assumptions, and question the legitimacy of the textual deconstruction, by showing that the alleged tensions in the text are actually the projections of conceptual tensions within the deconstructor, and thus that the deconstructor's deconstruction of the text would be illegitimate; and (3) that the deconstructionist's consciousness – insofar as this consciousness conceives of itself as being non-committed, neutral, and positionless – is a somewhat self-deceptive consciousness, since it claims to oppose all theory, but must always project a theory of its own which is definitive of its finite perspective as an acting and constantly interpreting human being.

Selected works of Jacques Derrida

1962 (age 32): *Edmund Husserl, L'origine de la géométrie* [*Origin of Geometry*]
1967 (age 37): (1) *L'écriture et la différence* [*Writing and Difference*]
    (2) *De la grammatologie* [*Of Grammatology*]
    (3) *La voix et le phénomène: Introduction au problème du signe dans la phénoménologie de Husserl* [*Speech and Phenomena*]
1972 (age 42): (1) *La Dissémination* [*Dissemination*]
    (2) *Marges – de la philosophie* [*Margins of Philosophy*]
    (3) *Positions*
1974 (age 44): *Glas*
1978 (age 48): *Éperons: Les styles de Nietzsche* [*Spurs: Nietzsche's Styles*]
1979 (age 49): *La vérité en peinture* [*The Truth in Painting*]
1980 (age 50): *La carte postale: De Socrate à Freud et au-delà* [*The Post Card: From Socrates to Freud and Beyond*]
1987 (age 57): *De l'esprit: Heidegger et la question* [*Of Spirit: Heidegger and the Question*]
1995 (age 65): *Mal d'archive. Une impression freudienne* [*Archive Fever: A Freudian Impression*]
1996 (age 66): *Résistances à la psychanalyse* [*Resistances of Psychoanalysis*]

13

Michel Foucault, Historian and Social Theorist (1926–84)

Life (1926–84)

It was a fateful coincidence that Paul-Michel Foucault shared with Friedrich Nietzsche (1844–1900) the same date of birth – October 15 – for Foucault reincarnated many of Nietzsche's ideas in the twentieth-century French style. Although Nietzsche's modest upbringing contrasted with Foucault's privileged family circumstances, both children grew up under the matter-of-fact assumption that they would continue the family heritage: Nietzsche's father and grandfather were Lutheran ministers, and during his childhood, Nietzsche was called 'the little pastor;' Foucault's father and grandfather were surgeons, and Foucault was accordingly steered toward the medical profession. Both fulfilled their families' expectations in oblique ways: after some early years in the comforting bosom of Christianity, Nietzsche became a hard-line anti-Christian; after working within the context of health-related organizations as a young man, Foucault became a trenchant critic of the medical, especially psychiatric, institutions, and a critic of rigid institutional structures in general. In their own times and in their own ways, both men transformed into intellectual rebels and revolutionaries.

At age twenty, Foucault entered the École Normale Supérieure in Paris. Such prestige carried with it a pressure to 'shine' and to be 'brilliant,' and Foucault worked diligently within this elite academic environment, suffering sometimes from serious bouts of depression. There were rumors of a suicide attempt when he was twenty-two, and these support the reflection that a driving and unsettling tension marked Foucault's personality – one that was probably complicated by his homosexuality. As a promising scholar in the late 1940s, Foucault's sexual inclinations stood in a collision path with the relatively conservative and restrictive French academic world of which he was a part, and within which he desired to excel.

Foucault joined the French Communist Party at age twenty-four, and although this membership was short-lived, a Marxist spirit endured within Foucault's later writings: just as Karl Marx campaigned forcefully against institutional powers that exploited the less economically privileged population, Foucault never lost his sympathy for the disadvantaged and marginalized members of society, directing many of his books and articles to the exposure of the mechanisms responsible for social oppression. It was Foucault's destiny to become the champion of the outsider.

By the time he had reached his late twenties, Foucault had completed a course in psychopathology, had attended clinical training sessions and lectures on psychoanalytic theory, and had become part of the Philosophy faculty at the University of Lille, where he taught philosophy and psychology. Foucault's knowledge of mental illness was enhanced by his work experiences at the Sainte-Anne mental hospital and the Centre National d'Orientation at Fresnes – a prison that housed the French penal system's chief medical facilities. At the Sainte-Anne mental hospital, Foucault drew up psychological–neurological profiles of the patients, administered specialized psychological tests and attended lectures on psychoanalysis given by Jacques Lacan, who was a member of the medical staff.

During the first half of the 1960s, Foucault was a Professor of Philosophy at the University of Clermont-Ferrand. Then for two years (1966–68), he lived abroad in Tunisia as a visiting professor at the University of Tunis – a position that kept him away from Paris during the turbulent and revolutionary May of 1968. Upon his return to France later in 1968, Foucault headed the Philosophy Department at the new University of Vincennes, and in 1969 he entered into the commanding echelon of French academic life with an election to the Collège de France. With this election, and choosing the title, 'Professor in the History of Systems of Thought,' Foucault joined the elite circle of Collège academics, which included Henri Bergson, Claude Lévi-Strauss, Maurice Merleau-Ponty, and Roland Barthes.

The 1960s were productive years for Foucault, and they issued in some of his best-known and most influential writings. Soon after *Madness and Civilization*, which traced the birth of the mental asylum, Foucault published *Naissance de la clinique – Une archéologie du régard médical* (*The Birth of the Clinic – An Archeology of Medical Perception* [1963]), which documented the rise of the mathematical, quantitative approach to medical problems and to human bodily functioning in general. 1966 was perhaps one of Foucault's best publication years, since *Les mots and les choses – Une archéologie des sciences humaines* [*The Order of Things – An Archeology of the Human Sciences*] – a book which examined the foundations of knowledge during the Renaissance, Enlightenment and Modern periods – became a bestseller. To cap the decade, Foucault published *L'archéologie du savoir* [*The Archeology of Knowledge*] in 1969, bringing into explicit thematization, the method of inquiry he had been adopting up until this point.

Foucault devoted the last fourteen years of his life to teaching and writing, frequently punctuating his daily affairs with leftist political activism, public lectures and mass media appearances. Among the latter is his November 1971 debate with the American linguist–philosopher, Noam Chomsky (1928–), shown on Dutch television. Chomsky had already established a reputation as a hard-fisted critic of the United States's military involvement in Vietnam and as a voice of social conscience, but his rationality-respecting approach to political strategy stood in domesticated contrast to Foucault's more forcefully iconoclastic and confrontational stance. A few years later, in 1975, as an intellectual and historical comment on contemporary prison conditions, Foucault wrote *Surveiller et punir – Naissance de la prison* [*Discipline and Punish – the Birth of the Prison*] – an account of the development of European penal systems. This work addressed not only the history of penitentiaries; it intended to enhance his readers' awareness of the oppressive institutional treatment received by groups of all kinds that are defined, relative to the status quo, as residing outside the social norm. Expanding on this theme, Foucault focused in his final years upon the historical construction of people's sexual identities, hoping to understand some of the fundamental institutional forces that shape the more feral aspects of the human psyche.

As the end of his life drew near, Foucault lectured frequently in the United States, visiting institutions such as Stanford University (1979), The University of Southern California (1981), The University of Vermont (1982), and the University of California at Berkeley (1979–83, on various occasions), where he continued to develop his work on human sexuality and the construction of human subjectivity. At an uncertain point during this time, Foucault contracted an immuno-deficiency disease, and his subsequent AIDS-related illness took his life on June 25, 1984, at age fifty-seven.

The experience of growth and liberation

To comprehend the intricate and nuanced texture of Foucault's writings, it is useful to reflect upon the experience of being released from a condition of bondage. This could be as dramatic as the day of liberation at the end of a long imprisonment, or it could be the release from oppressive working conditions at the end of a drudging week, or it could be the feeling of bright anticipation at the beginning of a long-awaited retirement. More abstractly, it could be the experience of being released, or of releasing oneself, from a stifling set of social relationships, or from one's former patterns of narrow-minded thinking. Each of these cases typically involves a mental expansion, a sense of greater openness to new possibilities, and a distinct feeling of stepping beyond one's former boundaries. Within Foucault's thought, the ecstasy of liberation flows as a steady thematic undercurrent – one which is comparable to Camus's emphasis upon the 'flame of life.'

Globally considered, Foucault's revolution-friendly outlook focuses more on liberty, than upon either equality or fraternity: most of his writings are understandable as parts of a multifaceted inquiry into the experience of liberation, undertaken by a powerful and complicated mind. On the constraint-related side of this experience, Foucault examined the various sorts of institutional cages that societies can impose upon people, along with the kinds of psychological cages within which people can suffer in isolation. Hence arose his interest in mental illness, both of the individual and the social sort. He investigated the historical construction of these enclosures, and implicitly revealed to his readers, ways to unravel, deconstruct, undermine, or otherwise dissolve their oppressive quality.[337] By understanding how a structure of social constraint has been constructed, one can understand how to disassemble it, and thereby perceive more distinctly how such a cage need not permanently endure. As they appear in Foucault's writings, such analyses embody a sophisticated revolutionary and carnivalesque tenor.

On the less rule-governed, or more unlawful, side of the liberation experience, Foucault's interest was drawn to extraordinarily creative individuals, such as avant-garde artists and writers, especially during the 1960s. He regarded such people, who are often dissenters, renegades, outcasts, and outlaws, as having the talent and courage to break apart one of the most invisible and most difficult-to-dissolve cages in which we live, namely, the cage of consciousness that is literally informed by the language we inherit. Foucault was distinctly aware that if the very language a person inherits is sexist and racist, for example, then the person is left with little choice but to formulate their outlook on the world through an atmosphere of sexist and racist values, implicitly present in even the simplest verbal communications. In such situations, the occasional need for the outright transgression of established values can be justified, and outrageous artists often exercise their freedom to this very end.

Some of Foucault's own inquiries intended, quite fundamentally, to undermine conceptions that have remained relatively unquestioned for centuries, and which have been so steadfast and 'natural,' that they have presented themselves as a second nature to most people, overlooked and remaining in the influential background. One of these – an idea that reaches back to ancient Greece, if not earlier – is the idea that there is an essence, or solid core, or basic self, or soul, to every human being, and that this core, moreover, is of a rational kind. Foucault also questioned the legitimacy of many entrenched social structures, challenging the idea that what a society labels 'normal,' or 'sane,' is of any everlasting validity. As did Roland Barthes, Foucault tended to dispute such claims, maintaining that the structures of societies, and of individual selves, are more arbitrary and malleable than most of us tend to imagine. Additionally inspirational to Foucault in this regard were the 'medical relativist' writings of Georges Canguilhem (1904–67), which argued that the concepts of 'normal' and 'pathological' were historically variable, value-steeped, and unavoidably charged with political, technological, and economic import.

Insofar as social structures are arbitrary, they are changeable. And insofar as they are changeable, less constraining possibilities remain open. So it might not follow that if a society defines a certain sexual practice – such as homosexuality – as 'wrong,' that it is necessarily, or is even reasonably, definable as such. Since socially dictated norms can nonetheless appear to be natural and written directly into the fabric of daily life, Foucault devoted much of his energy to showing, in very specific cases, that what is often taken to be natural is, in fact, no more than an alterable social fabrication. Within the regularities of our social world, he discovered more artistry, than natural law.

Foucault was also intrigued by the constructive significance of asymmetrical social relationships, especially within the context of clearly power-related interactions. His writings considered the standpoint of those in control, and they explored the mechanisms through which social discipline is maintained. In his later years, owing to Nietzsche's influence, Foucault investigated the ideas of *self*-control and *self*-discipline, noting that the distancing and control mechanisms that operate socially to dominate and oppress people are of a piece with the kind of control one can exert over oneself, although the latter may be used in a more constructive, creative, and self-liberating manner.

Upon first encounter, the array of subjects Foucault's writings encompass – medicine, madness, prisons, art, politics, sexuality, linguistics, history – forms a confusing and somewhat tangled fabric. Though diverse, he addressed most of these topics in connection with the idea of liberation, either by bringing to light constraints that are socially operative, but are nonetheless dimly perceived, or by revealing alternative styles of positive release from existing constraints. Foucault's particular and often peculiar choice of topics and historical episodes – among which includes an obscure story of a young man who mass-murdered his entire family in 1835,[338] and an unforgettably bloody account of a public execution in 1750s France[339] – is further explained in reference to his interest in telling the stories of marginalized groups in connection with value-shaking historical events.

The rationale behind Foucault's expository method also issued from psychoanalytic roots: as Sigmund Freud convincingly showed, bringing to light what has been forcibly silenced, or exposing what lies at the peripheries of 'normality,' is often more truth-revealing than what one obtains when keeping close to the sanitized surface, resting content to inspect only what has been allowed to manifest itself with the social stamp of approval. Highlighting non-privileged phenomena can be a kind of emancipatory act: giving voice to those who remain in the background, and who have been muted by the loci of established power, can liberate those people, or the ideas they represent, from institutional oppression, and indirectly reveal the issues which a society is too fearful to confront.

To appreciate the specific selection of topics upon which Foucault wrote, we can once again recall the influence of Friedrich Nietzsche, not only because the title of Nietzsche's first book, *The Birth of Tragedy* (1872), established a model for Foucault's studies of the birth of the mental institution, the birth of medical perception, and the birth of the prison, but because Nietzsche himself prescribed the very intellectual programme of study that Foucault appears to have adopted. Nietzsche wrote in *The Gay Science* (1882):

> *Something for the Hard-Working Ones* – To whomever now wants to make a study of moral matters, there opens up a monstrous field of work. All sorts of passions must each be thought through and traced, each through times, peoples, great and small individuals; their entire reason and all their values and examinations of things must be brought to light! Until now, everything that has given color to existence still has no history: for where has there been a history of love, of greed, of jealousy, of conscience, of reverence, of cruelty? Even a comparative history of law, or even of punishment, is completely missing. Has anyone yet made as an object of research the various partitions of the day, the consequences of a regular scheduling of work, festivities, and rest? Do we know about the moral effects of different kinds of food? Is there a philosophy of nutrition? (The fuss that continually breaks out over the pros and cons of vegetarianism already shows that there is no such philosophy!) Have the experiences of people who live together, for example, in monasteries, been assembled? Has the dialect of marriage and friendship been set forth as of yet? The customs of scholars, of businesspeople, artists, craftspeople – have these yet found their theorists? It is so much to think about! Everything that

until now people have considered to be their conditions of existence, and all of the reason, passion, and superstition involved in such considerations – has this been completely researched? Even the observation of the different growths which human instinct has had, and could have, in different moral climates, involves still too much work for the hard-working ones.[340]

It is striking to discover in this passing comment, a listing of key research topics taken up by Foucault during his later years. His book, *Discipline and Punish*, contains reflections on the history of cruelty and punishment, not to mention studies of regimentation and daily scheduling in connection with the development of the late eighteenth-century European soldier. In *History of Sexuality*, Foucault also thought through the histories of monastery life, friendship, and marriage relationships, and generally examined practices of self-care, which included nutritional practices and alternative styles of daily regimen. Inspirations from Nietzsche diffused even further into the details of Foucault's studies, as we shall see.

Martin Heidegger's influence

When Foucault gave his last interview in June of 1984, he mentioned that Martin Heidegger had always been for him, 'the essential philosopher.' What especially sparked his enthusiasm, Foucault added, was Heidegger's thought in conjunction with Nietzsche's. Foucault studied the work of both philosophers in the 1950s, and his first publication – an essay entitled, 'Dream, Imagination and Existence' – was clearly influenced by the Heideggerian outlook. To appreciate Foucault's intellectual development, it is important to once again recall some themes in Heidegger's earlier and later philosophy.

At the beginning of *Sein und Zeit (Being and Time*, 1927), Heidegger described the human being as one whose condition is special: unlike other living things, the human is a self-questioning being to whom its very existence presents itself as a problem. This ability to raise questions, as Foucault would say, amounts to a kind of power, for in questioning – especially in the questioning of authority – there resides a force of liberating change. And being able to question oneself, involves an implicit power to free oneself from one's former condition. If one is essentially self-questioning, then one is essentially self-freeing. Heidegger's characterization of the human being – an account that, as we have discussed earlier, seminally influenced the early twentieth-century French existentialist tradition in the figure of Jean-Paul Sartre – precipitates a lack of sympathy, not to mention a charge of inauthenticity, with views that have ceased to subject themselves to question. Quite unlike Socrates, who was famous for claiming ignorance of the ultimate truth, those who advocate positions that no longer put themselves into question often claim to know absolutely. Such manifestly dogmatic positions include those that essentialize, compartmentalize, and ossify the human being within a cage of rigid definitions.

Since according to Heidegger, much of 'what is' – Being itself – remains hidden, undisclosed and unthought of, ever-new possibilities remain latent within the field of Being, and to be authentically human involves being questioning, being creative, and maintaining an open mind and a receptive attitude to possibilities unseen and previously unrealized. As a complement, then, to the idea of the human being as a fundamentally questioning being whose own possibilities are virtually endless, Heidegger conjoined a conception of reality itself that is multidimensional and filled with possibility. His thought, Derrida's criticisms notwithstanding, is thereby intended to be opposed to monolithic, determinate, authoritarian systems that aim to regiment all of reality, and Heidegger hoped to resist those outlooks which present themselves as an end-all or absolute view. Part and parcel of this open-minded attitude is Heidegger's worried observation that the scientific, literalistic, object-oriented, quantitative approach to the world can assume a totalizing, absolutist quality, and he cautioned against adopting this scientific approach in an exclusive way, such that it ends up constricting human potentialities.

Despite the freedom of thought Heidegger's outlook promotes, he also remained fully aware that human beings are not phantoms, and do not dwell timelessly in the cosmic air: we are living, breathing, historical beings who are thrown into the world at a specific time and place, and who are impressed and informed with a distinctive linguistic style. In this flesh-and-blood situatedness, Heidegger noted that whenever we understand anything, we cannot avoid resting our understanding upon tacit presuppositions that direct our questioning, and that provide our questions with an internal coherence and initial social meaning. In short, as much as we try to remain receptive to new possibilities, our questioning remains guided by the background presuppositions we inherit, many of which remain opaque to our immediate reflection. As a way to reveal, or to open, new dimensions of Being, Heidegger emphasized the value of artistic expression, and poetic expression in particular. Foucault's thought follows closely along this line especially during the 1960s, when he held that the literary arts can enlarge the often-cramped and routine compartments of language, which Heidegger sometimes more reverently referred to as the 'house of Being.' Foucault also recognized historical studies as another such means of liberation, and he engaged primarily in this style of outlook-expansion.

Many of Heidegger's ideas are implicit in Nietzsche's texts, but Heidegger intensified, accentuated and developed Nietzschean insights with a distinctive emphasis upon existential, historical, and in his later period, linguistic, expression. These were ideas with which Foucault naturally sympathized, and one can imagine how the Heidegger–Nietzsche amalgam doubly impressed itself upon Foucault. Similarly, Foucault believed that we are fundamentally historical beings, and that if we are to gain any self-understanding, it is crucial that we identify the often-constraining background presuppositions that have been passed on to us by previous generations. Only then can we experience increased freedom and growth in a more self-aware manner, for Foucault held that it is imperative to question these historical inheritances, if only to allow ourselves as individuals the space to recreate ourselves and self-determine ourselves to a greater extent, in view of the necessity of some kind of social structuring that inevitably carries with it a certain degree of oppression.

Foucault as 'archaeologist'

Upon hearing that a person is an 'archaeologist' – someone whose work is to reconstruct a cultural lifestyle from a set of physical artifacts – it is easy to conjure up images of ancient ruins, pottery, arrowheads, cave paintings, stone temples, or mysterious tombs. As opposed to historical studies that center upon written texts, archaeology becomes crucial when a cultural group has left no written records. Some even believe that archaeology is more scientific and objective than the study of old texts, because so many of these texts – especially the ancient ones – express interests that are predominantly political or religious, as opposed to purely documentary. Describing one's work as 'archaeological' as opposed to 'historical,' then, can lend it an authority that is associated with the recognized authority of science, even if one's work is independent of scientific inquiries proper.

In Foucault's writings of the 1960s, the word 'archaeology' becomes increasingly more pronounced as the years pass. In 1963, he published a book whose subtitle was, 'an archeology of medical perception;' in 1966, he presented 'an archeology of the human sciences;' in 1969, he explored 'the archeology of knowledge' itself. With such works, Foucault came forth as a scholar on an 'archaeological dig,' searching for overlooked treasures among the dust-covered texts in the well-stocked French national library. Foucault's subtitles and titles also suggest that if we focus on the term 'archaeology,' we can gain a clear sense of the perspective from which he was writing during this important segment of his career.

In *The Order of Things*, Foucault characterized his idea of 'archaeology' as follows:

> Quite obviously, such an analysis does not belong to the history of ideas or of science: it is rather an inquiry whose aim is to rediscover on what basis knowledge and theory become possible; within what space of order knowledge was constituted; on the basis of what historical a priori, and in the element of what positivity, ideas could appear, sciences be established, experience be reflected in philosophies, rationalities be formed, only perhaps, to dissolve and vanish soon afterwards. I am not concerned, therefore, to describe the progress of knowledge towards an objectivity in which today's science can finally be recognized; what I am attempting to bring to light is the epistemological field, the *episteme* in which knowledge, envisaged apart from all criteria having reference to its rational value or to its objective forms, grounds its positivity and thereby manifests a history which is not that of its growing perfection, but rather that of its conditions of possibility; in this account, what should appear are those configurations within the *space* of knowledge which have given rise to the diverse forms of empirical science. Such an enterprise is not so much a history, in the traditional meaning of that word, as an 'archaeology.'[341]

Rather than revealing a people's daily lifestyle, as is done by traditional archaeologists, Foucault-as-archaeologist aimed to reveal a people's knowledge-style, bringing to light the guiding background assumptions that operate prior to any assertions that this or that fact happens to be known. From the philosophy of Immanuel Kant we can recognize the term '*a priori*' in Foucault's characterization of 'archaeology' – a discipline Foucault defined as belonging to neither history nor science in any straightforward way. Kant's inquiries, although they differed from Foucault's insofar as they professed to have a quality of universality and necessity for all human beings, were also neither historical nor scientific: already, in the late 1700s, Kant considered not bits and pieces of factual knowledge; he sought to unveil the underlying structures of the mind that constitute a network of conceptual presuppositions for human knowledge, against which, in terms of which, and by means of which, all contingent facts about the world could arise to begin with.

As much as Foucault was inspired by Kant, he gave Kant's search for the universal and necessary *a priori* conditions of human knowledge a modern twist, for he spoke of a 'historical' *a priori* to be uncovered by his archaeological investigations, rather than a traditionally universal and necessary one. This modification of Kant's terminology reveals Foucault's more unassuming view that there might not be a single, invariant knowledge-style that is common to all humans, or a common background of 'human nature,' but rather only a multiplicity of knowledge-styles that vary according to the specific time and place. Foucault's coining of the term, 'historical *a priori*,' in place of Kant's more timeless '*a priori*,' displays both Foucault's Kantian roots, side-by-side with Foucault's departure from Kant – a departure partially derived from Martin Heidegger's historical and existential sensitivity, and one that allowed Foucault to make later use of compatible insights from Nietzsche.

Specifically, as noted above, one of Heidegger's contributions to the theory of understanding and interpretation (also referred to as 'hermeneutics')[342] is the idea that whenever we understand something, or say that we know something, this understanding rests 'always already' upon interpretively guiding historical presuppositions. Owing to their generality and obviousness, these presuppositions tend to remain hidden from us, for Heidegger observed that our background presuppositions are often invisible, precisely because they are too close to us, as they function silently and unnoticeably. In a clear sense, then, these customarily overlooked presuppositions, or prejudgments, can be said to constitute a significant portion of our 'historical *a priori*.' Foucault's work of the 1960s can be regarded as a Kantian–Heideggerian attempt to reveal in detail exactly what these presuppositions were for various fields of knowledge and time periods. His work during this time was Kantian, insofar as it aimed to establish the *a priori* conditions for understanding in various fields. It was also Heideggerian, insofar as he conceived of the conditions for understanding as being historically rooted. 'Knowledge-styles,' in effect, became 'interpretation-styles,' within Foucault's view.

In *Madness and Civilization*, Foucault embarked forcefully on an archaeological exploration in search of the historical conditions underlying the emergence of some key institutions within European culture, and especially in France. He focused upon the various social definitions and attitudes that were directed toward a socially discredited group of outsiders, namely, those whom the prevailing society at the time labelled as 'mad.' Depending upon the historical period, Foucault observed, the group of individuals included within this category varied. During the Age of Enlightenment (also known as the 'Age of Reason,' or for Foucault, the 'Classical Age') this group included not only people who would today be classified as mentally ill; it included also the physically ill, the criminally active, the unemployed, and the aged. At a point that began roughly in the mid-1600s, all were grouped together and confined indiscriminately as 'the mad.'

That the Age of Reason was also the age of world-transforming scientific discovery is worthy of note, for Foucault draws our attention to the significant social fallout that issued from the very same mentality that led to indisputable and amazing advances in general knowledge and technological achievement. As the concept of 'reason' reached a level of cultural hegemony – a conception characterized by an impartial, disinterested, personally detached, measurement-centered, order-focused, regimenting style of thought – those 'unreasonable' people whose behavior did not measure up to this conception of reason were soon shouldered over to the peripheries of social legitimacy. Since humans were conceived of as rational beings, it was short work to define such non-typical people as subhuman, or as near-animals. In the 1700s, they were literally confined in cages within which, through active manipulation, they would be reformed, if possible, into hard-working, reasonable, predictable, law-abiding citizens. According to Foucault, the social role of 'absolute outcast' that had been assigned to the lepers in earlier ages, was played by the 'mad' in the Age of Enlightenment. In more recent times, on the political front, such outcasts have been referred to as 'guerillas'[343] or 'terrorists.'[344]

At the dawn of the 1800s, homestead-like mental asylums were born from an attitude that more discriminatingly distinguished the mentally ill from the criminals and from the physically ill. For Foucault, this change in general attitude did not imply any noticeably improved treatment for the mentally ill, since those confined were treated now as moral outcasts, even though they were no longer treated violently as subhumans. Rather than being manhandled into more socially conforming behavior through physical punishment, as had been the previous practice, the mentally ill were made to feel guilty as they became the victims of more subtle techniques of psychological abuse, such as the 'silent treatment.'

Madness and Civilization documented the social tragedy that arose when the classical idea that humans are essentially rational animals was intensified to the point where it became a tool of oppression and social exclusion. With this first book completed, and having described the position of those who were subjected to medical authority, Foucault then considered the flip-side of this situation in *The Birth of the Clinic*. Here, he observed how the growing authority of medical doctors paralleled the rise of scientific thinking, showing how their adoption of a supposedly impartial and deeply knowing 'medical gaze' provided them with an authority reminiscent of what was formerly held by the Christian priesthood.

In *The Order of Things – An Archaeology of the Human Sciences* (1966), Foucault extended his historical examinations to account for the birth of human sciences such as psychology, sociology, along with the analysis of literature and mythology. In this effort, he crystallized in greater detail the global knowledge-styles or '*epistemes*' of the respective Renaissance, classical, and modern periods, mainly to emphasize that if one is to understand history, social structures, and the individuals who operate within those social parameters, it is necessary to focus, not on timeless and unchanging essences, but upon processes of emergence, transformation, and erosion.

Foucault would later reconsider the validity of his sweeping references to three different 'ages,' each with its own peculiar, and permeating, knowledge-style, but in the 1960s he remained centered upon the project of identifying the global thought-categories relative to specific epochs – their respective historical *a priori* structures – just as Kant had tried to identify the *a priori* thought-categories relative to the human being in general. He claimed in particular that the knowledge-style of Western culture up until the end of the 1500s, was based on the ability to discern resemblances among things. Within this mode of thought, one could, for instance, hope to ease a headache by eating walnuts, because the brain-like shape of walnuts suggested that they might be related to the head. Or, one could hope to inflict damage on an enemy, or bring good fortune upon a friend, by inflicting damage upon or by taking care of, an effigy, because the negative or positive attention to the representation would be thought to be causally transferable to the intended object, owing to the resemblance between the effigy and the object it represented. According to Foucault, such an essentially anthropomorphic and quasi-magical knowledge-style was relatively unproductive, since resemblances can be perceived endlessly, and can be perceived in connection with the most practically unrelated things.

The classical period of the 1600s–1700s was the setting for the physical sciences, and in knowledge-style, Foucault distinguished this period as previously mentioned: the classical mind appeared to him to be order-focused, measurement-centered, abstracting, universalizing, and fundamentally impartial in its style of observation. A paragon example can be found in Galileo Galilei (1564–1642), whose theoretical understanding of nature took care to distinguish sharply between the directly measurable, relatively invariant qualities of physical objects (e.g., the weight of a cube of sugar) from their more variable subjective effects (e.g., the sweet taste of the sugar), and which led to the effective development of mathematical, objective expressions of physical laws. One of the ground-level assumptions of this knowledge-style is that the inquirer ought to, and can, remain completely disengaged from the object observed, such as to perceive the object as it is in itself, untouched and unaffected by the observer's presence. Within this scientifically oriented outlook, the observer turns into a ghostlike manipulator of situations and things, in an attempt to bring their material essence to measurable light. As the classical period extended forward in time, this scientific mentality was directed explicitly toward living things and to human beings, leading to the development of the biological, psychological, and sociological sciences.

The beginning of the nineteenth century marked the outset of the modern age – an age characterized by a more acute sense of history, and thereby, of a deeper sensitivity to the fluctuating features of human experience. With a more closely attuned awareness to the passing of time, modern thinkers experienced the breakdown of the classical quest for timeless universalities, and developed more provisional, conditional, and restrained outlooks that displayed a more pronounced awareness of the theoretician's own contingent existence and intrinsic finitude. Foucault himself often embodied this awareness, as he reflected on the status of his own writings as twentieth-century historical artifactual constructions, knowing full-well how time would eventually wash them away.

Foucault's final book of the decade, *The Archaeology of Knowledge* (1969), expresses the underlying investigative procedure of his earlier books in a linguistically focused manner: he speaks in a more explicit and concentrated way about various discourses and 'discourse formations' that are typical for different epochs, and refers to his search for the historical *a prioris* of different time periods as an inquiry into the underlying practices that constitute the prevailing discourses. What is distinctive about Foucault's description of his project at this stage, is not only his more accentuated linguistic focus, but also his growing awareness that language has an inexhaustible, complicated, if not convoluted and incongruous, multidimensional texture, and that it will not suffice to identify particular spirits of the various time periods. He began to realize more exactly how historical situations are thoroughly complicated: many tensions, alternative and interweaving strands of development, complementary themes, and variable rates of cultural change all figure into any concrete understanding of a historical subject matter, and these tend to foil the quest for global generalities. Foucault's understanding of historical complexity matched Derrida's and Barthes's multi-aspected understanding of linguistic complexity, in other words. A conviction that historical studies require an extremely discriminating awareness – an awareness which is also similar to that of a connoisseur or wine-taster – at this point began to develop a force in Foucault's work, and it led him to transform his earlier search for the historical *a priori* into a more self-conscious attention to nuance and detail that would be characteristic of an aesthete. It was the kind of discriminating mentality he found exemplified in the theorist of the 'will to power,' Friedrich Nietzsche.

Genealogy, power/knowledge, and surveillance

Foucault had a subtle, analytic mind coupled with a daring personality, and his lively awareness of the interweavings, incongruencies, tensions, and multivalences within linguistic phenomena was matched by a similar perception of cultural phenomena in general. For any historical subject – whether it concerned the notion of what an 'author' happens to be, or whether it concerned the development of penal systems – Foucault was able to reveal a complicated tissue of antecedent historical phenomena whose mutual influence and overlap could explain the emergence of that subject within some cultural context.

Such historical studies are comparable to tracing the blood-lineage of a person back for centuries into the ever-complicating and increasingly tangled roots of a genealogical tree – not for the sake of unveiling some single, original pair of ancestors such as Adam and Eve, but to show that any individual existence stems from hundreds, if not thousands, of often unrelated and often widely divergent, personal histories. And indeed, during the 1970s, Foucault described his style of intellectual inquiry as 'genealogical' in this very sense. The terminological inspiration was from Friedrich Nietzsche, whose *On the Genealogy of Morals* (1887) stood, in terms of his corresponding historical method, as exemplary for Foucault. Owing to Foucault's earlier influence by Kant, it is worth noting here that an antecedent to the Nietzschean idea of 'genealogy' is that of a legal 'deduction' – a term used philosophically and famously by Kant in the 1780s. In the centuries preceding Kant's lifetime, legal deductions were the official, sometimes book-length, inquiries into the history of a fought-over river or parcel of land, for the purpose of tracing the object back to some past owner and establishing a legal title thereby.

The most well-known work of this period is Foucault's *Discipline and Punish – the Birth of the Prison* [*Surveiller et punir – Naissance de la prison* (1975)]. This was a historical exposé and social critique of the French penal system, for among his many observations, Foucault noted that prisons do not diminish the crime rate, and that the overall stance of those who institute prisons has remained relatively unenlightened, not having changed much since the early 1800s. In connection with Foucault's theoretical approach, *Discipline and Punish* is important insofar as the idea of 'power' – another concept traceable to Nietzsche's influence – can be seen to have moved into the heart of his thinking, such that the notions of discourse formation and *episteme*, although not completely abandoned, faded into the background.

During this phase of his career, Foucault regarded the presence of power in society in a somewhat negative light, insofar as he understood social power to be fundamentally freedom-restricting and manipulative. It was not so much individuals, however, whose power he regarded as a force of domination; it was the power inherent in an institutional framework, constituted by a set of established social practices. It is these faceless social practices, deriving exclusively from no one in particular, and yet adopted by segments of the population in general – by 'them,' as Heidegger would say – that he saw as being responsible for molding people into various types suitable for the predictable and efficient functioning of the society.

A clear example of the social power Foucault had in mind, is illustrated in the formation of soldiers in the late eighteenth century. Before this time, if a person happened to have, among other qualities, a strong body, natural agility, and an alert manner, that person was regarded as naturally suited to be a soldier. Soldiers were found, rather than made. In later years, when 'the classical age discovered the body as the object and target of power,' people slowly became regarded as more akin to objects that could be manipulated, shaped, trained, and generally subject to use, transformation, and improvement. Social disciplinary practices of soldier-making thus became the norm, as people were increasingly seen as pieces of clay to be shaped. The practice of reforming prisoners by trying to reshape their mentalities was comparable, and was also generalizable: in a broad way, many social institutions, including the most well-intentioned ones, such as educational systems, could be understood as employing the oppressive and manipulative techniques of the prison.

In accord with the thought that many social institutions have a carceral, or prison-like, quality to them, Foucault observed that one of the essential functions of a prison-keeper is that of keeping the prisoners under surveillance. Within this context, Foucault gave an extended discussion of a remarkable architectural design for a perfect prison by the English philosopher, Jeremy Bentham (1748–1832). This 'panopticon' (all-seeing device) was a doughnut-shaped building at whose center was located an observation tower – one that allowed its occupant to keep simultaneous watch on all of the cells in the surrounding dormitories. Unlike the dark, private, dungeons of the old days, the prisoners' cells were to be completely illuminated for the purposes of perpetual monitoring 'like so many cages, so many small theatres, in which each actor is alone, perfectly individualized and constantly visible.'[345] The goal was 'to induce in the inmate a state of conscious and permanent visibility that assures the automatic functioning of power.'[346] Here, the observational standpoint's power tends towards an almost superhuman magnitude, since it intends to survey, record, control and assess, everyone's movements at once. Since the inmate is totally seen, while not being able to see the observer, and since the observer can always see everything without ever being seen, the inmate always feels the pressure of the observer's power, whether or not he or she is actually being observed.

Foucault's insights into the ways institutional structures maintain and perpetuate their power can be extended easily beyond the prison setting. To appreciate the contemporary applicability of Foucault's analysis, we can reflect upon the feeling of surveillance generated by one-way glass windows or video cameras in civilian settings – feelings generated quite independently of whether anyone happens to be behind the window or whether the camera is in fact operating – and the increasing technological advances that allow those with institutional authority to monitor telephone conversations and other kinds of electronic communications without detection. The principle is the same: social institutions exert their power by instilling the idea that those under control can be monitored, or placed under invisible surveillance at any time. In this respect, Foucault's analysis of panopticism – the principle of the all-seeing eye – continues to be of widespread relevance. Just as the classical-age physicist aimed to observe material things in a way such that his or her presence remained invisible and without affecting any changes upon the objects observed, the perfect social monitor, or technician of behavior, aims to observe people in a way such that his or her presence remains invisible to, and non-interacting with, those under surveillance.

It is important to note that in some situations, the panoptic frame of mind can be put to morally good use. It would be desirable in a hospital setting, for instance, where constant electronic monitors on all of the patients' bodily conditions were fully centralized at a central location for efficiency, thus shortening the response time in the case of emergency. Panopticism can become objectionable, though, when the surveillance style is used to control sectors of social activity where people have not chosen to sacrifice a major proportion of their autonomy.

Another of Foucault's influential ideas that took form during the 1970s is that 'power' and 'knowledge' always arise in an interdependency, reciprocity, and experiential amalgam with one another, just as 'color' always accompanies 'shape' in a visual experience. Part of the motivation for Foucault's association between power and knowledge issued from his concern with the political status of scientific knowledge. He observed that not only does scientific knowledge provide a power over nature, it provides an institutional power to those who develop, manage, and control the scientific knowledge.

The intellectual atmosphere of Foucault's approach is down-to-earth, and he retained an existentialist spirit. His analyses of key philosophical concepts such as 'truth,' 'power,' 'language,' and 'knowledge' are all grounded within the details of concrete historical contexts. Trying to detach some non-historical, timelessly true, completely literalistic, universal and unalterable conceptual structure from the infinitely complicated network of real-life happenings was antagonistic to Foucault's understanding, and in this respect, he resisted theorizing about absolute truths or about knowledge that is imagined to be completely detached from concrete circumstances. Since daily circumstances unavoidably involve social, political, and cultural dimensions, he insisted that any concrete understanding of knowledge and truth must recognize how these ideas are inextricably enmeshed within, infiltrated, and modified by changing historical conditions. He even recognized that the concept of 'power' – the central theme of his theorizing during the 1970s – remains empty if it is thought in the absence of articulating the specific kinds and circumstances of the power under consideration.

In 1977, in an interview on 'The History of Sexuality,' Foucault made a remark that has often been quoted and often misinterpreted. He stated that he was well aware that he had never written anything but fictions.[347] Standing by itself, this suggests that Foucault did not believe in 'truth,' and that his outlook is nihilistic. He continued in the next breath, however, to reveal a very different meaning by stating that he did not intend to say that truth is therefore absent. Which is to suggest that truth is expressible through fictional discourse, or, stated differently, that artistic, figurative, mythic, metaphoric, and literary expression can express truth equally as well, or perhaps even better, than purely literalistic language. This was also Nietzsche's position. It can also be attributed to Derrida.

If, indeed, the true state of affairs is multi-dimensional, allusive, fluctuating, and is not exhaustibly expressible within any finite linguistic framework, then we can read Foucault as someone who would have received with congeniality, the Daoist statement that 'the Way that can be spoken of is not the constant Way.'[348] Less remotely, we can read Foucault as a person who believed, with Nietzsche, and with Derrida, that the truth cannot be fully attained from a head-on, literalistic approach, but must also be brought forth with quiet charm, using indirect, artistic, and even mythic language.

In 1970 and in 1978, Foucault visited Japan, motivated in part by his interest in Zen Buddhism. Foucault's interest in Zen had at least three aspects, the first of which is that, like Zen, some forms of Christianity advocate stringent disciplinary techniques for the purposes of spiritual advancement. From the standpoint of comparative cultural practices, Foucault found that the Zen Buddhist monastic regimen stood in a striking parallel to Christian monastic discipline. In Zen as well, one can see embodied the Latin dictum, *laborare est orare*, 'to work is to pray.' Second, the Buddhistic position that all existence is conditioned or contingent, along with the Buddhistic denial of a substantial self – positions which are opposed to fixed conceptual definitions – are compatible with Foucault's anti-Cartesian, more nominalistic standpoint.

Third, that Zen is a way of life, and bears a kinship to Foucault's understanding of philosophy as a spiritual exercise or 'practice of freedom' – a practice to be grounded on the principle of self-detachment, or self-distancing – was another factor in Foucault's interest in Zen. Moreover, although the following point remains undocumented, one can also imagine that the specifically Zen Buddhist style of awareness – a 'being clearly aware of everything now at once' – could have been a further point of interest for Foucault, especially in connection with his interest in panopticism. The Zen Master, in being extraordinarily open to, and hyper-aware of, all perceptual details in a kind of wakefulness that is both childlike and wisdom-informed, can be regarded as a positive version of the panoptic mentality that preoccupied Foucault during this time period. In Zen, one aims to be absolutely observant for the purposes of apprehending the vivid, existentially fluctuating presence of the world; in panopticism, one aims to be absolutely observant for the purpose of maximizing one's control over what is observed. In the former case, one lets the world freely be, as Heidegger urged us to do in his later writings; in the contrasting panoptic mentality, one leans on the world heavily. Since Foucault was pragmatic to the core, and since he knew that Zen Buddhism was the religion of many samurai, one could expect him to have been fascinated by a practical kind of power that can stem from what is, on the face of things, an exceedingly spiritual mentality.

Self-control and self-artistry

In the late 1970s and early 1980s, Foucault developed his understanding of 'power' in a manner more consistent with his general assumption that the world is complicated, fluctuating, and multi-dimensional, rather than simple, static, and essentially definable. Although his historical investigations had embodied this idea well in their details, his guiding conception of power, as noted above, tended to be conceived somewhat monolithically as an oppressive and manipulative force impressed upon individuals by established institutional practices. In *The History of Sexuality*, volume I (*La volenté du savoir* [*The Will to Knowledge*], 1976), however, Foucault explicitly advanced a theoretically more informative and positive conception of power as a dynamic network of social forces. These were conceived of as diverse, overlapping, sometimes conflicting, and sometimes mutually supporting networks, operating in ever-changing 'matrices of transformation.' His view was that power, although everywhere, is not singular, and that one can never be 'outside' of power. To the contrary, one is always already enmeshed in specific power relationships.

The explicit theme for Foucault's final period – one that was implicit in his earlier work – can be expressed by the question, 'How is self-knowledge possible?' This is a traditional question, but Foucault's way of understanding it involved a unique mix of historical inquiry and philosophical depth: he considered, in usually meticulous detail, how fluctuating historical conditions have formed people's self-conceptions, and with this knowledge he reflected upon how people within such alternative historical constellations, have examined themselves. For example, in his study of the scientifically centered qualities of the modern period, he described how people were implicitly taught to regard themselves as potential objects of scientific inquiry, and how they thereby reproduced of their own accord, forms of self-understanding consistent with the idea that they were objects that could be thoroughly measured, predicted, and controlled.

Foucault's method is distinctive, not only in its attention to historical detail and its acute analysis of how self-images, or subjectivities, are constructed, but in its sensitivity to the self-reinforcing mechanisms of social-value perpetuation. Insofar as a person tends to reproduce the world in his or her own self-image, there arises the accompanying effect of the person's recreating, duplicating, and perpetuating the very social structures that significantly created that person's identity to begin with. This same kind of reciprocity-relationship, at one remove, can be seen in Foucault's conception of 'power-knowledge,' for power and knowledge are mutually reinforcing in a similar way: 'It is not possible for power to be exercised without knowledge, it is impossible for knowledge not to engender power.'[349]

Emerging from Foucault's focus upon the social construction of the subject was a more artistic and creative dimension to power, namely, the idea that people have a measure of self-control and can 'self-create' themselves according to their own designs. Although social practices can embody an implicit dominating force over the individual, power also flows through the individual and this can be expressed as a power of self-conquest, self-monitoring, self-formation, and self-legislation. So just as Foucault had explored the 'techniques of behavior' associated with the prison and the panoptic mentality, he later explored the 'technologies of the self' in an effort to understand the more creative side of how personal identities are constructed. In the year before he died, Foucault remarked: 'But couldn't everyone's life become a work of art? Why should the lamp or the house be an art object but not our life?'[350]

In his final years, Foucault complemented his more austere, detached vocabularies of 'strategies,' 'technologies,' and 'techniques,' with the more graceful and freedom-inspiring idea of an 'aesthetics of existence' or art of life, where the main concern was to give one's life a self-determined, aesthetic appeal, and unique style. Once again, Friedrich Nietzsche stands as the inspiration, for in the first section of *The Birth of Tragedy*, Nietzsche described how people themselves become works of art when engaged ecstatically in the musical activities of song and dance. A decade later, he reiterated the same theme, providing a detailed articulation to the thought later expressed only in passing by Foucault. Nietzsche wrote in 1882:

One thing is necessary – 'To give style' to one's character – a great and unusual art! Those who practice this have an overall view of what, in their nature offers strengths and weaknesses, and they then fit them together according to an artistic plan, until each appears as art and reason, where even weaknesses delight the eye. Here, a large mass of second nature is brought in; there, a piece of original nature is taken out – both with extended practice and daily work on it. Here, an ugliness which could not be taken out is hidden; there, it is given a new sublime interpretation. Much of what is vague, which resists being formed, is saved to be used for views far ahead – it ought to indicate what is wide and vast. Finally, when the work is completed, it becomes clear how the directing force of a single taste mastered over and formed everything large and small: whether the taste was a good one or a bad one, means less than one imagines – it is enough that it is a *single* taste![351]

Nietzsche's personalized and individualistic rendition of the art of life contrasts revealingly with Foucault's more socially and historically centered version. Although Foucault was also interested in the care of the self, he understood the construction of personal identity by focusing primarily on group behaviors, in keeping with his general thought that people are molded significantly from prevailing social forces. In Foucault, one reads less about the daily regimens of specific individuals, and more about the techniques of self-mastery employed by groups such as monastic and philosophic orders, whose common goal was to establish a shared hygiene and spirituality. In this respect, the idea of liberation that one encounters in Foucault's later works conveys less of an anarchistic tone, for it is tempered by the idea that rule-governedness is a condition for, and a path towards, freedom. One can say that Foucault took seriously Cicero's observation that freedom is the participation in power, rather than a self-isolating disengagement from it.

Liberation and social self-construction

Foucault's predominant intellectual style was masterfully discriminating. It could even be called 'atomizing' or 'disintegrating.' And as noted above, he had the ability to take virtually any, apparently clear, simply understandable and univocal concept, and, like an analytical chemist, reveal how its constitution was in fact complicated, not to mention changing and potentially unstable. In addition, Foucault was also an extraordinarily reflective individual: as one surveys his writings, one can see his own powers of discrimination being applied to his previous work – almost in an act of self-overcoming – to reformulate his views in a way that relied less and less upon univocal and universalizing categories. He became more authentically nominalist as time went on.

We have also seen that Foucault's transformation of thematic emphasis from the 1960s to early 1970s led to the emergence of the idea of power in his writings. But just as he initially conceived of time-periods and knowledge-styles in a univocal and conceptually smoothed-out manner, Foucault would initially conceive of power in a noticeably monolithic way as well, namely, as an oppressive power that was fundamentally antagonistic to freedom. As he became more discerning and discriminating in his reflections on power, Foucault soon re-expressed his view to reveal that power is an active, 'productive' energy within individuals, and that it manifests itself moreover, in dynamic and entangled constellations whose embodiment is not a matter incidental to understanding what power is, but is constitutive of power itself.[352]

Foucault made corresponding refinements in connection with the idea of knowledge: he believed that one cannot speak meaningfully of a specific time period's knowledge-style in the abstract, since an understanding of any knowledge-style must be located explicitly within a certain historical constellation of power. In the work characteristic of his final years, Foucault's discriminating outlook led him to speak not globally about subjectivity or about sexuality in general, but about many different subjectivities and different sexualities, all of which are linked into broad-based historical studies of the time and place within which they originated.

Insofar as Foucault's thought can be centered around the concept of liberation, his discriminating attitude of the conceptual connoisseur – if this is described more pragmatically as a 'disintegrationist' attitude – can be understood as a force directed toward revolutionary change. Disintegrating some given structure need not be construed as a purely destructive act, especially when the structure is as intangible as a conceptual structure, or is as malleable as a set of practices. To the extent that past forms can be kept in memory, Foucault's disintegrationist thought can expand our horizons, such that we can regard our previous conceptual structures as steps along the way to a more comprehensive awareness. Neither need such a view entail a progressive, linear, conception of human development, for myriad possibilities present themselves at each step of the way – artistic creation and influence is by nature unpredictable – and increased comprehension can occur along many alternative routes.

A standing problem for Foucault's thought, however, concerns whether his perspective is itself significantly constraining. That is, we can ask whether Foucault's efforts to explain our present styles of subjectivity in reference to the social forces that constructed them actually succeed in breaking away from the more self-centered Cartesian style of philosophizing that had been a continuing legacy in France. To be sure, Foucault had strong doubts about whether there is any invariant integrity to experiential subjects, and he also resisted exclusively analyzing the individual subject from the first-person, phenomenological, or 'inside' viewpoint. He clearly preferred to comprehend the individual consciousness in reference to various styles of historically constituted group-consciousnesses. The cluster of group-consciousnesses that constituted Michel Foucault, though, themselves appear to have determined him to prefer a group-centered and linguistically centered, as opposed to individualistically centered, style of understanding. Whether or not the parameters of his socially centered orientation provide for the possibility of significant self-transcendence remains a question, because the extent to which sociality and linguisticality are foundational remains debatable.

To appreciate the significance of the problem of self-transcendence in Foucault's thought as alluded to above, we can reflect upon Foucault's intellectual style, the mood of which is captured in the two words, 'discipline' and 'control.' These words convey an assortment of resonances, but the thoughts of manipulation, technique, domination, and perhaps also strategy and tactics – all of which figure prominently in Foucault's analyses – are close to the core. There is a distinct objectivity of temperament to be discerned here, arising even within Foucault's discussions of alternative attitudes toward oneself – discussions that center around the ideas of 'self-control,' 'self-discipline,' 'technologies of the self,' and 'self-regimentation.' In sum, the objectifying tone of cybernetic thinking can be seen to inhabit, and to inhibit, Foucault's discriminating and disintegrationist perspective, despite its emancipatory designs. Foucault was a reflective thinker, but in his efforts to understand and to transcend the objectifying mentality, he ended up taking an objectifying view toward the objectifying style of mind.

Looking down upon the objectifying standpoint in an intellectually cool, distanced, and non-committal manner, however, does not allow one to escape it, for the stance of analytic detachment is itself objectifying, and it reiterates the style of mind from which one seeks to be detached. In his life-long effort to achieve a balance between structured discipline of science and creative freedom of art, it would appear that discipline tended to prevail and that liberation remained only a more distant prescription. That Foucault was a true advocate of self-determination and practical self-mastery, though, will remain one of the inspirations of his legacy.

A constructive way to understand Foucault's attention to rule-governedness in connection with his interest in freedom, and a way to address some of Foucault's critics who regard his most thoroughly considered position as an amoral 'might makes right' variety, or as either anarchist, nihilist, or pessimist, is to regard his final work on the care of the self as an overture to a political philosophy, or 'care of the group.' The question has been often asked how Foucault can legitimate the political judgments he frequently made. Consistent with Kant and Hegel, and consistent with those contemporary theorists who, inspired by the ideals of the Enlightenment, insist upon invoking a universal rationality as a guide to political judgment, Foucault's association between rule-governedness and self-artistry would put him squarely on the side of those who claim that purely arbitrary, essentially whimsical, decisions are, in fact, unjustified, if no commitment to some set of rules will follow.

But just as Foucault spoke of a historical *a priori* in connection with the knowledge-styles of a time period, one can say that political styles are also historically variable. Moreover, the general idea that one is only free, if one acts consistently according to laws one has made oneself, or as a group, can be seen to be consistent with, and might even issue from, Foucault's thoughts on self-artistry. The main difference between Foucault and the Enlightenment-style thinkers would be his insistence that it is only possible to formulate rules or institute legislation that is suitable to the times and situation within which one lives. Exercising freedom within such a situation would not, then, be the anarchistic freedom to do whatever one wants whenever one wants, nor would it be a freedom in accord with a timeless pattern of rock-solid, self-evident, rationally grounded constants. It would be the freedom to act in accord with the historically specific laws one has made for oneself – laws whose optimal formulation require a sense of taste, discrimination, and most importantly, wisdom. That there are no determinate rules for either artistic genius or for political wisdom is a commonplace idea, and it remains part of Foucault's wisdom to insist that an allegiance to a mechanical and universalistic conception of reason reveals a distinct lack of wisdom, if only because circumstances change, and because changing circumstances make people who they are.

Selected works of Michel Foucault

1961 (age 35): *Folie et déraison. Histoire de la folie à l'âge classique* [*Madness and Civilization – A History of Insanity in the Age of Reason*]
1963 (age 37): *Naissance de la clinique – Une archéologie du régard médical* [*The Birth of the Clinic – An Archeology of Medical Perception*]
1966 (age 40): *Les mots and les choses – Une archéologie des sciences humaines* [*The Order of Things – An Archeology of the Human Sciences*]

1969 (age 43): *L'archéologie du savoir* [*The Archeology of Knowledge*]

1975 (age 49): *Surveiller et punir – Naissance de la prison* [*Discipline and Punish – the Birth of the Prison*]

1976 (age 50): *La volenté de savoir. Vol. 1 of histoire de la sexualité* [*The History of Sexuality, Volume I: An Introduction*]

1984 (age 58): (1) *L'usage des plaisirs. Vol. 2 of Histoire de la sexualité* [*The History of Sexuality, Volume II: The Use of Pleasure*]

(2) *Le souci de soi. Vol. III of Histoire de la sexualité* [*The History of Sexuality, Volume III: The Care of the Self*]

14

Jean-François Lyotard, Social Theoretician and Activist (1924–98)

Life and works

On August 10, 1924, Jean-François Lyotard was born in Versailles, near Paris. He attended excellent preparatory schools in Paris, and later studied at the University of Paris with a focus on literature and philosophy. After the Second World War and the completion of his education, Lyotard obtained a teaching position in 1950 at a secondary school in Algeria, and later, he continued teaching in France until 1959 at the *Pryanteé Militaire* in La Flèche – a school for children whose parents held military positions. During this time, at age thirty, Lyotard joined the political revolutionary association, 'Socialism or Barbarism' (*Socialisme ou Barbarie)* in 1954 when the political relationship between France and Algeria was becoming especially tense. Dedicating himself to this activist group for the next decade, Lyotard wrote often about Algerian and French politics. Beginning in 1959, he taught at the University of Paris, and also became familiar with the lectures and writings of Jacques Lacan. In 1966, at age forty-four, Lyotard began teaching at the University of Paris at Nanterre, and this located him at the originating center of the May 1968 student and civil protests. Lyotard finished his regular teaching career at the University of Paris VII, at Vincennes, retiring in 1987. Afterwards, he continued his scholarly life as a visiting professor and lecturer at numerous institutions in France and in the United States, notably at the University of California at Irvine and at Emory

University, in Atlanta, Georgia. In Paris, on the evening of April 20–21, 1998, Lyotard died from the effects of leukemia at the age of seventy-three.

Origins of the term 'postmodernism'

Although French thinkers have contributed to the contemporary theoretical understanding of 'postmodernism' (or 'the postmodern'), the initial use of the term 'postmodernism' stems from a context which is narrower in subject matter, but broader in its historical locale: it was initially used in reference to a dramatic change in architectural style which occurred during the early 1970s:

> By the 1950s, the world was familiar with the International Style, buildings expressing the simple geometrical intensity imagined by Gropius and van der Rohe.[353] It is this visible dominance which gave the 'postmodernist' reactions against the International Style, when they came, such clarity and definition. Charles Jencks, who is the single most influential proponent of architectural postmodernism, can therefore declare with absolute conviction that 'Modern Architecture died in St. Louis, Missouri on July 15, 1972 at 3:32 pm.'[354] This turns out to be the date on which the infamous Pruitt-Igoe housing scheme was dyna-mited, after the building had swallowed up millions of dollars in attempted renovation of the energetic vandalism it had suffered at the hands of vandals. For Jencks, this moment crystallizes the beginnings of a plural set of resistances to the hegemony of modernism.[355]

The International Style, as exemplified in skyscrapers of the 1940s and 1950s, is the paradigm of modernist architecture, and it is recognizable in its emphasis upon clear, functional, simple geometrical forms. This architectural style embodied the early to mid-twentieth-century emphasis on a coincidence of 'form' and 'function' in industrial design and it conveyed an impression of self-sufficiency insofar as the style resisted making any reference to other historical styles. At the same time, it remained impersonal and consistent with large-scale, quickly constructed units to be used by hundreds, if not thou-sands, of people at once.

To the emerging proponents of postmodernism, these features of modernist architecture were ideologically objectionable: they suggested a powerful dominance that was uncomfortably suggestive of totalitarianism and excessive authority. In reaction to this modernist 'iconography of power,' postmodernist architectural theory advocated values such as multiplicity of historical reference as opposed to self-sufficient unity; eclecticism of archi-tectural forms as opposed to a self-contained aesthetic of 'form follows function;' playfulness as opposed to the seriousness of power and political domination; smaller-scale construction as opposed to monolithic construction; complexity as opposed to simplicity, and internal contradiction of forms and subject matters, as opposed to formal coherency and unity of theme.

Through the contrast between modernist and postmodernist architecture, we can see reflected an assortment of prevailing themes within French poststructuralist thought. Perhaps the most universal of these is the resistance to oppressive authority and the celebration of individual freedom. As already noted, the theme has a long history, traceable at least as far back as the Protestant Reformation. Within early twentieth-century French philosophizing, we have seen it implicit in Sartre's characterization of consciousness as being absolutely free, and in Camus's emphasis upon individuality and defiance. Within French thought of the second half of the century, we have found it in Barthes's 1950s critique of capitalist mythologies, in his 1960s advocacy of the 'death of the author,' and in his 1970s emphasis upon the 'pleasures of the text.' The quest for freedom also characterizes Derrida's challenge to Western metaphysics insofar as Derrida maintains that it is impossible to construct a single, all-embracing account of the world; it is also an aspect of Foucault's related investigations into the historical, and hence changeable, foundations of the institutional power structures.

Each of the above thinkers can be interpreted as having been motivated by an ideal of freedom, usually in the form of freedom from oppressive authorities, whether that authority is taken to be a religious institution, as was true for Luther, an oppressive mode of thinking (as self-objectification and essentializing) as in Sartre, an oppressive religious/social ideology, as in Camus, an oppressive economic institution, as in Barthes, an oppressive mode of philosophical interpretation and understanding of language, as in Derrida, or an oppressive style of discourse and institutional organization, as in Foucault. Although the oppressive forces are variously defined from thinker to thinker, we encounter the common theme of emancipation. With respect to the theorists from Sartre to Foucault, the emphasis upon freedom and the rejection of any views that even remotely convey a totalitarian flavor is not surprising given that France was engaged in a life-and-death struggle with German totalitarianism during the Second World War. In a large part, the development of postmodernist theory in France is interpretable against this historical background, as it stands in conjunction with the equally subversive Freudian and surrealistic movements whose related focus was upon releasing people from oppressive forces that are harbored within the individual.

To appreciate the 'postmodern' mentality, we can consider an example with which Foucault begins his book, *The Order of Things* (1966). Reflecting upon a passage written by the Spanish author, Jorge Luís Borges (1899–1986), Foucault writes the following:

> This book first arose out of a passage in Borges, out of the laughter that shattered, as I read the passage, all the familiar landmarks of my thought – *our* thought, the thought that bears the stamp of our age and our geography – breaking up all the ordered surfaces and all the planes with which we are accustomed to tame the wild profusion of existing things, and continuing long afterwards to disturb and threaten with collapse our age-old distinction between the Same and the Other. This passage quotes 'a certain Chinese encyclopedia' in which it is written that 'animals are divided into: (a) belonging to the Emperor, (b) embalmed, (c) tame, (d) suckling pigs, (e) sirens, (f) fabulous, (g) stray dogs, (h) included in the present classification, (i) frenzied, (j) innumerable, (k) drawn with a very fine camelhair brush, (l) *et cetera*, (m) having just broken the water pitcher, (n) that from a long way off look like flies'. In the wonderment of this taxonomy, the thing we apprehend in one great leap, the thing that, by means of the fable, is demonstrated as the exotic charm of another system of thought, is the limitation of our own, the stark impossibility of thinking that.[356]

In the above, the various categories of animal are comparable to the many different categories of discourse and activity within the contemporary world. There are numerous communities, alternative value systems, cultural constellations, and linguistic differences, and there appears to be no common system that embraces them all. People often talk past each other, rather than to each other, and the contemporary world presents itself as more of a patchwork, than as a perfectly organized system. Daily life itself forms a pastiche, which Lyotard himself describes in his essay, 'What is Postmodernism:'

> Eclecticism is the degree zero of contemporary general culture: one listens to reggae, watches a western, eats McDonald's food for lunch and local cuisine for dinner, wears Paris perfume in Tokyo and 'retro' clothes in Hong Kong; knowledge is a matter for TV games. It is easy to find a public for eclectic works. By becoming kitsch, art panders to the confusion which reigns in the 'taste' of patrons. Artists, gallery owners, critics, and public wallow together in the 'anything goes,' and the epoch is one of slackening.[357]

With this general context in mind, we can now consider the more philosophical characterization of Lyotard's conception of the postmodern mentality.

The Postmodern Condition

Lyotard's *The Postmodern Condition: A Report on Knowledge* was commissioned by the Conseil des Universitiés of the government of Quebec, and the text's purpose was to provide an overview of contemporary societal conditions in a style that would be useful to legislators and university authorities. To understand the position of this work within Lyotard's intellectual development, it is helpful to know that it does not represent an outlook that he had held throughout his career up until that point. Rather, Lyotard went through some antecedent phases which, in some respects, were opposed to the theoretical foundations assumed in *The Postmodern Condition*.

Previous to this time, Lyotard tended to regard language as a fundamentally oppressive force (as did Barthes) that specifically needed to be transcended by refocusing our attention on visual imagery and upon sensation in general. As he later admitted, however, such an 'aesthetically' centered outlook could not effectively address questions of political justice, and this led him to abandon his earlier standpoint in favor of one that provided a more useful platform for the investigation of political questions. This was the source of his positive attention to language, and to the various discourses within which political power is embodied. Lyotard thus moved away from a position akin to Barthes's standpoint as expressed in 'the pleasures of the text,' and closer to Foucault's way of attending to modes of discourse as the embodiment of institutional power structures. His intellectual trajectory also matched how, during roughly the same time, Foucault was moving away from a 'negative' or oppressive conception of power to a more 'positive' or self-constituting and self-constructive conception of power.

But it was neither Barthes's nor Foucault's views on language which formed the more precise foundation for Lyotard's analysis of postmodernity. Rather, it was the Austrian philosopher Ludwig Wittgenstein who at this time influenced Lyotard the most. Lyotard's connection to all three of these thinkers, however, provides some background to the way he uses as a centerpiece, the concept of 'narrative,' as a way to characterize the postmodern mentality.

Lyotard gives a synopsis of his report in the introduction to *The Postmodern Condition*, and he states that his focus will be upon the 'discourses of legitimation' that operate within scientific knowledge. He is concerned with the form that knowledge takes within postmodern society, the way in which this knowledge acquires its authority, and the ways in which the specific form of this knowledge (viz., in a format compatible with computer technology) is likely to have repercussions within the structural organization of Western society as a whole. He defines his approach and central problematic as follows:

Science has always been in conflict with narratives. Judged by the yard-stick of science, the majority of them prove to be fables. But to the extent that science does not restrict itself to stating useful regularities and seeks the truth, it is obliged to legitimate the rules of its own game. It then produces a discourse of legitimation with respect to its own status, a discourse called philosophy. I will use the term *modern* to designate any science that legitimates itself with reference to a metadiscourse of this kind making an explicit appeal to some grand metanarrative, such as the dialectics of Spirit, the hermeneutics of meaning, the emancipation of the rational or working subject, or the creation of wealth.[358]

As the foundation for his definition of 'the modern,' to which he will contrast 'the postmodern,' Lyotard maintains first of all, that all forms of legitimation involve telling stories, or giving narratives. These legitimating narratives function to define a larger, meaningful, and seemingly non-controversial global context within which specific activities acquire their positive meaning, and hence, their legitimation. According to Lyotard, any activity which claims to present the truth, needs a legitimation in the form of a narrative, and the larger, more comprehensive, more complicated, more universal the narrative, the more powerful the legitimation will appear to be. This leads him to focus upon 'metanarratives' (narratives which are broad enough to include many sub-narratives) as those which have played a central role in the legitimation of scientific knowledge insofar as such narratives situate scientific knowledge within a universally meaningful context. These metanarratives are, in effect, philosophical accounts of the meaning of world history, or the meaning of human life in general. As a prime example of a metanarrative, he describes the 'Enlightenment narrative:'

> For example, the rule of consensus between the sender and addressee of a statement with truth-value is deemed acceptable if it is cast in terms of a possible unanimity between rational minds: this is the Enlightenment narrative, in which the hero of knowledge works toward a good ethico-political end – universal peace. As can be seen from this example, if a metanarrative implying a philosophy of history is used to legitimate knowledge, questions are raised concerning the validity of the institutions governing the social bond: these must be legitimated as well. Thus justice is consigned to the grand narrative in the same way as truth.[359]

As other examples of metanarrative, Lyotard cites philosophical views which maintain respectively that human society is becoming more and more mean-ingful over time in reference, alternatively, to spirituality, freedom, or wealth.

Such metanarratives are comparable in that each proposes a single important goal or end toward which all other activities are directed.[360] The Enlightenment narrative Lyotard finds especially prevalent – even within the postmodern period – and he makes a special effort to dispute its assumption that a harmonious consensus of opinion is possible among people.[361] In contrast to this modern mentality, Lyotard defines the postmodern perspective as one which, in a reflection of his disposition to reject any form of totalitarianism, actively resists the acceptance of any totalizing 'grand narrative' within which all human activities and values can be systematically comprehended:

> Simplifying to the extreme, I define *postmodern* as incredulity toward metanarratives ... The narrative function is losing its functors, its great hero, its great dangers, its great voyages, its great goal. It is being dispersed in clouds of narrative language elements – narrative, but also denotative, prescriptive, and so on. Conveyed within each cloud are pragmatic valencies specific to its kind. Each of us lives at the intersection of many of these. However, we do not necessarily establish stable language combinations, and the properties of the ones we do establish are not necessarily communicable.[362]

Lyotard continues with an observation regarding the way the decision-makers in contemporary society nonetheless continue to operate according to a metanarrative which, although it employs more fashionable terms, regards society as a large machine or unified system of ever-increasing power and efficiency:

> The decision-makers, however, attempt to manage these clouds of sociality according to input/output matrices, following a logic which implies that their elements are commensurable and that the whole is determinable. They allocate their lives for the growth of power. In matters of social justice and of scientific truth alike, the legitimation of that power is based on its optimizing the system's performance – efficiency. The application of this criterion to all our games necessarily entails a certain level of terror, whether soft or hard: be operational (that is, commensurable) or disappear.[363]

A main theme of *The Postmodern Condition*, then, is the way knowledge has become an item which is conceived to be thoroughly quantifiable, mechanizable, and computable. The study also focuses upon how this mode of packageable information prescribes a technological and totalizing mode of social consciousness which is tending to encompass all aspects of life. Insofar as Lyotard believes that this style of social understanding entails a certain level of terror, his discussion of the contrasting postmodern mentality stands as an effort to emancipate people from the oppressions of computer–technological thinking. His project is thus both descriptive of what he considers to be the new spirit of the times, and prescriptive of a way to overcome the potentially totalitarian aspects of the modernist outlook which he perceives are persisting within the postmodern era. He describes the postmodern historical period as involving dispositions toward both totalitarianism and emancipation.

The text begins by describing the development of computer technology as an event that compares in significance to the development of transportation systems and the mass media. In this respect, Lyotard sets forth a claim similar to what we find in Foucault's thought, namely, that different time periods (in this case, one defined by the widespread use of computers) carry with themselves a certain logic that determines which kinds of statements will count as knowledge. Lyotard's suspicion is that in due time, the belief will become widespread that if some alleged item of knowledge is not consistent with computer information systems, then that item does not count as real 'knowledge.'[364]

Lyotard refers to this as the 'exteriorization of knowledge,' 'the mercantilism of knowledge,' and 'the commercialization of knowledge,' as he observes how information in the form of computer data is packaged, bought, and sold. He also notes that multinational corporations, as opposed to nations, are gaining ever-increasing control over the large-scale computer information banks, and that investment decisions 'have passed beyond the control of nation-states.' The rise of corporate power and the development of the computer merge here to change the face of Western society.

Lyotard notes that with the computerization of knowledge, what counts as knowledge also becomes especially alienating in its exteriorization and objectification. Since scientific knowledge becomes more questionable as it assumes an increasingly depersonalized and inhuman guise, such knowledge faces a crisis of legitimation – its advocates begin to feel the need to provide a global justification of its role as knowledge, to compensate for this knowledge's alienating and dehumanizing aspect. Also, given the association between the control of this scientific knowledge and institutional bodies, Lyotard draws a connection between knowledge and power similar to the one that inspired many of Foucault's analyses. In this vein, Lyotard observes that governments are assuming a more pivotal role in the activities which define what knowledge is, and this acts as a force that has the effect of blurring the distinction between power and knowledge.

With respect to his method of interpretation, Lyotard adopts Wittgenstein's idea that key aspects of linguistic meaning are understandable upon analogy to playing games such as chess. According to Wittgenstein, the meanings of words amount to their prescribed uses within a community of speakers, just as the 'meanings' of the pieces within a game of chess are constituted by the rules for moving them on the board. Within the field of language, there are many different communities, and hence, many different 'language-games' (*Sprachspiele*) that people play, not all of which are commensurable with one another. There is no single language-game that everyone plays according to the exact same linguistic rules; there is only a multitude of overlaps and family resemblances amongst the many different language-games that are played.

> Wittgenstein, taking up the study of language again from scratch, focuses his attention on the effects of different modes of discourse; he calls the various types of utterances he identifies along the way (a few of which I have listed) *language games*.[365] What he means by this term is that each of the various categories of utterance can be defined in terms or rules specifying their properties and the uses to which they can be put – in exactly the same way as the game of chess is defined by a set of rules determining the properties of each of the pieces, in other words, the proper way to move them.[366]

Lyotard draws two implications from the above Wittgensteinian model: (1) language involves conflict, and that 'to speak is to fight,'[367] (2) language, insofar as it is constituted by many language games with differing rules, does not involve a rigid, lawlike, universal coordination of practice. Such features of language run counter to the modernist mentality, for in the Lyotardian–Wittgensteinian perspective, the actual practice of language entails that there will be multiplicity and variation over time, in the absence of any universal and constant language. Once again, as we have seen in the conceptions of language advanced by Barthes, Derrida, and Foucault, we encounter the idea that language is multidimensional, except that according to Lyotard, the sense of overlapping and criss-crossing, is expressed in reference to Wittgensteinian observations regarding the diversity of rules for the applications of words.

Lyotard observes that within contemporary society, there persists a modernist and scientistic tendency to understand social arrangements and social phenomena as 'systems.'[368] As an immense self-regulating system, society is conceived as a unified, machine-like entity whose inner directedness is toward greater and greater efficiency or 'performativity.' Quite independently of the theory's accuracy, Lyotard observes that once a theory such as systems theory is assumed to be the best description of society, certain implications for what counts as knowledge will immediately follow. Once it is accepted that society is a giant system, then it becomes more likely that machine-compatible information will count as the preferred style of knowledge. The acceptance of systems theory (as one among a number of possibilities) according to Lyotard, thereby serves indirectly to legitimate knowledge as exclusively machine-compatible information. He perceives, in effect, how certain philosophical views can serve as part of a legitimating ideology for science. The kind of observation compares to how Barthes showed that contemporary myths serve to legitimate and perpetuate the capitalist system.

As a counterforce to the rationalistic 'society as system' and 'knowledge as computability' outlook, Lyotard makes some Wittgensteinian observations about how languages operates in daily practice. Specifically he notes that the multiplicity of language games and the multiplicity of different kinds of utterance tend to resist the leveling that the 'knowledge as computability' outlook imposes upon communication. He claims that language, as it is actually used, contradicts the assumptions of the totalizing view of society-as-system, and that the latter, computer-and-information-centered view of society is therefore yet another ideology and fictitious metanarrative.

With a focus upon language as it is actually spoken, Lyotard identifies different kinds of knowledge in reference to various utterance-types. There is scientific knowledge, which corresponds to denotative utterances, but there are other kinds of knowledge as well, such as 'know-how' and 'knowing how to live' which correspond to performative and evaluative utterances. Lyotard claims that as it is traditionally understood, knowledge in general is constituted by at least these different kinds of specific knowledge, and that there is no one of these specific kinds in terms of which the others can be reduced.[369] Lyotard's view, then, is historical, language-centered, pragmatic, and pluralistic.

Lyotard also contrasts knowledge that is transmitted in the form of narrative (e.g., myths, fables, nursery rhymes, epics, historical anecdotes, personal histories, world histories, etc.) with knowledge that is transmitted in terms of denotative statements alone (i.e., scientific knowledge). He notes that narrative knowledge is more comprehensive insofar as it includes all kind of utterances – interrogative and evaluative, as well as denotative. Moreover, narrative knowledge is more vital to the social fabric than is scientific knowledge, since narrative is used to constitute societal bonds. In sum, Lyotard's analysis that knowledge expressed in the form of narrative is richer and more socially fundamental than scientific knowledge. As such, he notes how scientific knowledge is eventually led to legitimate itself in reference to some form of narrative knowledge, since the latter includes it and exceeds it in its indispensability to social organization.

Just as Derrida observed that language, in its concrete use, contains associative, literalistic, and metaphorical dimensions, Lyotard observes that narrative contains denotative, interrogative, and evaluative expressions. Both thinkers emphasize the concrete complexity of language, to show how abstract and one-dimensional the exclusive focus upon literalistic verbiage happens to be. Lyotard goes straight to the point, and claims that 'scientific knowledge requires that one language game, denotation, be retained and all others excluded,' adding that this kind of exclusion involves terror, and that it can be conceived as a form of cultural imperialism.[370]

> The scientist questions the validity of narrative statements and concludes that they are never subject to argumentation or proof. He classifies them as belonging to a different mentality: savage, primitive, underdeveloped, backward, alienated, composed of opinions, customs, authority, prejudice, ignorance, ideology. Narratives are fables, myths, legends, fit only for women and children. At best, attempts are made to throw some rays of light into this obscurantism, to civilize, educate, develop.
>
> This unequal relationship [between narrative and scientific knowledge] is an intrinsic effect of the rules specific to each game. We all know its symptoms. It is the entire history of cultural imperialism from the dawn of Western civilization. It is important to recognize its special tenor, which sets it apart from all other forms of imperialism: it is governed by the demand for legitimation.[371]

As noted above, Lyotard claims that scientific knowledge is exclusionary, insofar as it recognizes only one kind of utterance-type as knowledge. And for Lyotard, scientific knowledge is antagonistic to narrative knowledge, since it regards narrative knowledge as associated with fable, myth, and legend. He also argues that scientific knowledge is divorced from the social fabric, insofar as its sole emphasis upon denotation does not support a variety of communicative and evaluative interactions. Moreover, he maintains that narrative knowledge is inescapable and is necessary for any kind of social legitimation.

In this respect, Lyotard regards as inconsistent any view of knowledge that acknowledges only scientific knowledge as legitimate, for he holds that scientific knowledge must ultimately rely upon narrative knowledge to socially legitimate itself, even though it fails to regard narrative knowledge as proper knowledge at all. The defenders of the exclusivity of scientific knowledge are thus caught in a dilemma: either scientific knowledge recognizes other kinds of knowledge, and sacrifices its own claim to being the only true knowledge, or scientific knowledge holds on to its claim as being the only true knowledge, consequently negates narrative knowledge, and finds itself without any way to legitimate itself. In either case, it loses its status as the sole kind of knowledge.

On the more constructive side of things, Lyotard maintains that although there has been a diminished faith in the single, overriding, completely comprehensive metanarrative as a mode of legitimating and giving meaning to our cultural activities, there remains the possibility of providing smaller-scale narratives for this or that specific activity. Which is to say that although he believes that an absolute meaning for our lives cannot be given, a conditional and relative meaning can be provided by situating our activities within more local stories and accounts of what we happen to be doing. This defines a middle-path between the quest for absolute meaning and the recognition of utter meaninglessness.

It should be underscored that Lyotard is a thinker deeply concerned with social justice, and he observes in a more sinister note, that the present-day influence of the knowledge-as-computability, or knowledge-as-performativity viewpoint tends to serve the interests of those who have financial power:

> No money [e.g., for elaborate scientific instruments, research projects, etc.], no proof – and that means no verification of statements and no truth. The games of scientific language become the games of the rich, in which whoever is wealthiest has the best chance of being right. An equation between wealth, efficiency, and truth is thus established.[372]

> The production of proof, which is in principle only part of an argumentation process designed to win agreement from the addressees of scientific messages, thus falls under the control of another language game, in which the goal is no longer truth, but performativity – that is, the best possible input/output equation. The State and/or company must abandon the idealist and humanist narratives of legitimation in order to justify a new goal: in the discourse of today's financial backers of research, the only credible goal is power. Scientists, technicians, and instruments are purchased not to find truth, but to augment power.[373]

Within this picture of the 'mercantilization of knowledge,' Lyotard observes that the traditional question, 'Is it true?,' is nowadays being transformed into the question, 'Is it efficient?' – a question which is itself reformulated quickly into questions such as 'Is it useful?' or 'Is it saleable?' Accompanying the way in which knowledge is becoming a commodity, Lyotard links the institution of 'terror,' which he conceives of as the silencing of alternative and competing conceptions of knowledge. For him, 'terror' is a kind of violence inflicted upon a person or community whereby the individuals involved are not allowed to express what they perceive as wrongs committed against them, because the language-game or linguistic practice that would allow this expression is not recognized or is prohibited.

If, for example, some society believed that the only kind of legitimate knowledge is computational and informational, then anyone within that society who advocated any form of non-quantifiable knowledge would find it impossible to express their knowledge in the recognized and socially legitimate forms. They would, in effect, be silenced. The narrowness of the socially legitimate forms of knowledge operate to define alternative kinds of knowledge out of the conversation, and out of the mainstream social existence.

'Terror' arises, when one (or only a few) among a wide field of language-games becomes the only acceptably recognized language-game, where the rules of the linguistic game are narrowed to a point where dissenting voices are not given the means to express themselves. Just as Barthes stated in his final years that language is 'fascist' insofar as its categories are imposed upon us, Lyotard observes more concretely that a linguistic situation can become oppressive and terror-filled, when one community imposes the rules of its particular language games upon those whose form of life operates according to different linguistic rules. Which is to say that a profound form of terrorism is linguistic terrorism, which is exercised by the control others exert over the language one is allowed to speak and hear.

This theme of how subsections of the population can be excluded from legitimate society as a consequence of social definitions arises in Foucault's thought as well: he observed that with the rise of the Enlightenment view that reason is the final arbiter of all disputes, those who were deemed unreasonable became socially marginalized. People who were previously regarded as merely different and as having a strange kind of wisdom at times, were soon defined as being merely mad, and as subject to incarceration. And similar to Lyotard, Foucault sought a way to combat such styles of oppressive mentality by looking toward modes of aesthetic experience and to avant-garde artists who were able to express 'thought from the outside' of established norms.[374] In later years, inspired by Edmund Burke's (1757) characterization of the sublime as centered upon the experience of terror, Lyotard himself focused upon the aesthetic experience of the sublime – the attempt to 'present the unpresentable' – as a way to fight against a system of norms that terrorized people into silence. In this connection, sublimity becomes a revolutionary force in Lyotard's hands, and aesthetic experience assumes a general political relevance in the recognition that art can be politically liberating and can serve as a force to combat terror.

Critical discussion

The concluding chapters in *The Postmodern Condition* describe contemporary conditions in relation to the effects of computerization in the fields of education and scientific research. Both fields appear to be developing in service of the knowledge-as-computability and society-as-system outlooks: the values in education are gravitating toward practicality and information processing/producing techniques; the direction of scientific research is being determined by governmental and corporate bodies whose frequently predominating goal appears to be the increase of power. Lyotard, in effect, describes a powerful modernist ideology of systems theory that continues to prevail within the postmodern era.

Given the prevalence of modernist systems theory ideology, we can ask how such an ideology could prevail and could constitute a threat, in an allegedly postmodernist age – an age where such ideologies should no longer be taken seriously. This remains a puzzle within Lyotard's account. On the one hand, he emphasizes how there is a diversity of linguistic communities within Western society as a whole and within the scientific community in particular. In the face of such multiplicity and variation, Lyotard finds that any single, metanarrative, or universal language is an incredible possibility.

On the other hand, Lyotard admits that governmental bodies and multinational corporations operate according to an ideology of systems theory and according to an essentially mercantilistic and globalistic conception of knowledge that emphasizes denotative utterances alone. Insofar as the systems theory is a form of metanarrative, it would seem that our contemporary society is equally as modernist as it is postmodernist. We can ask, then, whether the social situation has changed much from the days when other kinds of metanarratives prevailed, and whether Lyotard has accurately captured the essence of the postmodern society, if indeed we are living within a substantially different social era.

In connection with Lyotard's identification of terror with social exclusion, we can also question whether the Wittgensteinian analogy between language and chess has not been overplayed to exaggerate the oppressiveness of language. The purpose of chess is to defeat the opponent, and it is a kind of fight. If language is regarded as a large chess game, then such an analogy can easily generate a view that regards language as a confrontational enterprise where the phrase 'to speak is to fight' is a fair enough description. Moreover, in chess, one useful strategy to defeat an opponent is to move one's chess pieces such that whatever move one's opponent chooses to make, one's opponent stands to lose. In psychological phraseology, to win at chess, one would do well to become a master of creating 'double-bind' situations.

What is interesting here, is that Lyotard identifies such double-bind situations as integral to the institution of terror, since a narrow set of social rules requires a person to either submit to the rules and thereby remain silent and unable to voice their objection, or violate the rules, and risk becoming defined as an insurgent, rebel, lawbreaker, or criminal. The person loses either way. The institution of terror often involves the institution of double-binds. To illustrate this principle of the double-bind, Lyotard gives the example of a rationale advanced in support of the claim that there were no Nazi gas chambers. The claim is that there are (supposedly) no direct witnesses for their existence, and hence, no good reason to believe that the gas chambers existed. The problem with the argument, as Lyotard reveals, is that it is posed as a 'no win' situation: if one supposes that every witness to the gas chambers entered the gas chambers and did not survive them, then there can be no witnesses, and hence, no evidence of the existence of the gas chambers.[375]

Indeed, the double-bind situation is especially apt for characterizing terroristic social situations, since it has been argued – by authors such as Gregory Bateson and R. D. Laing – that subjecting people to this kind of logic, especially within family and love-related contexts, has a tendency to drive their victims into a condition of mental disarray and confusion, if not mental illness. So Lyotard is asserting implicitly that any society that is excessively censorship-oriented and linguistically oppressive has the potential to develop a social consciousness that displays a pathological structure. Which is to suggest, conversely, that the less oppression and silencing of dissenting voices a society has, the healthier it is likely to be.

Lyotard's social and political message is of the highest value, but we can nonetheless question his emphasis upon how language can be terrorizing, if we wonder whether the Wittgensteinian analogy between the rules for word-use and the rules for chess, led Lyotard to perceive language as more conflictual and oppressive than it in fact happens to be. For we can also witness upon occasion, an inspiring amount of constructive interpersonal dialogue, peaceful resolutions to conflict, mutual fusion of horizons, consistent openness to other people's perspectives, and mixing of worldviews that occur in daily life.

Selected works of Jean-François Lyotard:

1954 (age 30): *La phénoménologie* [*Phenomenology*]
1971 (age 47): *Discours, figure* [*Discourse, Figure*]
1973 (age 49): *Dérive à partir de Marx et Freud* [*Driftworks*]
1974 (age 50): *Économie libidinale* [*Libidinal Economy*]
1979 (age 55): (1) *Au juste: conversations* [*Just Gaming*]
   (2) *La condition postmoderne: Rapport sur le savoir*
   [*The Postmodern Condition: A Report on Knowledge*]
1983 (age 59): *Le différend* [*The Differend: Phrases in Dispute*]
1988 (age 64): (1) *Heidegger et 'les juifs'* [*Heidegger and 'the Jews'*]
   (2) *L'inhumain: Causeries sur le temps* [*The Inhuman: Reflections on Time*]
   (3) *La Guerre des Algériens: Écrits 1956–63* [*Political Writings*]
1991 (age 67): *Leçons sur l'analytique du sublime* [*Lessons on the Analytic of the Sublime*]

15

Luce Irigaray, Feminist and Psycholinguist (1930–)

Life and works

Luce Irigaray was born in Belgium in 1930, remaining there for her early education and university studies, where she attended the University of Louvain. In 1955, she received a Master's degree from Louvain, and then taught in a *lycée* in Brussels from 1956–59. Moving then to France for further studies, Irigaray earned a Master's Degree in psychology from the University of Paris, and a year later, a diploma in psychopathology. During the 1960s she attended the seminars of Jacques Lacan, was trained in psychoanalysis, and in 1968 received a doctorate in linguistics from the University of Vincennes, which was published later as *Le langage des dements* [*The Language of Dementia* (1973)].

From 1970 to 1974, Irigaray was a member of the *École Freudienne de Paris*, a psychoanalytic school started by Jacques Lacan, and was also teaching at the University of Vincennes. It was during these times that she was also influenced by the feminist group '*Psychanalyse et Politique*' (known also as '*Psych et Po*') that was founded, in the wake of the 1968 social uprisings, by Antoinette Fouque – a person whom Irigaray analyzed in 1969. In 1974, Irigaray received a second doctorate from the University of Paris VIII, Saint Denis, the substance of which was published with a solid public reception as *Speculum de l'autre femme* [*Speculum of the Other Woman*]. The publication of this controversial book precipitated Irigaray's departure from her position at Vincennes. Irigaray was also questioning the views of Jacques Lacan at this time.

In the following years, Irigaray continued to write, research, and teach, and she was appointed in 1982 to a chair in philosophy in the Netherlands, at the Erasmus University in Rotterdam. Since 1985 she has worked at the *Centre National de Recherche Scientifique* (CNRS) in Paris. During these years, Irigaray became a key theorist in French and international feminist thought, and has been especially influential in Italy, where she has lectured and contributed to the newspaper of the Italian Communist Party.[376] Irigaray's essay on mother–daughter relationships, '*Et l'une ne bouge pas sans l'autre*' (1978)[377] ['*L'una non sogna senza l'altra*'; 'And the One Doesn't Stir without the Other'] has been of particular influence in Italian feminist circles.

The questionable domination of masculine values in Western society

For centuries, women have been denied the same rights as men within Western society in a wide range of cultural domains. To appreciate this fact, we need only consider the history of voting rights and land ownership to notice how women have been denied a political and financial voice on a par with men. Similarly, opportunities for securing jobs in influential social positions, along with the opportunity to participate equally in cultural spheres such as art and religion, have also been consistently denied to women. A central question, then, is not whether women have been denied social opportunities within a male-dominated society, but why this has happened.

Among the reasons that can account for the disadvantageous position in which women have found themselves, is an observation concerning the very languages we use: it can be shown that they implicitly and systematically subordinate values associated with women, and highlight values associated with men. This establishes and institutionalizes a prejudice against women from the linguistic start. In accord with the language-focused spirit of twentieth-century Western thought in general, Luce Irigaray investigates the languages we speak (focusing on French), and shows how male-oriented language dominates over the cultural symbols which, from infancy on, all members of the society must significantly share.

Just as Roland Barthes in his *Mythologies* reveals the implicit influence of capitalist and colonialist forces within contemporary culture, Irigaray reveals the implicit and prevailing male influence within Western culture as a whole.

As one important method of revealing this influence, she attends to the way the nouns in European languages tend to assign masculine grammatical genders to the more valuable, more important, and more powerful items. This is evident in the French language:

> Patient work on the gender of words reveals their hidden sex: this is not expressed immediately, and a linguist will quickly object that a lounge chair, *un fauteuil*, is no more masculine than an ordinary chair, *une chaise*. Apparently not, but a little thought shows that the lounge chair is more valuable than the ordinary chair. The chair, the feminine one, is simply more useful, and the masculine is more luxurious, ornamental, culturally signalled. A rigorous analysis of all the words in the dictionary will bring out their hidden sex; the computer, *l'ordinateur*, is of course masculine, whereas the typewriter, *la machine à écrire*, is feminine. It's a question of value.[378]
>
> Objects which are inanimate, deprived of life, inhuman, turn out to be feminine. This means that men have attributed to themselves subjectivity, and have reduced women to the status of objects.[379]

The above examples, taken individually, may appear to be of relatively minor significance, but when they are multiplied and surveyed as a whole, they reveal a tendency within European languages to assign a male designation to the items of acknowledged social value. Irigaray notes that the masculine privileging of the valued items in the world does not stop with everyday objects such as lounge chairs and computers; it extends to items like the sun and God – beings that occupy foundational positions within an array of natural and religious conceptual frameworks. This suggests that men, by having a linguistic, and hence a rhetorical, advantage that associates masculinity with divinity (for instance), are in a position to take advantage of such associations to minimize the power and the roles of women in society. For if God is a 'father,' then the foundation of the universe and the source of absolute value is conceived as being male-valued. Masculine ways consequently acquire a divine sanction and become ultimately authoritative within such a linguistic framework:

> The linguistic code, like the modes of exchange, like the system of images, and representation, is made for masculine subjects. Thus God is father; he begets a son, and for this purpose he uses a woman who is reduced to maternity. This has been the most abiding structure in our religious and civic traditions for centuries: a relation *between* men, or *in* man … through a woman. In such a culture the woman remains at home, and is the object of use and exchange between men. She is used for reproduction and for the material maintenance of life.[380]

For centuries, that which is considered to be of value has been of the masculine gender; what has been devalued is of the feminine gender. The sun, for example, *le soleil*, is masculine; the moon, *la lune*, is feminine. The sun is considered in our cultures to be the source of life; but the moon is seen as ambiguous, virtually sinister. The attribution of the masculine gender to the sun can be found throughout the history of human culture: the link between the sun and the god-man as well.[381,382]

Man as been the subject of discourse, whether in theory, morality, or politics. And the gender of God, the guardian of every subject and every discourse, is always masculine and paternal, in the West. To women are left the so-called minor arts: cooking, knitting, embroidery, and sewing; and, in exceptional cases, poetry, painting, and music. Whatever their importance, these arts do not currently make the rules, at least not overtly.[383]

If we multiply examples of the above kind, the evidence accumulates for the proposition that many of the central values of human life have been defined in reference to the male image, and that women have been largely excluded from the core of cultural definition thereby. In response to this one-sided situation – one that in Lyotard's terms would amount to a massive form of terror – Irigaray considers the sorts of action, reconception, and revaluation of values that would be appropriate to restore the balance between men and women, along with the voice of women, assuming that neither men nor women are unconditionally privileged with respect to the other.[384]

One classical strategy to alleviate the oppression of women, is to urge women to organize socially for the purpose of exerting an influence that will provide them greater access to the most powerful positions in society. Irigaray does not deny the importance of this pragmatic approach, but she believes that it fails to address a deeper problem: if the society in which women live is a society permeated with male values, then the most powerful positions in society will also be permeated with male values. So if a woman uncritically struggles to gain a powerful social role, then she could easily find herself obliged to behave in accord with masculine values. But insofar as such a woman supports such values, she would lose her specific identity as a woman.

It is therefore necessary to ask further what it would mean to be 'equal' to men, since one answer to this question is unsatisfactory. It should not mean that if women are to be equal to men, then women must allow themselves to be assimilated into a male-styled world. For to be 'equal to' men in a male-styled world would have the result of preserving that terrorizing masculine world. In a short essay written on the occasion of Simone de Beauvoir's death (spring 1986), Irigaray expresses this point:

Demanding equality, as women, seems to me to be an erroneous expression of a real issue. Demanding to be equal presupposes a term of comparison. Equal to what? What do women want to be equal to? Men? A wage? A public position? Equal to what? Why not equal to themselves?[385]

Certain tendencies of the day, certain contemporary feminists, are noisily demanding the neutralization of sex [*sexe*]. That neutralization, if it were possible, would correspond to the end of the human race. The human race is divided into *two genres* which ensure its production and reproduction. Trying to suppress sexual difference is to invite a genocide more radical than any destruction that ever existed in History [viz., the disintegration of female identity]. What is important, on the other hand, is defining the values of belonging to a sex-specific *genre*. What is indispensable is elaborating a culture of the sexual which does not yet exist, whilst respecting both genres … It is social justice, pure and simple, to balance out the power of one sex over the other by giving, or restoring, cultural values to female sexuality …

Equality between men and women cannot be achieved unless we think of genre as sexuate [*sexué*] and write the rights and duties of each sex, insofar as they are different, into social rights and duties.[386]

In a later interview (1990), Irigaray presents comparable ideas:

Neutralizing grammatical gender is equivalent to the annulment of the difference in sexual subjectivity, and it tends increasingly to exclude sexuality from culture. We will take a big step backwards if we abolish grammatical gender, a step backwards which our culture cannot afford. On the other hand, it is urgent and indeed imperative that equal subjective rights be given to men and women: 'equal' meaning, of course, different.[387]

With such observations, we arrive at Irigaray's emphasis upon 'sexual difference:' she maintains that although we are all human, there comes a significant point where men and women must be conceived as different kinds of beings, and that this difference is defined primarily in reference to their respective sexualities. She further claims that a complete fusion and merging of these two core identities is impossible, and that the equality and balance between men and women which is necessary for social justice must be achieved in recognition and in respect of these sexual differences, rather than in their dilution and elimination.

Sexual difference

How, then, are women different from men, according to Irigaray? As is obvious, there are physiological and structural differences between the male and female bodily forms, and Irigaray sometimes emphasizes this kind of physical difference. To reveal a distinctive women's identity, Irigaray also employs a mode of analysis similar to what she uses to reveal how men have appropriated language and cultural symbols: she examines the way women tend to speak about themselves and about others, and infers from these data that women tend to experience the world differently from men.

With respect to physiological and structural differences between men and women, Irigaray points out how prevailing, male-oriented conceptions of women define them as beings that are 'not men' insofar as women lack the male sex organ.[388] In accord with this negative conceptualization, women are regarded as 'incomplete' and (from Freud) as 'castrated males.' In this male-privileging and woman-negating characterization of women's sexuality, we can see once more how at a basic level of personal definition, men's sexuality is privileged, while women's sexuality is subordinated, if not invalidated.[389]

To counteract a male-centered characterization of women's sexuality – one which derives from a negative, and male-derived interpretation of the symbolic meanings of women's sexual organs – Irigaray offers an alternative and positive characterization:

> A remaking of immanence and transcendence, notably through this *threshold* which has never been examined as such: the female sex. The threshold that gives access to the *mucous*. Beyond classical oppositions of love and hate, liquid and ice – a threshold that is always *half-open*. The threshold of the *lips*, which are strangers to dichotomy and oppositions. Gathered one against the other but without any possible suture, at least of a real kind. They do not absorb the world into or through themselves, provided they are not misused and reduced to a means of consumption or consummation. They offer a shape of welcome but do not assimilate, reduce, or swallow up. A sort of doorway to voluptuousness? They are not useful, except as that which designates a *place*, the very place of uselessness, at least as it is habitually understood. Strictly speaking, they serve neither conception nor jouissance [sexual pleasure]. Is this the mystery of feminine identity? Of its self-contemplation, of this very strange word of silence? Both the threshold and reception of exchange, the sealed-up secret of wisdom, belief, and faith in all truths?
>
> (Two sets of lips that, moreover, cross over each other like the arms of a cross, the prototype of the crossroads *between*. The mouth lips and the genital lips do not point in the same direction. In some way they point in the direction opposite from the one you would expect, with the 'lower' ones forming the vertical.)

In this approach, where the borders of the body are wed in an embrace that transcends all limits – without, however, risking engulfment, thanks to the fecundity of the porous – in the most extreme experience of sensation, which is also always in the future, each one discovers the self in that experience which is inexpressible yet forms the supple grounding of life and language.[390]

In contrast to the male-centered definitions of female sexuality as being constituted by a fundamental 'lack,' Irigaray develops an alternative set of symbolic meanings for the female sex organs which assert a positive and unique characterization of women's sexuality. Among these meanings, perhaps one of the most philosophically and psychologically intriguing is her interpretation of the vaginal lips as 'strangers to dichotomy' in their being dual, and yet naturally always touching each other to form a unity. This image is reminiscent of the way Sartre characterizes pre-reflective consciousness as 'not dual,' but as the foundation for a reflectively generated, subject–object duality.

If this analogy holds, then Irigaray's interpretation of the female genitalia recalls a condition of consciousness akin to Lacan's 'imaginary' mode that is primordial, and more fundamental than the Lacanian male-centered symbolic and linguistic 'Name-of-the-Father' mode of consciousness. So Irigaray's interpretation suggests that the female sexual identity, at least in one sense, is the psychic foundation from which issues male identity, just as the pre-reflective consciousness is the foundation from which issues the reflective consciousness for Sartre, just as the imaginary mode of consciousness is the foundation from which issues the symbolic mode for Lacan, and perhaps more distantly, if we consider only the linguistic field, just as the narrative discourse is the foundation from which issues literalistic discourse for Lyotard.

Irigaray also characterizes women's identity by means of investigations into the way women tend to speak about themselves and others. This is a more sociological/linguistic mode of inquiry, and it intends to reveal some general evidence that there are some basic attitudinal differences between men and women. Irigaray lists these criteria in the following excerpt:

So, on the basis of my analysis of the data: first, women stress much more relations with the other sex. Men remain with each other. Secondly, women are much more interested in others in general. That's signalled in several syntactic procedures, particularly in the importance of transitive verbs, which animate personal objects. For example: 'I wash *him*,' 'I love *him*,' and so on. Thirdly, women are much more interested in the issue of place: they are alongside others, alongside things. Which recalls one of the Indo-European roots of the verb 'to be.' Women would make being, silently. Men would say 'I am.' Fourthly, women are much more interested in the qualities of people, of things, of the action taking place. Their discourse contains many more adjectives and adverbs than that of men ... Fifthly, women are more interested in the present, or the future, whereas men are interested in the past. Sixthly, women are more attentive in transmitting a message than men. They always make an effort to say something, even in an experimental situation. Men remain inert, unless their message is about the state of their soul.

I do not think that it is necessary to remove these characteristics of feminine discourse: on the contrary, women must be permitted to advocate their values publicly. Will they nevertheless lose these qualities? I don't think so. They are part of their sexual identity. The important thing is that they should become free subjects while remaining, or becoming, women, and not in endeavoring to become men.[391]

In this excerpt, Irigaray lists some criteria which she believes are characteristic of women's sexual identity: women are less self-absorbed than men; women are more in touch with the present and with the future than men; women are more sensitive to issues concerning 'place' than men; women transmit messages more attentively than men. Irigaray does not describe in detail her method of analyzing the linguistic data, so we cannot easily assess whether these criteria have the definitive status Irigaray attributes to them. A parallel can be drawn to the difficulties which attend Lévi-Strauss's use of the structuralist method in anthropology: there are many ways to interpret the anthropological data, and although some of Lévi-Strauss's analyses are plausible, the data remain complex, and it remains an open possibility that alternative construals of the same data could be equally convincing. Indeed, there is a poststructuralist question of whether any single interpretation of linguistic data can legitimately exclude all other alternatives. One might question, then, Irigaray's attempt to examine linguistic data such as to reveal a single, definitive female identity. Nonetheless, she shows convincingly that the male-oriented definitions of female sexuality as a kind of 'lack,' are neither necessary nor natural ones.

The ethics of sexual difference

In many accounts of the nature of morality, such as that of Immanuel Kant, a strong degree of mutual identity is postulated among human beings as the ground for explaining why they ought to do the right thing, why they should treat each other with respect, and why they share, and should pursue, a common good. Postulating a common human nature is one way to establish this identity among people. A central assumption within this approach to morality, is that it is wrong, or incoherent, to be self-destructive.

If self-destruction is wrong, and if other people are essentially like oneself, then it is wrong, or fundamentally incoherent, to destroy, take advantage of, or otherwise disrespect and abuse other people. Considered positively, moral consciousness issues from self-respect, along with the projective application of this positive quality to one's relationships with all other people, and perhaps to other human-like beings as well. We thus encounter principles such as 'do unto others as you would have them do unto you' or 'do not do unto others what you would not have them do unto you' (i.e., positive and negative versions of the Golden Rule), and the idea that one should always put oneself in the other person's place, when considering some action upon another person.

The above human-identity-based understanding of the foundations of morality conflicts to some extent with the idea that men and women have basically different sexual identities. If men and women are incommensurably different in their ways of understanding the world, each other and themselves, as Irigaray maintains, then it becomes impossible to ask a man to put himself in a woman's place, or to ask a woman to put herself in a man's place, because the respective identities remain inaccessible. Simply stated, if our personal identity is defined in reference to our sexual identity, and if a man cannot be a woman and a woman cannot be a man, then traditional moral consciousness becomes impossible to achieve:

> I shall never take the place of a man, never will a man take mine. Whatever identifications are possible, one will never exactly fill the place of the other – the one is irreducible to the other.[392]

Given this irreducibility of men to women or of women to men, we must then ask how a moral relationship between men and women is possible. If we are to establish some kind of moral relationships between men and women upon difference-respecting assumptions, it will be necessary to preserve the sexual differences between men and women, while explaining how equality, justice, and respect between men and women can nonetheless prevail in their social interactions. Advocating the human-identity-based foundation of morality obscures the significance of sexual difference, so if we recognize sexual difference, then we are led to doubt the human-identity-based foundation of morality. An emerging question is whether the acknowledgment of sexual difference necessitates the abandonment of moral relationships in favor of a power struggle between two fundamentally opposing kinds of being, namely, men and women.[393]

Irigaray develops an alternative foundation for moral relationships that avoids the above dilemma, and that appeals to the experience of men and women as they encounter each other as respectively different kinds of beings. Unlike Sartre, rather than emphasizing the hostility that often arises when individuals first encounter each other,[394] Irigaray emphasizes the sense of wonder and awe that can also attend such an encounter:

> To arrive at the constitution of an ethics of sexual difference, we must at least return to what is for Descartes the first passion: *wonder*. This passion is not opposed to, or in conflict with, anything else, and exists always as though for the first time. Man and woman, woman and man are therefore always meeting as though for the first time since they cannot stand in for one another ...
>
> Who or what the other is, I never know. But this unknowable other is that which differs sexually from me. This feeling of wonder, surprise and astonishment in the face of the unknowable ought to be returned to its proper place: the realm of sexual difference. The passions have either been repressed, stifled and subdued, or else reserved for God. Sometimes a sense of wonder is bestowed upon a work of art. But it is never found in the *gap between man and woman*. This space was filled instead with attraction, greed, possession, consummation, disgust, etc., and not with that wonder which sees something as though always for the first time, and never seizes the other as its object. Wonder cannot seize, possess or subdue such an object. The latter, perhaps, remains subjective and free?
>
> This has never happened between the sexes. Wonder might allow them to retain an autonomy based on their difference, and give them a space of freedom or attraction, a possibility of separation or alliance.[395]

We can describe Irigaray's model of the foundations of morality as a 'morality of the sublime.'[396] In the experience of what is sublime – an experience that Lyotard believed was capable of breaking through the silences that are imposed by linguistically centered terror – we are presented with another being that is awe-inspiring, overwhelming, incomprehensible, and 'beyond' ourselves in an unbridgeable way. In this respect, we can recall a traditional, Old Testament, model of the human being's relationship with God as filled with wonder and awe. What is morally salient in this relationship to God is the idea of respect: we naturally respect that which is beyond our comprehension.

Unlike the sublime human–God relationship, however, the sublime man–woman relationship does not include the idea of domination of women over men, or of men over women; men and women stand as equally sublime to each other and equally incomprehensible to each other. So within a morality of the sublime, human relationships would be grounded upon an atmosphere of respect, based on the mysteriousness to men of women's identity, and the mysteriousness to women of men's identity. In such a condition, members of one sex would be awe-inspired by the members of the other sex, and would therefore find themselves in a state of consciousness where dispositions toward manipulation, oppression, objectification, disrespect and exploitation of persons of the opposite sex would be virtually non-existent. In sum, Irigaray's conception of morality urges that men and women treat each other with a sense of divinity, insofar as they can thereby regard each other as male gods and female gods.

In the spirit of Roland Barthes's challenge to status quo social values that present themselves as being 'natural,' when in fact they are only mythic and constructed, Luce Irigaray challenges the specific, and yet socially permeating, myth of male-domination. One of her main strategies is to formulate what can be called a 'counter-myth,' where female sexuality is accorded an equal, and in certain contexts, a superior value, to male sexuality. By means of such imaginative constructions, she reveals how the male-oriented view is neither necessary nor natural, as its many advocates tend to assume. And in this enterprise of showing how social constructions are mostly fictional, Irigaray shares the position of many poststructuralist thinkers, namely, that there is more arbitrariness to the structure of our social world than we tend to imagine, and moreover, that the contrary assumption that the world is naturally divided, typically leads to oppression and injustice, once these so-called natural divisions are politicized.

As respectable as may be such motivations to reveal the truth, we can ask a basic question about the ethics of difference, or the 'morality of sublimity' as it has been termed here. Is not the difference between any two people as comparably as awesome as the more generic difference between men and women? Or, similarly, could not the difference between younger and older people be comparably as awesome, or, for that matter, the difference between people who live in rural communities, as opposed to people who live in city communities, and so on. There are many different pairs of oppositional categories in reference to which people can define themselves, and many of these pairs vary in intensity with each person, depending upon how the individual's personality has been formed. For some people, sexual differences are less important than religious or national or ethnic or various subcultural differences. One can question the assumption that sexual differences are fundamentally determinative of how a person defines her or his personal identity.

A benefit of comprehending the morality of sublimity in this more expanded manner, is that the occasions for experiencing the awesomeness of another person multiply with the number of oppositional categories one recognizes as relevant to the characterization of other people. For not only will a person, as a woman or man, feel an awesomeness with respect to the person of the other sex, a person who is immersed in a particular religious faith, will feel an awesomeness with respect to those who adhere to other faiths, and similarly for other categories. So as one becomes more concrete in one's thinking – as one multiplies the differentiating categories under which one conceives of another person – the ways for developing respect for them multiply. Such an expanded morality of sublimity might have the long-term effect of reducing the significance of sexual difference, but the trade-off may be an increase of mutual respect. The effect of this may improve the relationships between men and women, if not as such, then as a result of each person growing to respect each other person as a unique individual – a position which, when developed, returns us to the earlier existentialist views, and their associated celebration of individuality.

Selected works of Luce Irigaray

1974 (age 44): *Speculum de l'autre femme [Speculum of the Other Woman]*
1977 (age 47): *Ce sexe qui n'en est pas un [This sex which is not one]*
1980 (age 50): *Amante marine. De Friedrich Nietzsche [Marine Lover of Friedrich Nietzsche]*
1982 (age 52): *Passions Elementaires [Elemental Passions]*
1983 (age 53): *L'oubli de l'air chez Martin Heidegger [The Forgetting of Air in Martin Heidegger]*
1984 (age 54): *Ethique de la difference sexuelle [An Ethics of Sexual Difference]*
1990 (age 60): *Je, tu, nous: pour une culture de la difference [Je, Tu, Nous: Toward a Culture of Difference]*

16

Gilles Deleuze, Philosopher and Social Psychologist (1925–95)

Life and Works

Gilles Deleuze was born in Paris on January 18, 1925, and despite his family's conservative values, Deleuze gradually grew into sympathy with more radical and leftist positions as time went on. From 1944–48, he studied philosophy at the University of Paris, and after his graduation and teaching certification, he taught philosophy at various secondary schools until 1957. Deleuze then returned to the University of Paris as an instructor, teaching the history of philosophy from 1957–60 (ages 32–35). During a similar span of time as a researcher at the *Centre National de Recherche Scientifique* (CNRS) from 1960–64, Deleuze met Michel Foucault in 1962 while the latter was teaching at the University of Clermont-Ferrand. It was Foucault who, eight years later, would say that the twentieth century would perhaps someday become known as 'Deleuzean.'[397]

Deleuze taught at the University of Lyon from 1964–69, and proved himself to be one of the finest philosophical interpreters of his generation. In 1969 he completed his doctoral thesis, *Difference and Repetition*, and in the same year, he met the Lacanian psychoanalyst, Félix Guattari (1930–92), who would soon become Deleuze's intellectual collaborator. Their initial jointly authored books, *Anti-Oedipus* (1972) and *A Thousand Plateaus* (1980) – complementary works which constituted the two volumes of *Capitalism and*

Schizophrenia – brought international intellectual recognition to them both. From 1969 to 1987, Deleuze taught at the University of Paris VIII, at Vincennes, retiring at age sixty-two. In 1992, his health declined as a consequence of a serious lung ailment, and he died on November 4, 1995 after leaping from his apartment window in an act of suicide. He was sixty-nine.

Anti-Oedipus

Writing in the wake of the nation-immobilizing revolutionary events of May 1968, Deleuze and Guattari collaborated on *Anti-Oedipus: Capitalism and Schizophrenia, Volume I* (1972), a work which intended to reveal the ambiguous role of Freudian psychoanalysis in French intellectual circles. Freud himself believed that his style of psychoanalysis was revolutionary and subversive, and this opinion was adopted by those who succeeded him professionally and who were influenced by Freud's thought in general. The surrealists, for instance, fashioned themselves as revolutionaries, and social critics such as Roland Barthes later developed anti-capitalism-centered projects that took the form of an attempt to psychoanalyze the social consciousness, if only in an approximate and informal manner. Jacques Lacan, similarly, believed that Freudian thought opened a path to the liberation of the psyche. So by the time Deleuze and Guattari were writing, psychoanalysis had established itself as being among the preferred theories used by social critics. This was true not only in France, but in Germany, where the Frankfurt school of Critical Theory issued from both Marxist and Freudian inspirations.

Deleuze and Guattari, however, viewed psychoanalysis as having become a socially entrenched outlook, and as too closely associated with the status quo for it to have the revolutionary impact it once envisioned for itself. Their position noticeably recalled that of the Dadaist, Tristan Tzara, who stated in his 'Dada Manifesto' of 1918 that psychoanalysis is a dangerous disease because it systematizes the bourgeoisie, and who emphasized opposingly, that 'dada' is any phenomenon that is capable of becoming a negation of the family unit. In a related vein, Deleuze and Guattari believed that psychoanalysis conflicts with Marxist and communistic social ideals, because it is a fundamentally capitalism-supporting doctrine – one which supports 'bourgeois repression:'

> Hence, instead of participating in an undertaking that will bring about genuine liberation, psychoanalysis is taking part in the work of bourgeois repression at its most far-reaching level, that is to say, keeping European humanity harnessed to the yoke of daddy-mommy and making no effort to do away with this problem once and for all.[398]

Deleuze and Guattari's social vision specifies several forces of oppression, which include those of capitalism and the nuclear family. And it is in relationship to the latter that Freudian psychoanalysis becomes a target for their criticism, for they understand one of the central thematics of Freudian psychoanalysis – the Oedipus Complex – as set squarely upon the assumption that the nuclear family is the ground-zero locale for the development of human personality and sexual awareness. Much of *Anti-Oedipus* is consequently directed toward undermining the attraction of the triangular Freudian model of human development, where a person is understood to be engaged in a fundamental project of reconciling their feelings of sexual attraction toward the parent of the opposite sex, along with reconciling their feelings of rivalry toward the parent of the same sex.

Deleuze and Guattari do not dispute the overall truth of the Freudian model, but they point out how the model tends to restrict the conceptualization of a child's mental life by regarding immediate familial relations as the essential groundwork for psychological development. On their view, however, an exclusive focus upon the Oedipal-familial constellation of 'daddy-mommy-me' leads to the neglect of more general relationships and instinctual forces that are present in the child – forces which Deleuze and Guattari associate with the unconscious. Moreover, such a focus tends to interpret these energies in narrow reference to the nuclear family structure. Deleuze and Guattari emphasize, though, that instinctual energies are present in people independently of the family context and nuclear family structure, and that they need to be understood on their own terms, rather than through the Freudian Oedipal lens.

This attracts Deleuze and Guattari to the kind of personality type that has been notoriously resistant to Freudian psychoanalysis – the schizophrenic type – in order to discern the nature of pre-Oedipal, instinctual, energies in a style of human psyche that has not been amenable to civilized formation by the traditional family structure.[399] Their approach is comparable to that of Lévi-Strauss, who tried to focus on the 'wild' or 'natural' tribal peoples, in an effort to understand how we are as humans before the forces of mass-civilization make an impression upon our psyches. Similarly, Deleuze and Guattari focus their attention upon a 'non-Oedipalized' type of person, to understand what is 'wild' or 'natural' in the human unconscious. They accordingly develop a model of the unconscious based upon their understanding of the schizophrenic mentality:

> What the schizophrenic experiences, both as an individual and as a member of the human species, is not at all any one specific aspect of nature, but nature as a process of production.[400]
>
> The schizo has his own system of co-ordinates for sustaining himself at this disposal, because, first of all, he has at his disposal his very own

recording code, which does not coincide with the social code, or coincides with it only in order to parody it. The code of delirium or of desire proves to have an extraordinary fluidity. It might be said that the schizophrenic passes from one code to the other, that he deliberately scrambles all the codes, by quickly shifting from one to another, according to the questions asked him, never giving the same explanation from one day to the next, never invoking the same genealogy, never recording the same event in the same way.[401]

In this characterization of the schizophrenic type, we can discern a series of personal features that might appeal to an iconoclastic social critic. The schizophrenic lives according to his or her own codes, and these codes do not mesh with the prevailing social code. This attractively defines the schizophrenic as a social outsider who does not fit in. Also, in light of the schizophrenic's fluctuation, instability and scrambling of codes, this kind of person is difficult to understand, and therefore is resistant to dominating and classificatory rationalistic analysis. There is also a creative element in this kind of personality, which runs counter to the established rules of ordinary social behavior.

This set of features recalls Roland Barthes's prescription for continually shifting one's position which he outlined in his 1977 Inaugural Lecture. It also displays a kind of evasiveness and slipperiness that echoes the Derridean stance of not taking any particular stance, such as to use, in an 'intellectual-judo'-like manner, only the internal forces of opposing positions as a means to undermine those positions. It also recalls Sartre's apprehension of the contingent, accidental, overwhelming, and essentially incomprehensible nature of individual things – the items of daily life (seen in an estranged way) that stimulate his nausea. It also recalls Lyotard's celebration of the sublime, as that which is overwhelming and resistant to rational comprehension. In addition, resonating with Foucault's championing of the social outcast as a way to understand the nature of the society that casts such people away, Deleuze and Guattari's conception of the schizophrenic likewise provides an image of the absolute social outsider, whose alienated mentality is resistant, not only to typically civilized society, but also to one of the most powerful theories for understanding the human psyche, namely, psychoanalysis.

In speaking about schizophrenia, however, it is essential not to romanticize and idealize this mental condition, as Deleuze and Guattari sometimes do. The pain and suffering involved in having a schizophrenic mentality should be neither underestimated nor ignored. As a step toward this recognition, Deleuze and Guattari carefully underscore the extreme depersonalization and fragmentation involved in schizophrenic experiences, both introspectively and with regard to how the rest of the world appears.[402] On their analysis, the schizophrenic world appears as an aggregate of small-scale 'desiring-machines' – mouths, hands, stomachs, teeth, etc. – that mix and match, engage and disengage, like a shifting mosaic or disjointed marionette.[403] At the same time, this world also represents Deleuze and Guattari's view of what the truth of our world happens to be – it is an insane world, primordially ruled by instinctual desire – just as Sartre's nausea represents the absurd truth as Sartre perceives it.

This aspect of Deleuze and Guattari's vision is also comparable to Camus's apprehension of the absurd: the man in the telephone booth, talking rapidly and waving his hands wildly, is as comparably alienated and robotic, as is the schizophrenic. So in what appears to be a more contemporary schizophrenic model of the existentialist 'absurd person,' we witness once again the existentialist feeling of alienation and mechanization of the world, and themes that echo an assortment of existentialist writers. Deleuze and Guattari simply raise the level of existential absurdity to a higher level of intensity, expressing it in reference to a form of consciousness that would ordinarily be considered to be a form of serious mental illness.

There is also a practical, Marxist-inspired, aspect to Deleuze and Guattari's critique of psychoanalysis, for they claim that psychoanalytic theory is not linked to actual states of affairs and changing social conditions in a sufficiently concrete way. In short, they claim that psychoanalysis is too theoretical, which brings to mind Marx's remark that philosophers have only interpreted the world, whereas the point is to change it. According to Deleuze and Guattari, psychoanalysis has overlooked the productive aspect of the world:

> The schizoanalytic argument is simple: desire is a machine, a synthesis of machines, a machinic arrangement – desiring-machines. The order of desire is the order of *production*; all production is at once desiring-production and social production. We therefore reproach psychoanalysis for having stifled this order of production, for having shunted it into *representation*. Far from showing the boldness of psychoanalysis, this idea of unconscious representation marks from the outset its bankruptcy or its abnegation: an unconscious that no longer produces, but is content to believe.[404]

Deleuze and Guattari's interests are geared toward both liberation and practicality, and they express their views in reference to 'desire' – a force that they conceive of as productive – and in terms of 'machines,' which is a model that releases them from the association between 'system,' 'organic unity' and 'necessity.' For them, the social world is a sexually charged place whose central energy source is the unconscious, conceived as a storehouse of multiple and unceasing desires. They retain the Marxist ideal of personal liberation, along with the Freudian idea that sexual energies are fundamental to the individual and society, but they reject the Marxist ideal of a harmonious, well-organized, organically unified social system, along with the Freudian centrality of the family unit.

Regarding the nature of desire, Deleuze and Guattari differ from almost all theorists who preceded them, both in France and elsewhere. Traditionally – as we know from the views of Schopenhauer and Sartre, not to mention many versions of Buddhism and Upanishadic thought – desire is conceived of as a kind of 'lack' or condition which stands in need of fulfillment. To want something is, virtually by definition, not to have it, or to 'lack' it. This is especially evident in the case of craving, where there is a distinctive pain of frustration involved in not having what one craves to have.

The alternative Deleuzean conception of desire-as-productive, however, regards desire as a kind of energy-overflow that in its continued expansion, always 'wants more.' And if desire is considered to be a mode of willing, and if we appreciate that willing is a kind of action, then desire can be seen as a kind of 'becoming active,' as Deleuze and Guattari maintain. This yields a Nietzsche-inspired conception of desire as an expansive energy and power, contrary to age-old conceptualizations.[405]

Using this conception of desire-as-productive, Deleuze and Guattari regard desire as the fundamental social energy that becomes articulated into various social arrangements, all of which are crystallized into an ever-rearranging assemblage of machine-like structures. The picture is humanoid. As the flows of desire are blocked, diverted and transformed, the contours of the whole assemblage – considered to be a gigantic body without any systematically determined organs (i.e., it has no organic unity) – changes accordingly. Individuals which are themselves composed of smaller assemblages of machine-like forms (mouth, hands, legs, etc.) move within and across the larger assemblage in an arbitrary, unpredictable, indeterminate, and 'nomadic' fashion.[406] These nomadic subjects are assemblages that do not fit systematically, necessarily, organically, and perfectly into some larger social body; rather, each person has a merely aggregated, non-systematic, and non-necessary quality that resists rationalization and social homogenization. It is a non-rational dimension that, in its independence and resistance to external force, is also akin to the absolute freedom that Sartre identifies – a freedom which resists all efforts, either sadistic or benevolently intentioned, to manipulate it.

This brings us to the more central object of Deleuze and Guattari's social critique, which is neither Freudianism nor Capitalism. Their chief enemy is a set of social conditions and attitudes that stand in the way of liberation. It is the same enemy Roland Barthes attacks, who, in a manner different from Sartre, became nauseous upon apprehending the ossification and naturalization of what he perceived as nothing more than arbitrary and changeable social constructions, or 'myths.' In a word, Deleuze and Guattari are attempting to combat fascism – a force that terrorizes, rigidifies, oppresses, robs one of one's personal territory, and silences. Barthes conceived of language as being fascist, because it compels speech; Lyotard conceived of the predominant language-games as being terroristic, because they silence opposing speech. And Deleuze and Guattari conceive of the prevailing social system as fascist to the extent that it is repressive of desire. As things stand, every society is fundamentally repressive[407]

> If a society is identical with its structures – an amusing hypothesis – then yes, desire threatens its very being. It is therefore of vital importance for a society to repress desire, and even to find something more efficient than repression, so that repression, hierarchy, exploitation, and servitude are themselves desired ... desire does not threaten a society because it is a desire to sleep with the mother, but because it is revolutionary. And that does not at all mean that desire is something other than sexuality, but that sexuality and love do not live in the bedroom of Oedipus, they dream instead of wide-open spaces, and cause strange flows to circulate that do not let themselves be stocked within an established order.[408]

Despite their criticism of psychoanalysis, Deleuze and Guattari make the same point as did Freud in *Civilization and its Discontents* (1930), namely, that the preservation of social order requires that a muzzle be put upon people's aggressive and sexual energies, and moreover, that this requirement tends to generate a conflict between the individual's quest for freedom and the social rules of order. Deleuze and Guattari minimize Freud's insight, however, by aligning him with the forces of social order and with what they identify as the polar opposite of the schizophrenic type. This latter, anti-revolutionary style, specifically, is what they characterize (idiosyncratically) as the paranoid type, which seeks global system, domination, panopticism, predictability, control, a 'central sovereignty' and which, in the course of this project, attempts to remold foreign-appearing individuals into its own image. Deleuze and Guattari identify the paranoid type as a fascistic and terroristic type, and formulate their prescriptions and methods for revolutionary and liberating activity as directed against this type.

As alluded to above, the method of liberation that Deleuze and Guattari prefer is called 'schizoanalysis,' which Deleuze describes more fully in a later work, *Dialogues* (1977). He asks that for some phenomenon, we first consider the more rigid lines of force that hold the phenomenon together (e.g., like a body's skeleton). Then, we consider the more supple and flexible lines of force, along with their respective strengths (e.g., the musculature). And third, we consider the points of vulnerability, and points of volatility, along with the systematic links to outside forces and a consideration of their effects on the phenomena under consideration. The tendency here is to provide a mechanical analysis in terms of energy dynamics and functions.

In the background of his analyses, Deleuze adopts the vision of the social world described above, as an aggregate of machines. Furthermore, he imagines the interactions among these mechanical entities as following the pattern of a rhizome, contrary to the more familiar tree-like systems, as are typical of classically branching, genus–species styles of hierarchical classification. Any point of a rhizome can be connected to any other; rhizomes can be broken into parts, and each part can thereafter spread. Rhizomes can develop along subterranean pathways; rhizomes can be comprehended as being constituted mainly by lines of force, rather than by rigid structures with centers and peripheries. And rhizomes, finally, have a cancerous and unmanageable quality.

Critical discussion

Among French intellectuals, Deleuze had one of the most powerfully interpretive styles of thought. His vision of society was strong and dominating, and he developed his model of rhizomic-interaction in impressively rich detail. But Deleuze may have fallen victim to his own intense vision, for there are reasons to believe that society is not uniformly structured like a rhizome, and that people are not simply machine-like aggregates. Although the world does not appear to be the single, immense, living, and self-determining system that Hegel imagined it to be, there are recognizable dimensions of systematicity, rationality, and organic unity in our daily experience. Despite Deleuze's analysis, the healthy human body remains a paradigm of integrated systematic organization of a dynamic sort, as do the bodies of life forms in general.

Deleuze is not the only thinker subject to this sort of criticism. Within French thought, we find Jean-Paul Sartre in his existentialist writings, for instance, committed to the 'either-or,' bipolar, essentially mechanical style of logic – one that leads him to conclude that humans are necessarily frustrated beings. Camus also emphasized the mechanical nature of life in his uncomfortable feeling of the absurd. Saussure's structuralist linguistics was also grounded upon a bipolar, mechanical logic, as were the later views that adhered to a Saussurean linguistics – ones that tended to overlook the phenomenology of human experience in favor of externalistic analyses. And in Michel Foucault, there is a similar, somewhat cybernetic tone, which permeates his analyses of the human being. In this group of French thinkers, there is a notable sympathy with the seventeenth- and eighteenth-century idea that the world is a vast mechanism. Part of this can be explained in reference to the influence of Marxist interpretations of society that all of these thinkers had absorbed, which regards contemporary capitalist society as alienated, objectified, dehumanized, and thereby subject to mechanistic interpretation.

In these French theorists, we can discern the consequent submergence of the nineteenth-century German Idealist sentiment that the world is a being that is living, organically unified, and essentially harmonious with itself. Deleuze is especially memorable in that he takes the mechanical, alienated aspect of life to the extreme, and develops upon it nonetheless, a revolution-friendly and liberation-aimed position. What is paradoxical about Deleuze's antagonism to rigid thought-structures, is the way his world of rhizome-like structures is itself offered with a strong dose of dogmatic rigidity in its disregard for the systematic and organic aspects of experience.

Second, there is a question of whether the Deleuzean quest for liberation conflicts with his model of society as an assemblage of desiring-machines. On Deleuze's model, the 'self' is decentered, which is to say that it is difficult to say 'who' it is that is the subject of the liberation and freedom from paranoia, fascism and terrorism which is so pointedly sought. Just as Barthes disintegrates the 'reader' along with the 'author,' and introduces considerations that undermine his own view, Deleuze disintegrates the subject of experience into a schizophrenic and depersonalized set of 'desiring-machines.' His picture of the human being thus tends to render the idea of personal freedom far less meaningful than it is, for example, in Sartre's philosophy, where one can assert with less difficulty that there is a distinct and identifiable conscious individual who is free. That is, as one descends into the unconscious in search of a principle of freedom from oppression, one starts to lose the integrated ego who consciously experiences his or her freedom in the form of a distinct and autonomous individual.

So in general, there is a question of whether the quest for freedom and liberation that we find in many of the twentieth-century French intellectuals, is consistent with those theories that advance the idea of the 'decentered' self. Once again, Deleuze appears to exemplify this problem in a clear way, because he is straightforward about his conception of the human being as an aggregate and as an essentially disintegrated and non-systematic kind of being. To be sure, one can romantically associate the schizophrenic tendency toward shifting, creativity, and individuality with the idea of jazz improvisation, but there remains the question of whether one can say meaningfully that anyone in particular is doing the improvising, since the sense of integrated personality has been so weakened.[409]

Perhaps more disturbingly, it appears that instead of personal liberation of a healthy sort, Deleuze leads us into a triple-bind where, if we do not believe self-deceptively that we are organically unified and integrated personalities, we are left to gravitate into either paranoid fascism, or schizophrenic insanity. It cannot be denied, though, that Deleuze's exposition is ingenious: whatever path we choose within the theory's internal options, we end up at a dead end, and thereby in the very state of mental frustration that has been known to generate schizophrenic states.[410] Deleuze's theory can therefore be seen as having itself been designed to drive us mad, so that we can experience what he regards as the truth.

Selected works of Gilles Deleuze

1953 (age 28): *Empirisme et subjectivité: Essai sur la nature humaine selon Hume* [*Empiricism and Subjectivity: An Essay on Hume's Theory of Human Nature*]

1962 (age 37): *Nietzsche et la philosophie* [*Nietzsche and Philosophy*]

1963 (age 38): *La philosophie critique de Kant: Doctrine des facultés* [*Kant's Critical Philosophy: The Doctrine of the Faculties*]

1964 (age 39): *Marcel Proust et les signes* [*Marcel Proust and Signs*]

1966 (age 41): *Le Bergsonisme* [*Bergsonism*]

1968 (age 43): (1) *Différence et répétition* [*Difference and Repetition*]
  (2) *Spinoza et le problème de l'expression* [*Expressionism in Philosophy: Spinoza*]

1969 (age 44): *Logique du sens* [*The Logic of Sense*]

1972 (age 47): [with Félix Guattari] *Capitalisme et schizophrénie tome 1: l'Anti-Oedipe* [*Anti-Oedipe: Capitalism and Schizophrenia*]

1975 (age 50): [with Félix Guattari] *Kafka: Pour une litterature mineure* [*Kafka: Toward a Minor Literature*]

1980 (age 55): [with Félix Guattari] *Capitalisme et schizophrenie tome 2: Mille plateaux* [*A Thousand Plateaus: Capitalism and Schizophrenia*]

1983 (age 58): *Cinema-1: L'image-mouvement* [*Cinema 1: The Movement-Image*]

1985 (age 60): *Cinéma-2: L'image-temps* [*Cinema 2: The Time-Image*]

1986 (age 61): *Foucault*

1988 (age 63): (1) *Le pli: Leibniz et le baroque* [*The Fold: Leibniz and the Baroque*]
  (2) *Périclès et Verdi: La philosophie de François Châtelet* [*Pericles and Verdi: The Philosophy of François Châtelet*]

1991 (age 66): [with Félix Guattari] *Qu'est-ce que la philosophie?* [*What is Philosophy?*]

17

Jean Baudrillard, Sociologist (1929–)

Life and works

Jean Baudrillard, as he once stated, was born in the year of the Great Depression, on July 20, 1929, in Reims, France. His family came from the Ardennes–Champagne region, close to Belgium, and they were people who were making the transition from rural to city life. In Reims, Baudrillard's parents were civil servants, and he went to school in the city, eventually focusing upon the study of German language and literature. In later years, Baudrillard taught German from 1958–66 (ages 29–37), and thereafter (in 1966) he obtained a position teaching sociology at the University of Paris at Nanterre – the same year in which Jean-François Lyotard began working at the same institution, and which was the initial scene of the May 1968 student protests. In his early career, Baudrillard did translations into French of work by German writers such as Berthold Brecht (1956), Peter Weiss (1965), Karl Marx (1968), Wilhelm E. Mühlmann (1968), and Friedrich Engels (1969). He was also influenced by political events surrounding the Algerian War, Henri Lefebre's, *Critique of Everyday Life* (1958) and Guy Debord's, *The Society of the Spectacle* (1967), all within the context of having a strong interest in Marxism. Baudrillard was also involved editorially in the journals, *Traverses* and *Utopie*.

Soon developing his own original views after receiving his doctorate in sociology (his thesis became his first book, *The System of Objects* [1968])

Baudrillard continued teaching and writing numerous, widely influential books, remaining in his position at Nanterre until 1987 (age fifty-eight), at which point he had become one of the most internationally popular theorists of postmodern culture. Baudrillard's later interests (2001) have included a concentrated involvement in the theory and practice of photography.

Seduction

With an early interest in Marx, and as a sociologist who was familiar with semiological analyses of culture, Jean Baudrillard's work of the late 1960s and early 1970s combines both Marxism and semiology in an effort to understand our contemporary, mass-media-influenced society. As sophisticated as these analyses are, Baudrillard's scholarly work became even more influential during the late 1970s and early 1980s, in connection with his studies of postmodernist culture, emphasizing themes such as 'seduction,' 'simulations,' and 'hyperreality.' Since the late 1980s Baudrillard has expanded his theory of postmodernism by incorporating concepts from the most contemporary sciences (e.g., 'fractals') and themes from contemporary politics and sociology (e.g., race and gender issues).

In a 1979 work, *Seduction*, Baudrillard asserts that everything is seduction. To understand why he would make a head-spinning claim of this sort, and to understand what he means by 'seduction' in the theoretical sense, we can consider how he conceives of seduction in the ordinary sense. He describes seduction in the following ways:

> Thus in Kierkegaard's *Diary of a Seducer*, seduction takes the form of an enigma to be resolved. The girl is an enigma, and in order to seduce her, one must become an enigma for her. It is an *enigmatic duel*, one that the seduction solves, but *without disclosing the secret*. If the secret were disclosed, sexuality would stand revealed. The story's true meaning, if it had one, would be about sex – but in fact it doesn't have one. In that place where meaning should be, where sex should occur, where words point to it, where others think it to be – there is nothing. And this nothing/secret, this, the seduction's unsignified moves beneath the words and their meaning, and moves faster than their meaning. It is what touches you first, before sentences arrive, in the time it takes for them to fade away. A seduction beneath discourse, an invisible seduction, moving from sign to sign – a secret circulation.[411]

In the case of ordinary seduction, as exemplified in Kierkegaard's narrative, one (as seducer) attempts to make oneself attractive to another (the person seduced) by becoming alluring to the other person. This is done by presenting oneself as having something that the person seduced is expected to desire. Within seductive activity, communications operate 'beneath the surface' in a cloaked, disguised, subtle, secretive, or mysterious way. The important communications are not verbal, and each person stands before the other as an enigma.[412] The projected mystery perpetuates the seduction.

Baudrillard interprets the communications that operate 'beneath the surface' as being grounded upon an illusion that the seducer generates: in seduction, the seducer only intimates to the person seduced that he or she has something desirable, and the seduction can only proceed if that 'something' remains undisclosed, hidden, and implicit. Insofar as the mystery cannot be disclosed if the seduction is to continue, the process of seduction endlessly defers its disclosure.

This association between seduction and 'endless deferral' reveals a parallel between Baudrillard's conception of seduction and Derrida's conception of textuality. In the latter, words refer mainly to other words (or to items regarded as textual segments), and there is no 'transcendental (i.e., extra-linguistic) signified' that is recognized as an independently existing, sharply articulated reality existing beneath the language. In reference to the precise articulation of our experience, there is only language and the endless play of signifiers within writing, speaking, and thinking in general, just as within Sartre's theory of consciousness, even more radically, there is only the surface of conscious experience, without any hidden, underlying 'self' or 'thinking substance.'

Seduction, as Baudrillard uses the term in the more global sense, is similar: it is understandable as a principle which indicates that there is no fully articulated objective truth that remains hidden beneath the surface of language. The seducer, in other words, knows that the mystery he or she projects is empty. At the level of interpretation (if we extend the analogy of seduction into more literal areas), Baudrillard advocates a view similar to Derrida: he maintains that all traditional 'interpretation' – the act of seeking a single and determinate 'meaning of the text' – is misguided, just as the seducer knows that there is, in fact, no essential meaning to be discovered. The following excerpt from Baudrillard's 'On Seduction' shows a striking affinity to Derrida's view of language and interpretation:

> These appearances are not in the least frivolous, but occasions for a game and its stakes, and a passion or deviation – the seduction of signs themselves being more important than the emergence of any truth – which interpretation neglects and destroys in its search for hidden meanings. This is why interpretation is what, *par excellence*, is opposed to seduction, and why it is the least seductive of discourses. Not only does it subject the domain of appearances to incalculable damage, but this privileged search

for hidden meanings may well be profoundly in error. For it is not somewhere else, in a *hinterwelt* [world behind the scenes] or an unconscious, that one will find what leads discourse astray. What truly displaces discourse, 'seduces' it in the literal sense, and renders it seductive, is its very appearance, its inflections, its nuances, the circulation (whether aleatory and senseless, or ritualized and meticulous) of signs at the surface. It is that that effaces meaning and is seductive, while a discourse's meaning has never seduced anyone.[413]

Baudrillard's claim that everything is seduction thus makes sense in light of Derrida's view that language permeates all walks of life, along with Derrida's view that there is an endless deferral of meaning, or endless play, of signifiers within language. Seduction expresses the endless deferral and open-endedness of meaning, just as in an ordinary seduction the person seduced is continually 'led on' during the seductive process. Language is a seducer, in short, and the 'absolute and objective truth' compares to the sexual endpoint that does not exist. Which is to say that language itself entices us to believe in forever-unattainable, extra-linguistic, godlike foundations.

In addition to the parallelism between ordinary seduction and endless deferral, Baudrillard's emphasis upon seduction within the general linguistic context illuminates his view that rhetoric is more central than literal truth. On both Baudrillard's and Derrida's views, seeking the exclusively literal truth is believed to be an illusory goal. Upon realizing this, one's attention is thus drawn back to the 'surface' of language, which reveals the 'pleasures' of language (as we have seen in Barthes), along with its aesthetic and rhetorical quality. By speaking of 'seduction' and associating this with rhetoric, Baudrillard brings to the foreground the ways in which language is used to persuade and consequently to affect our behaviors and emotional life.

As revealing as Baudrillard's association between language and seduction happens to be, it remains to consider critically his claim that the meaning of an interpretive discourse has never seduced anyone. Baudrillard has in mind here Freudian psychoanalysis, which distinguishes between the latent (i.e., true and also threatening) meaning of a psychic manifestation such as a dream, and the manifest (i.e., disguised, publicly presented, and non-threatening) meaning of the same manifestation. The process of psychoanalysis aims to go beneath the superficial, manifest 'mask' in order to see the true meaning of the psychic contents. This is what Baudrillard refers to as 'interpretation,' which he contrasts to 'seduction.'

There is a tension within Baudrillard's account that resides in an ambiguous use of the term 'seduction.' On the one hand, he opposes seduction to interpretation, where seduction involves a reluctance to seek any hidden meanings, and to remain on the pleasurable, rhetorical surface of discourse. On the other hand, Baudrillard associates seduction with endless deferral – an idea which, at first, seems to be consistent with the emphasis upon rhetoric and surface qualities, but which introduces some problematic subtleties.

In his description of ordinary seduction, Baudrillard emphasizes how the person seduced's desire is continually focused upon an enigma or secret which, as long as the seduction continues, is never revealed. Indeed, Baudrillard plausibly claims that there is no substance to that apparent secret, and mainspring of the seduction. The arising problem is that the person seduced does not realize that there is no substance to what the seducer holds forth as a mystery; only the seducer realizes this. For only if one assumes that the seduced person believes that there is a reality to the seducer's mystery, can the person be seduced to begin with.

So although 'from the outside,' Baudrillard might be aware that there is nothing but seduction and rhetoric, a person who is being seduced must necessarily be oblivious to this absence of underlying meaning. Baudrillard's claim that everything is seduction can thus be effective in describing how people operate within language and within society, only on the condition that people do not have a perspective which would allow them to see that every-thing is seduction. Once this perspective is taken, seduction becomes no longer possible, for everyone will be aware that there are no hidden secrets or mysteries behind the scenes.

It is not clear whether Baudrillard fully appreciates the self-defeating nature of the claim that everything is seduction, but in subsequent writings, this concept becomes less central in his theorizing. Other related concepts that he develops at the time – ones such as 'simulations,' 'simulacra,' and 'hyperreality' – eventually become more clearly definitive of his analysis of contemporary culture, and of the style of thought for which he has become popular.

Simulations, simulacra, and hyperreality

Similar to the French structuralists and poststructuralists who were writing during the 1950s and 1960s, Baudrillard formulates his perspective with an emphasis upon the significatory features of language. He tends to use the Saussurean term, 'sign,' along with the term 'code,' which designates a system of signs. Also in the pattern of Foucault's analysis of knowledge in terms of *epistemes* which define the contours of knowledge within various outlooks, and also echoing Marx, Baudrillard identifies three major historical epochs as well. He characterizes each historical period differently, however, by distinguishing them in reference to three contrasting symbolic styles, or 'orders of simulation,' and by drawing the historical points of transition at different dates. Baudrillard writes:

> Three orders of simulation, parallel to mutations in the law of value, have succeeded one another since the Renaissance:
> 1. The *counterfeit* is the dominant scheme of the 'classical' epoch, from the Renaissance to the industrial revolution.
> 2. *Production* is the dominant scheme of the industrial era.
> 3. *Simulation* is the dominant scheme of the present phase of history, governed by the code.
>
> Simulacra of the first order play on the natural law of value; those of the second order play on the commodity law of value; and those of the third order play on the structural law of value.[414]

Baudrillard maintains that in caste, feudal, and archaic societies, the categories of social definition (e.g., class, occupation, etc.) are relatively fixed and clear: in such societies, 'each sign refers unequivocally to a (particular) situation and a level of status.'[415] In the transition from the Renaissance to the industrial revolution, however, there was a relaxation of social restrictions, and this led to greater class mobility and the emergence of fashion. During this period – which Baudrillard refers to as the era of the 'counterfeit' – signs expanded their application and became loosened from the earlier designations. For instance, as less affluent people became able to imitate more effectively the styles of the more affluent people, the signs that formerly operated within the sphere of the affluent alone began to circulate among the less affluent. In this sense, the signs of the affluent people became 'counterfeited' by those of other social classes.

The industrial revolution, with its development of mass production, and the accompanying technology of interchangeable parts, signals for Baudrillard a different style of symbolic interaction. He describes the new situation:

> [T]here is the possibility of two or of *n* identical objects. The relation between them is not that of the original to its counterfeits, or its analogue, or its reflection; it is a relationship of equivalence, of indifference. In the series, objects are transformed indefinitely into simulacra of one another and, with objects, so are the people who produce them.[416]

Some of the clearest examples of the interchangeability of signs arise during the later nineteenth century and beginning of the twentieth century, with the development of mechanical ways of reproducing not only clothing and other items of fashion, but visual imagery.[417] The printing of many photographs from a single photographic negative, along with processes of lithography, etching, woodblock printing, etc. all exemplify the kind of sign-production process which Baudrillard maintains became common during the industrial revolution and thereafter.[418]

Of crucial importance to Baudrillard's understanding of the postmodern world is the third order, which is characterized by what he calls the 'simulation.' This order of signs tends to generate a 'hyperreal' atmosphere – an atmosphere that is 'more real' than naturally occurring reality itself. Baudrillard characterizes this hyperrealistic condition in the following excerpts:

> Today, the real and the imaginary are confounded in the same operational totality, and aesthetic fascination is simply everywhere. It involves a kind of subliminal perception, a kind of sixth sense for fakery, montage, scenarios, and the overexposition of reality in the lighting of models. This is no longer a productive space, but a kind of ciphering strip, a coding and decoding tape, a tape recording magnetized with signs. It is an aesthetic reality, to be sure, but no longer by virtue of art's premeditation and distance, but through a kind of elevation to the second order, via the anticipation and the immanence of the code. An air of nondeliberate parody clings to everything – a tactical simulation – like an undecidable game to which is attached a specifically aesthetic pleasure, the pleasure in reading (lecture) and in the rules of the game.[419]
>
> At the conclusion of this process of reproduction, the real becomes not only that which can be reproduced, but that which is always already reproduced; the hyperreal.[420]
>
> Today abstraction is no longer that of the map, the double, the mirror, or the concept. Simulation is no longer that of the territory, a referential being, or a substance. It is the generation by models of a real without origin or reality: a hyperreal.[421]
>
> The real is produced from miniaturized cells, matrices, and memory banks, models of control – and it can be reproduced an indefinite number of times from these. It no longer needs to be rational, because it no longer measures itself against either an ideal or negative instance. It is no longer anything but operational. In fact, it is no longer really the real, because no imaginary envelopes it anymore. It is a hyperreal, produced from a radiating synthesis of combinatory models in a hyperspace without atmosphere.[422]
>
> Such would be the successive phases of the image:
>> it is the reflection of a profound reality;
>> it masks and denatures a profound reality;

it masks the *absence* of a profound reality;

it has no relation to any reality whatever: it is its own pure simulacrum.

In the first case, the image is a *good* appearance – the representation is of the sacramental order. In the second, it is an evil appearance – it is of the order of maleficence. In the third, it plays at being an appearance – it is of the order of sorcery. In the fourth, it is no longer in the order of appearance, but of simulation.[423]

In these various excerpts, Baudrillard characterizes the contemporary times as being in a hyperreal condition where what is taken to be provisionally foundational is in fact the product of some 'program' or 'code.' A machine-generated, artificial, reality has taken many of the social places raw nature once had. Owing to this extremely minimized reference to the 'real' (as raw nature), hyperreality assumes a 'floating' aspect: we operate within a layer of imagery that floats above (what used to be respected as) 'reality' and which has replaced it in its social importance.

Baudrillard's notion of 'hyperreality' compares to his characterization of 'seduction.' In connection with Derrida, we have seen how Baudrillardian seduction expresses the Derridean thought of an endless deferment of meaning, but achieves this in a more sensuous and aesthetic mode. Baudrillard's notion of hyperreality is similarly understandable in parallel with Derrida's notion of textuality. Since there is no linguistically transcendent and constant referent to be recognized within Derrida's view, language assumes a floating and foundationless quality as well. When we transport this idea into a more sociological context, and consider the aesthetic appearance of social events and media imagery, we can gain a sense of what Baudrillard means by 'hyperreality,' since there is no determinate interpretation to be reliably formulated, and since the media imagery appear to hover before us without any clear way in which they can be determinately tied down to actual reality. For all we viewers know, the media images could be computer-generated, as was demonstrated in the movie, *Wag the Dog* (1997).

To explain how our contemporary times differ from earlier times in reference to the way signs are used and understood, Baudrillard offers a four-stage model (cited above), much like his earlier three-stage model of symbolic modification. Although it resembles Foucault's own historical theorizing, there is a more revealing connection between Baudrillard's four-stage model – one which culminates in the suspension of traditional metaphysical thinking and the associated concept of the 'true world' – and Friedrich Nietzsche's reflections on the historical transformation of metaphysical thinking. In his *Twilight of the Idols* (1888) Nietzsche wrote:

How the 'True World' at Last Became a Fable

History of a Mistake

1. The true world, attainable for the wise, the devout, the virtuous one
   – he lives in it, *he is it.*
   (Oldest form of the idea, relatively clever, simple, convincing.
   Transcription of the sentence, 'I, Plato, *am* the truth.')

2. The true world, unattainable for now, but promised to the wise,
   the devout, the virtuous one ('for the sinner who does penance').
   (Development of the idea: it becomes more subtle, tricky, incomprehensible – *it becomes female*; it becomes Christian.)

3. The true world, unattainable, unprovable, unpromisable, but still,
   even as a comforting thought, a duty, an imperative.
   (Basically the old sun, but through fog and scepticism; the idea
   having become sublime, pale, northern, Königsbergish.[424])

4. The true world – unattainable? At least, unattained. And as
   unattained, also *unknown.* Therefore, also not consoling, redeeming,
   obligatory: how can we be obligated to something unknown?
   (The grey of morning. First yawnings of reason. Cockcrow of
   positivism.)

5. The 'true world' – an idea that no longer has a use, not a duty
   anymore – an idea grown superfluous and useless, and *therefore* a
   refuted idea: let's get rid of it!
   (Bright day: breakfast; return to good sense [*bon sens*] and cheer-
   fulness; Plato is red-faced with shame; the devilish racket of all the
   free spirits.)

6. We have gotten rid of the true world: which world is left over? the
   apparent world? … But no! *with the true world we have also gotten
   rid of the apparent world!*[425]
   (Noonday; moment of the shortest shadow; end of the longest
   mistake; high point of humanity; INCIPIT[426] ZARATHUSTRA.
   [Zarathustra begins.])[427]

In light of this passage from Nietzsche, we can see how Baudrillard's idea of
hyperreality and Derrida's discussions of textuality are not altogether new, and
that they both reiterate Nietzsche's rejection of the idea of a 'true world.' To
appreciate Baudrillard's particular formulation of this theme, we can note
some examples of hyperreal phenomena that Baudrillard has in mind. Aside
from the television media imagery referred to above, Baudrillard also refers us
to fantasy-parks in the United States, such as Disneyland, Marineland,
Enchanted Village, Magic Mountain, all of which are located in the Los Angeles

area. On Baudrillard's view, these fantasy-parks determine the interpretive horizon for the entire city. He describes the people in Los Angeles as acting out roles within a 'perpetual motion picture,' and as living a life which is 'unreal' (i.e., hyperreal):

> Los Angeles is surrounded by these imaginary stations that feed reality, the energy of the real to a city whose mystery is precisely that of no longer being anything but a network of incessant, unreal circulation – a city of incredible proportion but without space, without dimension. As much as electrical and atomic power stations, as much as cinema studios, this city, which is no longer anything but an immense scenario and a perpetual pan shot, needs this old imaginary like a sympathetic nervous system made up of childhood signals and faked phantasms.[428]

Another of Baudrillard's more important examples refers to the hyperreality of contemporary politics. He points out that, for instance, the responsibility for any given bombing remains indeterminate between a set of people: it could be the work of leftist extremists, or of extreme right-wing provocateurs, or of centrists who wish to bring both extreme views into disrepute, or of the police who wish to inspire appeals for more public security. In the hyperreality of political life, we encounter a discourse that is not merely ambiguous regarding what really happened. It has become no longer reasonable to expect that the disambiguation will occur and that the exact truth will ever be forthcoming.

In this regard, Baudrillard believes that we face a situation comparable to 'seduction' where there is an endless deferment of explanation from one alternative scenario to another, and where in principle, no explanation will ever be confidently fixed. There is a disengagement of the political discourse from what was formerly assumed to exist, viz., a 'political reality' or 'political truth.' In the past, it was commonly assumed that there was a determinately understandable and definable disposition of governmental entities toward each other and toward the population at large, that one could rely upon as the 'fact of the matter.' Within the contemporary world, however, Baudrillard claims that the expectation of such a determinate understanding has mostly dissolved, and that for any particular political event, the public can expect to be presented with an undecidable and never-completely understandable array of alternative scenarios, from which they will rationalize to and fro, without any final resolution. This leaves everyone without a credible, truth-bearing, historical account of what is now happening that can be passed on comfortably to future generations.

Criticisms of Baudrillard and some replies

Some criticisms of Baudrillard have been severe,[429] sometimes matching in intensity those which have been levelled at Lacan. Among them, we encounter the claims that Baudrillard continually undertheorizes his central concepts by failing to give clear examples and applications, that he is consequently led to sloganeering and superficial views, and that he is one-sided and misleading in his examinations of cultural phenomena. Worse yet, Baudrillard is said to be inconsistent in the way he claims that everything has become hyperreal while at the same time assuming a traditional theory of truth. The criticisms suggest that we ought not take Baudrillard seriously as a sociologist who attempts to offer an accurate and comprehensive portrayal of our contemporary world. Rather, it has been suggested that we should read Baudrillard as a science-fiction writer who offers entertaining, imaginative, and even ingenious, but nonetheless unrealistic and often theoretically inconsistent, construals of the contemporary scene.

To evaluate such criticisms, we should first specify the underlying criteria of evaluation that are being assumed, and whether Baudrillard would agree with such criteria. There are two general kinds of criteria operative in the above criticisms, namely, external and internal criteria. In the first case, Baudrillard is criticized as offering a theory that does not match the social facts. If we compare the world to how Baudrillard describes it, the allegation is that we do not obtain a close match. In the second case, Baudrillard is criticized as being inconsistent with his own principles.

Associated with the first case, is the criticism that Baudrillard does not provide a believable theory, insofar as his thought fails to embody those qualities that are required for a theory to express the truth well. An ideal theory of this sort would be theory consistent throughout in its use of terms. Such a theory, for example, would define its key terms such as to avoid ambiguity and vagueness. It would also elaborate the significance of each key term through the use of examples and show how the theory can explain a whole range of phenomena. A solid theory should be comprehensive, and admit as few counterexamples as possible; it should, as closely as possible, match reality – which, according to the criteria of what a good theory ought to be, must be assumed to be itself articulable in rationalistic terms.

If we are living in a world where 'reality' has become hyperreality, and where what used to be called 'reality' has been reduced virtually to a non-entity, then it would make sense for Baudrillard's own theory to exhibit hyperrealistic features, as opposed to what has been defined in the past as 'reality.' So in one sense, the above criticisms do not address Baudrillard on his own terms, but impose standards of criticism that Baudrillard does not fully recognize. What first appears as criticism reduces to a clash in fundamental worldviews and valuations.

To the extent that Baudrillard maintains that everything is seduction, his theory should itself be seductive, if he is to be self-referentially consistent. The more seductive his theory is, the better it will be as an embodiment of the postmodernist spirit. Conversely, once the theory begins to privilege the articulation of a hidden truth which would describe the postmodern world as it 'really is,' then it would sacrifice seduction for interpretation, and would become inconsistent with the assumed primacy of seduction. Now one can make a plausible case that Baudrillard's theory is seductive in its self-conscious use of cutting-edge, high-fashion terms from various sciences, and in its use of highly charged social concepts such as transvestism and transsexuality. If his goal is to be rhetorically seductive within the realm of 'theory,' then he appears to have achieved this goal to a respectable extent – an extent comparable to those 'successful' theories that operate according to traditional standards of truth.

This introduces the question of whether an internal criticism of Baudrillard would be more successful. Let us grant that if seduction is one of his primary values, then his theory should be seductive, and not primarily interested in some objective truth. We can ask, then, to what extent is Baudrillard nonetheless compelled to theorize about some objectively definable condition that can be referred to as 'postmodern'? Baudrillard often speaks – and he thereby does expose himself to the charge of inconsistency – as if he is offering a straightforwardly sociological theory: he provides descriptions of different historical phases that allegedly tell 'how things really were' in contrast to 'how things are now.' He describes different stages of the development of the sign, and suggests that these stages were actually historical. From this standpoint, then, Baudrillard's theorizing is not being hyperreal or primarily seductive. He employs theoretical terms from Marxism and semiology, and the resulting theory might even be construed not as seductive, but as 'boring' and interpretive in this respect.

A main problem in Baudrillard's presentation is thus the following: he offers a traditional sociological account of where we are today, which presents itself as historically accurate. At the same time, he situates himself within the contemporary postmodern standpoint – presumably to be faithful to his postmodernist times (since he is a historical product of them), and to communicate well with the majority of his postmodern-conditioned audience – and adopts a view that undermines the traditional, truth-oriented and reality-oriented perspective of his sociological account. This creates a dilemma, at least when it is formulated in logically abstract terms: either he accepts the allegedly outdated and non-postmodern view in order to validate his description of the postmodern condition as opposed to earlier conditions, or he fully entrenches himself within the postmodern value system and closes off the possibility of providing any historically accurate account of the post-modern condition in contrast to earlier conditions.

As things stand, Baudrillard oscillates between the two enterprises, and operates confusingly according to both assumptions. This lends his overall theory a quality of traditional objectivity mixed with a more fantasy-related incredibility. Which is to say that if one is a full-fledged postmodernist and hyperrealist, one is in the position of being unable to see how detached from traditional conceptions of naturally defined reality that perspective happens to be, because the traditional conception of a free-standing natural world has been mostly dissolved within the hyperrealistic outlook. Whereas the theory of seduction only made sense from a perspective that undermined the conditions for any seduction to take place,[430] the theory of hyperreality only makes sense from a traditional perspective that undermines the conditions for the post-modernist dissolution of the traditional idea of a naturally occurring world.

Baudrillard's theory consequently proceeds in a tension-filled way, by recognizing incompatible standards that attach, alternatively, to both tradi-tional, naturally determined truth and artificially determined seductiveness and hyperreality. When the objective standards of culture-independent truth are emphasized, Baudrillard becomes victim to the external criticisms discussed above upon those occasions when he presents himself in accord with postmodernist assumptions. But when Baudrillard operates in accord with the perspective of seductiveness and hyperreality, he loses the position from which he can justify the seduction-based or hyperreality-based standpoint as a legit-imate outlook. For only if he can describe the postmodern period in contrast to previous historical periods – only if he can offer a traditional sociological account – is it possible to show that either seductiveness or the idea of hyper-reality fits the spirit of the postmodern times.

Baudrillard's theoretical difficulties are not unique to his theory, however. They have plagued every historically sensitive outlook since the time when Heidegger maintained that our acts of interpretation are directed by predis-positions that are always already set by the culture and language within which we find ourselves initially immersed. This creates the bewildering problem of determining the extent to which our historically conditioned outlook has the power within itself to transcend itself, such as to apprehend truths that are culturally independent, non-artificial, and naturally occurring. It is a question of whether our historically, culturally, and linguistically conditioned outlooks allow us to see reflected only ourselves, or whether they allow us to see beyond ourselves to an independently existing, natural world. The tendency of postmodernist thought has been to remain almost completely self-enclosed within the structuring parameters of culture, language, or history – which is to say that the spirit of postmodernism has been significantly Kantian. Which is to say that the tensions inhabiting Baudrillard's thinking are not of his own making, but are reflections and embodiments of the twentieth-century hermeneutical situation.

Selected works of Jean Baudrillard

1968 (age 39): *Le système des objets: la consommation des signes* [*The System of Objects*]

1970 (age 41): *La société de consommation (Ses mythes, ses structures)* [*Consumer Society: Myths and Structures*]

1972 (age 43): *Pour une critique de l'économie politique du signe* [*For a Critique of the Political Economy of the Sign*]

1973 (age 44): *Le miroir de la productivité ou l'illusion critique du matérialisme historique* [*The Mirror of Production*]

1976 (age 47): *L'échange symbolique et la mort* [*Symbolic Exchange and Death*]

1977 (age 48): *Oublier Foucault* [*Forget Foucault*]

1979 (age 50): *De la seduction* [*Seduction*]

1981 (age 52): *Simulacres et simulation* [*Simulacra and Simulation*]

1982 (age 53): *À l'ombre des majorités silencieuses ou la fin du social suivi de l'extase du socialisme* [*In the Shadow of the Silent Majority*]

1983 (age 54): *Les stratégies fatales* [*Fatal Strategies*]

1986 (age 57): *America*

1987 (age 58): *L'autre par lui-même* [*The Ecstasy of Communication*]

1990 (age 59): *La transparence du mal: Essai sur le phénomènes extremes* [*The Transparency of Evil: Essays on Extreme Phenomena*]

1991 (age 62): *La Guerre du Golfe n'a pas eu lieu* [*The Gulf War Did Not Take Place*]

1992 (age 63): *L'Illusion de la fin ou la grève des événements* [*The Illusion of the End*]

1995 (age 66): *Le crime parfait* [*The Perfect Crime*]

18

Conclusion: Freedom, Language, and Existence

We can now survey some of the wider themes that integrate a large segment of twentieth-century French philosophy into an understandable narrative. To begin, we can recall the far-reaching, intellectual impact of the nineteenth-century 'death of God' thesis, and how this helped stimulate the rise of French existentialism. In the 1880s, Nietzsche complained that the presence of God was mentally and physically upsetting, because God shamelessly observed every thought and every move, and because God imposed moral constraints upon human activity, thereby stifling instinctual energies, the bulk of which Nietzsche regarded as requisite for health, but also as involving aggression and violence.

In principle, removing God from the scene leads to a greater sense of freedom of thought and action, since one is no longer panoptically observed; it leads to a greater sense of privacy and individuality; it leads to a release from moral constraints; it leads to a greater freedom of interpretation, or an increase in the multiple-interpretability of the world, since the 'absolute interpretation' and 'truth' of the world is removed. This idea was developed in postmodernist thought.

The death of God also leads, less positively, to a more intense feeling of personal isolation, since there is no longer an overseeing and guarding presence, along with a deeper sense of one's individuality and uniqueness, which carries with it a more profound and potentially disturbing sense of one's finitude and upcoming death. The death of God also leads to a more pronounced sense of there being no ultimate foundation to the world, or at least, of there being no ultimately intelligent and meaningful foundation.

The removal of God also leads to a positive release of previously stifled creative instinctual energies, many of which arise irrespective of rationalistic construals and moral valuations of the world. Which is to say that the removal of God supports the positive recognition of non-rational, non-scientific, non-mathematical, non-logical dimensions to human experience. All of this fits with the variety of intellectual trends that became popular in France during the first decades of the twentieth century: Dada and Surrealism emphasized non-rationality and instinctual, immediate expression; Freudianism similarly emphasized the unconscious, sexual, and non-moral instincts; French existentialism emphasized the absurdity and meaninglessness of existence, coupled with a strong feeling of being down-to-earth. It was also accompanied by a sense of one's aloneness, individuality, and contingency, all of which was associated with an awareness of death. A wide array of foundational French philosophical themes can be traced back to the death of God, and to the thought of Friedrich Nietzsche, who gave influential voice to that rebellious theme.

In conjunction with this cluster of intellectual trends, we can add the recognition that the twentieth century displayed in general, a strong interest in language. First, this interest appeared in turn-of-the-century developments in the artificial languages of logic and mathematics that are employed in scientific and technological inquiry. This was also a time when Saussure formulated his linguistic theory as a 'science,' and when he advanced the idea of a generalized 'science of signs' which he called 'semiology.' In the later parts of the century, a parallel interest in France developed in connection with the nature of literary language, and in the later 1950s and afterwards, a variety of tensions, blendings, privilegings, and mutual subordinations between literalistic and literary language characterized much of the intellectual debate in post-structuralist thought – a debate, in effect, which examined the respective virtues of literature versus science.

In the 1950s we can describe the first stages of this amalgamation between the Saussurean linguistic outlook and the earlier existential/phenomenological outlooks as a fusion between the linguistic field and the perceptual field. With this blending, especially in light of Saussure's view that 'the sign is arbitrary,' there precipitated an approach to the world which coordinated the distinctions between the things we perceive, with the distinctions that language determines by means of its vocabulary and grammatical structure. One could say that at this point in time these structuralist theorizations led their advocates to 'read' the perceptual field as if it were a text, as opposed to allowing the perceptual field to present itself in a less strongly interpreted manner, as was aimed for by traditional phenomenologists such as Husserl, and as was also described, albeit uncomfortably, by Sartre in his experience of perceptual nausea.

Reading the three-dimensional perceptual field within which one lives and acts as if it were an immense text – as one would read a dream, according to Freud's, and above all, Lacan's view – has its advantages and its drawbacks. On the level of basic practical activity, seeing-reading a table or a chair mainly in terms of the labels 'table' and 'chair' can increase one's efficiency of action, but it can also lead to a superficially oriented and stereotype-ridden consciousness that habitually overlooks the nuances of perceptual detail and which adheres too closely to the ordinary categorizations of things.

In practical life, to be sure, there is often no time to appreciate the aesthetic surface of the world. But by adhering to an outlook which weds one to the ordinary categories of things, and where the articulation of language is assumed to override any natural articulations that may be present in the raw perceptual field (e.g., physiologically grounded ones) – in one's adherence to a view through which one becomes 'blinded' by the fact that one uses only five words for designating color,[431] and thereby is in the habit of consciously registering only five different colors, instead of savoring the thousands of different perceptual shades in one's perceptual field – one is led into the danger of rendering the nauseating detail that Sartre experienced in his perceptual awareness close to impossible to appreciate. One is easily led to confuse the map of the territory with the territory itself.[432]

Perhaps more revealingly, such a structuralist outlook also softens the pain of perceiving the meaninglessness of things by rendering them meaningful through the rich lens of language and established cultural significations. It is remarkable to see how after 1950 there is very little complaint among French theorists about how meaningless the world happens to be. They seem to either ignore this upsetting existentialist apprehension or not be bothered by it.

Which is to say that French existentialism became tempered and transformed with the introduction of Saussure's linguistics into the intellectual scene. The world became more meaningful, as the meaninglessness of the raw perceptual field became inseparably infused with the endlessly resonant meanings of language. Nonetheless, though, the concrete-thinking-centered existentialist orientation was not completely lost: by the late 1950s, an existential sensitivity had been transported into the linguistic field itself by Jacques Lacan, Roland Barthes, Jacques Derrida, and Jean-François Lyotard, as they identified for us the many different dimensions that language holds within itself, such as the various voices through which a speaking subject can be phrased, language's various literalistic, associative, and metaphorical dimensions, and the multiple aspects of narrative speech. The existentialist emphasis upon concreteness, which generates an awareness of the complicated texture of perceptual experience, was preserved in the above poststructuralist thinkers in their conception of the rich and inexhaustible texture of language itself, and they used it as ammunition in arguments against the hegemony of scientific or literalistic thinking, charging such thinking with one-sidedness and superficiality. In this regard, one could call Lacan, Barthes, Derrida, and Lyotard, 'linguo-existentialists.'

But, as noted, these theorists and the majority of their contemporaries did not suffer from a perceived meaninglessness of the world; to the contrary, they wrapped themselves tightly in the blanket of textuality, as they swam in the endless field of meanings, forever resonating, that language itself afforded. The meaninglessness of the raw perceptual field was covered over, and the idea of multiple-interpretability was extended into the sphere of daily life, recalling the hermeneutic implications of God's death as the cosmic author and interpreter, and introducing an imaginary and fictive quality into the interpretation of the natural world at large. And in this way the principles of surrealism lived on, if only implicitly, for the surrealists had also advocated a blending of imagination and raw reality. As Baudrillard would observe, the emerging general outlook on the world – one taken not only by these poststructuralist and postmodern theorists, but apparently, by the prevailing culture at large – became 'hyperreal.' This spelled the demise of 'naturally defined reality' (the terrain) and the rise of 'artificially defined reality' (the map).

In advance of other postmodernist theorists, however, Baudrillard realized that living continuously within an excessively artificial reality inevitably leads people to realize that the artificially defined reality is in fact unreal, that they have been living in a kind of dream-world, and that it is only a matter of time before death and reality hit home. But in the meantime and amidst this uneasy condition of bad faith, it remains that owing to the immersion in virtual-reality devices and mass media imagery, there has been a surreal continuation of the nineteenth-century ideology of progress that has been taking place within this more imaginative, hyperrealistic field of experience, rather than in the more pleasure-principle-resistant, imagination-resistant and fantasy-resistant world of nature. In effect, Baudrillard observes that the existentialist and meaning-of-life-centered concern with authenticity and the need to confront one's upcoming death, has been defused and repressed as a result of the ready-satisfactions that contemporary electronics, media-imagery, and the abundance of consumer goods tends to supply. The poststructuralist emphasis upon textuality and multi-interpretability formed much of the ground from which this later sense of hyperreality and surreality grew.

Noting the realization that contemporary hyperrealistic modes of being are starting to become permeated with the feeling of meaninglessness that the early existentialists once perceived so poignantly, Baudrillard stated in 1996:

> The great philosophical question used to be 'Why is there something rather than nothing?' Today, the real question is: 'Why is there nothing rather than something?'[433]

This resurfacing of existential worry reveals the limitations of the quest for freedom that characterized much of twentieth-century French thought – a quest that one could call a 'negative' quest to be 'free from' oppressive forces.[434] The Dadaists wanted freedom from the science, rationality, and mechanistic-style of thinking that they believed was largely responsible for the First World War; the surrealists wanted freedom from the same kinds of rationalistic forces, and also wanted freedom from tired ways of creating art; Jean-Paul Sartre wanted freedom from ossified, essentialistic, rigid, and unchanging conceptions of the self and world; Roland Barthes, during his structuralist period, wanted freedom from the same kinds of essentialistic conceptions, which he conceived of as superficial 'myths' or as misleading stereotypes; Barthes, during his poststructuralist period, also wanted freedom from authorial dictates, and eventually, from language itself, which he eventually conceived of as 'fascist;' Derrida wanted freedom from any systems that laid a claim to absolute comprehensiveness and a finality of interpretation; Irigaray wanted freedom from male, sexist, terrorizing language; Lyotard wanted freedom from the domination of a model of knowledge defined exclusively in terms of computability; Foucault wanted freedom from social stereotypes and from dominating, manipulative political regimes; Deleuze and Guattari wanted freedom from instinctually restrictive Freudian and Oedipal family constellations, and from too tightly organized, fascistically terrorizing social structures.

All of these quests for freedom are well-aimed and are intended to make the world a better place in which to be with oneself and with others in a self-respecting way. But they are all fundamentally reactive to given, foreground-standing, oppressive situations, despite the contents of some of their visionary responses. 'Freedom from' some dominating species of oppression is a weaker kind of freedom than the 'freedom to' exert oneself in a direction that is defined more autonomously from a position of inner strength and solid self-determination.

In their more pragmatic and political orientations, as opposed to the predominantly textual orientations of other thinkers, it appears to this interpreter that among the theorists discussed in this survey, Foucault, Irigaray, and Lyotard have been the most directly oriented toward the 'reality-principle' and toward the exercise of self-legislating, positive-and-productive freedom, and have been less swayed by the surrealistic and hyperrealistic tenor of the latter part of the twentieth century. Aside from being more closely attuned to the presence of naturally occurring truth, albeit characterized optimally with literary or narrative language, their more realistic orientation is worth appreciating, since it might be an inspiration to review the social effects of the surrealistic–hyperrealistic atmosphere that appears still to prevail – an atmosphere which, according to some informed observers, has led to an alarmingly greater ease in the possibilities for immediately gratifying desires in a 'permissive cornucopia,' and which has the dangerous effect of generating political complacency.[435] Such complacency is reminiscent of Nietzsche's conception of the 'last man,' whose condition of contentment undermines the healthy interest in facing difficult challenges.

It is important to add that the hyperrealistic–surrealistic atmosphere that characterizes the postmodern period is not a phenomenon that exclusively derives from the widespread acceptance of poststructuralist theses regarding the multiple-interpretability of the natural and cultural orders. Just as one can note the influence of the structuralist–Saussurean amalgamation of linguistic structure with the perceptual field, and just as one can note the introduction of existentialist sensitivities to the poststructuralists' understanding of language itself, one can also note an influence that has entered from the opposing direction: even though poststructuralists have taken great pains to combat the hegemony of scientific and literalistic thinking, it remains that the multiple-interpretability thesis is all too receptive to being appropriated by instrumental–technological reason.

The latter form of rationality notoriously tends to use natural resources and people exclusively as a means, typically to an end conceived independently of any respect that might be accorded to the things and people that are being used. It becomes a non-moral way of thinking when it uses people without respecting them as being also ends in themselves. The manipulative feature of instrumental reason, when it is transferred into a linguistic sphere and culture that advocates multi-interpretability, invites the sophistical and rhetorical use of words. Instrumental reason 'uses words' with the intention of giving them a directed and distorting 'spin,' such as to achieve some extra-linguistic end. Within this regime of thinking, the phrase 'science of signs' becomes transformed into a 'technique' or 'technology' of signs, and the dispassionate search for truth and for the right words to express mind-independent realities, is transformed into an instrumental search for the right form of rhetoric to sway an audience's opinions and behavior. Such non-poststructuralist, technological, and instrumental forces also feed into the cultural situation to reinforce the sense of hyperreality that Baudrillard so insightfully described in his reference to the variety of unde-cideable political interpretations that can be given to terrorist bombings and other publicly reported events.

This leads us to a concluding generalization about the earlier and later halves of twentieth-century French philosophical thought in reference to their respective personal characters – a distinction which was captured well in a different context, and well ahead of his time, by Lionel Trilling in 1955.[436] Trilling contrasted the outlooks of Shakespeare and Kafka, and commented upon the respective sense of personal identity in each: in the Shakespearean world, we find a strong sense of wholeness, integrity and health; in the Kafkaesque world, we find a sense of personal identity that has been weakened, invalidated, destabi-lized, and alienated into a condition that approaches insanity.

If we recognize that a surrealist sentiment has permeated twentieth-century French thought in various guises, then we can refer accordingly to a healthy and reality-oriented surrealism which aims to tap into our instinctive energies for the purposes of exposing social ills, as opposed to a more imagi-nation-centered and pleasure-principle-oriented surrealism, which tends to obscure, not to mention deny the reality of, actual states of affairs, and which tacitly forbids us to determine what is happening as a matter of natural fact. The former kind of surrealism links with communistic and socialistic ideals and is typical of the earlier part of the century; the latter, more photorealistic style of surrealism, plays into the hands of forces that exercise control from the shadows, as the public consciousness is presented with a confusing and disori-enting array of conflicting interpretations of what is actually happening.

All of this implicitly argues for a revivification of those pre-poststruc-turalist, pre-postmodernist, and non-instrumentalist thinkers who adopted a third alternative, namely, to speak and discover the truth primarily for its own sake. In a more contemporary version, it argues for an acknowledgment of dialogue which remains receptively open,[437] and which aspires to realize an ideal speech situation[438] where participation is an open invitation, where ques-tioning of authority is allowed, and where terroristic silencing is prohibited.

Notes

1. In *Freud and Philosophy* (1970), Paul Ricoeur (1913–) identifies Marx, Nietzsche, and Freud as masters of 'suspicion' who, through their incisive powers of questioning, influentially dominated twentieth-century philosophical thought.
2. Marie-Jean-Antoine-Nicolas Caritat was Condorcet's actual name. He was a mathematician and social reformer who, during the time of the French Revolution, argued against the death penalty and helped institute influential changes in the educational system. Soon falling out of political favor, Condorcet was arrested during the Reign of Terror, and he died from uncertain causes during the first evening of his imprisonment in March 1794.
3. Comte was inspired by Henri de Saint-Simon (1760–1825), who first introduced the term 'positivism' into French theory within a sociological context. Comte is buried in Pére Lachaise cemetery in Paris – a cemetery which contains the graves of many well-known people such as Abélard and Héloise, Guillaume Apollinaire, Honoré de Balzac, Sarah Bernhardt, Georges Bizet, Frederic Chopin, Camille Corot, Jacques-Louis David, Eugene Delacroix, Isadora Duncan, Jean-Baptiste Moliere, Jim Morrison, Marcel Proust, Georges Seurat, Gertrude Stein, and Oscar Wilde.
4. This theme of demythologization is an undercurrent within twentieth-century French philosophy, and it is present in the thought of Jean-Paul Sartre, Albert Camus, Michel Foucault, and especially Roland Barthes in his writings of the 1950s. Claude Lévi-Strauss is an exception to this tendency, as is Jacques Derrida and the later Barthes, insofar as these latter theorists maintain that mythic, or metaphoric, thinking is fundamental to human awareness.

Contrary to formulations of twentieth-century French thought that sharply distinguish between 'structuralist' from 'poststructuralist' tendencies, and thereby tend to place Lévi-Strauss and Derrida in opposition, these two thinkers share an antagonism toward the more scientifically minded effort to demythologize and distill human ways of understanding the world into a more 'literal' and 'factual' form. In later chapters, we will see how these theorists compare and contrast with each other.

5. The source of Marx's own faith in progress stems, in significant part, from the views of the German Idealist philosopher, G. W. F. Hegel (1770–1831). Grounding his philosophy upon the dialectical structure of human self-reflection, Hegel anthropomorphically interpreted all of existence as a single, dynamic, intelligent being which is directed toward its own self-realization, self-awareness, and complete self-integration in the form of a perfect social organism and comprehensive consciousness.

6. For a concise expression of Marx's view, see the preface to his *A Contribution to the Critique of Political Economy* (1859).

7. For an interpretation of Marx's views that is inspired by French structuralist thought of the 1950s and which emphasizes Marx's later scientific and neutral approach to social change, see the work of the Algerian-born Louis Althusser (1918–90), and particularly his book, *For Marx* (1965).

8. See the work of Gottlob Frege (1848–1925), especially his *Begriffschrift* [Concept-Script] of 1879, whose mathematical conception of language led to a more versatile version of symbolic logic – one that reworked assumptions inherited from Aristotle. During the later twentieth century, this more quantificational system of logic became essential, for example, to understanding the theoretical limits of computer capabilities.

9. There was a comparable optimism at the beginning of the nineteenth century in Europe. This earlier optimism was generated in part by the technological success of the industrial revolution, and it was accentuated by the French Revolution (1789) and, thirteen years earlier, by the American Revolution (1776) – a social-political upheaval whose democratic aspirations reverberated throughout Europe.

Both Revolutions were inspired (in France, this inspiration was aided by the sentiments of French soldiers who had served to help the Americans) by the ideas that it is right to take up arms against tyranny, that all people should have liberal freedoms, that taxation should be appropriately and fairly levied, and that democracies are preferable to dictatorships.

10. One of Riemann's important precursors was Nikolai Ivanovich Lobachevski (1793–1856), who studied the geometry of hyperbolic surfaces. Lobachevski published 'Geometrische Untersuchungen zur Theorie der Parallellinien' ('Geometrical Researches on the Theory of Parallels') in 1836–38, which was one of the first essays in non-Euclidean geometry.

11. The title of Riemann's essay was 'Über die Hypothesen welche der Geometrie zu Grunde liegen' ('On the Hypotheses upon which Geometry is Grounded').

12. As signs of those times, there were related literary and philosophical works that speculated on what the perceptions of conscious beings would be like, if their

experiences were restricted to a flattened, two-dimensional space. The underlying philosophical motivation was to express the idea that beings such as ourselves, whose consciousness is comparably restricted to three-dimensional space, may be able to achieve *even higher* levels of consciousness, if we were to imagine what it would be like to experience an additional dimension. Two works in this genre are *Flatland – A Romance of Many Dimensions* (1884) by Edwin A. Abbott (1838–1926), and *Tertium Organum* (1920) by P. D. Ouspensky (1878–1947).

For the purposes of understanding geometrical curvature, the idea of imagining what a two-dimensional spatial consciousness might be like was explored initially by the mathematician Karl Friedrich Gauss (1777–1855). Another significant person in this history is Charles Howard Hinton (1853–1907), who considered the meaning of the fourth dimension in his *Scientific Romances* (1888).

13. Isaac Newton (1643–1727) published his scientifically revolutionary *Philosophiae Naturalis Principia Mathematica* in 1687, and he assumed the truth of Euclidean geometry, as did most people of his time.

14. Albert Einstein (1879–1955) published many ground-breaking papers in theoretical physics, one of the most famous of which was his 1905 paper, 'Zur Elektrodynamik bewegter Körper' ('On the Electrodynamics of Moving Bodies'), where he described the Special Theory of Relativity. In 1915–16 he formulated the General Theory of Relativity in a further series of publications.

15. One of the landmark paintings of cubism is Picasso's *Les Demoiselles d'Avignon* (1907).

16. Also aiming to capture the dynamism of perceptual experience within a still image – a dynamism which they also associated with modern technology, and which was expressed by their fascination with airplanes and propellers, racing cars and engines – the Paris-based, Italian Futurists were sympathetic to the scientific/technological atmosphere of progress, as they expressed a love for time itself. In this regard, we can recall F. T. Marinetti's statements in 'The Foundation and Manifesto of Futurism' (1908), which refer us to a new kind of beauty, namely the beauty of speed, race cars, and airplanes.

17. As early as 1794, Friedrich Schiller observed that the industrial revolution was leading to greater divisions of labor in society and to greater segmentation within the human mind itself. See his *On the Aesthetic Education of Man*, especially the Sixth Letter. Karl Marx's hope for a non-exploitative social system in the future was also tempered by his awareness of how industrial conditions can easily become unbearable for those who work in factories.

18. Walter Serner [Walter Eduard Seligmann] (1889–1942*), Austrian/Czech writer. (*Serner is presumed to have died in a concentration camp sometime after August 20, 1942.)

19. Jean Arp [also called Hans Arp] (1887–1966), Alsacian sculptor, poet, and painter.

20. Richard Huelsenbeck (1892–1974), German poet and writer.

21. The word 'dada' became linked with the group when Richard Huelsenbeck slipped a paper knife into a German–French dictionary, and the knife pointed to the word 'dada' by chance. The word 'dada' happens to mean 'hobby-horse,' but that particular meaning was not sought when the word was adopted.

22. Tristan Tzara (1896–1963), Romanian poet, essayist and author of several Dadaist manifestos.

23. Georges Hugnet, 'L'espirit dada dans la peinture,' *Cahiers d'Art*, 1932–34, quoted and translated in Maurice Nadeau, *The History of Surrealism*, trans. Richard Howard (London: Jonathan Cape, 1968), pp. 56–57.

24. G. W. F. Hegel, *Phenomenology of Spirit*, Section 205. (All translations from German-language texts have been done by the author.)

25. This is referred to by C. W. E. Bigsby, *Dada and Surrealism* (London: Methuen & Co. Ltd., 1972), p. 33.

26. Now inscribed and honored in almost every art-historical account of early twentieth-century art, and as such, completely contrary to the intentions of its perpetrator, one of the most well-known Dadaist acts was enacted in 1917 by the French artist, Marcel Duchamp (1887–1968), who had already been living in New York by the time that the Swiss Dadaist group was formed. In an act of defiance, mockery, and contempt, Duchamp submitted a common urinal to the New York 'Independent' show.

27. The word 'id' is Latin for 'it.' Part of the inspiration for Freud's use of the term 'id,' derives from the work of Georg Groddeck (1866–1934). See Groddeck's *The Book of the It* [*Das Buch Vom Es*] (1928).

28. Sigmund Freud, *New Introductory Lectures on Psychoanalysis* (1933), Lecture XXXI.

29. See Tristan Tzara's 1922 'Lecture on Dada' for these themes. Later, in the 1950s, Claude Lévi-Strauss similarly emphasizes the importance of attending to the 'wild' or 'savage' or 'uncivilized' state of the human mind, in an effort to understand the roots of the human psyche. This theme also appears in Deleuze and Guattari, who regard the schizophrenic state of mind as likewise aboriginal.

30. The adjective 'surrealist' was coined in 1917 by the poet and writer, Guillaume Apollinaire [Guillelmus (or Wilhelm) Apollinaris de Kostrowitsky] (1880–1918), in reference to his play, *The Breast of Tiresias*.

31. It will be suggested in later chapters that Jacques Lacan's style of lecturing had this surrealist, 'speaking from the unconscious,' quality, and that Lacan is best understood in connection with this surrealist influence.

32. The work of the Belgian painter, Jean Magritte (1898–1967), can stimulate this kind of awareness. See, for example, his *La condition humaine* (*The Human Condition*), 1934.

33. This Japanese movie is noteworthy, because its portrayal of ghosts hovers between representing them as actual beings on another dimension, and representing them as figments of the main characters' respective imaginations. This ambiguity highlights how the surrealists also referred to their movement as 'supernaturalism.'

34. This movie can be described as being within the surrealistic tradition, even though each of its episodes represents an actual experience. The editing style radically disintegrates the normal time sequence in order to simulate the confused psychological state of the main character, who suffers from a severe memory abnormality.

35. A salient feature of these later movies, beginning around 1990, is the portrayal within the film of a 'reality,' such that the audience, and not only the main character, becomes confused about what is supposed to be 'real.' The films create a

confused dream-reality state in the viewer, with respect to the interpretation of the film's representational contents.

36. The École Normale Supérieure (established 1794) has a history of being one of the best educational institutions in France, whose graduates form a long and impressive list of political and cultural figures.

37. Jean Jaurès (1859–1914 [assassinated]), an early leader of the French socialist movement, entered the school in the same year; Emile Durkheim (1858–1917), who was to become one of the most influential French sociologists, entered a year later. Jaurès is entombed in the Pantheon in Paris, alongside other great figures in French history such as Jean-Jacques Rousseau, Voltaire and Victor Hugo.

38. A *lycée* is a French secondary school that prepares students for university studies.

39. Immanuel Kant's main question in his *Critique of Pure Reason* (1781/1787) concerned the power of human reasoning and understanding to acquire metaphysical knowledge. Unlike Bergson, Kant concluded that the human mind in general is not powerful enough to give us absolute knowledge of things in themselves.

40. Henri Bergson, *The Creative Mind* [1903], trans. Mabelle L. Andison (Totowa, N.J.: Littlefield, Adams & Co., 1965), p. 159.

41. Ibid.

42. Ibid., p. 161.

43. Ibid., pp. 12–13.

44. In its general contours, Bergson's philosophical method compares with that of René Descartes, who also focused upon individual, first-person experience (viz., I think, therefore I am) in an effort to ground his philosophical standpoint. Descartes, however, attended to the reflective act of personal awareness, rather than to the experience of the flow of time. They were both introspectively oriented thinkers, but owing to the fact that each regarded a different aspect of their inner experience as basic, their respective philosophies assumed different forms.

45. Bergson, *The Creative Mind*, p. 162.

46. Ibid., p. 163.

47. Ibid., pp. 34–35.

48. Ibid., p. 189.

49. One of the most concentrated studies on this topic is Edmund Husserl's, *The Phenomenology of Internal Time-Consciousness* (1928).

50. Insofar as the passage of time involves change, time is also the ultimate death-force that brings beings to their point of termination.

51. This position is akin to Jean-Paul Sartre's view, to David Hume's view and to Buddhistic views, which deny that there is an everlasting personal self. It also resonates with 'decentered' and dynamically multi-aspected views of the self, as one finds in poststructuralist thought, and as one finds foreshadowed in Nietzsche.

52. Even this aspect of Bergson's view can be questioned, since photographs, motion pictures, and video images, although they are symbolic, external representations, can nonetheless sometimes convey very closely 'what it is like' to be perceiving an object from the standpoint of the photographer or the person with a video camera. The motion picture and video media are especially powerful in conveying, and

stimulating, the quality of another person's experience, and might serve this end better than simply performing an imaginative act of empathy.

53. The titles under which the stated work has been translated into English will be cited in square brackets, rather than a literal translation of the French titles.

54. Sartre's father was in the French navy, and he died of an intestinal disease [entercolitis] contracted while serving in South-East Asia.

55. Sartre's mother was born Anne-Marie Schweitzer, and she was a cousin to the humanitarian, Albert Schweitzer (1875–1965). (Her father's brother was Schweitzer's father.) Both Albert Schweitzer and Sartre were awarded Nobel Prizes. Schweitzer, who was thirty years older than Sartre, was awarded the prize for peace in 1954; Sartre was awarded the prize for literature in 1964 (Sartre refused the award).

56. Sartre's own interest in phenomenology was stimulated by Emmanuel Lévinas's early book, *The Theory of Intuition in Husserl's Phenomenology* (*Théorie de l'intuition dans la phénoménologie de Husserl*) which was published in 1930. Lévinas (1906–95) had visited Germany in 1928, where he encountered the views of Husserl and Heidegger (whose work, *Being and Time*, had been published only a year earlier). Sartre followed in Lévinas's footsteps five years later with a similarly inspiring visit to Germany.

57. The journal was named in recall of Charlie Chaplin's movie of the same name (*Modern Times* [1936]), and it included among its editorial staff Sartre's friend and philosopher, Maurice Merleau-Ponty (1908–61). Merleau-Ponty, who became known for his book, *The Phenomenology of Perception* (1945), resigned from the journal in 1952, owing in part to a difference of opinion with Sartre concerning the latter's supportive attitude toward the Soviet Union.

58. *The Flies* was an anti-Nazi play that was performed in Paris; *No Exit* is famous for the line, 'Hell is other people.'

59. The term 'existentialism' is partially inspired by the term 'existence-philosophy' ('*Existenzphilosophie*') that was coined by the German philosopher, Karl Jaspers (1883–1969).

60. Not wishing to be regarded as an 'institution,' Sartre also declined an appointment to the French Legion d'Honneur in 1945.

61. This cemetery is also the final resting place of Charles Baudelaire, Simone de Beauvoir (whose ashes are buried in the same grave as Sartre), Samuel Beckett, Constantin Brancusi, Eugene Ionesco, Guy de Maupassant, Pierre-Joseph Proudhon, and Camille Saint-Saens.

62. René Descartes. *Meditations on First Philosophy*, First Meditation, in *The Philosophical Works of Descartes*, trans. Elizabeth S. Haldane and G. R. T. Ross (Cambridge: Cambridge University Press, 1911), vol. 1 p. 144. All quotations from Descartes will be from this translation.

63. We encounter a related method of thought-experiment in Immanuel Kant's *Critique of Pure Reason*, in connection with Kant's efforts to differentiate and separate within his imagination, the constant, knowable *a priori*, forms of sensory experience (viz., space and time) from the variable, knowable only *a posteriori*, contents of sensory experience (viz., colors, sounds, tastes, etc.). See *Critique of Pure Reason*, B36/A22, 'Transcendental Aesthetic.'

64. Jean-Paul Sartre, *Being and Nothingness*, trans. Hazel Barnes (New York: Pocket Books, 1956), p. 4. The relevant passage from Nietzsche appears in *Twilight of the Idols* (1888), entitled, 'How the "True World" at Last Became a Fable.' This passage from Nietzsche is quoted below in the chapter on Baudrillard, and is from Nietzsche's later period.
65. Sartre, *Being and Nothingness*, p. 3.
66. Descartes, *Meditations on First Philosophy*, Second Meditation, in *The Philosophical Works*, p. 150.
67. Edmund Husserl, *Ideas – General Introduction to Pure Phenomenology*, Section 35.
68. Bergson's emphasis upon the underlying continuity of consciousness is also influential here, for within Bergson's view, the temporal continuity of consciousness serves similarly as a background for any specific act of self-conscious awareness.
69. Sartre, *Being and Nothingness*, p. 13
70. Sartre advances a second – and arguably more basic – argument for the existence of the pre-reflective *cogito*, which is that a consciousness without any self-awareness would be an unconscious consciousness, which is impossible.
71. As we shall see, the desire for being-in-itself also involves the search for an essence, which is a desire purely to be, and to escape from freedom.
72. Sartre, *Being and Nothingness*, p. 24.
73. One explanation for Sartre's interest in 'nausea' can be linked to Nietzsche, who discussed this idea in the *Birth of Tragedy* (1872). Nietzsche associated 'nausea' with the experience of apprehending the terrifying nature of reality – a reality which presents itself, Nietzsche believed, once we look under the pleasing, sanitized, idealized and innocuous surface of things.

    Sartre also experiences reality as terrifying, and his interest in the nauseating aspects of ordinary life can be seen as a transposition and relocation of Nietzschean 'nausea' up to the experiential surface of things. Since for Sartre, there is only the 'surface,' what Nietzsche apprehended 'beneath the surface,' Sartre must apprehend right upon the surface of human experience. And he finds such a nauseating 'reality' in the more repulsive, yet quite ordinary, phenomena of daily life – in mucus, slime, sweat, bad breath, etc.
74. These same ideas are expressed, almost verbatim, by Søren Kierkegaard in *Concluding Unscientific Postscript*. See especially 'Chapter III, Real or Ethical Subjectivity – The Subjective Thinker' in *Concluding Unscientific Postscript*, trans. David F. Swenson and Walter Lowrie (Princeton: Princeton University Press, 1941), p. 294. The distinction between human beings and inanimate material beings that appears centrally in Heidegger's *Being and Time*, is also expressed in this same passage from Kierkegaard.
75. Jean-Paul Sartre, *Nausea*, trans. Lloyd Alexander (New York: New Directions Publishing Corporation, 1964), p. 129.
76. Ibid., p. 131.
77. The experiences of the main character in *Nausea* express this well. When Roquentin experiences the incomprehensible sensory, contingent and accidental details of the world, he feels sickened, debilitated, 'flaccid,' weak, and meaningless. But when he imaginatively and selectively organizes these details into an organically unified

narrative or 'adventure,' he feels healthy, more powerful, 'rigid,' strong, and mean-ingful. Artistic illusion generates strength and a feeling of life, whereas appre-hending the meaninglessness and absurdity of the world generates weakness and a feeling of death. In short, the existential message of *Nausea* is interpretable in the Nietzschean terms of 'strength' versus 'weakness,' and 'health' versus 'sickness.'

78. Sartre, *Being and Nothingness*, p. 36.
79. Martin Heidegger, *Being and Time*, Introduction I, §2.
80. Ibid., §4.
81. When applied to the social sphere, this freedom to question anything and every-thing (recall the spirit of the Dada movement) opens up the possibilities of ques-tioning established social authorities and established values implicit in cultural practices. Sartre's questioning attitude (which is significantly inspired by Descartes's 'method of doubt') transfers readily to the social sphere. So although Sartre's position here focuses more on the individual person who self-questions, his view contains the seeds of a socially rebellious and revolutionary attitude – one which is later exemplified in thinkers such as Roland Barthes and Michel Foucault.
82. Sartre, *Being and Nothingness*, p. 124.
83. Ibid., p. 125.
84. Ibid., p. 140.
85. In this respect, there are affinities between Sartre's existentialism, classical Buddhism, and Schopenhauer's outlook.
86. Hegel's discussion of the 'Unhappy Consciousness' is located in his *Phenomenology of Spirit* (1807), §§207–230. We will consider Hegel's discussion more explicitly in the chapters on Cioran and Derrida.
87. Descartes, *Meditations on First Philosophy*, Second Meditation, in *The Philosophical Works*.
88. This is how Sartre tends to describe the situation. In fact, however, one might expe-rience an interference in one's world from the intrusion of wild animals, for example, if one were alone in the forest. It is not clear whether these would count as 'the Other' for Sartre, since one would probably not experience shame or pride – some of the central emotions that reveal other people to us, according to him – in front of a lion or tiger.
89. Ibid., pp. 341–342.
90. Ibid., p. 343.
91. Ibid.
92. Ibid., p. 345.
93. Ibid., pp. 347 and 349.
94. Ibid., p. 345.
95. Ibid., p. 347.
96. If Sartre's analysis is correct, it would invalidate Bergson's quest for empathic absolute knowledge of other people.
97. Sartre, *Being and Nothingness*, p. 147.
98. Ibid., p. 358.
99. Ibid., pp. 473.

100. Ibid., p. 566.
101. Ibid., p. 623.
102. This is why 'freedom' is not itself an 'essence.' Freedom does not restrict possibilities, but rather creates them.
103. Sartre, *Being and Nothingness*, p. 569.
104. Descartes, *Meditations on First Philosophy*, Fourth Meditation, in *The Philosophical Works* p. 175.
105. Satre, *Being and Nothingness*, p. 708.
106. In an odd coincidence of very close date, Nietzsche's collapse in Turin was on January 3, 1889.
107. Albert Camus, *The Myth of Sisyphus & Other Essays*, trans. Justin O'Brien (New York: Vintage Books, 1955), p. 3.
108. *Hamlet*, Act III, Scene I.
109. Decisions to commit suicide can also be done with the intent of lending one's life greater meaning, such as when one chooses to die for the sake of helping others, or for the sake of assisting one's nation while at war. The Japanese kamikaze pilots of the Second World War – the suicide-bombers of the Pacific – are an example of the latter kind of self-sacrifice.
110. Camus published *The Myth of Sisyphus* one year before (1942) Sartre published *Being and Nothingness*. Sartre's novel, *Nausea*, to which Camus indirectly refers, was published in 1938. Sartre and Camus first met in 1943, and their friendship reached a height soon after the Second World War ended, later falling apart in 1952.

     In *Nausea*, Sartre describes the feeling of the absurd in connection with suicide in the following:

     > And I – soft, weak, obscene, digesting, juggling with dismal thoughts – I, too, was *In the way*. Fortunately, I didn't feel it, although I realized it, but I was uncomfortable because I was afraid of feeling it (even now I am afraid – afraid that it might catch me behind the head and lift me up like a wave). I dreamed vaguely of killing myself to wipe out at least one of these super-fluous lives. But even my death would have been *In the way*. *In the way*, my corpse, my blood, on these stones, between these plants, at the back of this smiling garden. And the decomposed flesh would have been *In the way* in the earth which would receive my bones, at last, cleaned, stripped, peeled, proper and clean as teeth, it would have been *In the way*. I was *In the way* for eternity (*Nausea*, pp. 128–29).

111. Camus, *The Myth of Sisyphus*, p. 11.
112. The knowledge that everything will perish is a less arbitrary consideration than the experience of the feeling of life's absurdity. Not everyone will experience the feeling of the absurd as Camus does, and some might judge that this feeling represents a pathological, or at least an unhealthy, state of mind. But it is more difficult to dispute that time passes, that it erodes things, and that it will ultimately destroy the material formations that constitute our daily world. So it is not necessary to have the feeling of the absurd in order to appreciate what Camus describes as the

absurdity of life. It is necessary only to recognize that change permeates our world, that nothing is permanent and that this is the only world, thus rendering fruitless any search for absolute meaning.

113. Camus, *The Myth of Sisyphus*, p. 58.

114. The title of this book in Hebrew is *Qoheleth*, which signifies the 'words of someone who addresses an assembly.' The English title, 'Ecclesiastes,' is taken from *ekklesia*, which is the Greek word for 'church' (cf. French '*église*,' Spanish '*iglesia*,' and Italian '*chiesa*,' which all mean 'church').

115. Ecclesiastes 2:14–17, *The New World Annotated Bible*, ed. Bruce M. Metzger and Roland E. Murphy (New York: Oxford University Press, 1991), p. 843.

116. See also 'All the world's a stage ...' (*As You Like It*, Act II, Scene VII) and 'To be or not to be ...' (*Hamlet*, Act III, Scene I).

117. See *Macbeth*, Act V, Scene V.

118. We can compare Sartre's emphasis upon authenticity, which is closely related to Camus's conception of integrity.

119. Camus, *The Myth of Sisyphus*, p. 37.

120. Camus also refers to the views of the Russian existentialist, Lev Shestov (1866–1938), author of *Potestas Clavium* [Power of the Keys] (1923), *Athens and Jerusalem* (1938), and *Kierkegaard and Existential Philosophy* (1939). Bibliographical entries refer to him diversely as Lev Sjestov, Leo Sjestov, Leon Shestov, Lev Chestov, Léon Chestov, Leo Chestov, Leon Sestov, Leo Schestow, Lev Isaakovic Sestov, Lev Isaakovitsj Schwarzmann, and Leo Isaak Schwarzmann.

121. One can associate the nineteenth-century interest in freedom and the absurd with a return to a nominalistic, as opposed to rationalistic, conception of God. The former, nominalistic conception – as one finds in the fourteenth-century thought of William of Ockham – involves a more authoritarian and unpredictable style of deity. This conception of God was popular during the time of the Black Plague (mid-fourteenth century), when people appeared to contract the deadly disease at random, for no clear reason. See Michael Allen Gillespie's, *Nihilism Before Nietzsche* (Chicago and London: The University of Chicago Press, 1995). The same conception of God is mirrored (within the human being) in Sartre's theory of absolute freedom, for Sartre's absolute freedom is similarly unbounded by rationality.

122. Camus, *The Myth of Sisyphus*, p. 37.

123. Ibid., p. 23.

124. Ibid., p. 40.

125. The respect for fighting a losing battle also has a long history in Japanese culture. See, for example, *The Nobility of Failure – Tragic Heroes in the History of Japan*, by Ivan Morris (New York: The Noonday Press, 1975).

126. Camus, *The Myth of Sisyphus*, p. 42.

127. Ibid., p. 44.

128. In *The Stranger*, Camus's character, Meursault, contemplates what it would be like if he were suddenly released from his prison cell, and imagines the rush of joy that would bring tears to his eyes.

129. Camus, *The Myth of Sisyphus*, p. 47.
130. Ibid., p. 45.
131. For a rendition of the Kierkegaardian seducer and aesthete, see Kierkegaard's 'Diary of a Seducer' in *Either/Or* (1843). This theme of seduction will arise later in Roland Barthes's and Jean Baudrillard's views.
132. See Nietzsche's *Beyond Good and Evil*, 'What is Noble.'
133. Camus, *The Myth of Sisyphus*, pp. 88–89.
134. Ibid., p. 89.
135. Ibid., p. 91.
136. Sibiu is located in central Romania.
137. Cioran specifically studied philosophy, and wrote a thesis on Henri Bergson.
138. E. M. Cioran, *The Temptation to Exist* [1956], trans. Richard Howard (London: Quartet Books, 1987), p. 1.
139. As we have noted earlier, Tzara was a major influence in the Dada movement, as the author of numerous Dada manifestos.
140. Mircea Eliade was an internationally recognized specialist in comparative religions, and became known initially for his work, *Yoga, Immortality and Freedom*, which was his 1933 doctoral dissertation. In 1958, Eliade became chair of the History of Religions Department at the University of Chicago, where he continued to teach and write until his death in 1986.
141. Eugène Ionesco, playwright, is known as a leading representative of the post Second World War 'theatre of the absurd' during the late 1940s and early 1950s.
142. The *Evergreen Review* began in 1957, and published articles by Samuel Beckett, Jean-Paul Sartre, Albert Camus, Roland Barthes, Antonin Artaud, D. T. Suzuki, Jack Kerouac, William S. Burroughs, Henry Miller, Clement Greenberg, Karl Jaspers, and Boris Pasternak, among many others.
143. E. M. Cioran, *The Trouble With Being Born* [1973], trans. Richard Howard (London: Quartet Books, 1993), Section 7, pp. 118–119.
144. E. M. Cioran. *On the Heights of Despair* [1934], trans. Ilinca Zarifopol-Johnston (Chicago: The University of Chicago Press, 1992), 'On Death,' p. 22. Cioran continued his distaste for philosophical systems into his later years, describing Aristotle, Aquinas, and Hegel as 'three enslavers of the mind,' adding that 'the worst form of despotism is the *system*, in philosophy and in everything' (*The Trouble With Being Born*, Section 7, p. 117). As we shall see, Jacques Derrida shares the same anti-systematic sentiments in his criticism of 'logocentric' outlooks.
145. Ibid., 'The Contradictory and the Inconsequential,' p. 39.
146. As noted, Cioran wrote his undergraduate thesis on Bergson when he was studying at the University of Bucharest (1929–31).
147. Cioran, *On the Heights of Despair*, 'The Passion for the Absurd,' p. 11.
148. Similar sentiments are expressed in the concluding lines of Schopenhauer's first volume of *The World as Will and Representation*, where Schopenhauer states that from the standpoint of his detached and peaceful awareness, the world, with all of its shining galaxies, is unimportant. Unlike Schopenhauer, though, Cioran does not renounce life.

149. Cioran, *On the Heights of Despair*, 'Nothing is Important,' p. 33.
150. Cioran, alternatively, describes suffering from the objective standpoint:

> How is suffering rather than pleasure going to make me immortal? From a
> purely *objective* point of view, is there any significant difference between one
> man's agony and another's pleasure? Whether you suffer or not, nothingness
> will swallow you forever. There is no objective road to eternity, only a
> subjective feeling experienced at irregular moments in time. Nothing created
> by man will endure … so-called virtuous men are actually cowards who will
> disappear from the world's consciousness faster than those who have
> wallowed in pleasure. And even so, supposing the opposite were true, would a
> dozen or more years really count? (ibid., 'Eternity and Morality,' p. 63).

151. See Susan Sontag, 'Introduction' in E. M. Cioran, *The Temptation to Exist* [1956]
     (London: Quartet Books, 1987), p. 14.
152. Cioran, *On the Heights of Despair*, 'The Meaning of Grace,' p. 60
153. Ibid., 'On Death,' p. 25.
154. Cioran, *The Trouble With Being Born*, Section 4, p. 69.
155. Ibid., Section 5, p. 81.
156. Ibid., Section 10, p. 180.
157. Ibid., Section 10, p. 179.
158. Ibid., Section 8, p. 139.
159. The other woman was Marie Madeleine d'Aubray, Marquise de Brinvilliers
     (1630–76), who was known for, and executed for, the several murders (by
     poisoning) she committed. The Marquise was beheaded and burned. See *Drawn and
     Quartered*, 'Stabs at Bewilderment,' Section II, p. 104. St. Teresa and the Marquise
     combine in Cioran's thought to represent the themes of ecstasy and death.
160. His family lived in the Auvergne district, a few miles from Clermont, and they had
     a coat of arms which read, 'Fiery is their vigour, and of heaven their source.' The
     motto is from Virgil's *Aeneid*.
161. 'Voltaire' was a pen name. His actual name was François Marie Arouet.
162. It is instructive to compare Descartes's similar background, who also attended
     Jesuit schools when he was young. Both Teilhard and Descartes were trained in
     the contemporary science of the day and in the Catholic religion, and both
     philosophers can be seen as having come to terms with the tensions between
     science and religion.
163. Some of Teilhard's most important work focused upon the 'Peking man' [*Homo
     erectus*] in connection with the paleontological site at Zhoukoudian, China,
     located approximately 40km south of Beijing. *Homo erectus* is believed to have
     existed between 1.8 million and 300,000 years ago.
164. The Jesuit authorities did not allow Teilhard to publish his book, *The
     Phenomenon of Man* (1938–40), and, moreover, did not allow him to accept a
     professorial chair of high visibility and academic recognition at the Collège de
     France. Both of these official decisions were disappointing for Teilhard. But the
     Jesuit authorities believed that Teilhard's views bordered on heresy, and they

made decisions to locate him in overseas posts where he would be away from the centers of scholarly influence in Paris.

165. Teilhard de Chardin, *The Phenomenon of Man*, trans. Bernard Wall and Julian Huxley (New York and Evanston: Harper & Row Publishers, 1959), pp. 243–244.

166. Ibid., p. 268.

167. Schopenhauer expresses a similar view in his *The World as Will and Representation* (1818), although he does not emphasize any significant developmental or progressive dimension to human history, as does Teilhard. In this latter respect, Teilhard's view is more akin to that of G. W. F. Hegel.

168. De Chardin, *The Phenomenon of Man*, p. 56.

169. Ibid., p. 220.

170. Ibid., p. 220.

171. The word is taken from the Greek word '*nous*,' which means 'mind' or 'thought.'

172. De Chardin, *The Phenomenon of Man*, p. 244.

173. Ibid., p. 251.

174. In his early, more romanticist and theological writings of the 1790s, Hegel expressed a similar position regarding love and in connection with Jesus' essential message. See especially his fragment on love, 1797–98.

175. De Chardin, *The Phenomenon of Man*, p. 265.

176. It is in this context that his often-quoted remark that 'everything that rises must converge' reaches its total expression.

177. Which amounts to saying that human history develops between two points of reflection, the one inferior and individual, the other superior and collective. [This is Teilhard's own note within the text.]

178. De Chardin, *The Phenomenon of Man*, p. 287.

179. Ibid., p. 223.

180. When someone claims that an evil being (e.g., Satan, the devil) is responsible for evil, a parallel kind of problem arises, since one needs to explain why God would allow such an evil being to exist.

181. This sort of objection is voiced by Ivan Karamazov in Fyodor Dostoevski's novel, *The Brothers Karamazov*, where Ivan asserts that the final harmony of humanity, no matter how glorious, is not worth the tears of a single tortured child.

182. De Chardin, *The Phenomenon of Man*, p. 275.

183. An alternative way to express this objection is to point out that natural 'trends' are not the same as natural 'laws.' Teilhard carefully observes natural trends, but it remains an open question as to whether these refer to necessary and unchangeable patterns that will hold for the future. For a discussion of the distinction between natural trend and natural law, see Karl Popper, *The Poverty of Historicism* (London: Routledge & Kegan Paul, 1957), Part IV, who accordingly objects to theories similar to Teilhard's.

184. The summit of Mont Blanc (15,781 feet) was first reached on August 8, 1786 by Jacques Balmat and Michel Gabriel Paccard. Horace-Bénédict de Saussure described his own experiences in *Voyages dans les Alpes* (1779–86). The latter's description of the colors of shadows was referred to by Johann Wolfgang von

Goethe (1749–1832) in his 1810 work, *Zur Farbenlehre* [*Theory of Colors*], Section 74.

185. Ferdinand de Saussure, *Course in General Linguistics*, trans. Wade Baskin (New York, Toronto, London: McGraw-Hill, 1959), Part II, Chapter IV, p. 113

186. Ibid., Part I, Chapter I, p. 67.

187. Ibid., Part II, Chapter IV, pp. 111–112.

188. In the history of ideas, one encounters numerous parallelisms and analogies of this kind. For example, Plato understood the structure of society in terms of the structure of the individual human mind, and much later, the French sociologists, Émile Durkheim and Marcel Mauss, maintained that the predominant style of classification of objects in the world (e.g., genus-species hierarchies) reproduces the predominant style of classifications of people.

189. De Saussure, Part II, Chapter IV, p. 113.

190. Ibid., Part II, Chapter IV, p. 120.

191. Ibid., Part II, Chapter IV, p. 120.

192. Ibid., Introduction, Chapter III, p. 16.

193. Ibid., Introduction, Chapter IV, p. 18.

194. Ludwig Wittgenstein (1889–1951) has a theory of linguistic meaning that is in the same family as Saussure's. As does Saussure, Wittgenstein claims that the meaning of the word 'red' is not fundamentally explained in reference to some private sensory experience of a certain kind. Rather, Wittgenstein claims that the meaning of the word 'red' arises from the way the word 'red' is used in the language. So where Saussure speaks of a network of signs arranged in a bipolar network, Wittgenstein speaks of a set of linguistic practices. Both, however, deny that the meanings of words are fundamentally determined by private sensory experiences. Later, we will see how Jean-François Lyotard advocates Wittgenstein's theory of linguistic meaning.

195. The University of Paris was established in 1170, and later acquired its familiar name, the Sorbonne, from Robert de Sorbon, who established a college for theological studies in 1257. The University of Paris remained a centralized institution until 1970, when it was divided into thirteen independent institutions. It then became the University of Paris, IV (Sorbonne).

196. Lévi-Strauss marks the development of writing as a turning point in the development of human culture. After this development, he observes that there is a radical increase in the hierarchicalization of social groups, and a corresponding increase in the exploitation of one group in relation to another (i.e., a more distinct division of the society into a 'master' and a 'slave' group). See *Conversations With Lévi-Strauss*, ed. G. Charbonnier (London: Jonathan Cape, Ltd., 1969), p. 30.

197. Lévi-Strauss's book, *The Savage Mind* [*La Pensée sauvage*, 1962], expresses this idea in the very title of the work. It is worth noting that the translation of '*sauvage*' as 'savage' distorts Lévi-Strauss's meaning to some extent. The terms 'natural' or 'wild', insofar as they carry connotations of purity and being 'untainted by culture', more clearly express the intention of the book's title.

198. The example is adapted from one offered by Edmund Leach in his short, but excellent, book *Lévi-Strauss* (London: Fontana/Collins, 1970). Saussurean linguistics does not itself give a strong weight to the difference between what is natural and what is artificial, although a version of this distinction operates in a more salient manner in connection with Levi-Strauss's contrast between natural versus cultural sequences.

199. When set next to each other, red and green pigments produce a visual buzzing effect that arises as a consequence of their different wavelengths as they react upon the retina (i.e., the effect is explainable in physiological terms). Also, when red and green pigments are mixed together, they neutralize each other to result in a greyish color.

200. Leach, for example, points out (p. 22) that we use the color red to designate live electric wires, hot water taps, stop signs, etc.

201. The North American Chickasaw tribe was located originally in northern Mississippi, and was relocated to Oklahoma in 1832.

202. Claude Lévi-Strauss, *The Savage Mind* (Chicago: The University of Chicago Press, 1966), p. 118.

203. Sigmund Freud, *Introductory Lectures on Psychoanalysis*, Chapter X.

204. Ibid., Chapter X.

205. Ibid., Chapter X.

206. It remains unclear whether Lévi-Strauss was able to characterize the essence of humanity at this general level. He does, however, provide definite accounts of the central themes within various cultural groups. When generalizing from these groups, we encounter the basic theme of human culture attempting to reconcile itself with its (uncultured) natural roots.

207. Claude Lévi-Strauss, *Structural Anthropology*, trans. Claire Jacobson and Brooke Grundfest Schoepf (New York: Basic Books, Inc., 1963), p. 229.

208. Ibid., pp. 208–209.

209. Ibid., p. 225.

210. Saussure compared language to a musical symphony, so this procedure of interpreting myths upon analogy to reading musical scores traces back to a Saussurean insight.

211. Lévi-Strauss, *Structural Anthropology*, p. 224.

212. Ibid., p. 230.

213. Alexandre Kojève (1902–68) lectured influentially on Hegel from 1933–39 at the École Pratique des Hautes Études. These Marxist-toned lectures were published in France in 1947 as *Introduction à la Lecture de Hegel* (Paris: Gallimard, 1947). They appear in English as *Introduction to the Reading of Hegel*, assembled by Raymond Queneau, edited by Allan Bloom, and translated from the French by James H. Nichols, Jr. (New York and London: Basic Books, Inc., 1969).

214. Although Lacan's essay was originally delivered at the International Psychoanalytic Congress at Marienbad, it was not discussed at length by those who were present. Lacan gave his definite version of the essay in 1949 at the Zurich International Psychoanalytic Congress.

215. Lacan does, however, acknowledge that there is a 'thinking person' behind the scenes of linguistic formulations, however vague and indeterminately defined this being might be; he acknowledges an entire sphere of unconscious activity in a person.

216. For example, Lacan maintains that our gender identities (i.e., male and female roles) are largely a social construction. This arbitrariness in gender construction has been a feature of Lacan's view which has attracted contemporary feminists.

217. This view is expressed in Lacan's 'mirror-stage' essay, as well as in Sartre's theory of consciousness as stated in *Being and Nothingness*.

218. Implicit here is a theory of authentic communication, and a suggestion that mental illness involves a mode of distorted communication. In a more global vein, Jürgen Habermas (1929–) develops a general theory of society and postulates an ideal of authentic communication which echoes these Lacanian themes. See Habermas's, *The Theory of Communicative Action* (1984/1987). We will again refer briefly to Habermas in the concluding pages of the present study.

219. Sartre harbors the same attitude about basic human interaction: the first reaction to another person's presence is to perceive this presence as a threat. (See *Being and Nothingness*, p. 347)

220. As we have seen in the discussion of Sartre, one is always either 'master' (looking at someone) or 'servant' (being looked at by someone) during social interaction. So Hegel's conclusions about the unsatisfying nature of the 'master–servant' relationship can be seen to be conclusions about the human condition, if one assumes (as does Sartre) that we are always either 'masters' or 'servants.' Hegel himself disagreed with this assumption, and claimed that we could develop our perspectives so as to socially interact in a way where we mutually respected each other as equals, without the defining presence of dominance–submission relationships. Marx was of the same opinion as Hegel, as was de Chardin.

221. This was due to Lacan's reading of Lévi-Strauss's *The Elementary Structures of Kinship*, where – using a Saussurean linguistic framework – Lévi-Strauss interprets the taboo against incest in terms of a beneficially perceived social rule where women are obliged to marry members of other tribes, as opposed to marrying members within their tribe. This promotes larger organizations and ties between potentially warring factions.

222. Lacan's 'mirror-stage' can take place at six months of age, before the child can speak.

223. The 'real' is a primarily negative term in Lacan's terminology, and it designates whatever provides a resistance or whatever has been rejected from, or is outside of, the subject's structuring system. The 'real' varies according to the psychological structure involved, and does not refer to the 'real world' or the 'external world' within Lacan's view. It also sometimes refers to that which cannot be reduced to linguistic terms. In this context, Lacan refers to it as 'the impossible.'

224. In his *Phenomenology of Spirit* (Sections 125–128), Hegel identifies a similar kind of relationship that obtains among the objects in the perceptual (as opposed to linguistic) field, stating that the identity of any object in the perceptual field depends upon its being differentiated from the other objects within the field (i.e., its positive presence issues from its contrast with the background upon which it is

more generally located). Hegel's observation was reiterated by Edmund Husserl in his own analysis of the perceptual field – an analysis which, as we have seen, influenced Sartre's understanding of consciousness as having a pre-reflective, yet self-conscious, aspect. The main idea is that the background is prior to the foreground.

225. This, by the way, is the opposite of Kant's view, which claims that the integrity of objects, their coherence, wholeness, etc. arises from the projections of the (already-integrated) ego upon the world. Lacan turns things around, and says that the wholeness of perceived images (as in the mirror image of one's self) is used as a model for the integrity of the ego.

226. See Jacques-Alain Miller, 'Teachings of the Case Presentation,' in *Returning to Freud: Clinical Psychoanalysis in the School of Lacan*, trans. and ed. Stuart Schneiderman (New Haven: Yale University Press, 1980), pp. 42–54.

227. Jacques Lacan, *Le Séminaire*, vol. 3, *Les Psychoses* (Paris: Editions du Seuil, 1981), p. 172.

228. Freud, *Introductory Lectures on Psychoanalysis*, Lecture XI.

229. Ibid., Lecture XI.

230. Ibid., Lecture XXIII.

231. Metaphor and metonymy were first highlighted in the work of the structuralist, Roman Jakobson. See his 'Two Aspects of Language and Two Types of Aphasic Disturbances,' in *Fundamentals of Language* (1956).

232. For example, instead of saying, 'There were thirty ships on the horizon,' one says 'There were thirty sails on the horizon.'

233. Freud, *Introductory Lectures on Psychoanalysis*, Lecture XIX.

234. See 'Structure and Ambiguity in the Symbolic Order: Some Prolegomena to the Understanding and Criticism of Lacan' by Patrick Colm Hogan, in *Criticism and Lacan: Essays and Dialogue on Language, Structure, and the Unconscious*, ed. Patrick Colm Hogan and Lalita Pandit (Athens, GA: University of Georgia Press, 1990), p. 25. See also Masud Khan's book, *Alienation in Perversions* (New York: International Universities Press, 1979), pp. 178–180.

235. Hogan, 'Structure and Ambiguity,' p. 25.

236. For example, an indication of Lacan's unfortunate reception in the Anglo-American philosophical world is found in a publication offered by the American Philosophical Association, *The Philosophical Lexicon*. This *Lexicon* is a witty, entertaining, and self-consciously irreverent set of 'definitions' of newly coined words (that contain philosophers names and doctrines) that, in part, serves the function of indoctrinating new members into the profession. Through the use of humor, the *Lexicon* familiarizes people with what are regarded as important contemporary philosophical figures and, by implication, the prevailing values of the contributors to the *Lexicon*, some of whom are highly influential and respected members of the profession. The entry relevant to Lacan reads as follows:

> **lacanthropy**, n. The transformation, under the influence of the full moon, of a dubious psychological theory into a dubious social theory via a dubious linguistic theory.

The word-play upon Lacan's name involves the dictionary term 'lycanthropy' (this is derived from the Greek '*lykoi*' [wolf] and '*anthropos*' [human]). 'Lycanthropy' is the more scholarly term for the belief in werewolves. So in effect, the American Philosophical Association publication implicitly transmits the questionable message to newcomers that Lacanian psychoanalysis is akin to witchcraft, and that it is therefore not an intellectually creditable study.

237. The example of the leaping dancer is from Søren Kierkegaard's *Concluding Unscientific Postscript*, trans. David F. Swenson and Walter Lowrie (Princeton: Princeton University Press, 1941), pp. 112–113.

238. Moreover, as a matter of practical psychotherapy, psychotherapists do not always speak to patients in straightforwardly rational terms. Sometimes shocking and non-rational tactics are used. So Lacan's style of expression is also intended to evoke certain responses in his listeners and readers, rather than convince them purely by means of logical argumentation.

239. Roland Barthes, *Mythologies* [1957], trans. Annette Lavers (New York: Hill & Wang, 1977), p. 110.

240. Ibid., p. 69.

241. Ibid., p. 75.

242. During the 1950s (and also later), the Vespa was a popular style of motorscooter. For many people, it signified adventure, traveling to difficult-to-reach places, and personal independence. The Vespa company started in 1946 and celebrated its 50th anniversary in 1996.

243. Barthes, *Mythologies*, p. 53.

244. Ibid., p. 142.

245. Ibid., pp. 148–149.

246. Ibid., p. 61.

247. Roland Barthes, 'Science Versus Literature,' *The Times Literary Supplement* (28 September, 1967), p. 897.

248. Just as Lacan develops psychoanalysis in the direction of literature and away from quantitative science, Barthes argues that literature is a discipline that is more central than science.

249. Barthes, 'Science Versus Literature,' p. 897.

250. There is a sense, though, in which we use electrons to investigate electrons, or in which we use metal to investigate metal, if our scientific instruments are constituted by such materials. We also use thought to investigate thought, human consciousness to investigate human consciousness, human eyes to investigate human eyes, etc. So the problem Barthes is noting is not specific to the problem of investigating language with language. It is a general problem of self-reference.

251. Barthes, 'Science Versus Literature,' p. 898.

252. Ibid.

253. Ibid.

254. Jean-François Lyotard will make a similar claim about the virtues of narrative discourse, which is literary and multi-aspected. Lyotard comparably opposes

narrative discourse to scientific discourse, which be believes is more one-dimensional and exclusively literalistic.

255. France colonized Saigon in 1859, and Vietnam remained a French colony until it was taken over by the Japanese during the Second World War. After the war, Indo-China was provisionally divided between China and Great Britain for administrative purposes, with the intention to return Indo-China to France. Owing to the development of a strong Vietnamese nationalistic movement, France ended up fighting for control over the area, and they were finally forced to retreat in 1954, after the battle of Dienbienphu. It was not long before the Americans became involved in an effort to stabilize the area, and this effort accelerated into yet another war which lasted until 1972.

256. Roland Barthes, 'The Death of the Author,' in Roland Barthes, *Image, Music, Text*, trans. Stephen Heath (New York: Hill & Wang, 1977), p. 143.

257. Ibid., p. 148.

258. Ibid., p. 146.

259. Ibid.

260. Ibid., p. 143.

261. Ibid., p. 145.

262. See ibid., p. 142.

263. Ibid., p. 147. Note Barthes's reference to 'infinite deferral' – a theme that is developed by Jacques Derrida.

264. Ibid., p. 146.

265. Ibid., p. 147.

266. Ibid.

267. This marks a change from Barthes's earlier structuralist studies which tried to articulate the underlying meaning of contemporary myths by going beneath their surface meanings.

268. Barthes, 'The Death of the Author,' pp. 147–148.

269. To defend the idea that the meaning of a text is determined by the author's intended meaning, one can distinguish between the 'meaning' of a text and the 'significance' of a text. The text's 'significance' would include, for example, Freudian interpretations of *Hamlet*, but the core 'meaning' of *Hamlet* would nonetheless be what Shakespeare intended the play to mean. For a hermeneutic theory that is based on this distinction, see E. D. Hirsch, Jr.'s, *Validity in Interpretation* (New Haven and London: Yale University Press, 1967), which was published one year before Barthes's 'The Death of the Author.'

270. Barthes, 'The Death of the Author,' p. 148.

271. This is reported in a letter allegedly written by Mozart, although the authenticity of the letter has been questioned. The letter is reproduced in *The Creative Process*, ed. Brewster Ghiselin (New York: The New American Library of World Literature, 1955), pp. 44–45.

272. Roland Barthes, 'From Work to Text' (1971) in Roland Barthes, *Image, Music, Text*, trans. Stephen Heath (New York: Hill & Wang, 1977), p. 160–161.

273. Barthes, 'The Death of the Author,' p. 145. In Barthes's emphasis upon the 'here and now,' we should note the existential overtones of his view.
274. Barthes, 'From Work to Text,' p. 160.
275. See the beginning chapters of Nietzsche's *Thus Spoke Zarathustra* (1883–85). The first occurrence of the phrase 'God is dead' in Nietzsche's writings is in *The Gay Science* (1882), Book III, Section 108.
276. Nietzsche's father was a Lutheran minister, as was his grandfather. The connection between Nietzsche's call for the 'death of God' and Martin Luther's call for the elimination of Church authority is not merely coincidental.
277. In Nietzsche's philosophy, comparatively, this trans-individual power is played by 'life itself,' rather than God or language. Nietzsche sometimes wrote as if he imagined himself to be the inspired voice of life itself, which accounts for much of the prophetic quality of his writings.
278. An alternative postmodern aesthetic would advocate values such as wittiness, playfulness, indeterminacy, sublimity, pleasure, eroticism, profundity, and innovativeness.
279. Roland Barthes, *The Pleasure of the Text*, trans. Richard Miller (New York: Hill & Wang, 1975), p. 6.
280. Ibid., p. 43.
281. Ibid., pp. 66–67.
282. Roland Barthes, 'Inaugural Lecture, Collège de France' [1977], in *A Barthes Reader*, ed. Susan Sontag (New York: Hill & Wang, 1982), p. 459.
283. Ibid., p. 460.
284. Ibid.
285. Ibid., p. 461. Deleuze is also strongly opposed to fascism.
286. Ibid.
287. Ibid., p. 468. Barthes's idea of abjuring what one has written can be thought-provokingly condensed into the classically paradoxical sentence, 'This sentence is not true,' which, in effect, abjures itself. This semantic paradox will be mentioned once again in the discussion of Derrida's views on deconstruction.
288. Ibid., pp. 476–477. Note how Barthes's positive program uses the imagery of the mother and child, and how his earlier 'death of the author' imagery used a (negative) image of the father and child.
289. Within the existentialist tradition, we encounter the same recognition of inescapability in the claim that 'not to choose, is nonetheless to have made a choice.'
290. Barthes, 'Inaugural Lecture, Collège de France' [1977], pp. 473–474.
291. This was a presentation to the *Société française de philosophie* on January 27, 1968. It was published at the same time in the *Bulletin de la société française de philosophie*, July–September 1968, and also in *Théorie d'ensemble*, coll. *Tel Quel* (Paris: Editions du Seuil, 1968). It is one of Derrida's most important theoretical writings. As a sign of the turbulent times, we can note that the date of Derrida's presentation closely coincided with the Tet Offensive in the Vietnam War, which started only a few days later (January 30, 1968). The Paris events of May 1968 were also not far away.

292. Jacques Derrida, 'Différance,' in *Margins of Philosophy*, trans. Alan Bass (Chicago: The University of Chicago Press, 1972), p. 10.
293. Ibid., p. 11.
294. Ibid., p. 9.
295. See the beginning of Aristotle's text, 'On Interpretation.'
296. Derrida, 'Différance,' p. 3.
297. Ibid., p. 3.
298. In the earlier part of the twentieth century, philosophers who had literary inclinations tended to write philosophical works in the traditional, literalistic form while they also independently wrote novels and plays; in the later part of the century, philosophers who had literary inclinations tended to write philosophical works directly in a literary form, amalgamating the two styles into one. In the history of philosophy, Friedrich Schiller and Søren Kierkegaard exemplify the latter, philosophical–literary style of expression, and they are avant-garde figures in this respect.
299. Derrida, 'Différance,' pp. 3–4.
300. The association between *différance* and the concept of death is salient, and one could say that Derrida is a death-oriented thinker, insofar as 'death' has been traditionally linked to change, to nothingness, and to what cannot be experienced. Closely related to this, Heidegger states in *Being and Time*, that death cannot be surpassed, which is to say that he believes that beyond death, there is nothingness.
301. Derrida, 'Différance,' p. 4.
302. Shlomo Pines, 'Maimonides,' in *The Encyclopedia of Philosophy*, ed. Paul Edwards (New York: Macmillan Publishing Co., Inc. The Free Press, 1967), Vol. 5, p. 131.
303. Derrida, 'Différance,' p. 5.
304. Derrida here claims importantly that *différance* 'makes possible' the positive presentation of things. One could say, using more Kantian terminology, that *différance* is the 'condition for the possibility of' experiencing things that are present. This Kantian aspect of Derrida's notion of *différance* will be developed below.
305. Derrida, 'Différance,' p. 6.
306. Ibid., pp. 26–27.
307. Ibid., p. 22.
308. Heidegger, *Being and Time*, Section 1.
309. Ibid., Section 2.
310. Ibid., Section 2.
311. The method of Descartes's *Meditations* provides an example of the distinction. Descartes first proves *that* he is ('I think, I exist'), and then he proves *what* he is ('I am a thinking thing'). The latter kind of inquiry – one which focuses upon the 'what' or 'essence' of an individual – is what Heidegger characterizes as having been the predominant interest of Western metaphysics. But Heidegger himself is interested in the former, more primordial, sort of inquiry that focuses upon 'that-ness' or 'being-present.'

312. '*Sein*' = 'being;' '*vergessen*' = 'forgotten;' '*heit*' = 'ness.' Heidegger refers to the philosophical period of this loss of awareness of Being, as ranging from Aristotle to Kant (early Heidegger) or as ranging from Plato to Nietzsche (later Heidegger).
313. Heidegger, *Being and Time*, Section 44.
314. Ibid., Section 44.
315. Ibid., Section 52 (italics in original).
316. The mechanism here is parallel to (and part of the inspiration for) Sartre's conception of 'bad faith.' Just as we objectify ourselves in order to achieve some relief from the anxiety of apprehending our freedom, the 'they' objectifies the idea of death, which provides some relief from the anxiety of facing our actual death.
317. Derrida, 'Différance,' pp. 21–22.
318. Representatives of 'flux-theory' would include Heracleitus, Nietzsche, and Bergson. We could also associate the Hindu god Shiva – the destroyer – as representative of the spirit of such views. Some versions of Buddhism also emphasize the transitory nature of all things.
319. Since every noun in German is capitalized, Derrida's observation that 'Being' is expressed with a capital letter does not express his point well, which is that the positive idea of 'Being' stands at the solid center of Heidegger's philosophical outlook.
320. Derrida, 'Différance,' p. 17.
321. The procedure of 'conceptual inversion' was used by Hegel almost two centuries ago in his discussion of the philosophical dynamics of scientific theorizing. In the section of the *Phenomenology of Spirit* entitled 'understanding,' Hegel refers to the construction of an 'inverted world' which is the mirror-image of a supposedly 'completed' scientific theory. It is a world where 'negative' is 'positive,' where 'light' is 'dark,' and so on.
322. Barthes's structuralist revelations of the 'mythologies' that support capitalism operate in a similarly revolutionary way.
323. Recall Barthes's critique of science, for we encounter the same idea in that context. Barthes spoke of different 'voices' which the text can express; Derrida speaks of different literary dimensions within a text. The two are close in conception.
324. We find this concretist and anti-abstractionist theme in Berkeley's critique of Locke's doctrine of abstract ideas; Hegel's critique of Kant's 'formalism;' in Marx's critique of Hegel's 'idealism;' Kierkegaard's critique of Plato's attention to the spaceless–timeless 'Forms' in favor of Socrates's attention to real-life; and Heidegger's critique of Western metaphysics as having forgotten its existential foundation in Being.

     The basic idea is that those who engage in abstract, rationalized thought-constructions fail to recognize their concrete, material, existential (depending upon the theorist) roots, and that the abstract products of the thought-constructions – when taken to be descriptive of 'reality' – by ignoring these roots, inevitably falsify the true and more complicated state of affairs.
325. Specific illustrations require a close familiarity with the text at hand, and are difficult to otherwise appreciate. We can, however mention Derrida's analysis of

Plato's dialogue, *Phaedrus*, where he points out that a chain of words which have the same etymological root (*pharmakeia, pharmakon,* and *pharmakeus*), although mutually dependent upon each other in their meaning, are not regarded as having any meaningful connection within Plato's text. This is a 'contradiction' within the text. See his 'Plato's Pharmacy' (1972) which appears in English in *Dissemination,* trans. Barbara Johnson (Chicago: University of Chicago Press, 1981), pp. 61–84.

326. Jacques Derrida, 'Structure, Sign and Play in the Discourse of the Human Sciences,' *Writing and Difference,* trans. Alan Bass (Chicago: The University of Chicago Press, 1978), p. 292.

327. Derrida refers to remarks in Lévi-Strauss's *The Raw and the Cooked.*

328. A clear example is Derrida's deconstruction of Freud's *Beyond the Pleasure Principle* in his 'To Speculate – On "Freud"' (1980). In this study, Derrida examines the side-details and manifestly peripheral remarks in Freud's text, shows how they are in fact central to the book's meaning, and concludes that Freud's book is primarily an autobiographical text about Freud, rather than a theoretical text about the workings of the human mind in general.

329. Nietzsche faced a similar problem, when, in view of his claim that all perspectives were relative to an individual's psychology, physiology and overall level of power, he asked whether this, too, was also only an interpretation. The problem did not seem to bother him, for he answered, 'Well, so much the better' (See *Beyond Good and Evil,* §22).

330. The idea that *différance* cannot be surpassed, along with Derrida's claim that *différance* 'makes possible' the apprehension of presences, invites one to interpret Derrida in a Kantian manner. For Derrida appears to be seeking within the linguistic realm, what Kant (in his notion of categories of the understanding, among which was the category of 'negation') sought in the epistemological realm, and what Heidegger (in his notion of an *existentiale*) sought in the existential realm, namely, foundational notions linked with the idea of inescapability, universality, and necessity. Certainly, no text that was ever written, or that ever will be written, will escape the play of *différance.*

331. Alternatively, one could say that Derrida prefers more obviously metaphorical language to less obviously metaphorical language, if one ascribes to him a version of the view that all language is metaphorical.

332. In the more narrow distinction between 'presence' versus 'absence,' both presence and absence are positive terms, and are both 'presences' in the wider sense intended here. The 'versus' or differential relationship that draws the distinction is what Derrida prioritizes over and above the terms in the relation.

333. There are formulations of the Liar paradox that assume a double-sentence form, however, as when one writes on one side of a card 'the sentence on the other side of the card is false,' and writes on the other side of the card, 'the sentence on the other side of the card is true.' This sort of oscillation comes closer to the structure of skepticism that Hegel describes.

334. Hegel, *Phenomenology of Spirit,* Section 207.

335. Similarly, if I am discontented only when I am content, then if I am discontented, then I am content, and if I am content, then I am discontented. Parallel examples would be when I am happy only when I am unhappy, or am satisfied only when I am unsatisfied, or feel deep pleasure only when I am in pain, or feel close to people only when they remain distant, etc. These conditions characterize situations where emotions and feelings are present an unstable blend.

336. Kierkegaard contrasts Socrates with Plato, regarding Socrates as more existentially centered, realistic, and down-to-earth, and Plato as more unrealistic and otherworldly centered. The characterizations of Derrida in the present chapter, as both a 'linguo–existentialist' and as a 'linguo–Socrates' are inspired, in part, by Kierkegaard's conception of Socrates.

337. We saw a similar project in Roland Barthes's Inaugural Lecture, and in Derrida's advocacy of deconstruction. For Barthes, the constricting enclosures from which we should free ourselves, are the rigid structures of language itself. Foucault reiterates this theme.

338. See his *Moi, Pierre Rivière ayant égorgé ma mère, ma soeur et mon frère* [1973] trans. Aleon Frank Jellinik as *I, Pierre Rivière, Having Slaughtered my Mother, my Sister, and my Brother: A Case of Parricide in the Nineteenth century* (New York: Random House, 1975).

339. See the first few pages of Foucault's *Discipline and Punish: The Birth of the Prison,* trans. Alan Sheridan (New York: Pantheon Books, 1977 [1975]).

340. Friedrich Nietzsche, *The Gay Science,* §7.

341. Michel Foucault, *The Order of Things* (New York: Vintage Books, 1994), pp. xxi–xxii.

342. Hermeneutics, or theory of interpretation, arose in the wake of the Protestant Reformation, where a greater freedom to interpret the Bible became widespread. The discipline soon expanded from the theory of interpreting religious texts, to the theory of interpreting legal texts, to the theory of interpreting texts in general, to the theory of interpreting anything whatsoever.

   Some of the central figures in the history of hermeneutics are Friedrich Ast (1778–1841), Friedrich Schleiermacher (1768–1834), Wilhelm Dilthey (1833–1911), Martin Heidegger (1889–1976), Emilio Betti (1890–1968), Hans-Georg Gadamer (1900–2002), Paul Ricoeur (1913–) and Karl-Otto Apel (1922–).

343. The word 'guerilla' is connected initially with the Napoleonic campaign in Spain (1808–11) and was used by the Duke of Wellington in 1809. At that time, the English forces commanded by Wellington were helped by the Spanish peasants who waged a guerrilla war against the French army in Spain. '*Guerrilla*' is the diminutive of the Spanish word '*guerra*' and means 'little war,' 'small war,' or 'petty war,' signifying the style of warfare that is fought by small bands of militants, often against a larger, occupying force.

344. The word 'terrorist' derives from events surrounding the bloody aftermath of the French Revolution. It stems from the early-to-mid 1790s in France, and refers originally to an agent of the revolutionary tribunal during the Reign of Terror. The majority of initial references are to the 'terrorist' Jean-Baptiste Carrier, who carried out executions in Nantes (1793–94) by using barges as death-chambers,

loading people onto barges, sinking them, and then refloating the barges for further executions.

345. Michel Foucault, *Discipline and Punish – The Birth of the Prison*, trans. Alan Sheridan (London: Penguin Books, 1991), p. 200.
346. Ibid., p. 201.
347. See Michel Foucault, 'The History of Sexuality,' in *Power/Knowledge: Selected Interviews & Other Writings 1972–1977*, ed. Colin Gordon (New York: Pantheon Books, 1980), p. 193.
348. Laozi, *Daodejing*, Book I.
349. Michel Foucault, 'Prison Talk' [1975], in *Power/Knowledge: Selected Interviews & Other Writings 1972–1977*, ed. Colin Gordon (New York: Pantheon Books, 1980), p. 52
350. Michel Foucault, 'On the Genealogy of Ethics' [1983], in *Michel Foucault – Ethics*, ed. Paul Rabinow (London: The Penguin Press, 1997), p. 261.
  An intriguing example of a person who, throughout his mature life, consciously and deliberately attempted to blend art and life is the Japanese novelist and militant, Yukio Mishima [Kimitaka Hiraoka] (1925–70). To cap things off, in a blend of theatrics and political seriousness, and not wishing to die of decay, he committed ritual suicide (*seppuku*) at the very height of his career.
351. Friedrich Nietzsche, *The Gay Science*, §290.
352. Foucault's emphasis upon 'productive' power stems from Nietzsche's conception of an ever-expansive 'will to power.'
353. Walter Gropius (1883–1969) and Ludwig Mies van der Rohe (1886–1969) were German architects of the Bauhaus school (1919–33).
354. Charles Jencks, *The Language of Post-Modern Architecture*, 4th edn. (London: Academy Editions, 1984), p. 9.
355. Steven Connor, *Postmodernist Culture, An Introduction to Theories of the Contemporary* (Oxford: Basil Blackwell, 1989), p. 69.
356. Michel Foucault, *The Order of Things, An Archaeology of the Human Sciences* (New York: Vintage Books, 1994), p. xv.
357. Jean-François Lyotard, 'What is Postmodernism?' in *The Postmodern Condition: A Report on Knowledge*, trans. Geoff Bennington and Brian Massumi (Minneapolis: University of Minnesota Press, 1984), p. 76.
358. Jean-François Lyotard, *The Postmodern Condition: A Report on Knowledge*, trans. Geoff Bennington and Brian Massumi (Minneapolis: University of Minnesota Press, 1984), p. xxiii.
359. Ibid., pp. xxiii–xxiv.
360. This 'single-goal' style of thinking traces back to Aristotle. In his discussion of the meaning of human activity in his *Nicomachean Ethics*, he argues that there must be some single activity which is not a means to any end, but is an end in itself. This he defines as 'doing well' or (loosely translated) 'happiness.'
361. This ideal of achieving consensus is advocated by Jürgen Habermas, and Lyotard criticizes Habermas often, though usually indirectly, in *The Postmodern Condition*.
362. Lyotard, *The Postmodern Condition: A Report on Knowledge*, p. xxiv.

363. Ibid., p. xxiv.
364. We can witness this phenomenon in the view that understands the mind to be a very complex computer. On this view, if some feature of the mind cannot be expressed in mathematical and materialistic terms, and if it cannot in principle be embodied in an artificial intelligence, then that feature of the mind is not recognized as standing in need of explanation.
365. Lyotard is referring to Wittgenstein's later philosophy as expressed in *Philosophical Investigations* (1953).
366. Lyotard, *The Postmodern Condition: A Report on Knowledge*, p. 10.
367. Ibid. This agonistic view is not central to Wittgenstein's outlook, but is Lyotard's own emphasis.
368. Lyotard is implicitly referring to the German philosopher and systems theorist, Niklas Luhmann (1927–98). As an expression of Luhmann's mature views, see his 1984 book, *Soziale Systeme. Grundriβ einer allgemeinen Theorie* (*Social Systems*).
369. The argument here is comparable to Barthes's argument against the primacy of scientific knowledge. Barthes argued that language contains many 'voices,' of which the 'objective' and 'neutral' voice of science is only one among several.
370. Lyotard, *The Postmodern Condition: A Report on Knowledge*, p. 25.
371. Ibid., p. 27.
372. Ibid., p. 45.
373. Ibid., p. 46.
374. See Foucault's discussion of Maurice Blanchot in his, 'Maurice Blanchot: The Thought from the Outside' ['La pensée du dehors'] (1966), which originally appeared in *Critique*, 229.
375. See Lyotard's essay, 'Judiciousness in Dispute, or Kant after Marx,' published in *La Faculté de Juger* (Editions de Minuit, 1985).
376. One of the major founders of the Italian Communist Party in 1921 was Antonio Gramsci (1891–1937).
377. This essay appears in English (translated by Hélène Vivienne Wenzel) in *Signs: Journal of Women in Culture and Society*, 1981, vol. 7, no. 1, pp. 60–67.
378. Raoul Mortley (ed.), *French Philosophers in Conversation, Levinas, Schneider, Serres, Irigaray, Le Doeff, Derrida* (London and New York: Routledge, 1991), p. 66.
379. Mortley (ed.), *French Philosophers in Conversation*, p. 67.
380. Ibid., p. 64.
381. Ibid., p. 65.
382. Since moonlight is dimmer than sunlight and since it depends upon sunlight, one can interpret the metaphors sun-male, moon-female, as symbolically suggesting that women are less powerful than men and depend upon men.
383. Luce Irigaray, *An Ethics of Sexual Difference*, trans. Carolyn Burke and Gillian C. Gill (London: The Athlone Press, 1993), pp. 6–7.
384. In a physiological sense, for instance, men and women mutually depend upon each other for the continuation of the species.
385. Luce Irigaray, 'Equal or Different?' in *The Irigaray Reader*, ed. Margaret Whitford (Oxford: Blackwell Publishers, Ltd., 1991) p. 32.

386. Ibid., pp. 32–33.
387. Mortley (ed.), *French Philosophers in Conversation*, p. 65.
388. The intellectual practice of defining women negatively in reference to men has a history that traces back to the times of Aristotle. He stated, for example, that the female is, as it were, a 'deformed male' (*Generation of Animals*, 2.737a: 27).
389. Such observations ground Irigaray's criticisms of Freud and Lacan, who follow this male bias in defining women's sexuality via a negative comparison to male sexuality. Irigaray does, however, retain Freud's and Lacan's general outlook insofar as she identifies sexuality as a central feature of human self-definition.
390. Irigaray, *An Ethics of Sexual Difference*, pp. 18–19.
391. Mortley (ed.), *French Philosophers in Conversation*, p. 77.
392. Irigaray, 'Sexual Difference,' in *The Irigaray Reader*, pp. 171–172.
393. The question here concerns whether the 'human-identity' which one postulates as the basis of morality (e.g., reason, moral feeling, common moral intuitions) will be the condition of, will define, or will override any specific morally relevant differences we might acknowledge between men and women. To accommodate both a general morality along with a recognition of sexual difference, one could maintain (as would a utilitarian) that the central and universally binding moral prescription is to maximize pleasure in the world (with due consideration to issues of just distribution), while acknowledging that men's pleasures and women's pleasures can be very different. This allows one to acknowledge a common human identity in the affirmation of universal moral principles, while also acknowledging as significant, and morally relevant, differences in identity between men and women. Irigaray appears to take a more radical route which, although acknowledging the basic value of justice, emphasizes the centrality and necessity of sexual difference.
394. Hegel's discussion of the 'life-and-death struggle' in his *Phenomenology of Spirit* (as discussed in the chapter on Lacan) provides a paradigm analysis of the hostile reactions that can attend the initial face-to-face encounter between two individuals. Prior to Hegel, Thomas Hobbes (1588–1679) similarly described the state of nature as a situation where each person is at war with every other person. See Hobbes's *Leviathan* (1651).
395. Irigaray, 'Sexual Difference,' in *The Irigaray Reader*, pp. 171–172.
396. The inspiration for Irigaray's view comes from the thought of the French philosopher Emmanuel Lévinas, whose ethical views rest on the idea that the Other is never fully known. His two main works are *Totality and Infinity* (1961) and *Otherwise Than Being or Beyond Essence* (1974).
397. See Foucault's essay 'Theatricum Philosophicum' (1970), which appears in *Language, Counter-Memory, Practice*, ed. Donald F. Bouchard (Ithaca, NY: Cornell University Press, 1977).
398. Gilles Deleuze and Félix Guattari, *Anti-Oedipus: Capitalism and Schizophrenia* [1972], trans. Robert Hurley, Mark Seem, and Helen R. Lane (Minneapolis: University of Minnesota Press, 1983), p. 50.
399. This aspect of the Deleuzean picture conflicts somewhat with R. D. Laing's view (see further below) on the origins of many cases of schizophrenia.

According to Laing, the human psyche can be deformed, rather than positively formed, by the imposition of certain kinds of confusion-filled family structures, where schizophrenic reactions are the result. In such cases, the schizophrenic type of person would not exist prior to the family structure and would not clearly exhibit a more primordial state of mind, but would originate from within the family structure itself. In some remarks, however, Deleuze and Guattari follow Laing's basic account insofar as they recognize that the dehumanizing effects of capitalism can also drive people mad.

400. Deleuze and Guattari, *Anti-Oedipus*, p. 3. Deleuze and Guattari's emphasis upon the concept of production has an intentional Marxist ring.

401. Ibid., p. 15. This also describes the literary style Deleuze and Guattari employ, as it exemplifies 'nature as a process of production' in the very text that they write. Their method is comparable to how Lacan tried to speak with the multidimensional and polymorphous voice of the 'unconscious.' It is also comparable to how Derrida writes with the semantic multidimensionality of texts in mind, and how Irigaray writes with the voice of woman in mind. Each theorist self-consciously tries to achieve an exemplificational consistency between the content of their theoretical views and the form of expression through which they express those views.

402. In Laing's terminology, this condition of depersonalization is referred to as 'ontological insecurity.' See his *The Divided Self – An Existential Study in Sanity and Madness* (1959).

403. Arthur Schopenhauer also conceives of individual body parts as manifestations of desire: 'teeth, throat and digestive canal are hunger objectified; the genitals are the sex drive objectified; grasping hands and swift feet correspond to more indirect strivings of the will, which they represent' (*The World as Will and Representation*, Section 20). Schopenhauer also speaks of 'bodies without organs' [... *Körper ... ganz ohne Organe* ...] (Section 23). I am grateful to Saffron Toms for pointing out these affinities between Deleuze and Schopenhauer.

Deleuze is rarely associated with Schopenhauer, but it stands that one of Deleuze's most well-known books – *Nietzsche and Philosophy* (1962) – was on Friedrich Nietzsche, who was himself strongly influenced by Schopenhauer.

404. Deleuze and Guattari, *Anti-Oedipus*, p. 296.

405. Deleuze's analysis of desire stems from his analysis of 'active' and 'reactive' forces in connection with Nietzsche's views on the will to power. See Deleuze's, *Nietzsche and Philosophy*.

406. In Deleuze and Guattari's writings published after *Anti-Oedipus*, the image of the nomad is given greater emphasis.

407. This is akin to Foucault's view that social institutions tend to operate like prisons.

408. Deleuze and Guattari, *Anti-Oedipus*, p. 116.

409. A similar problem arises in Buddhist philosophy in reference to the question of 'who' is enlightened, if the reality of the ego is denied.

410. The work of R. D. Laing, as inspired by Gregory Bateson (1904–80), explores the relationship between double-bind situations and the development of schizophrenia within family contexts. One of Laing's central ideas, as alluded to previously, is that

contradiction-ridden schizophrenic symptoms are often direct reflections of contradictory patterns of behavior in the family. See, for example, his *Sanity, Madness and the Family* (1964).

411. Jean Baudrillard, *Seduction*, trans. Brian Singer (New York: St. Martin's Press, 1990), p. 80.
412. Baudrillard's conception of seduction parallels, albeit in a perverse way, Irigaray's ethics of sublimity, where two people also stand as mutual mysteries to each other (with, of course, very different attitudes toward their mutual inscrutability).
413. Baudrillard, *Seduction*, p. 53–54.
414. Jean Baudrillard, 'Symbolic Exchange and Death' in *Jean Baudrillard – Selected Writings*, ed. Mark Poster, (Stanford, Ca: Stanford University Press, 1988), p. 135.
415. Ibid., p. 136.
416. Ibid., p. 137.
417. It is not, however, as if such techniques were absent until the industrial period. Woodblock printing, for instance, has had a long history. The issue concerns the prevailing cultural modes of symbolization at some given time.
418. As a landmark analysis of this mode, Baudrillard refers to 'The Work of Art in the Age of Mechanical Reproduction' (1936), by Walter Benjamin (1892–1940).
419. Baudrillard, 'Symbolic Exchange and Death,' pp. 146–147.
420. Ibid., pp. 145–146.
421. Jean Baudrillard, *Simulacra and Simulation*, trans. Sheila Faria Glaser (Ann Arbor, MI: The University of Michigan Press, 1994), p. 2.
422. Ibid., p. 2.
423. Ibid., p. 6.
424. Nietzsche's reference is to Kant, who lived in Königsberg.
425. This line of argument was set forth earlier by G. W. F. Hegel in his *Phenomenology of Spirit*, in the section of the book entitled 'Force and the Understanding.'
426. The word '*Incipit*' refers generally to the opening words of a medieval manuscript or early printed book.
427. Friedrich Nietzsche, *Twilight of the Idols* (1888).
428. Baudrillard, *Simulacra and Simulations*, p. 13.
429. For example, see Steven Best and Douglas Kellner, *Postmodern Theory – Critical Interrogations* (New York: The Guilford Press, 1992), pp. 128–140.
430. To recall, this is because one cannot be seduced, if one knows that there is no hidden truth that the seducer is keeping secret.
431. In the *Daodejing*, there is a remark that 'the five colors blind the eye.' This can be read as stating that the five color words that we ordinarily use, owing to their superficial categorizations, do not allow us to appreciate fully the rich sensory texture of our perceptual field. I am grateful to Chad Hansen for this example and interpretation of the Chinese text.
432. The phrase, 'a map is not the territory,' is from the Poland-born semanticist and mathematician, Alfred Korzybski (1879–1950). See his influential book, *Science and Sanity: An Introduction to non-Aristotelian Systems and General Semantics* (1933). Baudrillard employs the distinction between 'map' and 'territory' and he

characterizes 'hyperreality' as a situation where one can recognize only the 'map,' and where sight of the terrain has been lost.

433. Jean Baudrillard, *The Perfect Crime*, trans. Chris Turner (London/New York: Verso, 1996), p. 2.

434. This conception of liberty has a long history. In 1651, for example, Thomas Hobbes defined liberty as the absence of external impediments that prevent someone from doing what he or she wants. See his *Leviathan*, Chapter XIV.

435. See Zbigniew Brzezinski, *Out of Control: Global Turmoil on the Eve of the Twenty-first Century* (New York: Collier Books, 1993).

436. See Trilling's *The Opposing Self* (London: Secker & Warburg, 1955).

437. This openness of dialogue is developed in the philosophy of Hans-Georg Gadamer, as inspired by the later philosophy of Martin Heidegger. See Gadamer's *Truth and Method* (1960).

438. The notion of an 'ideal speech situation' was developed by Jürgen Habermas. See Habermas's, *The Theory of Communicative Action* (1984/1987).

Acknowledgments

I would like to thank Professor Daniel Dennett, for permission to quote from *The Philosopher's Lexicon*; Cambridge University Press, for permission to quote from *The Philosophical Works of Descartes*, Volume I (1911), translated by Elizabeth S. Haldane and G. R. Ross; the Division of Christian Education of the National Council of the Churches of Christ in the USA for permission to quote from the book of Ecclesiastes, used by permission, all rights reserved; Rowman & Littlefield Publishers, Inc. for permission to quote from *The Creative Mind* (1965), by Henri Bergson, translated by Mabelle L. Andison, published by Littlefield, Adams & Co.; the University of Chicago Press, for permission to quote from *On the Heights of Despair* (1992), by E. M. Cioran, translated by Ilinca Zarifopol-Johnston, *The Savage Mind* (1966) by Claude Lévi-Strauss, *Writing and Difference* (1978) and *Margins of Philosophy* (1972), by Jacques Derrida, both translated by Alan Bass; the University of Michigan Press, for permission to quote from *Simulacra and Simulation* (1994), by Jean Baudrillard, translated by Shiela Faria Glaser; Verso, The Imprint of New Left Books, Ltd., for permission to quote from *The Perfect Crime* (1996), by Jean Baudrillard, translated by Chris Turner; Farrar, Straus and Giroux, L.L.C. for permission to quote from *A Barthes Reader*, by Roland Barthes, edited by Susan Sontag, *Image/Music/Text*, by Roland Barthes, translated by Stephen Heath, *Mythologies*, by Roland Barthes, translated by Annette Lavers, and *The Pleasure of the Text*, by Roland Barthes, translated by Richard Miller; Random House, UK, for permission to quote from *The History of Surrealism*, by Maurice Nadeau, translated by Richard Howard; Random House, Inc., for permission to quote from *The Myth of Sisyphus*, by Albert Camus, translated by Justin O'Brien, copyright © 1955 by Alfred A. Knopf, a division of Random House, Inc., used by permission of Alfred A. Knopf, a division of Random House, Inc.;

Random House, Inc., also for permission to quote from *Power/Knowledge*, by Michel Foucault, edited by Colin Gordon, copyright © 1972, 1975, 1976, 1977 by Michel Foucault, this collection © by The Harvester Press, used by permission of Pantheon Books, a division of Random House, Inc.; Penguin Books Limited, for permission to quote from *Discipline and Punish: The Birth of the Prison*, by Michel Foucault, translated by Alan Sheridan (first published as *Surveiller et punir: Naissance de la prison* by Éditions Gallimard 1975, Allen Lane 1975) Copyright © Alan Sheridan, 1977; New Directions Publishing Corporation, for permission to quote from *Nausea*, by Jean-Paul Sartre, translated by Lloyd Alexander, copyright © 1964 by New Directions Publishing Corp.; University of Minnesota Press, for permission to quote from *The Postmodern Condition*, by Jean-François Lyotard, translated by Geoff Bennington and Brian Massumi (English edition published by University of Minnesota Press, 1984), originally published in France as *La Condition postmoderne: rapport sur le savoir*, copyright © 1979 by Les Éditions de Minuit, English translation and Foreword copyright © 1984 by the University of Minnesota, all rights reserved; The Perseus Books Group, for permission to quote from *Structural Anthropology*, Volume I, by Claude Lévi-Strauss, English translation copyright © 1963 by Basic Books, a member of Perseus Books, L.L.C.; Routledge and Thomson Publishing Services, for permission to quote from *French Philosophers in Conversation – Levinas, Schneider, Serres, Irigaray, Le Doeuff, Derrida* (1991), interviewed by Raoul Mortley; HarperCollins Publishers, for permission to quote – all of these quotations appear in the present work in chapter 6, "Pierre Teilhard de Chardin, Priest and Paleontologist" – from *The Phenomenon of Man*, by Pierre Teilhard de Chardin, and translated by Bernard Wall, introduction by Julian Huxley, Copyright 1955 by Éditions de Seuil, Translation and Introduction copyright 1959 by William Collins Sons & Co., Ltd. and Harper & Brothers, © renewed 1987 by Harper & Row, Publishers, Inc., reprinted by permission of HarperCollins Publishers, Inc.; Palgrave Macmillan, for permission to quote from *Seduction*, by Jean Baudrillard, published by St. Martin's Press, 1990; Continuum International Publishing Group, for permission to quote from *An Ethics of Sexual Difference*, by Luce Irigaray, translated by Carolyn Burke and Gillian C. Gill, © The Athlone Press, London, 1993; Blackwell Publishing, for permission to reprint the chapter entitled, "Michel Foucault" (with minor alterations) by Robert Wicks, which originally appeared in *The Blackwell Guide to Continental Philosophy*, edited by Robert C. Solomon and David Sherman, Oxford, Blackwell Publishing, Ltd., 2003, pp. 243–264; Éditions Gallimard, for permission to quote from *Dits et écrits* (Ethics) by Michel Foucault, © Éditions Gallimard, Paris, 1994; Thomson Gale/The Gale Group, for permission to quote from The *Encyclopedia of Philosophy*, edited by Paul Edwards, Macmillan Library Reference, © 1967, Macmillan Library Reference, Reprinted by permission of the Gale Group; Penguin Putnam, Inc. for permission to quote from *Anti-Oedipus*, by Gilles Deleuze and Feliz Guattari, translated by Helen Lane, Mark Seem, and Robert Hurley, copyright © 1977 by Viking Penguin, Inc., English Language translation, used by permission of Viking Penguin, a division of Penguin Group (USA) Inc.; Philosophical Library, New York, for permission to quote from

Course in General Linguistics, by Ferdinand de Saussure, ed. by Charles Bally and Albert Sechehaye in collaboration with Albert Riedlinger, translated, with an introduction and notes by Wade Baskin, © 1959, by The Philosophical Library, Inc., reprinted by McGraw-Hill Book Company by arrangement with The Philosophical Library, Inc.; Philosophical Library, New York, for permission to quote from *Being and Nothingness*, translated by Hazel Barnes, copyright © 1956 by The Philosophical Library, Inc.; Cornell University Press, for permission to quote from *An Ethics of Sexual Difference*, by Luce Irigaray, translated by Carolyn Burke and Gillian C. Gill, © Cornell University Press, Ithaca, 1993, used by permission of the publisher, Cornell University Press; Éditions Gallimard, for permission to quote from E. M. Cioran, *La tentation d'exister* and *De l'inconvénient d'être né*, © Éditions Gallimard, Paris.

I would also like to acknowledge my requests to the following publishers and individuals, for permission to quote from the various sources named. Éditions du Seuil, for permission to quote from *Le phénomène humain*, by Teilhard de Chardin, © Éditions du Seuil, 1955, *Image/Music/Text*, by Roland Barthes, and *The History of Surrealism*, by Maurice Nadeau, © Éditions du Seuil, 1964; Monsieur Jacques Boncompain of the Camus Estate for permission to quote from *The Myth of Sisyphus*, by Albert Camus; Weidenfeld & Nicholson and The Orion Group, for permission to quote from *The Savage Mind*, by Claude Lévi-Strauss, © Weidenfeld & Nicholson, 1988; Georges Borchardt, Inc., for permission to quote from Roland Barthes, "Science versus Literature"; Penguin UK, for permission to quote from *The Order of Things*, by Michel Foucault; Random House, UK, for permission to quote from *The Barthes Reader*, by Roland Barthes and for permission to quote from *Mythologies*, by Roland Barthes; Arcade Publishing, for permission to quote from *The Trouble with Being Born*, by E. M. Cioran, © Arcade Publishing, 1998, originally published by Éditions Gallimard; The University of Chicago Press, for permission to quote from *The Temptation to Exist*, by E. M. Cioran, © The University of Chicago Press, 1998; Penguin UK, for permission to quote from *Structural Anthropology*, by Claude Lévi-Strauss, © Penguin, UK, 1972; and Manchester University Press, for permission to quote from *The Postmodern Condition*, by Jean François Lyotard, © Manchester University Press, 1984.

Every effort has been made to trace and acknowledge ownership of copyright. If any required credits have been omitted or any rights overlooked, it is completely unintentional; the publisher and author will be glad to make suitable arrangements with any copyright holder whom it has not been possible to contact.

Index